CURIES

Cross University Research in Engineering and Science (CURIES) is a working group on research and praxis concerning women and gender in science, engineering, and mathematics. We came together in 1991 from four colleges and universities which had been active in fostering women's participation in scientific and technical fields: Carnegie Mellon University, the University of Michigan, the University of Washington, and Wellesley College. Cinda-Sue Davis, Angela B. Ginorio, Carol S. Hollenshead, Barbara B. Lazarus, and Paula M. Rayman formed the CURIES Working Group in order to guide the development and implementation of CURIES activities. From these efforts grew the 1994 CURIES conference which ultimately resulted in the writing and publication of *The Equity Equation* as well as a national research and policy agenda. This project was administered by the University of Michigan Center for the Education of Women under the direction of Carol Hollenshead. CURIES conference arrangements were coordinated by the Wellesley College Center for Research on Women and overseen by Paula Rayman and C. Y. Loker. Throughout the project the CURIES Working Group has collectively guided project efforts. An advisory committee of experts and leaders in the field assisted CURIES with its work throughout the project.

The Equity Equation

The Equity Equation

Fostering the Advancement of Women in the Sciences, Mathematics, and Engineering

Cinda-Sue Davis

Angela B. Ginorio

Carol S. Hollenshead

Barbara B. Lazarus

Paula M. Rayman

and Associates

Jossey-Bass Publishers • San Francisco

Substantial discounts on bulk quantities of Jossey-Bass books are available to corporations, professional associations, and other organizations. For details and discount information, contact the special sales department at Jossey-Bass Inc., Publishers (415) 433–1740; Fax (800) 605–2665.

For sales outside the United States, please contact your local Simon & Schuster International Office.

TCF Manufactured in the United States of America on Lyons Falls Pathfinder Tradebook. This paper is acid-free and 100 percent totally chlorine-free.

Library of Congress Cataloging-in-Publication Data

Davis, Cinda-Sue, date.
    The equity equation: fostering the advancement of women in the sciences, mathematics, and engineering / Cinda-Sue Davis. . .[et al.].
        p.   cm. — (The Jossey-Bass higher and adult education series) (The Jossey-Bass education series)
    Includes bibliographical references and index.
    ISBN 0–7879–0213–6 (alk. paper)
    1. Women in science. 2. Women in mathematics. 3. Women in engineering. I. Title. II Series.
Q130.D39 1996
305.43'5 — dc20   96–3994
                                                                                        CIP

FIRST EDITION
HB Printing 10 9 8 7 6 5 4 3 2 1

A joint publication in
The Jossey-Bass Higher and
Adult Education Series
and
The Jossey-Bass Education Series

Contents

Preface

Whether our study of gender equity in science, mathematics, and engineering focuses on girls or women, at school or at work, various sociocultural and methodological issues emerge. It has become clear that barriers to full female participation arise in large measure from institutional practice.

It has also become apparent that a full understanding of women's experience requires a vision of diversity that goes beyond gender to race/ethnicity, class, age, sexual orientation, and disability. It also requires more complex approaches to research and policy development. This translates into greater use of diverse kinds of evaluation, including qualitative as well as quantitative methods. Today's researchers combine multiple approaches to single topics of study to provide a more complete analysis of the issues.

Along with these methodological shifts, we have seen a call for greater accountability. Funders can play a critical role in directing funds to institutions with an active commitment to achieving equity. Scarce resources must be wisely used and targeted to programs with clearly demonstrated results.

Today's focus on equitable access for women comes at a challenging time, when many worry that we may be producing more scientists than the labor market can use. Yet there are still many reasons to encourage women to enter engineering, math, and science. In spite of somewhat reduced academic and research opportunities, scientific and technical occupations still present greater opportunities and rewards for women than more traditional fields. Moreover, women—as well as men—should have the full range of career choices available to them. As we point out in Chapter Ten, regardless of what size the supply of scientists should be, the proportion of women at every level of scientific and technological education and work should be equitable.

It is also important to enlarge our vision of the purposes and outcomes of science education. Americans need a better general understanding of science and technical applications in order to participate fully and flourish in our increasingly technologically complex society. In addition, programs in science, mathematics, and engineering, particularly at the graduate level, need to take a broader view of their fields so their students will acquire skills applicable to a range of occupations. It is no longer acceptable to prepare students only for traditional academic careers.

While many barriers to a diverse work force arise early in life—from the toys parents choose to the K-12 curriculum—higher education remains the true gatekeeper to technical careers. Higher education defines criteria for entry and credentials required to be a scientist or engineer; higher education teaches the teachers who work in our schools; higher education affects the attitudes of parents and future parents. To change opportunities for women in engineering and science, we must focus in large measure on the role of higher education.

As discussed in Chapter Ten, *The Equity Equation* emerged from a conference sponsored by the Cross University Research in Engineering and Science (CURIES) group on gender issues in May 1994. This conference, supported by the Alfred P. Sloan Foundation, came at a key point in the development of the study of gender issues in science. By necessity, during the past decade, intervention and policies on women in science, mathematics, and engineering have moved ahead of research; most programs have relied on personal experience, tradition, or anecdotal evidence of need and effectiveness. Now, after a decade of work with intervention programs, program directors are calling for better evaluation and for greater ties between intervention and relevant research. Simultaneously, an increase in the numbers of women in the field has enabled more thorough statistical analysis, while the use of diverse methodologies is yielding more sophisticated research design. It has also become more evident that the barriers women face arise from the institution and not the individual; because of this, solutions need to focus on institutional change.

It is our hope that *The Equity Equation* will serve to ground future intervention and funding on a firm research base. Programs tied to research will increase our understanding of the social systems of science, mathematics, and engineering and of *all* women in these fields. This book aims for the development of a culture where both men and women can have productive and satisfying careers in all fields of scientific and technological endeavor.

The Equity Equation begins with a chapter analyzing the critical role of public policy in education and in the support of scientific research. Daryl E. Chubin and Shirley M. Malcom argue for reinventing science to take advantage of our nation's full human resources, and they conclude that it is a national imperative to ensure equal opportunity in the scientific enterprise.

Chapter Two, by Betty M. Vetter, provides hard numbers to spell out the realities of women's role in science, mathematics, and engineering. Tracing progress in the last two decades, Vetter concludes that the increases in women's participation in science seen in the 1970s and early 1980s have leveled off in most areas. She documents lower salaries, higher unemployment rates, and slower progress toward advancement or tenure for women.

The next five chapters examine the educational pipeline for girls and women. Chapter Three, by Jane Butler Kahle, discusses K-12 education, opening with a review of the controversy over mixed versus single-sex instruction. It moves on to questions of gender and racial/ethnic difference in educational experience and the effects of differential schooling on girls' achievement and options.

Chapter Four, by Helen S. Astin and Linda J. Sax, examines the college years. The authors review previous research and suggest directions for curricular and pedagogical transformations in undergraduate education. They point out that higher education cannot reverse the influence of socialization on women's career decisions, so educators must maintain the aspirations of women already committed to science, mathematics, and engineering and keep the door open for others to rediscover science in college.

In Chapter Five, Carol S. Hollenshead, Stacey A. Wenzel, Barbara B. Lazarus, and Indira Nair discuss graduate education. They trace the history of discrimination against women and examine the assumptions and norms that shape the graduate experience. In assessing our state of knowledge about graduate education, the authors review research on access, funding, and institutional environment, as well as the nature of scientific disciplines, the intersection of gender with other sources of discrimination, and the success of intervention programs. They conclude with a call for greater institutional accountability and systemic change.

In Chapter Six, Beatriz Chu Clewell and Angela B. Ginorio review studies covering topics ranging from individual influences to complex sociocultural issues. The authors examine the impact of the educational and work setting on girls and women of color, lesbians, disabled women, and women of different classes. Examining these multiple levels and populations is critical, the authors contend, to a full interpretation of any research findings on girls and women in science, and they therefore call for research that accounts for the experiences of every woman, no matter which, or how many, of these populations she belongs to.

Cinda-Sue Davis and Sue V. Rosser examine intervention programs and curriculum reforms in Chapter Seven. Such efforts are widely regarded as key to increasing women's participation in science, mathematics, and engineering. Yet they are rarely evaluated, leaving faculty and program directors with little sense of what works and what doesn't. The authors stress the importance of such evaluation and describe potentially "female-friendly" curricula.

The book then turns to scientific and technical careers. In Chapter Eight, Mary Frank Fox finds that "the higher the fewer" still holds true for women in the ranks of academic faculty. She examines the institutional factors that contribute to this phenomenon, the implications for policy, and the future prospects for women's attainment in academic science and engineering.

Paula M. Rayman and Jennifer S. Jackson explore the status of women in nonacademic careers in Chapter Nine. They note where women are found in industry and examine barriers to employment and success through case studies. Raising the questions "Science by whom, for whom?" they review theories explaining patterns of inequity and conclude with implications for research and policy.

Chapter Ten, by Carol S. Hollenshead, Stacey A. Wenzel, Margaret N. Dykens, Cinda-Sue Davis, Angela B. Ginorio, Barbara B. Lazarus, and Paula M. Rayman, summarizes the recommendations emerging from the CURIES conference. Intended as a blueprint for research and policy development, the chapter stresses the importance of sustainable institutional change to promote equity.

It proposes changes in data collection, intervention program evaluation, and other key issues.

The Equity Equation can help build and maintain a climate that welcomes girls and women in science, mathematics, and engineering. It is a sourcebook for change, aimed toward a culture where all intellectual styles reach full expression and diversity adds to excellence. The research and ideas it presents can serve as practical resources for individuals and institutions seeking to improve conditions. In a very personal sense, we hope our work will help open doors for our daughters and granddaughters, as well as for those who come after them.

January 1996

Cinda-Sue Davis
Angela B. Ginorio
Carol S. Hollenshead
Barbara B. Lazarus
Paula M. Rayman

*To Betty M. Vetter, whose work made our work possible
and whose life enriched our lives*

Acknowledgments

Neither the CURIES project nor this book would have been possible without the generous support of the Alfred P. Sloan Foundation. We are grateful to the Foundation not only for making this project possible but also for their continuing commitment to the advancement of women in science, mathematics, and engineering. Ted Greenwood, Sloan Project officer, deserves special thanks. He believed in our vision, advocated for our project, and supported us at each step along the way.

We are also grateful to the staff of the Center for the Education of Women, the Center for Research on Women, the Northwest Center for Research on Women, and the Carnegie Mellon Associate Provost's Office whose dedication and labor made the CURIES project successful. Linda Stoker of Michigan and C. Y. Loker of Wellesley worked over and above the call of duty to help make the conference and project run smoothly. Lisa Gubaci of Michigan has provided ongoing administrative support and financial management. Larry Baldwin of Wellesley, Stacy Wenzel of Michigan as well as Michelle Elekonich of Washington and Deborah Harkus of Carnegie Mellon provided invaluable assistance.

The CURIES working group also owes a great debt to all the other individuals and groups who helped to shape the CURIES project and *The Equity Equation*. The CURIES Advisory Committee assisted in defining the scope of the project and the topics to be addressed at the conference and in the book. Following the conference many individuals reviewed drafts of the research and policy agenda and provided insightful comments and advice. Throughout the process the book's chapter authors gave endlessly of their time and expertise. Not only did they complete their work with the highest standards of scholarship and sensitively review the work of their colleagues, but they also served as valuable associates throughout the project. Their collective wisdom defined the research and policy agenda and we sought their advice again and again on all matters large and small. We thank them for their time, their spirit of collaboration, and their patience. The participants in the CURIES conference contributed their remarkable range of expertise; they gave generously of their time, their knowledge, and their insights. In this regard, we are especially grateful to Lotte Bailyn, Alan Fechter, M.R.C. Greenwood, Lilli Hornig, Nancy Kolodny, and Vivian Pinn for their contributions.

In addition to the chapter authors, a number of other individuals deserve recognition for their thoughtful reviews and helpful comments. We owe thanks to Jacquelynne Eccles, Alan Fechter, Ted Greenwood, Scott Long, Devamonie Naidoo, Willie Pearson, Jr., Helen Remick, and Elaine Seymour.

Many hands and minds are needed to transform a set of interesting and provocative papers into a coherent manuscript and ultimately a published work. *The Equity Equation* would not exist without the faith and efforts of Gale Erlandson and Pamela Berkman of Jossey-Bass, the editing skills of Hilary Powers and copyeditor Michele Jones, the untold hours of work in manuscript preparation by Center for the Education of Women staff Mary Penet and Judy Stentzel, and research and reference checking by Margaret Dykens and Michelle Bejian.

Last but hardly least we want to thank our families for their understanding and support as well as their willingness to listen as we wrestled with ideas and problems.

C.-S. D.

A. B. G.

C. S. H.

B. B. L.

P. M. R.

The Editors

CINDA-SUE DAVIS has an undergraduate degree in chemistry from Grand Valley State University and a M.S. (1972) and Ph.D. (1976) in biological chemistry from the University of Michigan. She spent several years as a postdoctoral scholar and research scientist in the Neurotoxicology Research Laboratories, Environmental and Industrial Health, School of Public Health, University of Michigan.

Since 1984, Davis has directed the University of Michigan Women in Science and Engineering Program of the UM Center for the Education of Women. The WISE program encourages and supports girls and women, from elementary school through graduate school, to consider and pursue degrees and careers in science, engineering, mathematics, and technical fields. Davis has developed and implemented a number of innovative programmatic efforts, including "Summerscience for Girls," a residential hands-on summer science program for middle school girls; "Science for Life," a high school internship program in the biomedical sciences; and the "Pipeline Program," an undergraduate program designed to encourage high-achieving women engineering students to pursue graduate degrees. She was the on-site host for the 1987 Gender and Science and Technology Conference (GASAT) as well as for the first national Women in Science and Engineering Conference, also in 1987, held in collaboration with the American Association for the Advancement of Science. She has authored numerous papers on WISE issues and frequently gives presentations on this topic.

Davis is the recipient of numerous awards, including the "Can-Doer" award from the Michigan Technology Council and a Congressional Resolution of Appreciation and Merit from the Committee on Science, Space, and Technology. She is a member of the Women in Engineering Advocates Network (WEPAN) national board.

ANGELA B. GINORIO is director of the Northwest Center for Research on Women, assistant professor in Women Studies, and adjunct assistant professor in the Psychology Department of the University of Washington in Seattle. She teaches courses on women and science and women and violence.

Her research focuses on issues of women in science, sexual harassment, and racial and ethnic identification. Her most recent publications are the 1995 monograph "Warming the Climate for Women in Academic Science" published by the American Association of Colleges and Universities, "Psychological Issues for Latinas" with L. Gutiérrez, A. M. Cauce, and M. Acosta in *Bringing Cultural Diversity to Feminist Psychology,* and "Dealing with the Sexual in Sexual Harassment" with H. Remick, forthcoming in *Initiatives.*

Ginorio is currently principal investigator of a grant from the NSF's Programs for Women and Girls for a project with rural high school girls, their science teachers, and their counselors. She is a fellow of the American Psychological Association and incoming chair of its Committee on Women in Psychology.

CAROL S. HOLLENSHEAD is director of the University of Michigan Center for the Education of Women (CEW) and University of Michigan chair of the President's Advisory Commission on Women's Issues. An expert on women in higher education, Hollenshead has been a member of the board of directors of the National Council for Research on Women since 1991 and has served as chair of the council since 1994.

As director of the Center for the Education of Women, she oversees service programs, research, advocacy, and policy development focused on higher education and careers for women. Reaching over 10,000 women a year, the center has been in the forefront of the efforts to increase educational access for women for thirty years. The center's Women in Science and Engineering Program was established in 1980 and has served as a model for many other programs throughout the country.

Hollenshead is director or co-director of research and education initiatives concerning women in science, mathematics, and engineering, as well as women's leadership, education, and careers, funded by the National Science Foundation, National Institutes of Health, the Sloan and Kellogg Foundations, and other agencies.

She has lectured and published on many issues of concern to women, including women's education and career patterns, women in the sciences and engineering, the status of women in higher education, and women, work, and aging. Her recent publications focus on career planning for college women, sources of satisfaction and dissatisfaction among graduate students, and women graduate students in mathematics and physics.

Hollenshead is active in a variety of educational and professional organizations. She serves as a reviewer for various journals and as a commentator for Michigan Public Radio.

BARBARA B. LAZARUS is associate provost for academic projects at Carnegie Mellon University. An educational anthropologist, she received her bachelor's degree (1967) from Brown University, her master's (1969) from the University of Connecticut, and her doctorate (1973) from the University of Massachusetts, Amherst. At Carnegie Mellon, she is responsible for coordinating academic programs and policies for undergraduates and graduate students. She serves on the university's Academic Council and the University Education Council and chairs two councils of the seven colleges' associate deans. Dr. Lazarus has teaching appointments in the Department of History and the Heinz School of Urban and Public Affairs. Her research focuses on women in nontraditional occupations in the United States and Asia, and on the impact of illness on paid work. Her most recent book, with M. Karlekar and the Committee for Women's Studies in Asia, is *Changing Lives: Narratives of Asian Pioneers in Women's Studies* (Feminist Press, 1995). She is currently completing *No Universal Constants: Personal Stories of Women in Science and Engineering* (working title), with S. Ambrose, K. Dunkle, D. Harkus, and I. Nair (forthcoming, Temple University Press, 1997).

Lazarus serves on the executive committee of Women for Asian Development (WADEV), on the board as chair of the International Action Committee of Women in Engineering Program Advocates Network (WEPAN), and on the editorial board of the Committee on Women's Studies in Asia.

PAULA M. RAYMAN is director of the Public Policy Institute at Radcliffe College and an instructor at the Harvard Graduate School of

Education. She holds a joint doctorate in economics and sociology from Boston College. A former associate professor of sociology at Wellesley College, Rayman has also served as director of the Women and Sciences Project at the Wellesley Center for Research on Women. She is the former chair of the Older Worker Task Force for the Massachusetts Jobs Council and presently serves as chair of the Council's Science and Technology Task Force. She was a member of the Science and Technology Commission for the Fourth World Conference on Women in Beijing.

Rayman is editor of Temple University Press's *Labor and Social Change* series. Her published works include *Pathways for Women in the Sciences: Part I* (Alfred P. Sloan Foundation, 1993); *Out of Work: The Consequences of Unemployment in Hartford's Aircraft Industry* (National Institute for Mental Health, 1982); *The Israel Kibbutz: Community and Nation Building* (Princeton University Press, 1981); and *Non-Violent Action and Social Change* (Wiley, 1979). She recently received a National Science Foundation Grant to convene a working conference in the fall of 1996 on science careers, the economy, and gender equity.

The Contributors

HELEN S. ASTIN, a psychologist, is professor of higher education and associate director of the Higher Education Research Institute at the University of California, Los Angeles (UCLA). She served as interim director of the UCLA Center for the Study of Women between 1990 and 1992 and as the associate provost of the College of Letters and Science at UCLA from 1983 to 1987. Astin is a recipient of the Carolyn Wood Sherif Award of the American Psychological Association and in 1988 was named by the association a Distinguished Leader for Women in Psychology.

She is also a recipient of the award for Outstanding Contribution to Research and Literature of the National Association of Student Personnel Administrators, of the Bread and Roses Award of the Los Angeles Westside National Women's Political Caucus, and of several honorary degrees. Astin has served as a trustee of Mt. St. Mary's and Hampshire Colleges. In 1994–95 Astin served as chair of the board of the American Association for Higher Education.

Astin's major books include *Women of Influence, Women of Vision; Human Resources and Higher Education; The Women Doctorate in America; The Power of Protest; Higher Education and the Disadvantaged Student; Open Admissions at CUNY; Women: A Bibliography on Their Education and Careers; Sex Roles: An Annotated Research Bibliography; Some Action of Her Own: The Adult Woman and Higher Education; Sex Discrimination in Career Counseling and Education; The Higher Education of Women; Essays in Honor of Rosemary Park.*

DARYL E. CHUBIN has been division director for research, evaluation, and dissemination in the Education and Human Resources Directorate of the National Science Foundation since September

1993. Chubin began his career in federal service in 1986 as senior analyst, and later as senior associate, in the Science, Education, and Transportation Program of the Office of Technology Assessment, U.S. Congress. Prior to that he was professor in the School of Social Sciences at the Georgia Institute of Technology (1977–1986). Since 1990, he has served as adjunct professor in the Cornell-in-Washington program. He earned a Ph.D. in sociology from Loyola University, Chicago, in 1973.

Chubin has published numerous articles, chapters, and commentaries, as well as six books, including *Peerless Science: Peer Review and U.S. Science Policy* (with E. J. Hackett; SUNY Press, 1990) and *Rethinking Science as a Career: Perceptions and Realities in the Physical Sciences* (with S. Tobias and K. Aylesworth; Research Corp., July 1995). He was project director for the OTA reports *Educating Scientists and Engineers: Grade School to Grad School* (Government Printing Office, June 1988) and *Federally Funded Research: Decisions for a Decade* (May 1991).

Chubin serves in an array of editorial roles for five journals. He is also a founding member of the Society for Social Studies of Science (4S), was elected a fellow of the American Association for Advancement of Science (AAAS) in 1990, and was elected in 1992 to the policy council of the Association for Public Policy Analysis and Management (APPAM).

BEATRIZ CHU CLEWELL is a principal research associate at the Urban Institute in Washington, D.C. She received her B.A. (1970) in English literature and her Ph.D. (1980) in educational policy planning and analysis, both from Florida State University. Her main research activities have focused on factors that encourage or impede equal access to educational opportunity for members of racial/ethnic minority groups and women. One area of specialization has been research on the access of members of underrepresented racial/ethnic groups and women to science, mathematics, and engineering fields.

Clewell's publications include *Women of Color in Mathematics, Science, and Engineering: A Review of the Literature* (with B. T. Anderson, 1991); *Building the Nation's Work Force From the Inside Out: Educating Minorities for the Twenty-First Century* (with S. V. Brown, 1991);

Breaking the Barriers: Helping Female and Minority Students Succeed in Mathematics and Science (with B. T. Anderson and M. E. Thorpe, 1992); and "Asian Americans in Mathematics and Science" in *The Asian American Almanac* (1995).

MARGARET N. DYKENS has worked at the University of Michigan Center for the Education of Women as information specialist and publications editor since 1993. She received her master's degree (1980) in biology from the College of William and Mary and her master's (1993) in information and library studies from the University of Michigan. At the Center for the Education of Women, she serves as an expert resource for information regarding women's education and employment, as well as women in science issues. With over fourteen years' experience in research laboratories and herbaria, she has written and edited numerous articles for scientific journals. Throughout her career she has also illustrated scientific monographs and textbooks, both as staff illustrator at Harvard's Arnold Arboretum and as a freelance artist.

MARY FRANK FOX is professor of sociology, School of History, Technology, and Society, Georgia Institute of Technology. She received her Ph.D. (1978) in sociology from the University of Michigan. Her research focuses on women and men in academic and scientific organizations and occupations, and her current project, supported by the National Science Foundation, is a study of women in doctoral education in five scientific and engineering fields. She is the co-author of *Women at Work* (1984), editor of *Scholarly Writing and Publishing* (1985), and author of articles in over twenty different scholarly journals and collections. She is associate editor of *Sex Roles* and co-founder and past associate editor of *Gender & Society*. Currently, she is on the Council of the Section on Sex and Gender of the American Sociological Association (and past chair of the section) and is president (1995) of Sociologists for Women in Society.

JENNIFER S. JACKSON served as a research associate on the Pathways Project for Women in the Sciences from 1991 to 1995. She received her B.A. (1993) in psychology from Wellesley College and her M.Ed.

(1995) from the Harvard Graduate School of Education. She is currently employed as a senior research analyst for the Center for Educational Leadership and Technology in Marlborough, Massachusetts.

JANE BUTLER KAHLE is Condit Professor of Science Education at Miami University, Oxford, Ohio. Kahle's current research concerns the development and testing of a theoretical model to guide scholarship concerning the recruitment, retention and success of girls and women in non-traditional courses and careers. As co-principal investigator, she has made equity the cornerstone of Ohio's statewide systemic initiative to improve the teaching and learning of science and mathematics. Recently she completed a study to assess changes in learning environments, teaching practices, and learning outcomes throughout the state of Ohio.

Kahle has received national awards and several international fellowships for her research. She is the author of more than eighty articles, four monographs, thirteen book chapters, and six books and has served on the editorial review boards of more than a dozen scholarly journals. She has also served as chair of the National Science Foundation's Committee on Equal Opportunities in Science and Engineering, as a member of the American Association for the Advancement of Science's Committee on Opportunities in Science, and as an expert witness for congressional committees and task forces. In addition, she has served as chair of the board of directors of the Biological Sciences Curriculum Studies and of the Gender and Science and Technology Association. Kahle has been president of the National Biology Teachers Association and the National Association for Research in Science Teaching.

SHIRLEY M. MALCOM is head of the Directorate for Education and Human Resources Programs of the American Association for the Advancement of Science (AAAS). The directorate includes AAAS programs in education, activities for underrepresented groups, and fostering public understanding of science and technology. Malcom was head of the AAAS Office of Opportunities in Science from 1979 to 1989. Malcom received her doctorate (1974) in ecology from Pennsylvania State University; her master's degree in zoology from the University of California, Los Angeles; and her B.A. degree with distinction in zoology from the University of Washington. In addition she holds six honorary degrees.

Malcom serves on several boards, including those of the American Museum of Natural History, the Carnegie Corporation of New York, and the National Center on Education and the Economy. In addition, she has chaired a number of national committees addressing education reform and access to scientific and technical education, careers, and literacy.

She served on the Clinton-Gore team, chairing the task group on vocational/technical education for the Departments of Education and Labor. She was recently appointed by President Clinton and confirmed by the Senate as a member of the National Science Board and named to the President's Committee of Advisors on Science and Technology.

INDIRA NAIR is associate professor and associate department head in Engineering and Public Policy at Carnegie Mellon University in Pittsburgh, Pennsylvania. Her research interests include environmental problems, risk analysis, risk communication, and uncertainty in science; ethics and technology; science teaching, public education, educational administration, and student development. Nair received her B.Sc. (1960) in physics and mathematics and her M.Sc. (1962) in physics from the University of Bombay, India. She received a M.S. (1969) in physics from Kansas State University and a Ph.D. (1972), also in physics, from Northwestern.

At Carnegie Mellon, she teaches several interdisciplinary courses, including "Radiation, Health, and Policy" and "Science, Technology, and Ethics." Her service activities there include membership in committees for programs for women in science and engineering, student quality of life, and faculty and student ethics. She also founded the CMU chapter of Student Pugwash, an international organization devoted to student explorations of scientific, technological, and social relationships and responsibility. She received the 1993 Doherty Prize, the highest award at Carnegie Mellon for contribution to teaching and education.

Nair chaired the advisory panel for the U.S. Congress Office of Technology Assessment on "green design" and co-authored an OTA report on biological effects of power-frequency electric and magnetic fields. She works with several high school and precollege teacher resource programs.

SUE V. ROSSER received her Ph.D. (1973) in zoology from the University of Wisconsin, Madison. During 1995, she served as senior program officer for women's programs at the National Science Foundation. She is currently the director for the Center on Women's Studies and Gender Research at the University of Florida, Gainesville, where she is also professor of anthropology. From 1986 to 1995 she served as director of women's studies at the University of South Carolina, where she was professor of family and preventive medicine in the medical school.

Rosser has edited collections and written approximately sixty journal articles on the theoretical and applied problems of women and science and women's health. Author of the books *Teaching Science and Health from a Feminist Perspective: A Practical Guide* (1986), *Feminism within the Science and Health Care Professions: Overcoming Resistance* (1988), *Female-Friendly Science, Feminism and Biology: A Dynamic Interaction, Women's Health: Missing from U.S. Medicine,* and *Teaching the Majority,* she also served as the Latin and North American co-editor of *Women's Studies International Forum* from 1989 to 1993. From 1992 to 1994 she held a grant from the National Science Foundation for "A USC System Model for Transformation of Science and Math Teaching to Reach Women in Varied Campus Settings." During the fall of 1993 she was visiting distinguished professor for the University of Wisconsin System Women in Science Project.

LINDA J. SAX is associate director of the Higher Education Research Institute (HERI) and the Cooperative Institutional Research Program (CIRP) at UCLA. In that capacity, she is responsible for CIRP's ongoing national studies of college students and faculty. She received her B.A. (1990) in political economy from the University of California, Berkeley, and her Ph.D. (1994) in higher education from UCLA. Sax teaches graduate courses at UCLA in research methodology, evaluation of higher education, and gender issues in higher education. She also serves on the editorial board for *Research in Higher Education.*

Sax's research focuses on gender differences in college student development, particularly with respect to how college influences mathematics and science confidence, persistence, and career choice. She has given numerous presentations at national conferences and has authored book chapters and monographs. She has recently published articles on the development of mathematics self-concept during college, gender differences in mathematics and science persistence, and the effects of the gender composition of the major.

The late BETTY M. VETTER served as a director of the Commission on Professionals in Science and Technology (CPST, formerly the Scientific Manpower Commission) from 1963 to 1994. In this capacity she planned and administered a program concerned broadly with providing accurate information about the characteristics of and opportunities for U.S. scientists and engineers, with fostering excellence in their education, and with their utilization in the national interest. The program included analysis and publication of data delineating the supply of and demand for these specialists, their salaries, their career opportunities, and their demographic characteristics. Biennial symposia, most recently in 1992 on *Preparing for the Twenty-First Century: Human Resources in Science Technology*, and the resulting *Proceedings*, were planned and carried out under her guidance.

She was the author of many publications for the commission dealing with scientists and engineers and the military draft, the supply of and demand for technical personnel, the demographic characteristics of today's scientists and engineers and of those in varying careers in these disciplines.

The first significant project concerned with women and minorities in science and engineering resulted in publication in 1975 of the first edition of *Professional Women and Minorities: A Manpower Data Resource Service*. That enlarged report is now in its tenth edition. The studies resulted in the publication of *Labor Force Participation of Women Trained in Science and Engineering and Factors Affecting Their Participation* (1979); *The Production, Testing and Evaluation of an Audio-Visual Presentation on Career Opportunities for Women in Science and Engineering* (1981); *Opportunities in Science and Engineering* (1984); *Guide to Data on Scientists and Engineers* (1984); and

Measuring National Needs for Scientists to the Year 2000 (1989). With assistance from various staff members, Ms. Vetter carried out the research involved and authored the ensuing reports of all these projects.

From 1964 to 1994, Ms. Vetter served as editor and principal author of *Scientific, Engineering, Technical Manpower Comments,* a thirty-two-page digest published nine to twelve times a year by the Scientific Manpower Commission (now CPST).

Her experience included both the collection and analysis of data for specific studies and the analysis of data from other sources. She was the author of more than 150 published reports and articles, and was a frequent lecturer in these subject areas.

STACY A. WENZEL received her Ph.D. in Higher and Postsecondary Education from Michigan in 1995. She currently serves as research associate at the Center for Research on Women and Gender of the University of Illinois at Chicago. She is the author or co-author of a number of studies focusing on the success and satisfaction of engineering and science faculty and graduate students. Her most recent work is a qualitative analysis of the careers of women engineering faculty.

In addition to her research on engineering and science faculty and graduate students, Wenzel has conducted studies on the retention of women faculty at research universities and on faculty publication performance. She actively presents her work through the Association for the Study of Higher Education, the American Educational Research Association, the American Society of Engineering Education, and the Women in Engineering Programs Advocacy Network.

Throughout her graduate career at Michigan, Wenzel was awarded a number of scholarships recognizing her commitment to excellence in her work. Prior to her graduate studies, she earned a B.S. (1985) in chemical engineering. She has worked in industry as a process engineer and in university administration providing academic guidance to first-year engineering students.

Chapter One

Policies to Promote Women in Science

Daryl E. Chubin, Shirley M. Malcom

Public policy works to promote social goals. However, good intentions can lead to bad public policy, and good public policy can lead to bad practice. Many—scholars, policy makers, and ordinary citizens alike—are wary of policies and programs, especially when directed by the federal government. They warn of creeping regulation, which all too often seems to beget an equally disruptive and costly deregulation, as in transportation and trade.

Sometimes the fear is warranted. For example, policies designed to ensure that students targeted for Title I support were served by the programs it funded actually counteracted its benefit. Title I was established in 1965 as a Great Society program to support educational remediation of students from economically disadvantaged situations. The scope of the program expanded over time to include a larger target audience and broader range of social services. But regulations provided disincentives for success: if student performance improved, schools lost funding (Legters &

Note: We are grateful to Alan Fechter and Paula Rayman for comments on earlier drafts. The views expressed here are the authors' own and do not reflect those of the American Association for the Advancement of Science (AAAS), the National Science Foundation (NSF), or the National Science Board (NSB). This chapter is dedicated to the memory of Betty M. Vetter.

Slavin, 1994). Conditions that produced the need for remediation in the first place were neither challenged nor changed, and the innovation represented by Title I gradually eroded to its present status of district entitlement. This is policy gone awry.

Is there a way to strike a balance between interference and disregard? Can government implement innovative programs that produce intended effects and benefit the national interest?

We reply with an unequivocal yes: the nation's human resources are amenable to policy intervention. Federal policy has already increased the presence of underserved populations in the professions, including science and engineering. Nevertheless, women, minorities, and persons with disabilities remain underrepresented in science and underserved by it. Without the participation of these growing groups, the health of U.S. science inevitably suffers.

Policy Rhetoric and Reality

The linkages among law, policy, and cultural change are hard to trace. Public law alone is no panacea; it can create opportunities with so much stigma and suspicion attached that they inhibit larger social changes. For example, consider federal set-aside programs that limit a pool of eligible competitors to those with a targeted attribute, such as age, gender, or race. Such programs, despite the good they do, often marginalize their beneficiaries. The need for sheltered competition is invariably interpreted as lack of ability to compete. In the language of public discourse, this interpretation is called "blaming the victim." Nonetheless, program floors easily become ceilings used to steer even the most meritorious members of the defined population to the meager set-asides.

In these days of reexamination, some are questioning the legacy of affirmative action. That phrase, of course, is a misnomer. We need to change the discourse of affirmation as well as the resulting action. If programs designed to increase participation in science on the basis of merit diminish that merit, then the result is not a benefit. Anything that compromises quality is detrimental to the health of science.

The term *affirmative action,* as applied in an employment context, muddles both the purpose and the operation of programs designed to increase opportunity *among those equally qualified.*

Affirmative action in science must combine a quality screen and certain collective characteristics to fulfill the intent of the program. For example, the Small Business Innovation Research Act of 1982 specifies a set of agencies to determine the merit in proposals from small firms to perform federally funded R&D. This targeting to increase diversity of research participants and strengthen the health of science should not be confused either with guaranteed funding or with a weakening of the federal portfolio—proposals must reach a quality threshold before the question of funding arises.

Public policy is a blunt instrument. It seeks to transform institutions from the inside out, but usually intervenes on behalf of outsiders trying to get in. The difference is not subtle: the latter kind of public policy is a wedge that lets people seep into essentially unchanged institutions; the former is a mandate that declares how institutions shall act and urges them, along with the culture at large, to accept change. In fact, both individuals and institutions must be readied for change. The dual burden of public policy is to force an examination of individual behavior and, in the process, to change institutions to accommodate the intent of policy.

This book's focus is on women, but the problem is the system within which they function. Viewed systemically, the issue is one of creating opportunities for all to prepare and compete for careers in science and engineering. Underpinned by federal law, institutionalized change, or what has been called structural reform (Matyas & Malcom, 1991), would eliminate the need to speak of nontraditional occupations (those in which women rarely participate) or to create targeted set-aside programs. Structural reform aims for coursework, pedagogy, institutional climate, and recruitment and retention systems that work together in a supportive administrative structure. However, until increased participation has been built into the system, targeted programs will remain a critical strategy for working toward reform.

Donna Shavlik, of the American Council on Education, wrote in 1989, "Before, it was women doing the changing, the adapting. Now women are demanding that it's time for institutions to do the adapting" (Pearson, Shavlik, & Touchton, 1989). This is the state of affairs—a system of education linked to the workplace, opportunities for career development congruent with national needs—

that we have in sight. Increasing the preparation of any group for degree-taking is wasted motion if they have no opportunity to participate in the work force. From a policy perspective, there is another wrinkle, too: targeting the *majority* of the population is contradictory. If the majority is ill-served, then the overall policy is flawed, not just for one group but for society at large. This is what Etzkowitz, Kemelgor, Neuschatz, Uzzi, and Alonzo (1994) recently termed "the paradox of critical mass."

Put another way, if the culture of a workplace—academic, corporate, or governmental—is unwelcoming, even the best human resources will not be drawn to it. The education process is fraught with negative cues for women. They are seen as lacking aptitude or fortitude and thus neither valued nor developed as a recruitable resource for science (Hewitt & Seymour, 1991). If they survive to enter the work force, their presence is greeted with ambivalence even by the few women who have preceded them (Etzkowitz et al., 1994). Opportunities for development, recognition, and career advancement remain in doubt.

First and foremost, this is a cultural issue. Science has resisted women as equal partners. And public policy has helped sustain this resistance. We need to develop new ways for public policy to intercede in the culture of the scientific workplace. Rather than concentrating processes such as recruitment and reward, public policy can diversify them, and it can suggest ways to reshape institutional actions to fortify the health of science.

Changes in Practice: Increasing the Policy Pressure

Whether prohibiting discrimination, providing direct student funding, underwriting institutional programs, disseminating model materials, or supporting state and local agencies, the federal government is a major force in education (U.S. Congress, 1991, ch. 7; Browning, 1992; Stromquist, 1993; Matyas & Malcom, 1991), particularly in science, engineering, and technology. The influence began with the pre-equity stage of the National Defense Education Act of 1958, continued through Title VII of the Civil Rights Act of 1964 and the Higher Education Act of 1965, blossomed into Title IX of the Education Amendments of 1972 and the Science and Technologies Opportunities Act (reauthorizing the NSF) in 1980 that targeted specific groups, and led to the economic competitiveness rationale signaled by the Perkins Vocational Education Act of 1984 and subsequent legislation (Leggon & Malcom, 1994).

As the U.S. Congress Office of Technology Assessment (1988a) put it:

> Federal legislation, in particular Title IX . . . has provided leadership, law, and most importantly a national commitment to sex equity, and has impelled substantial social and economic changes. Title IX eliminated overt discrimination and encouraged equitable treatment of men and women both inside and outside education. The greatest gains of women in science . . . were made during the early days of Title IX, during broad interpretation of the legislation, vigorous enforcement, national leadership, and social fervor.
>
> Since its passage, enforcement of Title IX has lessened, grant support for its implementation under the Women's Educational Equity Act has been reduced, and its applications have been narrowed by Federal and court rulings. . . .
>
> The past clear success of Title IX in . . . encouraging women to enter non-traditional fields argues that . . . the Nation recommit itself to equity. . . . This should require little new funding; most of the achievements of Title IX were made through changes in practice rather than Federal appropriations for new programs [pp. 100–101].

"Changes in practice" speak to the barriers that women find: a chilly climate on campus, too few role models, and a perception (reinforced by mounting data) that access to career opportunities and salaries may be even more gender linked in science and engineering than in business or law (U.S. Congress, 1989, p. 9; American Council on Education, n.d.; Dix, 1987; Hall & Sandler, 1982).

In government and industry, the phrases *glass ceiling* and *mommy track* have come to denote career-truncating biases (U.S. Department of Labor, 1992). Between scholarly, historical, and biographical accounts of women scientists (Holloway, 1993; Abir-Am & Outram, 1987) and federal reports on underemployment and promotion and salary differentials (National Science Foundation [NSF], 1994), we see pervasive forces keeping women out of the boardroom and off the path to it. Stereotypes about capabilities and choices—not performance—continue to define advancement.

Stereotyping alone does not explain the underrepresentation of women in science. Girls and women make their own choices, but they are surrounded by expectations about appropriate behavior: self-fulfilling prophecies do the rest. Simultaneously, however, policy pressures build through the accumulation of small informal injustices and large social trends. Consider, therefore, some countertrends that can shape the future:

1. *Demographic change* has increased the number of women pursuing higher degrees and entering the work force (Dix, 1993). The greater the number, the harder to isolate and conquer. For example, the growing presence of senior women on boards, committees, and policy-making bodies reinforces the impression of professional communities and society at large that there is more than tokenism at work: these women's contributions are valued.

2. *Dual-career couples* (and especially dual Ph.D.'s) create new demands on their employers (for the timing of promotion and tenure review, and for child care), as well as on the couples themselves (regarding what one is willing to sacrifice in professional opportunities for the career of the other) (Crease, 1993; Foster, 1993; Lubchenco & Menge, 1993; Wake, 1993).

3. *Workplace sensitivity* to qualitative issues of climate, harassment, and power has been increasing in science and engineering (for example, see Brennan, 1993; Etzkowitz et al., 1992). Investigative journalism often targets sites of alleged bias and tension, spreading the word and simultaneously giving hope to some and striking fear in others (for example, see Mann, 1994a, 1994b). Note the rise of ombudsmen and the visibility of equal opportunity offices (e.g., Swisher, 1994; Tilghman, 1993; Angier, 1991).

4. *Professional societies* and nongovernmental organizations such as the Women Chemists Committee of the American Chemical Society, the American Physical Society Committee on the Status of Women in Physics, and the National Academy of Sciences Commission on Women now monitor equal opportunity for all their members and the involvement of formerly underparticipating groups in official business and intellectual programs (for example, see Fehrs & Czujko, 1992; Hoke, 1992).

In addition, groups such as the Association for Women in Science sometimes intervene in workplace disputes through investigation, censure, or legal recourse.

5. *Political vigilance* (congressional hearings, caucuses, lobbying) accompanies the threat of lawsuits (U.S. House of Representatives, 1992). Legal cases centered on individual disputes often lead to remedies available more broadly, or to corrective efforts designed to avoid similar litigation. (For a discussion of disputes over allocation of lab space, budgets, and personnel to male and female investigators at the National Cancer Institute, see Seachrist, 1994; for disputes on women's health issues in research deficits and clinical trials, see Pinn, 1992.)

Such changes confront and slowly erode assumptions about practice. The force of law depersonalizes and recalibrates as offensive behavior that may have been seen as idiosyncratic and even whimsical. The issue, at one level, is compliance with the law; at another it is heeding the cultural message "beware, discrimination will not be tolerated." Does the institution make an accommodation? Or does the burden fall squarely on the individual? A recent title captures the current situation: *The "Problem" of Women in Science: Why Is it So Difficult to Convince People There Is One?* (Tobias, 1993).

Answers will derive from stretching the social fabric. Changes, however, must be made locally—in the classroom and the workplace—and early in the life cycle (for example, see Baker, 1992; Clewell, Thorpe, & Anderson, 1987) if girls and women are not to be limited by the attitudes and expectations of teachers, supervisors, and opinion leaders. Data and analysis differ from decisions on how to act (Layzell, 1990). We must remain mindful that measuring the extent of discrimination does not remove it. Such measurement, however, can supply evidence useful to those who must first convince colleagues of the problem and then set mechanisms in place to monitor progress toward its remedy.

Asking the Right Question: How Far Have We Come?

Since 1985, the Office of Technology Assessment (OTA) (U.S. Congress, 1985, 1988a, 1988b, 1989, 1991) has monitored the changing face of human resources for science and engineering. These path-breaking reports triggered a wave of scholarly literature, as disciplines and professional societies became more self-conscious and analytical about the fate of their new practitioners. Reviewing this literature, as the Commission on Professionals in Science and Technology (CPST) has done, reporting monthly in *CPST Comments*, prompts assessments of how various groups move through the formal U.S. education system and what they encounter after their training is complete. To capture the plight of women in science, we quote CPST's late executive director, Betty Vetter (1992): "ferment: yes, progress: maybe, change: slow."

Many interventions focus on increasing women's participation in the science and engineering pipeline—an unfortunate metaphor often used to denote the process of refining a supply of potential talent into competent, credentialed specialists. From the focus on supply, we have learned that launching a career in science demands preparation in content and nurturance of spirit and aspiration, and we have begun to understand what type of curriculum and mentoring and apprenticeship programs provide the necessary preparation and support. However, we also need an environment where women and people of color can find appropriate jobs in academic and industrial science, or we perpetuate an insidious feedback loop. If the face of science remains predominantly white and male, talent is clearly being diverted to other fields. Translation to the student: diversity is valued more by other professions so I should go elsewhere.

Thus, no matter how sophisticated our data and analyses, it is the way our evaluations and interpretations are used that counts. The best data, the most reasoned analysis, and the most compelling policy alternatives may have no impact at all on the creation of new legislation or the reauthorization of old. To put it bluntly, just because we know better doesn't mean we *do* better. The question of use is beyond the control of any analyst and can seem overwhelming, but research must continue regardless—state-of-the-art knowledge is a necessary condition for progress, even if not sufficient to ensure it.

Research by the American Association for the Advancement of Science (Matyas & Malcom, 1991) and professional societies

("Women in Science," 1992; Kenschaft, 1991) indicates that women continue to struggle for access to tenure-track positions in research universities. More women work in non–tenure-track slots or part time, often on short-term funding, than men. Women earn less at every stage of the scientific career, and the disparity increases at the highest levels of experience. These hard data are embedded in a well-documented anecdotal record of climate factors deterring women from pursuing or completing undergraduate degrees, or seeking graduate degrees in science and engineering, or flourishing even with the right credentials in the academic workplace (Healy, 1992). Meanwhile, the record is silent on the causes of student indecision about major fields; on the transitions between stages of education that are especially forbidding to women; and on who applies, who reviews, and who decides in selecting and hiring practices, and who is ultimately appointed.

Nevertheless, congressional oversight, as well as the work of such support agencies as the General Accounting Office and the OTA and of policy and planning offices in the executive R&D agencies, suggest that the federal government has institutionalized "professionalized scrutiny" (Chubin, 1994, p. 129). Systematic, quantitative data on underrepresentation of women in enrollment, financial support, degree taking, and early career awards provide benchmarks that raise legislative awareness and adjust targets in federal programs designed to increase merit-based participation in science (see, for example, U.S. Congress, 1989, pp. 168–171; U.S. Congress, 1991, pp. 206–208; Carson & Chubin, 1993). The availability of disaggregated information, nationally or in discipline-, sector-, or industry-specific databases, can help determine the effort (and perhaps resources) needed to address and redress subtle and not-so-subtle practices from the classroom to the boardroom to the courtroom (Chubin, Hackett, & Solomon, 1994).

One of the purposes of gathering new data and performing new analyses is to help motivate changes in practice. Such changes can open up the tenure process, shape career paths, influence the criteria and rewards for professional achievement, and improve the climate of the workplace. Whether this is done in the name of equity, avoiding waste of talent, or complying with the law, the purpose is to enhance the motivation to welcome qualified women to the workplace. What, then, is the appropriate role for various stake-holders, from Congress to the local institution, beyond document-ing, explaining, or defending the factors that restrain full participation of women in science and engineering?

H.R. 467, a bill introduced by Rep. Constance Morella (R-MD) early in the 103rd Congress, outlines one congressional response. The bill would establish a commission on the advancement of women in scientific fields. Near the end of the 103rd Congress, in August 1994, Sen. Orrin Hatch (R-UT) proposed a counterpart (S. 2356) bill, focused on the problems associated with retaining women in science, mathematics, and engineering careers. The Hatch bill details membership for a seventeen-member commis-sion: five presidential appointees, seven congressional appointees, two representatives, two senators, and the director of the Office of Science and Technology Policy (OSTP).

The charge to the commission Morella seeks to create, which may be one step closer to reality given Hatch's action, includes a formidable research agenda.

1. Identify the number of women in the U.S. science and engi-neering work force and the specific types of occupations in which women scientists and engineers are underrepresented.
2. Examine the preparedness of women to pursue careers in science and engineering and to advance to positions of respon-sibility in academia, industry, and government.
3. Describe the practices and policies of employers and labor unions relating to the recruitment, retention, and advance-ment of women scientists and engineers.
4. Identify the opportunities for, and artificial barriers to, the recruitment, retention, and advancement of women scientists and engineers in academia, industry, and government.
5. Describe the employment situations in which the recruitment, retention, and advancement of women scientists and engineers are comparable—and those not comparable—to those of men.
6. Compile a synthesis of available data on practices, policies, and programs that have led to the successful recruitment, reten-tion, and advancement of women in science and engineering, including training programs, reward programs, employee ben-efit structures, and family leave policies.

7. Examine such other issues and information relating to the advancement of women in science and engineering as determined by the Commission to be appropriate.
8. Issue recommendations that government (including Congress and appropriate federal agencies), academia, and private industry can follow to assist in the recruitment, retention, and advancement of women in science and engineering. (H.R. 467, 1993, pp. 4–5)

Data and analysis coupled to such a national commission could indeed inform and prescribe possible policy actions.

Targeted and Structural Remedies

For many years, efforts to address the participation of women and minorities in science have been undertaken through special or targeted programs, usually localized and small in scale. We have learned valuable lessons about feasibility and effectiveness from these efforts (for summaries, see U.S. Congress, 1988b; Federal Task Force, 1990). But they were never designed to produce, and have never yielded, sweeping national improvements. A targeted approach necessarily features modest efforts relative to the size of the problem and to the resources deployed by the rest of the system to maintain the status quo. What is good—and different—is all too easily crowded out before attention turns to scaling up.

Targeted approaches have other problems as well:

- Volatility due to dependence on outside money. "Hard budget times" often excuse cutting special or experimental programs.
- Overdependence on volunteer labor by faculty and staff, especially where the work does not count toward promotion, tenure, or merit raises for performance.
- Resistance to perceived outside mandates that undercut grassroots (department, college) control. The institutional commitment is seen only as financially driven, not prompted by convictions and activism germinating in the local culture.

Clearly, these factors point up the difference between real change and change embraced for extrinsic and transient reasons. Small targeted programs cannot generate structural reform, but they can help generate ideas. The bumper sticker might read: "Think bigger, act structurally." Figure 1.1 outlines the relationships among individual and institutional commitment and funding that must evolve to create structural reform.

Matyas and Malcom (1991) report that the institutions of higher education they studied evidenced no enduring structural change. Rather, each was at a foundational stage of restructuring through the establishment of centers and the coordination of programs. Indeed, no institution had formulated or implemented a promotion and tenure system that gave adequate weight, value, and attention to the human resources activities of departments. Budget considerations were based on head counts (input) instead of student success (output), and no effort was made to connect student outcomes to faculty outcomes.

Figure 1.1. Model for the Evolution of Intervention Programs.

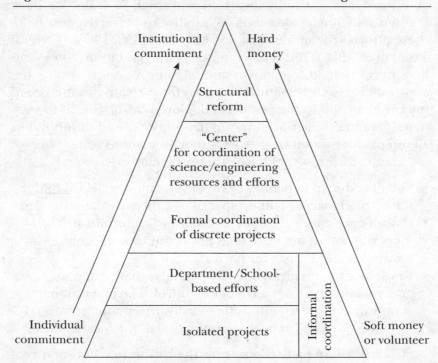

Source: Matyas and Malcom, 1991, p. 144.

In many research universities and other institutions, the reward system has become distorted. Claiming to value teaching, it penalizes those who spend time trying to teach well. And the federal government, wittingly or not, has allowed its research funding policy to promote this effect. Knowledge generation has been severed from—and perversely pitted against—education and human resource development. Simply put, how do faculty spend their time? What earns rewards for them? Who is their primary clientele? The answers are all too clear: research; research and entrepreneurship; other researchers and sponsors. Somehow we must reintegrate research, education, and human resource development.

If new knowledge is the only product valued by research universities or is perceived to be all that government is buying, then disincentives confront every other activity. Faculty are discouraged from mentoring, serving as role models, and devoting time to undergraduate instruction and community service aimed at younger students contemplating scientific careers. Students get channeled into very limited areas, instead of gaining experience in a variety of professional settings. They find their doctorates delayed while they work on research for their professors, and they must participate in a system devoted to the compulsive weeding out of undergraduates whose performance in freshman gatekeeper courses makes them seem unsuitable for research careers. No one has any incentive to draw students into science from nonscience fields, as such students would require intellectual and time commitments to repair deficiencies in their preparation, and having been courted and persuaded to transfer, they would tend to be less tolerant of the institutionalized labor system. The fields of science, mathematics, and engineering thus suffer from the waste of human resources at all levels of university life.

The slowing of growth in federal R&D funding further stifles academic human resource development by intensifying competition for research grants. Many faculty are forced to compete for funds to support graduate students; they find that the resulting tension turns teaching undergraduates into a diversion and developing a diverse faculty and student body into a gamble. It is clear that the way federal funds are awarded affects a range of outcomes valued by the nation, and it should therefore support all the things we value, not just knowledge generation.

It is time to reexamine the systematic tensions between undergraduate teaching and research and to reconsider research support mechanisms and models. For example, we need an alternative to the current endless proposal writing, and we need to promote competition among (and thereby excellence in) collaborative units rather than among individuals (U.S. Congress, 1991: ch. 7). The individual-investigator system leads to the practice of using nonfaculty researchers to ghostwrite proposals for faculty. Ostensibly, funded proposals sustain momentum in the professor's research program. But at what cost? Such funding also supports postdoctoral or nonfaculty researchers—a legion of soft-monied but credentialed laborers, often female—in a spiral of intellectual servitude. Many institutions refuse to accept research proposals from nonfaculty personnel, so these ghostwriters cannot establish independent track records. Their identity is submerged in the professor's team, lab, and reputation.

Another source of tension that should be amenable to public policy intervention is the call to reduce production of young physicists (and increasingly, mathematicians) in the face of an indifferent-to-sluggish labor market. Faculty may inadvertently feed students' sense of betrayal by preparing them for a market that no longer eagerly employs new Ph.D.'s (Holden, 1994). If Ph.D. production is to be restricted in the short term, then how can the federal government induce institutions and departments to cut back voluntarily? Should certain institutions be targeted? Should recent employment rates for new Ph.D.'s be adopted as the guide for sanctioning production levels? Or (as discussed by Magner, 1994, and Kirby & Czujko, 1993) do we wait and hope that market forces will reverse, prospects brighten, and hiring rebound? In a new book, Tobias, Chubin, and Aylesworth (1995) answer with a resounding no. If recent downturns indicate a more permanent, global structural change rather than a cyclical trough, then we urgently need information on the demand for scientific personnel and on ways to influence that demand and deploy trained personnel to benefit a broad array of national and corporate goals.

The worry is that federal intervention may have consequences far more grave than a laissez-faire approach (Fechter, 1990, 1994). What is at risk? We face a dilemma of underparticipation versus overproduction. How do we justify policies to increase participa-

tion of women and others in the face of an apparent glut of
Ph.D.'s? How do we demonstrate the strength in diversity among
women and U.S. minorities without casting a nervous eye on the
growing proportions of foreign citizens who earn Ph.D.'s in engineering, mathematics, and computer science? In terms of financial support alone, it is difficult not to conclude that the presence
of foreign nationals in our graduate departments reduces the
recruitment of women and U.S. minorities. Federal policies, especially immigration law, maintain the imbalance between underparticipating groups and overproduced groups. Can new policy
reduce the imbalance in nondiscriminatory ways while preserving
institutional latitude to serve disciplinary, sectoral, local, national,
and international interests?

Although we cannot do such questions justice here, it is useful
to discuss a deeper cultural issue that can muffle or amplify policy
interventions. We need to temper our individualist science ethic
by greater appreciation for teamwork, cooperation, and shared
meanings and outcomes. Collaboration receives a great deal of lip
service, and yet collaborative behavior is neither taught nor
rewarded. (For a nonacademic view, see Schrage, 1990; also Alper,
1994; and Gibbons, 1994.) Negotiation and compromise are still
seen as business skills, not as creative tools. Sharing ideas and weav-
ing them into a cloth distinctive from the output of one brain is
seen as fortuitous and anomalous, not a thing to be routinely
achieved. More cynically, submerging one's brilliance in group
effort, especially across disciplines, is considered a dilution of excellence, a search for a tolerable lowest common denominator. (For
studies of interdisciplinarity, see Chubin, Porter, Rossini, & Connolly, 1986; "Interdisciplinary Studies," 1989; and Kates, 1991.)

One could argue that the culture of science and engineering,
outside high-energy physics and large-scale clinical trials, inhibits
or blocks collaboration. Rewarding teams as well as individuals
would pose its own measurement difficulties, even if the culture
favored collective performance appraisal. In academic research,
how is a solo contribution distinguished from that of the group
and rewarded accordingly? Careers are made of such discrimina-
tions. The reward system of science is geared to priority and nov-
elty in research. The built-in injunction runs: be first, be different,
be right, and when more than one scientist is involved, think as

one. It is as if the sum of the parts cannot exceed unity—classic zero-sum game logic. Yet collaboration sometimes conjures bigger and richer thoughts—a larger pie, not smaller slices. Why does this bias persist? Would it not be ironic if scientists didn't trust their ability to measure group performance? Many today argue that measuring individual teaching proficiency at the undergraduate level is futile, so multiplying the task and raising the stakes may seem that much more daunting (Mooney, 1991).

Structural reform is an ongoing process that requires wholesale rethinking of the system. We must change what is in our heads, what we see as normal, what we expect of the institutions that employ us and the colleagues with whom we work, before we prescribe specific remedies for change in the way science looks and acts. (For various examples, see Benditt, 1993; Harding, 1991; Rosser, 1990; Tobias, 1990; Keller, 1985.)

Stating the Obvious: Nurturing Women into Science

In 1992, Radcliffe College president and chemist Linda Wilson put it this way:

> The design features of our academic research enterprise . . . were built on assumption of a context that permitted single-minded devotion to task, rather than a context for persons with multiple competing responsibilities spanning work and home.
>
> What has changed is the diversity of roles of the players in the enterprise itself, where faculty are educators, researchers, entrepreneurs, policy advisors, peer reviewers, public relations managers, financial managers, and personnel managers, and in the diversity of roles played outside the enterprise. . . .
>
> We need to tap the entire pool of talent to strengthen, replenish, and renew our science and engineering work force. But the new "immigrants" to . . . [this] work force, women and minorities, bring some differences in expectations, some of which are based on caregiving responsibilities that have been traditionally assigned in a differentiated way. Redistribution of roles among men and women will take place, but the cultural roots are very deep and the stakes are very high. . . .
>
> Our near-term decisions therefore will involve personal attitudinal change, organizational change, and systemic change. These

decisions themselves are interdependent, a set of human resources issues of a scope larger than we have had to address for many years. . . .

We are confronting a new era. "Business as usual" will not be a winning strategy. We could choose to pursue a definitive course, or elect to bob and weave, or default and drift. I recommend we confront the question of our future as knights, not pawns [p. 11].

Wilson's remarks drew retorts all too familiar to proponents of equity and change: that she was devaluing the competitiveness of research and, in turn, diluting the quality of that research as detected and rewarded through peer-based decision making. Wilson, of course, proposed no such compromise. Rather, she suggested that some of the problems facing science "may be linked to the existing ground rules of competition" (Mervis, 1992: p. 3). In short, macho science, as it has been called, belongs to a bygone era, when men were men, scientists were men, and science was all about the mastery of nature, control of the universe, and variants on the themes of domination, exclusivity, and presupposition, not harmony, inclusivity, and participation.

Wilson asks us to inspect the root values of the research university enterprise. The federal policy anchoring many of those values likewise warrants reflection. It is not that the values are wrong, but they may be maladaptive for the times, speaking to a once-homogeneous research community that has become ethnically, demographically, and intellectually as heterogeneous as any of us ever imagined was possible. Do we seize this variety and exploit it, or continue to deny its existence and potential contributions to the enterprise? The winning strategy, to paraphrase Wilson, is one of participation. Once again, federal policy must forge an ethic of participation and intervene for the good of science and the nation. Perhaps a program of career development awards, patterned on the annual Presidential Awards for Excellence in Science and Mathematics Teaching (at elementary and secondary levels), would fulfill this need for recognition and retooling at critical career junctures.

Although many things have changed for women in science, all too much remains the same. As a recent study (Rayman & Brett, 1994) shows, women continue to be weeded out and not cultivated into science. The study describes a learning environment that promotes women's continued engagement with science by providing opportunities to do research as an undergraduate and to have informal interaction with faculty; it would include candid career advice, informed parental support, confidence-building work experiences, and a valuing of difference. Some institutions already have this kind of support infrastructure, notably liberal arts, traditional women's, and historically black colleges, as well as universities with special programs and institutes—the latter typically funded by soft money from federal agencies and private foundations and located within or between what are often otherwise hostile departments. And many more colleges and universities have yet to develop a useful support structure of any kind. Ultimately, what is most likely to change the constellation of environment, perception, and treatment we describe is to get more women into science: as tenured and tenure-track faculty, as researchers with full status as principal investigators and reviewers, and as advisers and mentors who affect the way men and women view science as well as do science.

Consider, too, that the gender-blind-as-male policies in clinical science were questioned only recently, and then more as an element of policy rather than from concern about the quality of research data from clinical trials that exclude or largely ignore the female half of the population. Some diseases are not gender blind. Yet only when Congress intervened did the issue of generalizing treatment, drug regimen, and health recommendations from white-male-only clinical trials become a funding concern and in turn a concern of the biomedical research community. Perhaps this lesson as much as any other points to the power of public policy to change behavior. But the continued reports of women's impaired health and treatment caused by health practitioners' differential response to their symptoms remind us just how serious are the repercussions of not being taken seriously.

Research support criteria can be adjusted to promote desired policy outcomes. If the nation demands a positive learning environment for its postsecondary students, a rethinking of the reward and tenure system in institutions of higher education, a climate that supports teaching, and the advancement of women in science, public policy remedies of the type used heretofore may prove indirect and slow. The federal role in fomenting cultural change has been to communicate its concerns in its *research* funding decisions. This is far slower than direct financial aid to affected parties. On the other hand, it is also more feasible in science and engineering than in many fields because federal funds are more plentiful here—and thus more influential, because of the expectations attached to them. It would be desirable to quicken the pace for change even here. But how?

Reinventing Agency Criteria for Human Resources Development

There are two ways to utilize federal funding to affect the behavior of complex systems: reward what is desired and punish what is not, or the proverbial carrot and stick. While we always prefer the carrot, it typically yields incremental change, tinkering at the margin of a problem. Therefore, it is necessary at times to raise the cost of undesirable behavior to rivet people's attention to the goal at hand.

In a dramatic example of a well-applied stick, the assistant director for biological, behavioral, and social sciences at the NSF issued an important notice in 1991: conference organizers need not apply for support if no women were included as invited speakers (Clutter, 1991). This simple edict cost the agency nothing, but had a profound symbolic effect. It declared that the NSF valued the participation of qualified women, that men in the fields it supported needed to be aware of their outstanding but often overlooked female colleagues, and that federal dollars would not perpetuate discriminatory practices. The funding policy affected fields where women were already numerically strong and conducting leading-edge research and moved them from the bleachers onto the conference stage.

The civil rights movement of the 1950s and 1960s taught us that the laws of the land must be enforced despite resentment, disagreement, and resistance. Otherwise, people lose respect for the rule of law. Law may not change hearts, but it can change behavior.

We earlier argued against relying on targeted programs, commending instead the support of structural change. For K–12 education, wholesale transformation of the development and delivery of teaching and learning is now supported by Goals 2000 legislation, which assigns the U.S. Department of Education an impressive bootstrapping operation. Higher education needs a similar reform strategy. How can the current federal investment in colleges and universities support systemic reform?

In the current budget climate, it is unlikely that much new discretionary money will appear. Instead, granting agencies need to look at existing programs and stop funding those of marginal utility that feed inequities or do not develop human resources. But most of all, they need to reexamine the meaning of technical merit and reaffirm federal support of faculty and institutions that do the right thing while respecting merit. At least at the NSF, the lead executive agency for science education and human resources, mechanisms exist in the current review and decision-making structure to accomplish these ends.

Over a decade ago, the National Science Board (NSB), the NSF policy-making body, established four criteria for the selection of research projects: performer competence, intrinsic merit, utility/relevance, and effect on the infrastructure of science and engineering. "This last criterion relates to the potential of the proposed research to contribute to better understanding or improvement of the quality, distribution, or effectiveness of the Nation's scientific and engineering research, education, and manpower base" (NSF, 1990, pp. 8–9).

Considerations involved in criterion four include "questions relating to scientific, engineering, and education personnel, including participation of women, minorities, and disabled individuals; the distribution of resources with respect to institutions and geographic area; stimulation of high quality activities in important but under-developed fields; support of research initiation for investigators without previous Federal research support as a Principal Investigator or Co-Principal Investigator; and interdisciplinary approaches to research or education in appropriate areas" (NSF, 1990, p. 9).

According to the OTA, criterion four "defines the bases for using other criteria in addition to scientific merit in mainstream allocations of research funds, and within set-aside programs. . . . [Further,] every research program at NSF now impacts on human resources for science and engineering. This should remain foremost in mind when weighing policies for research programs" (U.S. Congress, 1991, p. 16).

Clearly, the four NSF-wide criteria should be revisited. Criterion four has been weighted inconsistently in agency decision making. There are many plausible explanations for this. Perhaps peer reviewers do not value human resource development, a sad commentary on the culture of science. Or perhaps program officers look at nothing but scientific merit in allocating scarce resources, abandoning the NSF's commitment to advance its twin and intertwined missions of research and education in all its funding decisions. Or narrow definitions of merit may prevail, because reviewers understand only the technical matter at hand and have no special competence to judge proposals on other criteria, including human resource factors.

Reinventing science to develop human resources could begin with federal funding criteria that make the human infrastructure more than an afterthought. It must be seen as integral to the future health of science. The process could proceed as follows:

1. *Conduct an inventory of values and practices,* much as has been done in response to research misconduct cases, of what to keep and what to drop in the portfolio of science. An inventory would clarify both the knowledge base (variations across disciplines and institutional types) and the core values of the system.

2. *Identify accountable units of change* in the education and knowledge-production system.

3. *Design a coherent strategy* that recasts and unites research, teaching, and apprenticeship; service and outreach; knowledge-driven disciplinary specialization and client-driven interdisciplinary syntheses.

4. *Raise other structural issues for debate:*

   - Tenure. Can institutions still afford to commit faculty positions for life? Do federal agencies have any regulatory or mediating role to play?
   - Graduate student support. Are there support mechanisms other than traineeships that would decouple the fortunes of students from the research funding of their professors?
   - Preparation for careers. How are skills imparted? What makes Ph.D.'s versatile enough to respond to emerging opportunities?

- Proposals by nonfaculty researchers in their own names. Does exclusion from competition consign a significant pool of professionals to perpetual second-class citizenship? Are there public policy incentives that could change institutional policy on this score?
- Career redefinition. If reinventing science from the inside out means that the culture of and expectations for institutions and disciplines must change, who takes the lead?

5. *Look at the whole portfolio of an R&D agency:*

- Think not of individual research projects, but the agency's mission, goals, and objectives. How can the research enterprise be diversified by sector and skills and be made more attractive, hospitable, and communal in its incentives and rewards? A mechanism for this is in place already—the Government Performance and Results Act of 1993 specifies that agency budget proposals beginning in fiscal year 1997 must include explicit performance goals, objectives, and indicators of progress. These goals can easily be required to include a human resources component.
- Consider the strategic issue from a national perspective. How do agency programs contribute to synergy on campuses and in states and regions that represents national value beyond the aggregation of individual projects?
- Invent means to support dual-career couples. How do we create flexibility in job options; enhance mentoring, networking, and support groups; root out institutional sexism; and encourage climate surveys? (For a description of climate surveys, see Sussman, 1994.)

Prospects

The NSF plays a dominant role in fundamental research and science education budgeting, but it is a minor player in the total R&D enterprise. The NSF is dwarfed by federal agencies with different missions and (except for the Departments of Labor and Education) highly specialized work force needs. In terms of coordination on federal principles and the programs that serve them (including education and human resources development), the Executive

Office of Science and Technology Policy is clearly the most influential player. By wielding its significant symbolic capital, it can drive a policy wedge into issues that require coherence and accountability across the federal government.

This chapter advocates combining the principles of quality and inclusion to attract an influx of talent. We envision a very different system, in customs and practice, from the one that created the current inequities of opportunity. At the same time, we recognize that either at its origin or in its implementation, public policy can miss the mark or exacerbate the situation its well-meaning creators intended to improve.

In an environment where an ever-shifting configuration of policy actions unfold, any intervention can turn sour due to unforeseen events or political diversions. Good programs do not guarantee good results. With this in mind, however, we still see policies for human resources development that have increased, and seem likely to continue to increase, the diversity of the scientific and engineering work force. As was recently observed: "Participation of all groups in society is a basis for the public support of science. The legitimation of science, the moral injunction to achieve equity, and the strategic national interest in utilizing talent to its fullest extent are reasons for change" (Etzkowitz et al., 1994, p. 54).

Equity is not just a federal or personal issue; it is a national imperative. And public policy leads the way. The interagency National Science and Technology Council has pledged to develop a national human resources policy, with special emphasis on underrepresented groups (Office of Science and Technology Policy [OSTP], 1994). Announcing such a policy is itself a symbolic act, able to inspire action not just for women in science but for everyone who passes through, aspires to join, or contributes to the institutions of science. Public policy, in sum, can reduce the size of underserved populations, by helping institutions reexamine old practices and reinvent the human infrastructure of science.

References

Abir-Am, P. G., & Outram, D. (Eds.). (1987). *Uneasy careers and intimate lives: Women in science, 1789–1979.* New Brunswick, NJ: Rutgers University Press.

Alper, J. (1994). Job-hopping to greater career heights. *Science, 265,* 1924–1925.

American Council on Education. (n.d.). *The new agenda of women for higher education.* A report of the ACE Commission on Women in Higher Education, Washington, DC.

Angier, N. (1991, May 21). Women swell ranks of science, but remain invisible at the top. *The New York Times,* pp. C1, C12.

Baker, D. (1992). I am what you tell me to be: Girls in science and mathematics. *ASTC Newsletter, 5–6,* 14–15.

Benditt, J. (Ed.). (1993). Gender and the culture of science. *Science, 260,* 384–430.

Brennan, M. B. (1993, February 8). Women scientists, engineers seek more equitable industrial environment. *Chemical & Engineering News, 71,* 13–16.

Browning, G. (1992, Mar. 21). Everyone loses this battle of the sexes. *National Journal,* p. 1724.

Carson, N., & Chubin, D. E. (1993, March 25). *Women in science: The transition from school to work.* Office of Technology Assessment draft.

Chubin, D. E. (1994). How large an R&D enterprise. In D. H. Guston and K. Keniston (Eds.), *The fragile contract: University science and the federal government* (pp. 118–144). Cambridge, MA: MIT Press.

Chubin, D. E., Hackett, E. J., & Solomon, S. (1994, Feb. 21). *Peer review in the courts, or when scientists "get real."* Paper presented at the annual meeting of the American Association for the Advancement of Science, San Francisco, CA.

Chubin, D. E., Porter, A. L., Rossini, F. A., & Connolly, T. (Eds.). (1986). *Interdisciplinary analysis and research.* Mt. Airy, MD: Lomond.

Clewell, B. C., Thorpe, M. E., & Anderson, B. T. (1987, May). *Intervention programs in math, science, and computer science for minority and female students in grades four through eight.* Princeton, NJ: Educational Testing Service.

Clutter, M. E. (1991, October 15). *Support of conferences, meetings, workshops, and international congresses.* NSF/AD/BBS Circular No. 14.

Crease, R. (1993). Fallout from paper on working mothers. *Science, 259,* 1530–1531.

Dix, L. S. (Ed.). (1987). *Women: Their underrepresentation and career differentials in science and engineering.* Washington, DC: National Academy Press.

Dix, L. S. (Ed.). (1993). *Women scientists and engineers in industry: Why so few?* Washington, DC: National Academy Press.

Etzkowitz, H., Kemelgor, C., Neuschatz, M., Uzzi, B., & Alonzo, J. (1992).

Athena unbound: Barriers to women in academic science and engineering. *Science and Public Policy, 19*(3), 157–179.

Etzkowitz, H., Kemelgor, C., Neuschatz, M., Uzzi, B., & Alonzo, J. (1994). The paradox of critical mass for women in science. *Science, 266*, 51–54.

Fechter, A. (1990). Engineering shortages and shortfalls: Myths and realities. *The Bridge, 20*, 3–6.

Fechter, A. (1994). Future supply and demand: Cloudy crystal balls. In W. Pearson, Jr., & A. Fechter (Eds.), *Who will do science? Educating the next generation* (pp. 125–140). Baltimore, MD: Johns Hopkins University Press.

Federal Task Force on Women, Minorities, and the Handicapped in Science and Technology. (1990). *Changing America: The new face of science and engineering.* Washington, DC: U.S. Government Printing Office.

Fehrs, M., & Czujko, R. (1992, August). Women in physics: Reversing the exclusion. *Physics Today,* pp. 33–40.

Foster, M. S. (1993). A question of jobs—The two-career couple. *BioScience, 43*, 237.

Gibbons, A. (1994). Making the grade as a scientific manager. *Science, 265*, 1937–1938.

H.R. 467. Bill establishing the Commission on the Advancement of Women in the Science and Engineering Work Forces. U.S. House of Representatives, 103rd Congress, 1st Sess. (1993).

Hall, R. M., & Sandler, B. R. (1982). *The classroom climate: A chilly one for women.* Washington, DC: Association of American Colleges.

Harding, S. (1991). *Whose science? Whose knowledge?* Ithaca, NY: Cornell University Press.

Healy, B. (1992). Women in science: From panes to ceilings. *Science, 255*, 1333.

Hewitt, N. M., & Seymour, E. (1991). *Factors contributing to high attrition rates among science, mathematics and engineering undergraduate majors.* Report to the Alfred P. Sloan Foundation. Boulder: University of Colorado.

Hoke, F. (1992, August 17). Survey: More women entering chemistry, but career advancement poses problems. *The Scientist,* pp. 1, 4–5.

Holden, C. (1994). Science careers: Playing to win. *Science, 265*, 1905–1906.

Holloway, M. (1993, November). A lab of her own. *Scientific American, 269*, 94–103.

Interdisciplinary studies: Defining and defending [special section]. (1989, Spring). *National Forum, 69*, 2–41.

Kates, R. W. (1991, May 17). The great questions of science and society do not fit neatly into single disciplines. *The Chronicle of Higher Education*, pp. B1, B3.

Keller, E. F. (1985). *Reflections on gender and science.* New Haven, CT: Yale University Press.

Kenschaft, P. C. (Ed.). (1991). *Winning women into mathematics.* Mathematical Association of America.

Kirby, K., & Czujko, R. (1993, December). The physics job market: Bleak for young physicists. *Physics Today, 46,* 22–27.

Layzell, D. T. (1990, October 24). Most research in higher education is stale, irrelevant, and of little use to policy makers. *The Chronicle of Higher Education,* pp. B1, B3.

Leggon, C. B., & Malcom, S. M. (1994). Human resources in science and engineering: Policy implications. In W. Pearson, Jr., & A. Fechter (Eds.), *Who will do science? Educating the next generation* (pp. 141–151). Baltimore, MD: Johns Hopkins University Press.

Legters, N., & Slavin, R. E. (1994, April). *Elementary students at risk: A status report.* New York: Carnegie Corporation.

Lubchenco, J., & Menge, B. A. (1993). Split positions can provide a sane career track—A personal account. *BioScience, 43,* 243–248.

Magner, D. K. (1994, April 27). Job-market blues. *The Chronicle of Higher Education,* pp. A17–20.

Malcom, S. M. (1991). More than market forces: Policies to promote change. In M. L. Matyas & S. M. Malcom (Eds.), *Investing in human potential: Science and engineering at the crossroads* (pp. 141–145). Washington, DC: American Association for the Advancement of Science.

Mann, J. (1994a, Sept. 28). Women in science: Getting them there. *The Washington Post,* p. B1.

Mann, J. (1994b, Sept. 30). Bringing girls to the front of the class. *The Washington Post,* p. E3.

Matyas, M. L., & Malcom, S. M. (Eds.). (1991). *Investing in human potential: Science and engineering at the crossroads.* Washington, DC: American Association for the Advancement of Science.

Mervis, J. (1992, January 20). Radcliffe president lambastes competitiveness in research. *The Scientist,* p. 3.

Mooney, C. J. (1991, May 8). Professors feel conflict between roles in teaching and research, say students are badly prepared. *The Chronicle of Higher Education,* pp. A15, A17.

National Science Foundation. (1990). *Grants for research and education in science and engineering: An application guide.* Arlington, VA: Author.

National Science Foundation. (1994). *Women, minorities, and persons with disabilities in science and engineering: 1994.* (Reprint). Arlington, VA: Author.

Office of Science and Technology Policy. (1994, August). *Science in the national interest.* Washington, DC: Author.

Pearson, C. S., Shavlik, D. L., & Touchton, J. G. (1989). *Educating the majority: Women challenge tradition in higher education.* New York: Macmillan.

Pinn, V. W. (1992). Women's health research: Prescribing change and addressing the issues. *Journal of the American Medical Association, 268,* 1921–1922.

Rayman, P. M., & Brett, B. (1994, March 21). Clearing the path for women scientists. *The Scientist, 8*(6), 11.

Rosser, S. V. (1990). *Female-friendly science: Applying women's studies methods and theories to attract students.* Elmsford, NY: Pergamon Press.

Schrage, M. (1990). *Shared minds: New technologies of collaboration.* New York: Random House.

Seachrist, L. (1994). Disparities detailed in NCI division. *Science, 264,* 340.

Stromquist, N. P. (1993). Sex-equity legislation in education: The state as promoter of women's rights. *Review of Educational Research, 63,* 379–407.

Sussman, E. (1994, May). *Women in the science workforce: A policy analysis.* Unpublished paper, Cornell-in-Washington Program.

Swisher, K. (1994, March 18). Medical school, researcher settle sex bias lawsuit. *The Washington Post,* pp. G1–G2.

Tilghman, S. M. (1993, January 25). Science vs. the female scientist. *The New York Times,* p. A17.

Tobias, S. (1990). *They're not dumb, they're different: Stalking the second tier.* Tucson, AZ: Research Corporation.

Tobias, S. (1993). The "problem" of women in science: Why is it so difficult to convince people there is one? In D. Fort (Ed.), *A hand up: Women mentoring women in science* (pp. 150–159). Washington, DC: Association for Women in Science.

Tobias, S., Chubin, D. E., & Aylesworth, K. (1995). *Rethinking science as a career: Perceptions and realities in the physical sciences.* Tucson, AZ: Research Corporation.

U.S. Congress. Office of Technology Assessment. (1985, December). *Demographic trends and the scientific and engineering work force.* Washington, DC: U.S. Government Printing Office.

U.S. Congress. Office of Technology Assessment. (1988a, June). *Educating scientists and engineers—Grade school to grad school.* Washington, DC: U.S. Government Printing Office.

U.S. Congress. Office of Technology Assessment. (1988b, December). *Elementary and secondary education for science and engineering.* Washington, DC: U.S. Government Printing Office.

U.S. Congress. Office of Technology Assessment. (1989, March). *Higher education for science and engineering.* Washington, DC: U.S. Government Printing Office.

U.S. Congress. Office of Technology Assessment. (1991, May). *Federally funded research: Decisions for a decade.* Washington, DC: U.S. Government Printing Office.

U.S. Department of Labor. (1992, August). *Pipelines of progress: An update on the glass ceiling initiative.* Washington, DC: U.S. Government Printing Office.

U.S. House of Representatives. Committee on Education and Labor. (1992). *Hearing on sexual harassment in nontraditional occupations.* 102nd Congress, 2nd Session. Washington, DC: U.S. Government Printing Office.

Vetter, B. M. (1992). Women in science III—Ferment: Yes, Progress: Maybe, Change: Slow. *Mosaic, 23,* 34–35.

Wake, M. H. (1993). Two-career couples—Attitudes and opportunities. *BioScience, 43,* 238–240.

Wilson, L. (1992, March 16). U.S. universities now confront fateful choices. *The Scientist,* p. 11.

Women in science. (1992). *Science, 255,* 1365–1388.

Chapter Two

Myths and Realities of Women's Progress in the Sciences, Mathematics, and Engineering

Betty M. Vetter

Women made remarkable inroads into the community of scientists and engineers during the seventies and early eighties, but the increase leveled off in most areas well before women achieved demographic parity or occupational equality with men. The obstacles that remain are formidable, but women increasingly influence all occupations by their presence. Some of the barriers to their participation are dropping, and others are at least being recognized—the first step toward elimination.

Girls find science and mathematics attractive or repellent due not only to their own aptitudes and interests, but also to their reaction to the attitudes of their teachers, their parents, and their peers. There is no evidence that girls are born less inclined to mathematics or mechanics than boys, but there is strong evidence that society believes this to be the case and encourages a division

Note: Following the untimely death of Betty Vetter, invaluable assistance in editing this chapter was provided by Eleanor L. Babco, deputy executive director of the Commission on Professionals in Science and Technology.

between boys and girls. Classroom attitudes of teachers, books written for children, and subtle but constant parental and societal pressures persuade children that boys are better at science, engineering, and mathematics than are girls and that girls are better with words than are boys. These are among the many stereotypes that affect U.S. children and the choices they make, both in school and during their working years.

A recent pilot study of about five hundred engineers by the Society of Women Engineers (Ellis & Eng, 1991) found that, by far, the most important reason women selected for their choice of field was that they were good in math and science. Only 32 percent of the men named that as the most important reason, compared with 44 percent of the women. But boys and men are far more likely than girls and women to believe they are good in math and science, even when their grades are the same or lower (Adelman, 1991).

This difference in self-confidence is not an accident, nor is it the result of genetic differences. It comes, instead, from conditioning. From infancy, people are presumed to have different capabilities solely because of their sex, and so they are treated differently throughout their childhood and school years, and on into the world of work. Mathematical and mechanical talent are assumed to be sex linked, and girls learn very early that they are believed to have less of these talents than boys have. Their toys emphasize these attributes of gender. Boys, of course, get the same message—not always subliminal—and grow up believing that they are superior to girls in math and science, even when their grades do not support this assumption.

Precollege Years

Mathematics is the single most important factor in determining admission and success in science and engineering careers, and girls score as well as boys through the early teens. However, with little to encourage their participation, many girls drop out of mathematics as soon as they can, and this lowers their scores by age seventeen (Dossey, Mullis, Lindquist, & Chambers, 1988). In the most recent (1990) National Assessment of Educational Progress (NAEP), young women showed some improvement relative to the men in their age group, as mathematics course taking for girls again came into favor.

Science is a different matter. As Figure 2.1 shows, the NAEP science assessment shows a sex gap even at age nine. Further, between the first science assessment in 1970 and the one in 1986, the sex gap doubled for thirteen-year-olds. Girls scored 1.5 percent below boys in 1970, but 3.6 percent below them by 1986. There was some recovery among thirteen-year-olds by 1990, when the gap was 2.6 percent. However, seventeen-year-olds showed a 3.5 percent gap in 1990, only slightly narrower than the 1986 gap for this cohort.

Teacher behavior partially explains the problem. K-8 teachers, almost all women, tend to suffer from inadequate science preparation. They fear teaching it and lack confidence in their ability to do it effectively (Weiss, 1993), and thus provide unfortunate role models. A teacher's feelings of fear and helplessness about science

Figure 2.1. Science Proficiency.

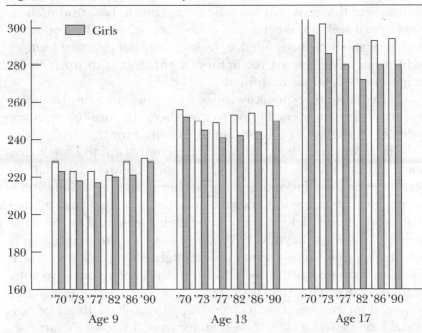

Source: National Assessment of Educational Progress. Graph by Commission on Professionals in Science and Technology (CPST).

or mathematics say that it is natural for girls not to like or be good at these subjects.

Moreover, teachers of all ages and both sexes discriminate in the classroom (Sadker & Sadker, 1994). They share society's expectations about science and mathematics. They call on and praise boys more than girls and let boys interrupt girls, but praise girls for being polite and waiting their turn (Eccles & Jacobs, 1986). Even now, when barriers are being broken and some genuine change is occurring, both overt and insidious forms of gender bias continue to distort the education of girls and young women, from kindergarten through graduate school. Sexual harassment now starts in grade school, with taunts, physical touching, and grabbing. School officials have failed to stop this behavior (American Association of University Women [AAUW], 1993).

But teachers are not solely to blame. Recent studies (AAUW, 1992) find that preteen girls are self-confident and generally equal to boys in mathematics, but that as they enter adolescence their confidence erodes, often almost to the vanishing point, as society shows them that girls and women are inferior to boys and men in intellectual abilities, mechanical or mathematical skills, and leadership qualities. Self-confidence, by itself, cannot guarantee either achievement or reward for achievement. But without it, high achievement is far more difficult.

Many parents, especially those with sons, also discriminate against their daughters, failing to give them the most elementary training in the use of tools to build or repair mechanical things (Mullis & Jenkins, 1988). Most U.S. parents accept the myth that sons, simply because of their sex, are more talented than daughters in mechanics and mathematics. They praise their daughters' *hard work* in getting good grades or honors in science and mathematics but express delight at the *talent* their sons reveal by the same accomplishments (Keynes, 1989). Verifying this parental bias, it is interesting that women who choose engineering as a career are likely to have no brothers (LeBold, n.d.). Parents with no sons seem to endow daughters with the supposedly masculine abilities required for engineering. As a group, parents have lower educational aspirations for daughters than for sons. To no one's surprise, women high school graduates have lower educational aspirations than their male classmates (Adelman, 1991).

Nonetheless, in a national longitudinal study of the high school graduating class of 1972 (U.S. Department of Education), women were found to have continued education at the same rate as men, earned more scholarships than men, completed both associate and bachelor's degrees at a faster pace than men, and earned better grades, even on a course-by-course basis. Whatever they studied, women earned consistently higher grade point averages in college than men in the class, and the differences were greatest in the traditionally male fields of engineering, science, and business. Self-selection does play a major role in determining which women major in those fields, but men do just as much self-selection of majors.

Although boys are more confident than girls of their ability to learn mathematics, girls earn better grades. In calculus, 23.6 percent of boys and 36.3 percent of girls earned an A or A-; 37.5 and 32.0 percent a B or B-; 33.0 and 26.5 percent a C or C-, and 5.9 percent of boys and 5.1 percent of girls earned a D or F.

This experience of achievement had a striking impact on the plans of women in the class of 1972. When resurveyed in 1976, the proportion aspiring to graduate degrees vaulted over that of men and remained higher through the 1979 survey. Success renewed their self-confidence. But long before they have a chance to discover their ability, many girls absorb the message that they cannot do as well as boys in mathematics—and drop out to avoid disgracing themselves (U.S. Department of Education). In high school, students with higher math scores tend to take chemistry, the higher the math scores, the larger the fraction who do so. When considered by math achievement level, males and females are approximately equal in chemistry enrollment. Physics, however, is a different story. Regardless of mathematical excellence, women are much less likely than men to take physics, so some other factor must be at work (Czujko & Bernstein, 1989).

It is hard to understand how parental attitudes about the talents and abilities of sons and daughters can continue to reflect gender myths when the evidence of their falsity is so clear. (The individual talents of children, having little or nothing to do with their sex, may cloud the picture.) Whatever the cause, by the tenth grade, only 10 percent of girls, compared with 25 percent of boys, express interest in the natural sciences. By the end of high school, only 5 percent of the girls indicate a potential career interest in these fields, while about 20 percent of the boys still do so (Shakhashiri, 1990).

Undergraduate Education

Over the past two decades, the proportion of U.S. women going to college has increased significantly, as has their presence in math-based majors. Fields such as engineering and physics that used to have few, if any, women saw even greater gains. However, women remain less than one-sixth of the graduates in these fields, even at the bachelor's level (National Center for Education Statistics [NCES], 1994a).

But the forces that turn women away from science do not vanish at the end of high school. Of the women who enter college planning to major in engineering or a physical science, already a very small fraction, more than one-third do not complete those plans. For example, among freshman women in 1988, 2.6 percent planned engineering majors (Astin et al., 1988). But among the women earning bachelor's degrees in 1992, only 1.5 percent were in engineering (NCES, 1994a). Of course, there is also a drop-off of men, but until very recently, it was a little less pronounced. Among the men in that same freshman class, 17.5 percent planned an engineering major, but only 9.9 percent of the men in the 1992 graduating class earned engineering degrees.

Of course, this is a crude measure of retention, as it does not say how many freshmen actually went on to earn a bachelor's degree in engineering. Many students join engineering programs as juniors from two-year colleges and were not counted as freshmen. Obviously, the true retention rate, if we had the data, would be somewhat lower than the contrived rate, which seems mostly to allow observation of differences by sex and by race/ethnicity. Indeed, the Asian-American retention rate was for several years above 100 percent—so few left engineering that the junior year input was larger than the number who dropped out. However, actual retention rates in any field are difficult to find, and we can rarely tell whether those who leave move to other majors (in or out of the science/engineering [SME] grouping), change schools, or drop out of school altogether. Chapter Four discusses one study that addressed this question, finding a considerable amount of transfer among SME majors. We sorely need additional studies of retention and dropout rates of science and engineering freshmen, including those in two-year courses, from their first year of undergraduate study through the B.S. degree.

One recent study of undergraduate SME majors (Hewitt & Seymour, 1991) finds that the students who stay vary little from those who move out before completing undergraduate degrees. They have the same complaints about the undergraduate program, but the student who leaves is more likely to be drawn away by another force, such as peer pressure or interest in another major. Relatively few women leave engineering because of bad grades.

Despite the substantial drop in U.S. college-age population that began in the early 1980s, there has been no drop in total baccalaureate production, and none is expected before 2000 (NCES, 1994b). However, the numbers of bachelor's degrees awarded in the natural sciences and engineering (NS/E) have been dropping, for both men and women, from a high of 214,000 in 1986 to 160,600 in 1991—a 25 percent drop in just five years (Vetter, 1994). Thus, the NS/E fields have dropped from 21.3 percent of all bachelor's degrees in 1986 to 14.7 percent in 1991. Had it not been for the increasing proportion of women earning degrees in those fields, by 1991 the proportion of degrees in NS/E fields would have been about the same level as in 1971.

For the female graduating class, the proportion of NS/E bachelor's degrees has fallen from 12.3 percent in 1986 to 9.1 percent in 1991, while the percentage in social and behavioral sciences has risen steadily. As Figure 2.2 shows, women have not achieved parity with men even at the bachelor's level in any natural science field except the biosciences, despite earning a majority of all bachelor's degrees by 1983. Because their decrease is less than for men, women have increased their percentage of NS/E degree awards from 29.1 percent in 1986 to 33.6 percent in 1991.

Although they have not reached parity either in NS/E or in total SME (which includes the social and behavioral sciences), women now earn more than half of all bachelor's and master's degrees awarded and almost 40 percent of the doctorates. In 1991, they earned only 33 percent of the natural science and engineering bachelor's degrees, 27 percent of the master's, and 22 percent

Figure 2.2. Percentage of Women NS/E Bachelor's Graduates.

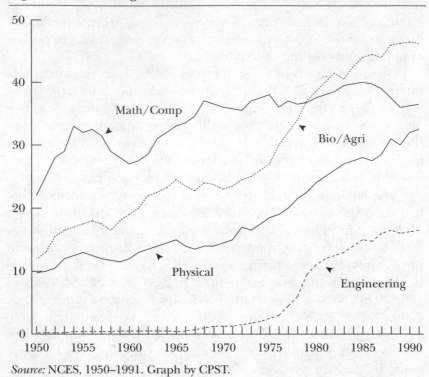

Source: NCES, 1950–1991. Graph by CPST.

of the Ph.D.'s. Including the social and behavioral sciences raises the percentages significantly.

If we look just at engineering degrees, we can see some of the changes more easily. Women increased their representation among B.S. graduates at a steady rate from 1976 to 1986, when they reached almost 15 percent of the graduating class. But they held steady between 15 and 16 percent of the graduates for the next six years. Finally, in 1993, they increased their share of B.S. graduates to 16.1 percent. The figures are somewhat distorted by double-counting of women from racial/ethnic minorities, who appear in the overall total twice (once for each status), but the numbers involved are very low. Figure 2.3 graphs other data that do allow us to look at sex and race separately.

Women earn a higher percentage of the engineering degrees awarded to minorities than of those earned by white students.

Figure 2.3. Percentage of Women Among B.S. Engineering Graduates, 1993.

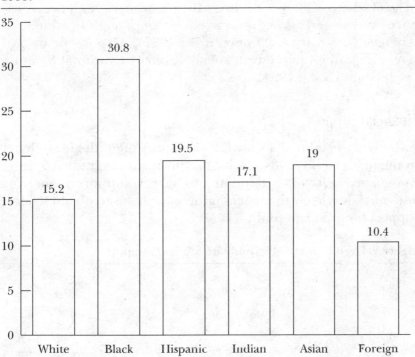

Source: Engineering Workforce Commission, 1993, p. x. Graph by CPST.

Among blacks, women earn about twice the percentage of engineering bachelor's degrees as do women of other racial and ethnic groups. Foreign students show the smallest representation of women, and the foreign students become an increasingly important factor at the graduate level.

Graduate Education

Enrollment

Graduate SME enrollment continued to climb through fall 1992, but much of the increase was made up of foreign students, who comprised 29.8 percent of full-time enrollment. At that time, women, including those with foreign citizenship, were 33.9 percent of all full-time graduate students, ranging from 14 percent in engineering to 67 percent in psychology. Women were 24 percent of full-time students in physical sciences; 30 percent in mathematical sciences; 32 percent in earth, atmospheric, and ocean sciences and also in agricultural sciences; 20 percent in computer sciences (down from 25 percent in 1982); 45 percent in biosciences; and 43 percent in social sciences (National Science Foundation [NSF], 1994).

Financial Support

Although, as Figure 2.4 shows, the majority of graduate students in the math-based fields receive funding in their graduate years, women are more likely than men to have to support themselves and much less likely than men in the same fields to obtain federal support for graduate study.

Figure 2.4. Full-Time SME Graduate Student Support.

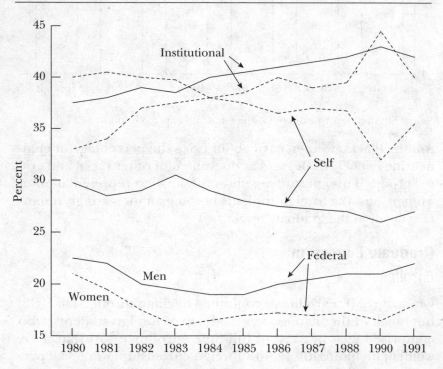

Source: National Research Council, 1982–1993. Graph by CPST.

In 1990, for the first time, women were somewhat more likely than men to have institutional support, usually teaching assistant jobs (TAs), but by fall 1991, the proportion of support once again favored men. Men also are more likely than women to get support in the form of research assistantships, rather than TAs, thus furthering their opportunities for a research career.

Master's Degrees

The master's degree is difficult to evaluate. It is sometimes awarded as an indicator of progress toward a Ph.D., and sometimes it is either a terminal degree or a consolation prize awarded to students who do not complete the Ph.D. Women are more likely than men to seek a master's degree without planning further graduate study. Indeed, women make up 47 percent of full-time SME graduate students in master's-granting institutions but only 32 percent of those in the more prestigious Ph.D.-granting institutions. Lack of self-confidence may be one reason for this discrepancy, and lack of support may be another.

Although women earned over half of the master's degrees and doctorates in the biological sciences and over half of the bachelor's, master's, and Ph.D. degrees in psychology, they earned 14 percent of the master's, 15 percent of the Ph.D.'s, and only 9 percent of the bachelor's degrees in engineering. Women earn a slightly lower percentage of master's degrees than bachelor's degrees in natural sciences, and a larger drop occurs at the Ph.D. level.

Doctoral Degrees

The number of women earning SME Ph.D.'s defines the baseline for their presence among top researchers and faculty. In most math-based fields, those numbers continue to be well under a quarter of the total, as shown in Figure 2.5. In 1992, women earned about a third of the life and social science doctorates awarded by U.S. universities, and they exceeded half only in psychology (National Research Council, 1993). The increasing numbers of foreign nationals among doctoral recipients in the math-based fields further reduce the percentage of women graduates.

Figure 2.5. Percentage of Women Among U.S. SME Ph.D.'s by Field.

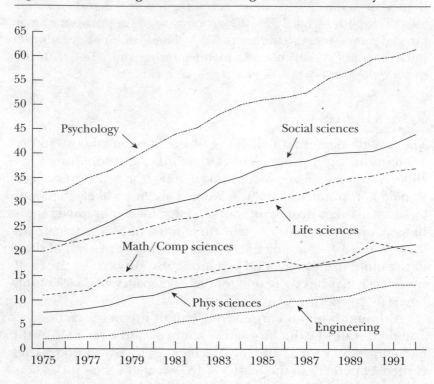

Source: National Research Council, 1977–1994.

Looking only at U.S. citizens, one sees that women earned 26.3 percent of 9,428 NS/E doctorates in 1992, including 281 in engineering; 86 in physics and astronomy; 356 in chemistry; 140 in earth, atmospheric, and marine sciences; 97 in mathematics; and 69 in computer science. Of these women, 11 were American Indians, 143 were Asian Americans, 35 were African Americans, and 71 were Hispanic, for a total minority representation of 11.3 percent. In contrast, 7,857 foreign citizens, mostly male, earned Ph.D.'s in these same fields in 1992 from U.S. universities. Women are better represented among doctorate recipients in life sciences, social sciences, and behavioral sciences; foreign citizens have their largest representation in engineering, physical sciences, and mathematics/computer sciences.

Barriers to Women in the Work Force

Although still relatively low in the physical and engineering sciences, the numbers of women earning doctorates in all SME fields have been rising steadily but slowly for two decades. Why are so few women achieving professional status in these fields? Although the answer is complex, some of the explanation lies in the many barriers, both apparent and hidden, to interest and participation of women. As noted earlier, those barriers begin almost at birth, but new barriers appear at the beginning and end of each stage of education and at entry into the work force. Women aspiring to science careers face a triple penalty of cultural, attitudinal, and structural impediments (Cole, 1979). This accumulation of disadvantages results in higher attrition rates and lower achievement for most of those who remain. It also substantially restricts the number qualified to choose a scientific career. Some of the barriers are deeply ingrained in societal values, and immense effort will be required to effect change. Although disentangling the web of causality is immensely complex, some barriers would be relatively simple to remove, if employers wanted them changed, if the government wanted them changed, if academic administrators or faculties wanted them changed, or if the majority of the population wanted them changed. When only women (and not always even a majority of women) want change, it comes about very slowly, if at all.

Barriers to Entry

There are many other gross inequities in the SME work force. Women and men do not seem to have equal employment opportunity—if they did, people with similar qualifications in a field would have similar unemployment rates. However, women have higher unemployment rates at all levels, and—while there doubtless are reasons other than discrimination, including women's greater responsibilities for children and in some instances their lesser mobility—discriminatory practice also plays a part.

Women in science are more than twice as likely to report being unemployed and seeking employment as are men with similar credentials. In spite of a relatively low unemployment rate among doctoral scientists and engineers—averaging only about 1 percent overall in 1989 and 1.4 percent in 1991—unemployment rates in every biennial survey of the doctoral population from 1973 to 1991 were two to five times higher for women than for men in the same field (NSF, 1973–1991).

When overall unemployment is highest, the gap between the unemployment rates of men and women is greatest. Where women are a larger proportion of working Ph.D.'s in a field, the gap is lowest. Figure 2.6 details unemployment rates in various fields, illustrating that fields with relatively few women (physics, engineering, and chemistry) show the largest gap. In physics/astronomy, for example, which had the most unemployment in 1991, the rate for women was three times higher than for men.

Figure 2.6. Ph.D. Unemployment Rates by Sex, 1991.

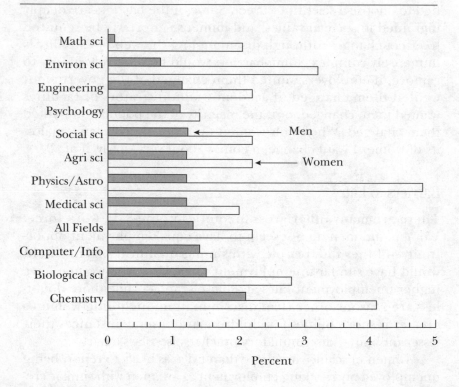

Source: NSF, 1993. Graph by CPST.

Barriers to Advancement

Once employed, women scientists and engineers advance more slowly than men, thus holding back salary increases and widening the salary gap. Sometimes, women's inability to advance results from paternalism, as supervisors refuse to expose women to activities that may be required for advancement. Some of the delay has to do with the preconception that a woman may leave before completing a project. She might get married and leave; if already married, she might leave when her husband gets transferred, or she might get pregnant and leave. Although there appear to be no verified data indicating that women scientists and engineers voluntarily change employers more often than men, this belief is part of the mythology associated with women in the workplace.

Salary Differentials

Differential salaries—and the statement they make—pose a major barrier to women. In a democracy, salaries tend to be equated with worth. Like men, women need assurance that society values their abilities, their work, and their achievements. Many factors affect salary, including education, specialty, experience, type and size of employer, geographic location, and supply of workers with similar qualifications. But when all of those have been controlled, the differential that remains is related to the sex of the worker. In a national longitudinal study of 1972 high school graduates, more women than men believed they benefited from higher education. Unfortunately, their belief was not supported by the labor market, "where evidence of women's superior educational performance and commitment was discounted" (Adelman, 1991). Between ages twenty-five and thirty-two, substantially more women than men experienced unemployment, regardless of education—and the lowest unemployment rates for women to age thirty-two were for those with no children who had earned less than a bachelor's degree by age thirty. Even though, as Table 2.1 shows, women with bachelor's degrees had better grade point averages than men in all major fields, women graduates experienced higher rates of unemployment.

Table 2.1. Average Undergraduate GPA for Bachelor's Recipients.

Major	Women	Men
All	3.07	2.92
Engineering/Computer science	3.17	2.96
Science and math	3.18	2.98
Business	2.96	2.79
Education	3.05	2.89
Humanities	3.16	3.10
Arts	3.13	3.08
Social sciences	3.08	2.95

Source: Adelman, 1991.

When employed, women were found disproportionately in low-paying and traditionally female occupations such as nursing and health technology (11 percent), school teaching (22 percent), and office and financial services support (9 percent).

It appears that women achieve near pay equity in some occupations as a correlate of the amount of mathematics they studied in college. If one looks only at those who earned more than eight credits in college-level mathematics, gender-based salary differentials drop from 9.1 percent to 2.6 percent among accountants. Among engineers, the difference drops from 5 percent to 1.9 percent, and in financial institutions, wholesale or retail trade, or manufacturing, the drop is even greater (Addman, 1991). The message for young women is obvious, but the importance of mathematics to their future earnings is a well-kept secret when girls are making choices about courses to take.

Although women earn less than the men with whom they work, women working in male-dominated fields such as engineering will earn more than women working in female-dominated fields such as elementary education, because women's fields are assumed to be worth less than men's. This has little or nothing to do with demand for workers, job responsibility level, or any shortage or surplus of supply. This occupational differential, determined by the proportion of women in the field, explains the data in Table 2.2. Among full-time workers in 1990, women with four or more years of college earned average salaries ($28,017) only slightly above those ($26,653) of men with high school diplomas and well below those of men with bachelor's degrees ($39,238) (U.S. Bureau of the Census, 1992).

Starting salaries in most fields are slightly lower for women than for men (College Placement Council [CPC], 1994), and the gap widens over time. Even in female-dominated fields, men earn more than women, from the very beginning. For example, 1994 starting salary offers in nursing averaged $29,357 for men and $28,886 for women (CPC, 1994). Some years, women in chemistry or physics show slightly higher average offers than the men with whom they graduated, but by the next year, women have slipped behind again. Engineering is an exception. Here women have earned slightly higher starting salaries than men for several years, but that advantage quickly disappears. According to the Society of Women Engineers, "Before they reach the age of thirty, men engineers move ahead of women and continue to move ahead throughout their careers" (Society of Women Engineers, 1993).

Doctoral scientists and engineers show a salary gap in the first postdoctoral job, and the gap continues to widen over time. Further, after about twenty to twenty-four years of experience, women's salaries drop off, while men's continue to rise (NSF, 1991). Some of the differential may stem from women leaving for a time to raise children. But most women with Ph.D.'s work through pregnancy and child rearing, just as men do. The overall salary gap between men and women doctoral scientists in 1991—about $12,000 per year—was less in some fields than in others and

Table 2.2. Median Income* by Education and Sex, 1990.

Education	Women	Men	Women as % men
Less than high school	12,251	17,394	70.4
Some high school	14,429	20,902	69.0
High school graduate	18,319	26,653	68.7
Some college	22,227	31,734	70.0
Bachelor's degree	28,017	39,238	71.4
1+ years graduate	33,750	49,304	68.5

*For year-round, full-time workers, 25 years and older.

Source: U.S. Bureau of the Census, 1992, Series P-60, No. 174.

was less among those with comparable experience. For example, women chemists with five to nine years of professional experience earned median salaries of $53,900, compared with $55,500 for men with the same experience. Median salaries of biological scientists with fifteen to nineteen years of experience were $63,000 for men and $55,500 for women.

Ideally, each salary survey would include a large enough sample to control for field, degree level, years of professional experience, type and size of employer, work activity, and all other known determinants of salary. Any remaining differential, attributable to sex, could then be measured with greater accuracy. Actually, it is rarely possible to find salary data that are presented by more than two of these determinants.

Over a lifetime, the salary differential does substantial damage to women scientists. They pay the same school fees and tuition as their male classmates; and they pay the same prices as men for food, mortgage loans, cars, and all other essential goods and services. The salary difference among Ph.D.'s extends across all science fields and changed very little over the ten biennial surveys carried out by the National Science Foundation from 1973 to 1991.

Sexual Harassment

Sexual harassment and outright sexual discrimination form a major barrier to advancement. At the least, harassment deflects a woman's energy from her work. If she complains, fellow workers may avoid her. If she tries to handle it herself, she must be always on guard. As was evident to all after the televised nomination hearings of Supreme Court Justice Clarence Thomas, men and women do not necessarily see the same thing when they examine sexual harassment or other forms of workplace bias. Some recent reports from groups of women scientists illustrate how this affects women's opportunities.

In a survey of the American Astronomical Society, 40 percent of the 250 women responding reported experiencing or witnessing discrimination against women within their profession. In a second survey focusing exclusively on the society's female members,

71 percent reported being victims of discrimination or harassment at some point in their careers, including 26 percent who had been sexually propositioned on the job (Manpower Comments, 1991). Although women scientists say that sexual harassment is rarely discussed in professional circles, this continuing barrier to their advancement is common in groups of scientists and engineers, particularly those with a small proportion of women.

Women ecologists face disadvantages at each career stage, cumulatively lowering their productivity and advancement, according to recent research (Primack & O'Leary, 1993). The survey sample was 105 women and 229 men who had been selected by the Organization for Tropical Studies (OTS) to attend courses in Costa Rica between 1966 and 1979 and who had since earned their Ph.D.'s. The group was considered in four parts: senior men and women who earned Ph.D.'s in 1976 or earlier, and junior scientists of each sex who earned their Ph.D.'s after 1976. The sample was further split by family status (single, single with children, married, and married with children). They found that women faced greater disadvantages than men at every career stage, regardless of family status. Women reported less satisfactory relationships with their doctoral advisers, difficulty in finding suitable mentors, sexual discrimination in the workplace, nomadic employment, lack of institutional empowerment, disruptions caused by moving to advance a career or to accommodate a spouse, and family responsibilities. As a result, women showed more limited career advancement and consistently lower salaries than men did. Only 43 percent of senior women and 16 percent of junior women earned more than $40,000, in contrast with 59 percent of senior men and 26 percent of junior men. Women have less job security and lower scientific productivity as disadvantage accumulates from stage to stage of their careers.

A recent report (Russell Reynolds Associates, 1990) says that two-thirds of leader-style women in corporate line or staff positions perceive hostility from their superiors, while only 2 percent of the leader-style men perceive any hostility to women in the workplace. Only a third of the women believe their company actively encourages their career while three-fourths of the men believe their company encourages women's careers. More than half the women believe that men have more opportunities than women to exercise power and authority, but two-thirds of the men believe women have equal opportunity for power and authority.

A survey of engineers (Ellis & Eng, 1991) asked explicitly if they were "personally aware of instances where females have been overlooked with regard to career opportunities." Among the women, 56 percent said yes, compared to 15 percent of the men.

Among chemists surveyed by the American Chemical Society in 1990 (Roscher, 1990), women saw less chance of advancement, either professional or managerial, than men; and their views appear to be true. Among chemists in industry, women generally perceive better opportunities for promotion if another woman has preceded them or is their supervisor.

The Glass Ceiling

A Catalyst survey of chief executives reported in the *Washington Post* (Feb. 20, 1990) found that three-fourths conceded that a glass ceiling prevents women from reaching the executive suite. Barriers included stereotyping and preconceptions (81 percent), reluctance to take risks with women in line positions (49 percent), and lack of career planning and planned job assignments for women (47 percent). The findings ran counter to the prevailing assumption that women change jobs, leave the work force, or start their own business because they want to raise their children. The report notes that the working mother may be more a convenient excuse than a reality for failing to promote women, adding that when women leave the work force, companies call it a family problem—when, in fact, it is likely to be because their opportunities weren't challenging enough.

Women in science are in neither a better or worse situation regarding advancement to top positions than women in other fields requiring similar amounts of education and dedication. Less than 3 percent of top jobs at Fortune 500 companies were held by women in 1990; only 175, or 2.6 percent, of the 6,502 corporate officers employed at the nation's largest companies in 1992 were women; only 4.5 percent of the corporate board seats of Fortune 500 companies were held by women (Ball, 1991). As shown in Table 2.3, only 17 women were on the boards of the nation's top ten industrial companies in 1993 (Catalyst, 1993).

Table 2.3. Number of Women on Boards of Top Ten Industrial Companies.

Company	Number
Chevron	2
DuPont	2
Exxon	1
Ford	1
General Electric	2
General Motors	2
IBM	2
Mobil	2
Philip Morris	2
Texaco	1
Total	17

Source: 1993 Catalyst Census

Women in Government

Federal agencies employ a higher proportion of women scientists and engineers than either industry or academia. However, as in other settings, entry levels are lower and advancement is slower for women. Grade levels (and thus salaries and responsibility) lag well behind men of similar background.

The National Institutes of Health, for example, is still what Estelle Ramey, professor emeritus at Georgetown University Medical School, described as a "cloistered aristocracy" of white men, and many believe sex discrimination there to be worse than at universities or hospitals. An NIH task force reports that although 30 percent of the postdoctoral fellows at NIH during the past decade were women, they still are only 18 percent of tenured scientists and are "significantly under-represented at the most senior managerial levels," numbering only 17 percent of section chiefs and 4 percent of lab chiefs—both positions critical to deciding what gets funded at NIH. The report concludes, "There are inequities for NIH intramural women scientists with regard to pay, tenure, promotion and visibility" (Manpower Comments, 1993, p. 19).

The NIH is not alone. Federal women scientists, wherever they work, typically rank two or more salary grades below men in the same field, earning $6,000–$12,000 less (Babco, 1993). While some of this may be due to greater job longevity among men, that is not sufficient to explain the difference.

Women in Industry

In January 1993, the National Research Council's Committee on Women in Science and Engineering held a conference on their fields' employment record in industry (Dix, 1994). The conference subtitle was "Why So Few?" Some of the women engineers and scientists attending the meeting noted that not only had they come on their own, without corporate support, but that they would not want their employers to know they were there. Employers do not encourage networking and support groups for women. Because of the macho image of engineering in their companies, these women felt they had to be careful of what they said and who knew they had attended the meeting, to avoid trouble with management.

Even some "good companies for women" refuse to tell their staff how many women engineers or scientists they employ. They do not encourage women to form support groups or participate in other networking practices. Companies say they want women but give their own women professionals no promotional credit for recruiting, speaking about issues, or advising women about science and engineering careers.

Companies have double standards for men and women, so that women and their contributions are perceived differently than those of their male colleagues. For example:

- Companies often reward men and penalize women for the same action, whether it is parenthood or leadership. Having children indicates stability in male employees, but lack of dedication to the job for women. A confident woman is likely to be considered "too aggressive." Women are promoted only after they have already proven that they can perform the tasks required in a new position, whereas men are promoted based on their perceived potential.

- Women often do not understand what is needed for promotion and assume that excellent work will be noted and rewarded. They must learn to point out their contributions to management, take the lead on projects, and create a visible role for themselves, both in their company and in their field. At the same time, they must not be seen as aggressive, boastful or blowing their own horn, since these are not "feminine" characteristics.

Women's share of Ph.D. science jobs more than doubled from 10 percent in 1973 to 22 percent in 1991 (NSF, 1973–1991), as shown in Figure 2.7. Women make up about a third of all working scientists and have been available in larger numbers for many years in the lower and middle ranks of science. But they have been unable to pierce the upper strata in anything beyond token numbers.

Figure 2.7. Women as Percentage of Employed SME Ph.D.'s, 1991.

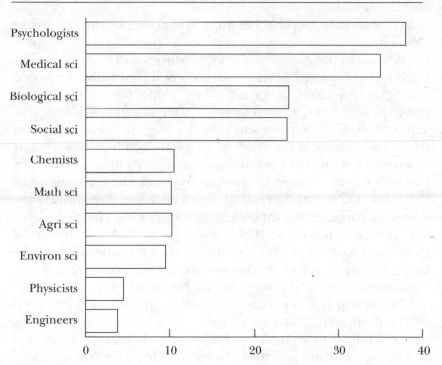

Source: NSF, 1993. Graph by CPST.

Some characteristics of science may make it more difficult for women to enter, including its extreme insularity. The need to be in a working network to ensure hearing of vital new results before competitors do handicaps women, since they are rarely part of the key communications patterns. They tend to be excluded from scientific meetings and collaborations, as well from the gossip loop. Women also get fewer chances to present their findings and ideas to powerful audiences of their peers, as revealed by the speakers list for any large scientific meeting.

Academic Employment

Among doctoral scientists and engineers employed in academic institutions, women were 20.5 percent of the 1991 total. However, they still earn less than men at every rank, in every type of institution, and in every field. It is also more difficult for women than for men to find permanent academic employment, to achieve tenure, and to advance in rank.

For example, at the 1993 annual meeting of the American Council on Education, a panel examined "Twenty Years of Progress for Women in the Academy: Personal Stories and Perspectives on Institutional Change." Beverly Ledbetter of Brown University noted that before the 1970s, the decade when gender was added to Executive Order 11246, women were an afterthought in affirmative action. Mills College president Janet Holmgren McKay described the developments of the 1980s as characterized by establishment of women's centers at institutions, attention to the issue of child care, pressures to control sexual harassment, the opening up of the sciences, and the creation of women's studies programs. Women's participation on college faculty doubled between 1975 and 1985, but in the mid 1980s, women held thirty-two thousand part-time faculty positions and men only ten thousand. Despite large inroads into academia, women have not become tenured or tenure-track faculty in proportion to their availability.

In the top ten departments of mathematics in the United States, there were 303 tenured men and 4 women in 1993. Harvard, MIT, Princeton, Yale, Stanford, Cal Tech, and the University of Chicago had no tenured female faculty. The University of California, Berkeley, which had two, was being sued (successfully) for sex discrimination by Jenny Harrison, who had been denied tenure. Women earned 19 percent of mathematics Ph.D.'s in 1991, so the persistence of such faculty imbalance suggests the continued existence of a bias against women in many top-level mathematics departments.

The picture in chemistry is similar. Women have earned an increasing percentage of the doctorates in chemistry every year since 1970 (including more than one-fourth of 1992 awards), but faculty has not grown commensurately. Indeed, women made up only 5 percent of tenured faculty in 1991 and 16 percent of tenure-track faculty, although they have earned more than 9 percent of the Ph.D.'s awarded by these departments in every year for the past two decades. Doctoral women chemists who are employed in academic institutions earn substantially less than their male counterparts with the same rank—$6,500 less among full professors in 1990, $2,926 less among associate professors, and $1,873 less among assistant professors (American Chemical Society, 1992). These differences exist regardless of experience level—for example, among full professors twenty to twenty-four years after the B.S., men average $65,675; women, $61,868 (Roscher, 1990).

Among academic chemists, there continue to be few women in the upper ranks at any type of institution. At every rank, women are more likely than men to be employed in institutions awarding A.A. and B.S. degrees, but much less likely to be in those awarding Ph.D.'s. Among men, 75 percent have tenure or are in a tenure track, compared with 59 percent of women.

Conclusion

From its beginnings, the United States has been a sexist, racist society that generally subscribes to the myth of white male superiority. Changing these beliefs is a real battle, but until we do, we can never be the best we could be. Myths about gender-based characteristics of girls and women and their roles are slow to change, but they are changing. Most families now recognize the importance of preparing their daughters for independence rather than solely for marriage and motherhood.

The barriers of prejudice and custom that impede progress for women in science persist, but some of them are slowly being edged aside. The isolation experienced by women working in engineering and science has decreased as more women enter these fields. It may take another decade or more to end such practices as paying lower salaries in occupations dominated by women; but in the meantime, salaries for women in male-dominated fields will continue to exceed those in other fields. As the recession passes, job opportunities should increase, and women may expect to get a reasonable share of those in science and engineering.

Adelman (1991) writes, "The United States will enter the next century with a remarkable edge over its global competitors. U.S. women, of all races, are the best educated and trained in the world and will constitute 64 percent of the new entrants to the workforce over the next 10 years" (p. 1). It will be up to us to capitalize on that edge.

References

Adelman, C. (1991). *Women at thirtysomething: Paradoxes of attainment.* Washington, DC: U.S. Department of Education, Office of Educational Research and Development.

American Association of University Women. (1991). *Shortchanging girls, shortchanging America.* Washington, DC: Author.

American Association of University Women. (1992). *How schools shortchange girls.* Washington, DC: Author.

American Association of University Women. (1993). *Hostile hallways: The AAUW survey on sexual harassment in America's schools.* Washington, DC: Author.

American Chemical Society. (1992). *Domestic status, discrimination, and career opportunities of men and women chemists.* Washington, DC: Author.

Astin, A. W., Green, K. C., Korn, W. S., Schalit, M., & Berz, E. R. (1988). *The American freshman: National norms for fall 1988.* Los Angeles: Cooperative Institutional Research Program, University of California.

Babco, E. L. (Ed.). (1993). *Salaries of scientists, engineers and technicians* (16th ed.). Washington, DC: Commission on Professionals in Science and Technology.

Ball, K. (1991, August 26). Study finds few women hold top executive jobs. *The Washington Post,* p. A11.

Catalyst. (1993). *Women on corporate boards: The challenge of change.* 1993 Catalyst Census. New York: Author.

Cole, J. R. (1979). *Fair science: Women in the scientific community.* New York: Free Press.

College Placement Council. (1994, July). *Salary survey.* Bethlehem, PA: Author.

Czujko, R., & Bernstein, D. (1989). *Who takes science? A report on student coursework in high school science and mathematics.* New York: American Institute of Physics.

Dix, L. S. (Ed.). (1994). *Women scientists and engineers employed in industry: Why so few?* Washington, DC: National Academy Press.

Dossey, J. A., Mullis, I.V.S., Lindquist, M. M., & Chambers, D. L. (1988). *The mathematics report card: Are we measuring up? Trends and achievement based on the 1986 national assessment.* Princeton, NJ: Educational Testing Service.

Eccles, J. S., & Jacobs, J. E. (1986). Social forces shape math attitudes and performance. *Signs, 11,* 367–380.

Ellis, R., & Eng, P. (1991). *Women and men in engineering.* (Engineering Manpower Bulletin 107). Washington, DC: Engineering Workforce Commission of the American Association of Engineering Societies.

Engineering Workforce Commission. (1993). *Engineering and technology degrees 1993.* Washington, DC: American Association of Engineering Societies.

Hewitt, N. M., & Seymour, E. (1991). *Factors contributing to high attrition rates among science, mathematics and engineering undergraduate majors.* Report to the Alfred P. Sloan Foundation, University of Colorado, Boulder.

Keynes, H. B. (1989, Spring). UMTYMP: Recruiting girls for a more successful equation. *ITEMS,* University of Minnesota Institute of Technology.

LeBold, W. (n.d.). [Annual reports on freshmen in engineering at Purdue University.] Unpublished reports. Purdue University, West Lafayette, IN.

Mullis, I.V.S., & Jenkins, L. B. (1988). *The science report card: Elements of risk and recovery.* Princeton, NJ: Educational Testing Service.

National Assessment of Educational Progress. (1991a). *NAEP 1990 technical report.* Princeton, NJ: Educational Testing Service.

National Assessment of Educational Progress. (1991b). *Technical report for the 1990 Trial State Assessment.* Princeton, NJ: Educational Testing Service.

National Center for Education Statistics. (1950–1987, 1992–1993). *Earned degrees conferred by U.S. colleges and universities.* [Annual series, 1950–1993 (data for 1988–1991 unpublished)]. Washington, DC: U.S. Government Printing Office.

National Center for Education Statistics. (1994a). Degrees and other formal awards conferred. 1990–91 survey reported in B. M. Vetter (Ed.), *Professional women and minorities: A total human resource data compendium* (11th ed., pp. 70–72). Washington, DC: Commission on Professionals in Science and Technology.

National Center for Education Statistics. (1994b). *Projections of education statistics to 2002: An update* (NCES 91–683). Washington, DC: U.S. Government Printing Office.

National Research Council. (1972–1994). *Doctorate recipients from United States universities.* [Annual summary reports, 1972–1994]. Washington, DC: National Academy Press.

National Science Foundation. (1973–1991). *Characteristics of doctoral scientists and engineers in the United States.* [Biennial reports]. Arlington, VA: Author.

National Science Foundation. (1994). *Selected data on graduate science/engineering students and postdoctorates, fall 1992* (NSF 94–301, pp. 8, 11–12). Arlington, VA: Author.

Primack, R. B., & O'Leary, V. E. (1993, March). Women in ecology. *Bioscience, 43.*

Roscher, N. M. (1990). *Women chemists 1990.* Washington, DC: American Chemical Society.

Russell Reynolds Associates. (1990). *Men, women and leadership in the American corporation.* New York: Author.

Sadker, M., & Sadker, D. (1994). *Failing at fairness: How America's schools cheat girls.* New York: Charles Scribner's Sons.

Shakhashiri, B. (1990). U.S. science education. In B. Vetter & E. Babco (Eds.), *Human resources in science and technology: Improving U.S. competitiveness* (pp. 59–69). Washington, DC: Commission on Professionals in Science and Technology.

Society of Women Engineers. (1993). *A national survey of women and men engineers: A study of the members of 22 engineering societies.* New York: Author.

U.S. Bureau of the Census. (1992). *Education and income.* Series P-60, No. 174. Washington, DC: U.S. Government Printing Office.

U.S. Department of Education. *National longitudinal survey of high school seniors of 1972* (NLS-72). Washington, DC: Author.

Vetter, B. M. (ed.). (1991). *Manpower Comments* (Vol. 28, No. 1). Washington, DC: Commission on Professionals in Science and Technology.

Vetter, B. M. (Ed.). (1993). *Manpower Comments* (Vol. 30, No. 5). Washington, DC: Commission on Professionals in Science and Technology.

Vetter, B. M. (Ed.). (1994). *Professional women and minorities: A total human resource data compendium* (11th ed.). Washington, DC: Commission on Professionals in Science and Technology.

Weiss, I. (1993). *Science and mathematics education briefing book* (Vol. 4). Chapel Hill, NC: Horizon Research.

Opportunities and Obstacles: Science Education in the Schools

Jane Butler Kahle

Recently, the press has been full of articles drawing connections between the education of girls and women and the health and welfare of nations. Scholarly papers have presented evidence of gender-based educational differences, especially in science, mathematics, and engineering, for several decades. Popular and scholarly articles alike argue for increased emphasis on the education of girls and women, both in terms of justice and in terms of economic and social progress. This chapter reviews the quality of elementary and secondary schooling for girls and women in science, mathematics, and engineering. It analyzes the forces that attract girls to scientific fields and those that inhibit their entry to or persistence in those fields, and it explores the overall effect of the pipeline on girls' achievement and advancement in scientific and technical careers. It also reviews several models for research in gender equity and recommends areas for continued research.

This chapter is based upon the premise that equity is a prerequisite for a strong and just nation (Fennema, 1990a), and its definition of equity is broad and encompassing. Equity is not merely a matter of educating equal numbers of boys and girls or appropriate proportions of majority and minority students to a specific level of competence, in this case, in mathematics and science. Rather, it includes equity in access (who studies technical subjects); equity in education (who has the curricula, materials, and instruction for optimal education); equity in outcomes (who achieves to his or her ability); equity in resources (who has optimal and equal facilities and other types of support); and equity in leadership (who has access to and success in a myriad of leadership roles).

The discussion primarily addresses mathematics and science, because few U.S. K-12 schools have any courses in engineering. And because socioeconomic status confounds results in private schools, the review centers on public, coeducational schools. There is some assessment of work with factors unique to minority populations, but the reader is also referred to Chapter Six for an in-depth exploration of the information available on effects of sex, race/ethnicity, and class on girls' educations.

Girls in School

Analysis of national data bases and individual research suggests that girls and boys experience different educations. The differences may be subtle, such as who is called upon more often in a given class or lesson, or they may be overt; for example, who is recommended or encouraged to take advanced science and mathematics classes. In either case, the differences are cumulative as girls move through school and, eventually, they contribute to overall gender-related differences in attitudes, self-confidence, and achievement.

The long debate about mixed or single-sex education is still unresolved. One issue has been whether to address progress for individual girls (usually assumed to be enhanced in single-sex settings) or societal change (assumed to depend on attitudes, perspectives, and stereotypes of both men and women). This section traces the general educational experiences of girls in mixed and single-sex settings, then summarizes findings about girls' scientific and mathematics education from kindergarten through high school—the pipeline to scientific and technological careers. It also examines some similarities and differences in the science and mathematics education of girls of color.

Beyond the social and educational factors discussed in this chapter, biological differences are often cited as influencing success in mathematics and science. To summarize briefly, Kahle and Danzl-Tauer (1991) report that in 1981, Gray claimed a biological basis for differences in spatial test scores of females and males. He postulated a sex-linked, recessive, spatial superiority gene on the X chromosome and described an inheritance pattern that would result in the observed female-male spatial ability difference. Although this hypothesis would predict a bimodal distribution of female scores on spatial ability tests, Gray's observations indicated a unimodal distribution. Nonetheless, the hypothesis has been used to support a biological basis for sex difference in mathematics and science. (See Kahle & Danzl-Tauer, 1991, and Linn & Peterson, 1983, for a more complete discussion.)

Coeducational Schools

Generally, research on girls in school has focused either on interaction patterns found across different types of classes and levels of schooling, or on specific teaching/learning strategies such as laboratories or textbook usage common in mathematics and science instruction. This section focuses on classroom experiences. When possible, any self-concept or achievement differences that may be related to those experiences are described. However, those relationships are not consistent nor significant across studies.

A fair amount of research has examined gender differences in classroom interaction patterns, particularly in mathematics and science (Sadker & Sadker, 1985; American Association of University Women [AAUW], 1992). Over the past ten years, studies have attempted to identify, categorize, and interpret the results of the experiences girls and women have in mathematics and science classrooms (Tyack & Hansot, 1988).

This research provides partial support for the hypothesis that gender differences in attitudes and achievement levels stem from differential treatment of girls and boys in their classrooms (Jones & Wheatley, 1990; Kahle, 1990; Lee, Marks, & Byrd, 1994; Morse & Handley, 1985; Tobin & Garnett, 1987). For example, boys are more likely than girls to initiate interaction with teachers, to volunteer to answer teacher questions, to call out answers, and to receive praise, criticism, or feedback for their responses. The disparity in interaction results in greater opportunities for boys to learn science and may reflect differential teacher expectations for boys and girls (Kahle, 1990).

Gender differences are most pronounced in whole-class activities. Tobin and Garnett (1987) report that such activities tend to be dominated by what they call target students, who are usually male. In junior and senior high school science classes, Tobin and Gallagher (1987) have found a ratio of four male to one female target student. In calculus, chemistry, English, and U.S. history classes in both mixed and single-sex schools, Lee and her colleagues (1994) report that the major source of sexism was boys' domination of discussion and teacher interaction. The most blatant examples appeared in the chemistry classes in the study. Because of boys' ability to dominate interactions, Kelly (1988) noted that "On average, teachers spend 44 percent of their time with girls and 56 percent of their time with boys" (p. 13). She concluded that, on the whole, boys receive approximately 1,800 more hours of teacher instructional time than girls during twelve years of schooling.

Besides different classroom interaction patterns for girls and boys, researchers have noted gender-related differences in the use of materials and manipulatives. In 1983, Kahle and Lakes analyzed student responses to the 1976–77 National Assessment of Educational Progress (NAEP) science survey and documented for the first time that boys generally have more opportunity than girls to use scientific equipment, to perform experiments, and to take science-related field trips. Their findings were supported by Kelly (1985) and Whyte (1986) in the United Kingdom as well as by numerous U.S. studies. In 1992, the American Association of University Women issued a report, *How Schools Shortchange Girls,* which summarizes the situation, noting that by third grade, 51 percent of boys but only 37 percent of girls have used microscopes, and that by eleventh grade, 49 percent of boys but only 17 percent of the girls have used electricity meters.

Performance differences between girls and boys (favoring boys) provided the impetus for studies of interaction patterns in mathematics classrooms. Koehler (1990) summarized progress of that work along a continuum. Initially, studies looked for external factors such as sex-stereotyped remarks, sex of teacher, or sex-biased texts. When neither causal nor correlational relationships could be drawn, researchers next examined the interactions between teachers and students; for example, what types of questions are asked and who is called upon to respond, how incorrect responses are handled and who receives praise or criticism, and who asks for and who receives help. Koehler characterized such studies as *differential treatment* studies and concluded that, on the whole, boys and girls are treated differently from elementary through high school and that those differences usually favor boys. However, she identified two limitations in those studies: first, achievement outcomes are usually not considered; second, the scope of the classroom processes observed is rather narrow.

Eccles and her colleagues have observed junior high and middle school mathematics classes for over a decade. Recently, she summarized their findings about differences in amount and type of teacher interactions with girls and boys. She reports finding less evidence of differential treatment than expected. Further, she notes that when differences are found, students usually initiate action, not teachers. On the whole, males get more teacher attention, especially criticism. In mathematics, as in science, target students are more likely to be males. The studies, which often combined parental interviews with classroom observations, found that girls and minority students fare better when teachers contact parents; this finding suggests that stereotyping exists at home. In addition, the proportion of girls who continue to study advanced mathematics is increased when teachers do specific compensatory activities (Eccles, 1992).

Eccles' observations (1992) suggested that increased use of cooperative, hands-on, and practical problem-solving activities improved participation and achievement for girls and minority students in mathematics classes. Other differential treatment studies also suggested that girls preferred cooperative instructional strategies (Koehler, 1990; Peterson & Fennema, 1985).

A decade ago, Kahle (1985) described strategies in high school biology classes that were found to increase the number of girls (including minority girls) who continued to study science in high school and college. Those strategies paralleled the ones identified in mathematics and included the increased use of laboratories and discussions; educational and career counseling; inquiry, creative, and basic-skill activities; and field trips and other out-of-school science activities. In addition, the biology teachers studied used multiple curricular sources (in lieu of a single text) and developed many of their own curricular materials in order to include information about women in science.

Extensive observational studies suggest that active learning and cooperative learning groups motivate young women to study mathematics and science. Other studies report that most girls prefer cooperative rather than competitive learning activities and take a more active role in them (Baker, 1990; Eccles, 1989; Johnson & Johnson, 1987; Kahle, 1990; Peterson & Fennema, 1985; Smail, 1985). In addition, researchers such as Gilligan (1982), Noddings (1984), and Belenky, Clinchy, Goldberger, and Tarule (1986) have suggested that females are more willing than males to make exceptions and accept innovations, are less competitive, and are more likely to make moral judgments based on compassion. There is little empirical evidence that boys prefer competitive or individualistic learning situations, and some studies (for example, Johnson & Johnson, 1987, or Johnson & Englehard, 1992) suggest that cooperative learning experiences promote higher achievement for all students.

However, there is also evidence suggesting that cooperative learning may not always increase girls' participation and achievement. For example, in mixed-sex, small groups in mathematics classes, girls are less likely to receive help from boys; and, if there is only one girl in a group, the boys usually ignore her (Koehler, 1990). Although research found that boys outperformed girls in above-average, ninth-grade mathematics classes using small cooperative groups, no significant difference in performance was found in similar below-average classes (Webb, 1984; Webb & Kenderski, 1985). Recently, Rogg (1990) reported that achievement gains were not associated with increased cooperative group work for either girls or boys in average-ability high school biology classes.

Regardless of classroom organization, opportunities to participate and to build their own knowledge enhance students' learning in mathematics and science (von Glasersfeld, 1989; Wheatley, 1991). However, both observations and survey responses indicate that instruction in high school mathematics and science tends to rely on a whole-class format. For example, students and teachers cite lectures as the prevalent form of instruction (83 percent of the time in junior high school and 84 percent of the time in senior high school science classes). Further, when students are asked to report the frequency of science instructional strategies, 68 percent of seventh graders and 54 percent of eleventh graders rank "reading the textbook" highest—occurring several times each week. Only 14 percent of seventh graders and 18 percent of eleventh graders cited "experimenting in groups" as occurring several times a week (Horizon Research Inc. [HRI], 1989). Science instruction at the secondary level is primarily textbook based, and lecturing, accompanied by reading the text, is the basic instructional strategy.

In mathematics, students also have reported the frequency of various types of instruction (HRI, 1989). For example, in Grade 7 the activities cited as occurring daily by the most students are listening to the teacher (82 percent), working problems alone (81 percent), and using mathematics textbooks (77 percent). Most students say cooperative and/or manipulative activities seldom or never occur in their classes. For example, most seventh graders say they never do reports (81 percent) and projects (78 percent), or have mathematics laboratory activities (81 percent). In eleventh-grade mathematics, using the text (76 percent) and listening to the teacher (74 percent) are the most common daily activities, while the percentage of students who report that they never do projects or reports rises to 87 percent, and those who report never doing mathematics lab activities increases to 82 percent (HRI, 1989). These daily activities reported by students for science or mathematics classes do not match the ones researchers identify as motivating for girls and non-Asian minority students.

Gender differences in classroom interactions and activities show some relationship to gender differences in confidence and in self-concept in science (Kahle & Rennie, 1993; Rennie, Parker, & Hutchinson, 1985). In a comprehensive review of the literature, Kahle and Meece (1994) conclude that there is increasing evidence that differential experiences affect the attitudes, if not the achievement, of girls in science. However, similar studies in mathematics have yielded inconsistent results. Although Fennema and Sherman (1977, 1978) found that sixth- through twelfth-grade males are more confident than females of their ability to learn mathematics, the difference was not related to classroom interaction. Other studies suggest that students' attitudes and achievement levels in mathematics seem to be context specific, because gender effects are not observed in some classroom settings (Eccles & Blumenfeld, 1985; Eccles [Parsons], Kaczala, & Meece, 1982).

In mathematics, differences in the attributions of females and males are often cited as reasons for enrollment and performance differences. Extensive research indicates that girls tend to attribute success in mathematics to effort, while they blame failure on lack of ability. Boys, on the other hand, attribute success to ability, and failure to lack of effort. There is some evidence that many teachers explain results in the same terms (Eccles [Parsons], Kaczala, & Meece, 1982; Fennema & Sherman, 1978). Leder (1990b) suggests that girls' lower mathematics performance levels are largely a function of girls' internalizing and conforming to expectations of others rather than the result of different classroom interactions. She states, "Students capable of continuing with mathematics but who *believe* that the study of mathematics is inappropriate for them may select themselves out of mathematics or perform at a level they believe others consider appropriate for them" (p. 19, Leder's emphasis). Eccles (1989) predicts a relationship between students' perceived value of and success in a subject and their subsequent persistence and performance in that subject. Kloosterman (1990) cautions that "while attributions are important, they have not, at this time, been shown to be the key to understanding differential achievement of females and males" (p. 124).

The experiences of girls and boys in science and mathematics classes—from kindergarten through high school physics—are strongly influenced by sex-role stereotypes that many teachers may hold, many children bring to school, and many parents wittingly or unwittingly foster at home. Kelly (1985), Lee, Marks, and Byrd (1994), and Parker (1995) hypothesize that schools are social institutions that reinforce gender-appropriate behavior, interests, and occupations. Perhaps the greatest concern about the subtle yet pervasive gender socialization in schools is that it limits opportunities for some children to learn. As discussed earlier, classroom patterns involve more frequent interactions with boys, fewer challenging questions posed to girls, fewer opportunities for girls to use manipulatives or equipment, and more examples and exemplars related to masculine activities. Unfortunately, such experiences are cumulative, resulting in deficient mathematics and science education for many girls, particularly in the capstone courses of calculus and physics.

Single-Sex Schools and Classes

Although many comparisons of the efficacy of mixed and single sex education are confounded by differing student socioeconomic levels, Lee and her colleagues (1994) have done a controlled and comprehensive analysis. They studied eighty-six classrooms in twenty-one private schools, seven all boy, seven all girl, and seven mixed. In each school, they observed classes in calculus, chemistry, English, U.S. history, and one other subject, chosen by the school administration. In assessing the frequency of sexism, they used as the unit of analysis a "gender-related *incident*" (author's emphasis) that could be either positive or negative.

They found that the number of gender-related incidents was similar across the three types of schools, but the kinds of incidents were different. The most overt and negative ones were reported in boys' schools, where female activities and/or accomplishments were ridiculed. On the other hand, "a pernicious form of sexism" was common in girls' schools, where gender-related incidents fostered academic dependence and weakened instructional rigor. In coeducational schools, the number of gender-related incidents was higher in chemistry than in other classes observed. Further, as the ratio of males to females rose in chemistry classes, the number of gender-related incidents also rose. Generally, gender-related incidents occurred in 37 percent of the observed classes in boys' schools, virtually all teacher initiated. Gender-related incidents occurred in 45 percent of the girls' classes, with teachers initiating the majority. Although the percentage of gender-related incidents was highest in mixed classes (54 percent), teachers initiated only two-thirds of them.

Science and mathematics instructors in girls' boarding schools describe students as reluctant to take risks in class or to enter national science or mathematics competitions. They hypothesize that many girls have been socialized away from science and to a lesser extent mathematics before entering their classes. It appears that the gender-socialization that affects girls' participation in science and mathematics in mixed settings is also a factor in single-sex schools (Polina & Gould, 1992).

In spite of these concerns, there is a general perception that girls fare best in mathematics and science in single-sex settings. That perception stems from research findings that women undergraduates in single-sex colleges develop higher levels of self-esteem, while the self-esteem of women in mixed colleges actually deteriorates. Women in female colleges score higher on standardized tests, are more likely to choose nontraditional majors, and are more likely to graduate than those in mixed colleges. Similarly, women who have attended a female college are more likely to hold higher positions in their careers as well as to earn more money than those who attended coeducational schools. (See, for example, Astin, 1993; Rice & Hemmings, 1988; Smith, 1990.) However, it is not altogether feasible to generalize from these findings. Because many women's colleges are highly selective and expensive, studies that control for student ability and economic status are needed.

To test the efficacy of single-sex settings, all-girl mathematics and science classes have been formed in mixed schools. Because of legal concerns about special opportunities based on sex or race, three California public schools have set up single-sex classes in mathematics and science for both girls and boys. Although there have been no controlled studies of achievement or outcome, anecdotal evidence suggests that girls respond enthusiastically to the option. However, reactions from boys and teachers are mixed, as many decry the loss of the calming and steadying influence of girls in the all-boy classes (Gross, 1988).

A summary of research in this area concludes that "evidence to date does not warrant an unreservedly enthusiastic advocacy or adoption of long-term gender-segregated mathematics classes" (Leder, 1990a, p. 16). Likewise, a recent analysis of equitable educational practices concludes that the hypothesis "that some types of gender segregation may be better for some females" needs further investigation (Klein et al., 1994, p. 17). Hollinger's (1993) review suggests that the conflicting evidence concerning the efficacy of single-sex versus mixed classes and schools may be due to gender equity policies and practices rather than to the gender composition of the class or school. For example, Eccles (1989) notes that when students reflect about their experiences, they emphasize the importance of having close friends in class, not the gender composition of the class itself. Neither anecdotal evidence nor research findings yet provide a basis for advocating single-sex education in mathematics and science.

In both mixed and single-sex situations, research has found that schooling does not overcome gender socialization, although there is some evidence that socialization affects racial groups differently. Furthermore, studies by Whyte (1986), Kahle and Rennie (1993), and Meyer and Koehler (1990) suggest that sex-role stereotypes about appropriate activities for, and aptitudes of, girls are held more firmly by boys than by girls. However, some findings argue that sexism is present even in all-girl schools (Lee et al., 1994; Polina & Gould, 1992). Research is needed to determine if single-sex environments enhance the learning of science and mathematics for girls and boys.

Pipeline Issues by Educational Level

Interviews with kindergarten boys and girls three weeks after they enter school suggest that they come to school with different ideas about science. None of these children can define science, but— even without that knowledge—more boys than girls reply that they want to be scientists, that they are good in science, and that they have done science (P. Campbell, personal communication, November, 1993). The importance of those attitudes is reflected in Baker's (1990) hypothesis that gender differences are established as early as kindergarten. She states, "Socialization acts as a filter for what students remember about their science instruction in terms of topics and pedagogy and in terms of instructional preferences. These early memories and preferences seem to influence subsequent course taking behavior" (p. 7).

In a study designed to help curriculum developers produce material of equal interest to girls and to boys, Shroyer and her colleagues found that by Grade 6 girls and boys reflected gender stereotyping of science in their topic choices. (Girls chose life sciences; boys chose physical sciences.) Furthermore, gender affected the reasons they gave for their choices. Girls more frequently attributed their selections to what they *should* know. Boys, on the other hand, based their choices on what they *wanted* to know (Shroyer, Powell, & Backe, 1991). More recently, Kahle and Rennie (1993) found gender-related responses about preferred science topics among fourth-grade children. However, when Bunderson and Baird (1994) compared fifth and sixth graders' science fair projects, they found high correlations between the choices of girls and boys within subject areas (0.94 for life sciences, 0.87 for physical sciences, and 0.73 for earth sciences). They suggested that girls with a broad range of topics to choose among, as well as experience with a variety of science activities, made choices that were less sex-role stereotyped.

Others have drawn attention to the need for equitable teaching and science experiences in the elementary grades if girls are to participate equally in science (Harlen, 1985; Rennie et al., 1985). Furthermore, it has become evident that interest and performance in science interacts with students' out-of-school activity (Johnson, 1987; Kahle & Lakes, 1983). Bunderson and Baird (1994) relate boys' more varied and interesting science fair projects to the broader and more frequent opportunities that boys have to do science out of school.

Recent work has focused on elementary school, where girls' attitudes and self-confidence in science and mathematics begin to decline. Researchers note that formation of student interest is related to the amount and kind of science and mathematics taught in elementary school (Kelly, 1981; Meece, Parsons, Kaczala, Goff, & Futterman, 1982; Ormerod & Wood, 1983). Other studies describe how teachers influence students' perceptions of and confidence in doing mathematics and science (Eccles, 1992; Kahle, Anderson, & Damnjanovic, 1991; McMillan & May, 1979; Meyer & Koehler, 1990; Simpson, 1978). Teachers may hold stronger sex-role stereotyped views than students about the appropriateness of specific science activities for girls and boys. For example, Fennema (1990b) discusses the effect of perceived sex-role congruency and the study of mathematics, noting "While research on beliefs about appropriate behavior of males and females by teachers is scanty, there seem to be indications that teachers do perceive and evaluate females and males differently and that these beliefs do influence classroom behavior of teachers as they interact with females and males" (p. 180). Likewise, Bunderson and Baird (1994) have found that teachers' responses concerning science fair topics selected by girls and boys were more sex-role stereotyped than were students' actual selection of topics.

By the time they reach adolescence, children have a well-defined identity. Eccles (1992) reports that gender differences in the type of mathematics courses taken begin to occur in Grades 8 and 9. She especially notes the effect of parental stereotypes on students' choice of mathematics classes as well as on out-of-school activities. For example, parent perceptions affect girls' and boys' own perceptions of their ability and determine parent interactions with daughters and sons. Parents buy more mechanical games and computers for sons than daughters. Other studies suggest that differences in leisure-time activities affect career expectations of girls and boys (Leder, 1990b). In 1983, Kahle and Lakes found that girls preferred more science-related activities and experiences (both in school and during their leisure time) than they actually had. Empirical research since that time has not provided evidence to the contrary.

Further, studies show that girls' regard for science begins to decline in junior high school. Equal percentages of third-grade girls (67 percent) and boys (66 percent) respond that what they learn in science classes is useful in everyday life. In seventh grade, both boys' and girls' responses continue to be fairly high (54 percent and 57 percent). However, boys retain that attitude through high school, while girls' perceptions of the utility of science fall by 11 percent. The same is true of interest in a career in science. Boys and girls respond the same in the seventh grade, but many girls have lost interest by the eleventh grade (Mullis & Jenkins, 1988). The deterioration in girls' view of science is reflected in their enrollments in elective science courses in high school. Although the last few years have seen a substantial increase in the number of young women enrolling in high school chemistry, they continue to be underrepresented in physics. There is also some indication that girls' increased chemistry enrollment may be due to increased science requirements for high school graduation, and that much of the increase is found in nonacademic chemistry courses (National Science Foundation [NSF], 1992).

However, there is little or no decline in girls' perceptions of the value of a career in mathematics or in the usefulness of mathematics between ages nine and seventeen (Mullis, Dossey, Owen, & Phillips, 1991). Both girls and boys (over 70 percent at ages thirteen and seventeen) express consistently positive views of the usefulness of mathematics for solving everyday problems. Furthermore, equal percentages of fourth-grade girls and boys (66 percent) think "almost all people use mathematics in their jobs." That percentage rises as students proceed through school. In junior and senior high, over 73 percent of girls and boys respond positively (strongly agree or agree) to that item (Mullis et al., 1991). Eccles and others have shown a positive relationship between perceived value and usefulness of a subject and student enrollment and achievement in that subject (Eccles et al., 1982; Meece et al., 1982).

Girls' positive attitudes about the value and usefulness of mathematics seems to have affected their course-taking patterns, eliminating gender differences in all courses except precalculus and calculus. Fennema (1994) attributes this disparity to girls' tendency to score lower than boys on complex mathematics tasks and to have lower math self-confidence and less willingness to take risks to solve problems. However, recent data (Vetter, 1994a) indicate that the gender gap is closing in both calculus and physics. Between 1987 and 1993, the percentage of women taking calculus rose by four points, those taking physics by seven, and those taking chemistry by nine. For men, the comparable figures were a two-point rise in calculus, no change in physics, and a four-point increase in chemistry.

Science and Mathematics Education for Girls of Color

Any discussion of the scientific and mathematics education for girls of color is hampered by the limited availability of data disaggregated by sex and racial/ethnic group. While Chapter Six reviews the existing literature concerning women of color in depth, some additional commentary is in order here. Although the evidence is sparse, it suggests that in several racial/ethnic groups, gender differences in achievement, interest, and attitudes favor girls, not boys (Kahle & Damnjanovic, 1994; Pollard, 1993; AAUW, 1992).

Kahle's analysis of the 1976–77 NAEP science data was the first to examine racial differences in responses; however, she was unable to report sex-by-race differences because the data were aggregated. Briefly, she found that African-American children were more enthusiastic both about school science and about science careers than were their majority peers. Compared to white students in all age groups (nine-, thirteen- and seventeen-year-olds), they were more confident both of their own future in science and of science's ability to solve world problems (Kahle, 1979). A decade later, analyses of NAEP responses by racial groups (Hispanic, African American, and white) yielded similar findings (Jones, Mullis, Raizen, Weiss, & Weston, 1992).

While the NAEP provided evidence of positive responses for all minority children, a few researchers explored gender differences within racial/ethnic groups. For example, Ascher (1985) found that African-American boys were more likely than girls to have high science self-concepts and to state preferences for careers in science, even though their science achievement test scores were equivalent. When Khoury and Voss (1985) assessed the impact of different factors on the science concentration decisions made by tenth-grade African-American and white students, they found that females and all African-American students tended to avoid advanced and more quantitative science courses. Furthermore, although girls achieved higher grades in science classes than boys in their own racial group, they expressed less enjoyment in learning science than boys did. An important finding was that, regardless of race or sex, motivation and usefulness of science were the most important predictors of future course enrollments.

Recently, Pollard reported on two studies of urban, African-American junior and senior high school students. The first study explored factors related to the successful academic achievement of economically disadvantaged minority adolescents (Pollard, 1989). The second involved structured interviews seeking detailed information on the school experiences of selected participants (Pollard, 1993). The primary purpose of the second study was to identify any gender-related differences in the school experiences of African-American students. Although the findings are disaggregated by sex and race, they are not discipline specific.

Pollard found that girls, on average, had higher achievement levels than boys, a finding supported by the work of Mickelson (1989) and Nelson-LeGall (1991) with African-American students. However, she found no gender differences with respect to self-perception, reporting that academic self-concept was more closely related to achievement than to gender. By contrast, work with whites indicates that, regardless of grades received, boys consistently rate their abilities higher than girls do in science (Linn & Peterson, 1985) and in mathematics (Eccles, 1992).

Pollard's findings (1989; 1993) describe differences in the educational experiences of African-American girls and boys in urban schools that enroll predominately minority students. For example, she reports that African-American girls are twice as likely as boys (nearly 70 percent versus almost 31 percent) to receive specific help from teachers with their school work. On the other hand, more African-American boys (60 percent) than girls (40 percent) respond that teachers provide them with personal support such as: s/he listens to and understands me; lets us get to know him/her; or jokes around with us (Pollard, 1993). However, she reports no other sex difference in students' descriptions of their school experiences.

Another study that spanned all subject areas identified differences in teacher expectations for African-American girls and boys. The study differed from earlier ones because it controlled for ability and other personal attributes (Ross & Jackson, 1991). Briefly, teachers read twelve case histories of hypothetical African-American fourth graders. They were asked to predict the students' current and future academic performance and to indicate their preference for having each student in their class. The findings suggested a distinct bias in favor of females; that is, given identical case histories, teachers gave higher academic performance ratings to girls than to boys and generally selected more girls than boys for other classes.

Howe (1982) studied classroom behavior of African-American and white students in junior high school science classes and found no systematic race or sex differences. Students' entering mathematics and reading scores were the best predictors of final grade, but *active learning behavior* (as opposed to passive learning or non-attending behavior) also contributed significantly. She concluded that for many urban students, obstacles to achievement in science were not related to race and sex but rather to poor basic skills and failure to participate in the classroom.

A more recent study of African-American and white fourth and fifth graders (Kahle & Damnjanovic, 1994) did analyze data by race and sex. The study involved a preassessment of attitudes, followed by a week of inquiry instruction in electricity, followed by a postassessment of attitudes. Prior to instruction, there was no difference by race: girls anticipated enjoying biology more than physical science, while boys expressed more interest in physical science. Significantly more boys—regardless of race—expected to enjoy the electricity unit. However, for girls of both races, enjoyment of electricity improved significantly after doing the activities. This finding supports Parker's (1985) premise that girls' negative attitudes and expressed dislike for certain science topics may be based on lack of experience.

In the Kahle and Damnjanovic (1994) study, gender-based differences favoring boys also were found for other responses, including self-confidence and perceived difficulty of the tasks. However, the gap was greater for white than for African-American children, suggesting that gender socialization was stronger in the white sample. In addition, compared to African-American girls and boys and white boys, white girls expressed significantly lower levels of self-confidence and ability and also ranked the electricity activities significantly more difficult. Overall results suggested that white girls in upper elementary school already hold stronger sex-stereotyped views of their own ability and interest in physical science than African-American girls do.

Irvine's (1986) study of student-teacher interactions offers an explanation for the lack of confidence found by Kahle and Damnjanovic (1994). White girls in both lower and upper elementary grades received less teacher feedback and attention than did African-American girls and boys or white boys in her study. However, although African-American girls were actively engaged in the lower elementary grades, as they proceeded to upper grades Irvine found they received significantly less total teacher feedback, less positive feedback, and fewer public response opportunities. She warns of a "decline over time in the salience of African-American female students in the classroom" (p. 20).

Other studies have analyzed the effects of various factors on interest or achievement levels of high school students. For example, Thomas (1986) looked at the effects of race or gender on students' expressed interest in science and mathematics. The results showed that being African American or female was not significantly related to students' expressed interest in high school science. However, having a science hobby was strongly related to interest in high school science for girls and boys, regardless of race. While the next two most important factors for girls were encouragement to major in science and performance on standardized tests, for boys they were childhood aspiration of being a scientist and high school grades in science. When the results were considered by race, high school grades and standardized test scores were significant variables for white students but not for African Americans. The results also suggested that although white males and females differed significantly in their interest in high school science, African-American males and females did not.

Another study statistically analyzed participation and achievement levels of African-American, Hispanic, and white high school students in mathematics, science, and advanced technology programs in all schools in Virginia. Analyses found that African-American and Hispanic students participated and achieved at rates lower than white students did. Females in all racial groups were on a par with male students in their racial group (Ayers, Bryant, Cotman, Firebaugh, Keeling, Parsons, & Willcox, 1992). However, another study of Hispanic students found that a strong positive attitude about gender roles correlated with grades in science and mathematics for Hispanic adolescents (Valenzuela, 1993). Those attitudes were generally in contrast to many traditional attitudes about girls and women in Hispanic culture.

Ortiz-Franco (1990) divided a Hispanic sample into two groups and studied the reliability of seven tests of mathematics ability and their interrelationships with English- and Spanish-speaking Hispanic students. Gender was not included as a factor in the analysis because the number of females was deemed too small for meaningful results. Results showed marked differences in the reliability of the tests for English-speaking and non-English-speaking

Hispanic students, suggesting that there might be a difference between the way higher-order mathematics abilities are related to each other among more acculturated and less acculturated Hispanic students. Moreover, the marked differences found between the two populations of students in both the item analysis and the correlational analysis indicated that Hispanic students are not a homogeneous group.

Another study of Hispanic students investigated attitudes toward high school chemistry (Crawley & Koballa, 1991). It found that the students were motivated to enroll in chemistry because they held favorable attitudes toward the subject and that family support had no significant impact on their intentions. These findings contrasted with those of Sabogal, Marin, and Otero-Sabogal (1987), who reported family support as a critical factor for enrollment in elective science courses for Hispanic students.

Findings for the traditional group of Asian Americans (first- and second-generation Chinese and Japanese) contrast with most findings reported for other racial groups. First, traditional Asian Americans are overrepresented in science and mathematics courses and careers. They lead all groups in national assessments and standardized tests of achievement in science and mathematics. Furthermore, in individual studies of attitudes, they tend to have the most positive attitudes of all racial groups about the usefulness and value of science and mathematics. Campbell and his colleagues have completed a series of investigations about the attitudes of Asian-American and white Westinghouse Science Talent Search semi-finalists. Although their findings indicate no significant differences among white males, Asian-American males, and Asian-American females, significant differences separate white females from the other groups. White females, compared to the students in the other three groups, rank lowest on scales assessing self-concept, attribution for success, and persistence in science as well as mean scores on the Scholastic Aptitude Test in Mathematics (SAT-M). Campbell concludes that white girls are more influenced by gender socialization than are Asian-American girls (Campbell, 1991; Campbell & Connolly, 1987).

Huang and Waxman (1993) compared Asian-American and white students' motivation in mathematics and their perceptions of mathematics learning environments in middle school. Results indicated that compared with white students, Asian Americans demonstrated greater pride in their class work, stronger desire to succeed in class, and higher expectations for success in mathematics. They also expressed more enjoyment of mathematics classes and assignments than white students did. Generally, Asian-American students were more participative and attentive in class activities, and their parents were usually more interested and involved in what their children were doing in mathematics than white parents were. Stevenson and Stigler (1992) have reported on a decade of work comparing Chinese, Japanese, and American students' attitudes, confidence, and achievement levels in mathematics in their home countries. Generally, results mirror those found for Asian-American students in the United States.

Discussion of the schooling of Native American children in mathematics and science is hindered by an almost complete lack of data. First of all, the sample is too small for the NAEP to report results separately for Native Americans. Second, few researchers have studied Native American students in science and mathematics, and a thorough search of the literature yielded only one report that included results by gender. In a review of junior and senior high school Menominee Indian students in computer-related classes, Grignon (1993) found that girls took different classes using different types of software and that they generally came away with a less useful education than the boys did. Chapter Six discusses this study in more detail.

Effects of Differential Schooling on Achievement

As described earlier, girls and boys tend to develop different attitudes and interest levels in science and mathematics. Research has not yet established direct relationships between student attitudes and interests and number of science courses taken. However, recent longitudinal analyses of NAEP data track the effects of differential schooling on achievement and, ultimately, on the options of girls and boys. The NAEP does not disaggregate data by sex and race, so one must look at one or the other. This chapter deals with the reported gender differences, and Chapter Six returns to the longitudinal studies to discuss findings regarding various racial/ethnic groups.

Science analysis covers two decades of testing (1970 to 1990); mathematics analysis covers slightly less than two decades (1973 to 1990). The NAEP reports performance at ages nine, thirteen, and seventeen. It lists results as an average proficiency level and also as the percentage of students who reach each of five proficiency levels. Using a stratified random sample design, surveys reached between seventy-four thousand (1977) and seventeen thousand (1986) students in science and between sixty-five thousand (1978) and seventeen thousand (1986) in mathematics (Jones et al., 1992; Mullis et al., 1991). Science surveys were done in 1970, 1973, 1977, 1982, 1986, and 1990, and mathematics surveys were done in 1973, 1978, 1992, 1986, and 1990.

Comparisons of male and female science scores show few changes across the two decades. For example, there were no gender differences in the average proficiency of nine-year-olds in any of the six science assessments. However, at ages thirteen and seventeen, girls' average 1990 science proficiency level was significantly lower than the boys'. Furthermore, a gender gap has existed for seventeen-year-olds since 1970 and for thirteen-year-olds since 1977. In the past two decades, the gender gap in average science proficiency level between seventeen-year-old males and females has not narrowed significantly. There was a non-significant change between 1982 and 1990, but it was due to a slight increase in average female score, while the average male score remained unchanged. Some have attributed that effect to the intervention programs for girls that occurred between those two test dates.

In both science and mathematics, NAEP proficiency scales range from 0 to 500. To anchor the results, the NAEP defines student performance at five levels along the proficiency scale and reports percentages of students who reach each level. The science proficiency levels involve the following competencies:

150   Knows everyday science facts

200   Understands simple scientific principles

250   Applies general scientific information

300   Analyzes scientific procedures and data

350   Integrates specialized scientific information

By comparing the percentage of children scoring at each level in 1977 and again in 1990, researchers obtain proficiency level trends. In 1990, there were marked improvements at the 150 and 200 proficiency levels compared to 1977, but no significant increase in the percentage of students (all grades and all racial groups) reaching the upper proficiency levels in the same period.

Analysis by sex reveals differences among older students. There are no gender differences at any proficiency level in either 1977 or 1990 for nine-year-olds. Significant differences favor male thirteen-year-olds at levels 250 and 300 and male seventeen-year-olds at levels 300 and 350. Those differences remained constant from 1977 to 1990.

The NAEP also reports course-taking frequency for students taking each assessment. Generally, the percentage of students reporting physical science, earth/space science, biology, and chemistry courses increased between 1982 and 1990, with the largest increases in biology and chemistry. For example, 45 percent of U.S. girls enrolled in high school chemistry in 1990, compared to 30 percent in 1982 (Jones et al., 1992).

In mathematics, increases in average scores occurred earlier (Mullis et al., 1991). Both boys and girls gained significantly in average proficiency between 1973 and 1990, with the greatest improvement occurring in the 1980s. There is essentially no difference between the average proficiency scores of nine- and thirteen-year-old boys and girls in mathematics today. The scores of seventeen-year-old males declined during the 1970s and the scores of seventeen-year-old females increased in the 1980s, so the gender gap in average proficiency score has narrowed at that age level.

The mathematics proficiency levels involve the following competencies:

150   Simple arithmetic facts
200   Beginning skills and understandings
250   Numerical operations and beginning problem solving
300   Moderately complex procedures and reasoning
350   Multi-step problem solving and algebra

At the 200 level, nine-year-olds showed significant progress from 1978 to 1990. The percentages of girls and boys at the first three levels (150, 200, and 250) were remarkably similar across this time period. Between 1978 and 1990, the only significant gain was at level 300 for seventeen-year-old girls, a change that helped close the gender gap, as boys did not show a similar improvement.

Between 1978 and 1990, the percentage of both girls and boys taking mathematics through Algebra II significantly increased. The only other significant change in course taking was a decrease in the percentage of students of either sex reporting that they had taken no mathematics beyond prealgebra or general mathematics (Mullis et al., 1991).

Generally, NAEP data trends suggest that the gender gap in average scores as well as in percentages of students reaching the lower proficiency levels have improved, especially in the 1980s. However, gender gaps persist and grow, both in average proficiency and at the higher proficiency levels, as students move through school. Those results suggest that schools continue to shortchange girls in mathematics and science education.

Effects of Schooling on Girls' Options

Although few direct studies have been done, evidence suggests that the schooling of girls in mathematics and science both discourages and disadvantages them in their career aspirations and college admissions. Based on a national sample, Matyas (1984) reported that the best predictor of science career interest for girls was positive feelings about science classes. Gordon (1990), using a sample from the 1980 *High School and Beyond* study, compared two cohorts of students who graduated from college by 1986: those majoring in one of the natural or physical sciences, mathematics, or engineering (SME majors) and those in other fields. Most of his findings were not gender specific, but he noted that there was a higher proportion of men than women in SME majors, that among SME graduates, men were more likely than women to have identified a potential SME major in high school, and that women with high grades who took calculus in college were less likely than men with similar backgrounds to graduate with a SME major. Generally, both reports emphasize the importance of K–12 schooling on the choice of college major and career.

Grandy (1987) examined ten-year trends in SAT scores of high school seniors planning SME majors. She found that (1) numbers of examinees planning to major in SME increased until 1983 and has fallen since then; (2) examinees planning SME majors in 1986 had verbal scores averaging 19 points above the average for all examinees; (3) average SAT-M scores of 1986 potential SME majors were 38 points above the average for all test takers; (4) examinees intending to study pre-medicine, classics, comparative literature, philosophy, classical languages, Chinese, Latin, Russian, education of the gifted and talented, and mathematics education had higher SAT-V and SAT-M means than those interested in SME majors; (5) SAT-V and SAT-M scores for potential computer science majors have declined 26 and 40 points respectively in the past decade; (6) more males than females intend to enroll in SME majors; (7) among prospective electrical, mechanical, and civil engineering majors, women have higher average SAT-M scores than men; and (8) mean SAT-M scores of African Americans planning SME majors have risen considerably over the past decade.

Benbow (1988) and Benbow and Minor (1986) examined the subject choice, standardized test–taking patterns, anticipated and actual college majors, postgraduate educational plans, and career aspirations of girls and boys who were part of the Study of Mathematics Precocious Youth (SMPY). Gender differences emerged in all areas. For example, in subject choice, slightly more girls than boys took high school biology, while almost 20 percent more boys than girls took physics. Substantially more boys than girls took both the advance placement test and a College Board examination in biology, chemistry, or physics. More males (71 percent) than females (59 percent) anticipated a college SME major, and more males (59 percent) than females (37 percent) subsequently enrolled in such a major. Five years after high school graduation, 38 percent of the men but only 24 percent of the women were enrolled in doctoral programs, while another 41 percent of the men and 27 percent of the women reported doing graduate SME work. Overall, twice as many men as women (40 percent to 20 percent) anticipated a career in mathematics or science.

Scoring levels show gender differences on three widely used standardized tests: the Preliminary Scholastic Aptitude Test (PSAT), the Scholastic Aptitude Test (SAT) (both of which are administered by the Educational Testing Service and the College Board), and the American College Testing Program Assessment (ACT). All three report verbal and quantitative scores, and all directly affect college admission and scholarship support.

Recently, the American Civil Liberties Union and the National Center for Fair and Open Testing have filed a federal civil rights complaint charging the ETS and College Board with gender bias in the PSAT. National Merit Scholarships, awarded solely on the basis of PSAT scores, go disproportionately to boys. That is, 55 percent of the test takers are girls, yet boys win 60 percent of the scholarships, which total more than $30 million each year (Beck, 1994). In addition, the National Center for Fair and Open Testing has charged the National Academy for Science, Space, and Technology with sex bias for awarding its national scholarships solely on the basis of ACT scores. In 1993, boys won three out of every four of the science, space, and technology scholarships (352 boys and 84 girls). The total pool of money is $2.2 million, and the awards are renewable until graduation (Winerip, 1993). The complaints are based on the lack of predictability of the tests for women's future achievement in mathematics courses.

SAT and ACT scores play a large role in college admission decisions. Briefly, on the mathematics section of the SAT (800 total points) boys outscore girls 501 to 460, while boys score 0.2 points ahead of girls on the 36-point ACT test. Yet a study by Wainer and Steinberg (1992) involving forty-seven thousand students showed that among students who took the same college mathematics course and received the same grade, the women had scored approximately 33 points lower than the men on the SAT-M. That is, compared to men, women's SAT-M scores underpredicted performance levels. Others (Hyde, Fennema, & Lamon, 1990; Hyde, Fennema, Ryan, Frost, & Hopp, 1990) have noted that the SAT-M also underpredicts grade point averages of freshman and sophomore women. They question its validity in admission decisions for women—but it continues to be used. These reviews provide a strong indication that K-12 mathematics and science education leaves girls less able than boys of similar potential to deal with standardized gatekeeping tests and so has far-reaching effects on their opportunities and aspirations.

Future Research

Recently, Klein et al. (1994) summarized the research needed to continue progress toward gender equity. Although they noted eight areas, the list can be clumped into three main categories. They emphasize the need to analyze the effects of differential representations of various groups in school texts, children's literature, and content curricula as well as to study the integration of equity into education courses and programs. They also point out that research is needed to evaluate alternative assessments and see if they are less biased than standardized ones. Finally, they focus on the need for more research on single-sex environments. What factors make women's colleges effective? When, where, and for whom are single-sex environments most effective? What are the critical transitions from segregated to integrated environments? They close by stating, "It is important to establish coordinated research and action efforts in all areas that contribute to increasing gender equity" (p.19).

This chapter also identifies critical areas for research, and it reiterates the need for coordinated studies that lead to action. Our knowledge base has substantial gaps, particularly in the matter of disaggregated data. Only recently have researchers (Campbell, 1991; Campbell & Connolly, 1987; Kahle & Damnjanovic, 1994; Khoury & Voss, 1985) had access to—or collected—data that allow them to examine gender differences in various populations. Studies disaggregated by sex and race begin to provide insight into the effect of sex-role stereotyping in various cultures. However, no one has yet examined the effects of socioeconomic status on the attitudes, confidence, and achievement levels in mathematics and science of girls and boys, regardless of race. Current demographics suggest that studies that disaggregate data by sex, race, and economic status are urgently needed.

In addition, although much is said about boys' preferences for certain types of learning environments, tests, and teaching, few of the implicit assumptions have been tested or studied. A thorough search of the literature on cooperative and competitive learning environments found no studies of boys' preferences for either type of environment. Similarly, research is needed on single-sex and mixed learning environments. Most research on single-sex schools and classes is confounded by socioeconomic level, and the current enthusiasm for single-sex mathematics and science classes seems to be based on anecdotal evidence. As Klein et al. (1994) suggest, comprehensive research is needed in this area. For example, future research should examine both gender composition and policies in schools, classes, and small groups.

Other chapters in this book identify the critical pipeline transitions and entry points for girls and women in science, mathematics, and engineering. Research is needed concerning the effect of those transitions and entry points on girls' educations and women's careers. Furthermore, research is needed to identify how, when, and by whom girls' choices are affected.

Perhaps the most critical area for future work is research examining how children (both girls and boys) learn mathematics and science. After examining that factor for over a decade, Carpenter and Fennema (1992) have developed and tested a curriculum based upon their findings. Friedman's work (1995) also has contributed to our understanding of how spatial and verbal abilities contribute to the learning of mathematics. Similar studies are needed in science, and this promising area of research should be continued in mathematics.

Most important, we need models upon which to base research. That is, paradigms need to be proposed, tested, and revised or rejected. Models will provide the structure needed to advance our knowledge and improve the efficacy of intervention efforts. It is worth looking at several models in mathematics and science that have been proposed to describe interconnections among various social, cultural, and educational factors in the education of girls. (For further discussion, see Eccles et al., 1982; Fennema & Peterson, 1985; Kahle, Parker, Rennie, & Riley, 1993.)

Eccles delineates four types of factors that contribute to differential achievement and interest levels of girls and boys in mathematics: first, causal attribution patterns for success and failure; second, the input of socializers; third, sex-role stereotypes; and fourth, individual perceptions of various tasks. Her research indicates that the interaction among those four factors affects girls' choices by affecting the perceived value of an activity. If an activity involves mathematics or science, girls tend to undervalue it. In addition, the four factors affect student expectations for future success. According to Eccles' Academic Choice Model, both perceived value of an activity and expectation for success in it influence the amount of effort expended on the activity, the performance level that can be achieved, and the decision to participate in or continue the activity (Eccles, 1989).

Likewise, the Autonomous Learning Behavior (ALB) model of Fennema and Peterson (1985) investigates the influences of past achievement and gender on mathematics tasks requiring high cognitive ability. They hypothesize that certain behaviors, such as persistence and willingness to work on difficult problems, are necessary for success in mathematics. In the ALB model, such behavior responds to internal and external variables including confidence, perceived usefulness, attribution for success and failure, and sex-role congruity. Both models have been critical to the explication of factors affecting girls and women in mathematics, particularly in elementary and secondary schools.

Fennema, Carpenter, and Peterson (1989) have developed a model for the influence of teacher knowledge and beliefs on students in mathematics. The final outcome—student learning—is directly influenced by children's cognitions and behaviors, which are in turn influenced by classroom instruction. This classroom instruction is determined by teachers' decisions, grounded in their knowledge and beliefs. As Fennema (1990b) concludes, "Partly based on what teachers know and believe about gender differences in mathematics, decisions are made about what each female and male should do in the classroom; these, in turn, influence what that female or male learns in mathematics" (p. 172).

Similarly, Kahle and her colleagues (1993) have proposed a model to study relationships between gender and science. They draw upon evidence that teachers and students construct such relationships under the influence of previous educational and sociocultural experiences. In science classrooms, teacher beliefs and attitudes affect teaching behavior and may result in inequitable learning opportunities for girls and boys. In turn, those experiences serve either to strengthen or modify science-related attitudes and beliefs that students hold based on their own previous experiences and gender socialization. The model hypothesizes that student beliefs and attitudes concerning gender and science directly affect student outcomes in science.

The models suggest the intricate interrelationships among society and its gender socialization of girls and boys, teacher beliefs and behaviors, student beliefs and behaviors, and final student outcomes in mathematics and science. Although any of the models may be changed or rejected as a result of future research, they are all valuable theoretical frameworks for ongoing work. In addition, testing the models through further research enhances the possibilities of comparing results and coordinating action.

Conclusion

A reviewer raised a provocative question: "To what extent are the observed performance differences between boys and girls the result of sex-role stereotyping and to what extent are they the result of innate differences in girls' and boys' learning styles and interests?" He suggested that radically different solutions were needed depending on the answer to that question. If stereotyping dominated, equal opportunity and treatment would be called for. However, if there were innate differences, different but appropriate opportunities and treatment would be needed.

Clearly, the evidence presented in this and other reviews points to early and pervasive sex-role stereotyping. Kahle and Danzl-Tauer's review (1991) of transmission genetics, sometimes said to be a biological basis for innate differences, indicates that past studies were flawed. No new evidence has emerged on that topic. However, research continues to document the interaction between sociocultural variables and girls' interest in, performance in, and attitudes about science and mathematics.

It is difficult to see where gender differences arise, because some behaviors occur so early and some are so consistent. For example, when does a girl first learn to smile prettily or to act demure? When does a boy learn that risk taking is rewarded? How are active and passive roles learned and when are they internalized? Recent studies at the University of Minnesota suggest that boys and girls learn appropriate behavior by twenty-four to twenty-six months.

At that early age, male and female stereotypes are set, and boys, more rigidly than girls, define what they will and will not do (Vetter, 1994b). Even after the human genome is completely mapped, we will not have the answer, because training and environment as well as heredity influence human potential.

It seems to me that the question is not one of innate differences or stereotyped expectations, but of what interactions lead to the observed outcomes. And the solutions are not based either on equal treatment and opportunities or on appropriate treatment and opportunities. Treating girls and boys equally can further disadvantage the group with lower skills, knowledge, or interests. Meanwhile, gender-based treatment can strengthen differences—as when it led women's colleges to double the importance they placed on verbal SAT scores in relation to mathematics scores in making admission decisions. The inevitable result was that more of their graduates were interested in the humanities, arts, and social sciences—fields often stereotyped as women's disciplines—than mathematics and science. Recent research also suggests that gender-based treatment may lead to coddling of girls (Lee et al., 1994).

Although further research is needed, the conclusion from current studies is that gender differences are related to common, ordinary differences in the schooling that girls and boys receive in science and mathematics: differences that contribute to different interests, attitudes, achievements, and enrollments during junior and senior high school. The negative effect of those differences does not stop with high school graduation. Rather, young women on the whole are disadvantaged in attaining prestigious scholarships and are cautious about selecting scientific, mathematics, or engineering majors. In today's schools, equity is not the same as equality. Rather than equal treatment, equity may mean differential treatment and opportunities in order to compensate for one groups' lack of experience, skills, knowledge, or confidence.

References

American Association of University Women. (1992). *How schools shortchange girls.* Washington, DC: Author.

Ascher, C. (1985). *Increasing science achievement for disadvantaged students.* Washington, DC: National Institute of Education. (ERIC Document Reproduction Service No. ED 253 623)

Astin, A. W. (1993). *What matters in college? Four critical years revisited.* San Francisco: Jossey-Bass.

Ayers, D., Bryant, S., Cotman, T., Firebaugh, J., Keeling, D., Parsons, S., & Willcox, G. (1992). *A study of the participation and achievement of Black, Hispanic and female students in mathematics, science and advanced technologies in Virginia secondary schools.* (ERIC Document Reproduction Service No. ED 354 296)

Baker, D. (1990). *Gender differences in science: Where they start and where they go.* Paper presented at the meeting of the National Association for Research in Science Teaching, Atlanta, GA.

Beck, J. (1994, March). Scores don't add up for high-school girls. *The Cincinnati Enquirer,* p. G3.

Belenky, M. F., Clinchy, B. M., Goldberger, N. R., & Tarule, J. M. (1986). *Women's ways of knowing: The development of self, voice, and mind.* New York: Basic Books.

Benbow, C. P. (1988). Sex differences in mathematical reasoning ability in intellectually talented preadolescents: Their nature, effects, and possible causes. *Behavioral and Brain Sciences, 11,* 169–232.

Benbow, C. P., & Minor, L. (1986). Mathematically talented male and females and achievement in high school sciences. *American Educational Research Journal, 23,* 393–414.

Bunderson, E. D., & Baird, J. H. (1994). *Teachers' perceptions of topics selected by boys and girls for science fair projects.* Paper presented at the annual meeting of the National Association for Research in Science Teaching, Anaheim, CA.

Campbell, J. R. (1991). The roots of gender inequity in technical areas. *Journal of Research in Science Teaching, 28,* 251–264.

Campbell, J. R., & Connolly, C. (1987). Deciphering the effects of socialization. *Journal of Educational Equity and Leadership, 7,* 208–222.

Carpenter, T. P., & Fennema, E. (1992). Cognitively guided instruction: Building on the knowledge of students and teachers. In W. Secada (Ed.), [Special issue] *International Journal of Educational Research* (pp. 457–470). Elmsford, NY: Pergamon Press.

Crawley, F. E., & Koballa, T. R., Jr. (1991, April). *Hispanic-American students' attitudes toward enrolling in high school chemistry: A study of planned behavior and belief-based change.* Paper presented at the annual meeting of the National Association for Research in Science Teaching, Lake Geneva, WI. (ERIC Reproduction Service Document No. ED 337 353)

Eccles, J. S. (1989). Bringing young women into mathematics and science. In M. Crawford & M. Gentry (Eds.), *Gender and thought: Psychological perspectives* (pp. 37–57). New York: Springer-Verlag.

Eccles, J. S. (1992, January). *Girls and mathematics: A decade of research.* Report presented to the Committee on Equal Opportunities in Science and Engineering. Arlington, VA: National Science Foundation.

Eccles, J. S., & Blumenfeld, P. C. (1985). Classroom experiences and student gender: Are there differences and do they matter? In L. C. Wilkinson & C. B. Marrett (Eds.), *Gender influences in classroom interactions* (pp. 79–114). New York: Academic Press.

Eccles (Parsons), J., Kaczala, C. M., & Meece, J. L. (1982). Socialization of achievement attitudes and beliefs: Classroom influences. *Child Development, 53,* 322–339.

Fennema, E. (1990a). Justice, equity, and mathematics education. In E. Fennema & G. C. Leder (Eds.), *Mathematics and gender* (pp. 1–9). New York, NY: Teachers College Press.

Fennema, E. (1990b). Teachers' beliefs and gender differences in mathematics. In E. Fennema & G. C. Leder (Eds.), *Mathematics and gender* (pp. 169–187). New York: Teachers College Press.

Fennema, E. (1994). *Mathematics, gender, and research.* National Center for Research in Mathematics and Science Education, Wisconsin Center for Education Research. Madison: University of Wisconsin.

Fennema, E., Carpenter, T. P., & Peterson, P. L. (1989). Teachers' decision making and cognitively guided instruction: A new paradigm for curriculum development. In K. Clements & N. F. Ellerton (Eds.), *Facilitating change in mathematics education* (pp. 174–187). Geelong, Victoria, Australia: Deakin University Press.

Fennema, E., & Peterson, P. L. (1985). Autonomous learning behavior: A possible explanation of gender-related differences in mathematics. In L. C. Wilkinson & C. B. Marrett (Eds.), *Gender-related differences in classroom interactions* (pp. 17–35). New York, NY: Academic Press.

Fennema, E., & Sherman, J. A. (1977). Sex-related differences in mathematics achievement, spacial visualization and affective factors. *American Educational Research Journal, 14,* 51–71.

Fennema, E., & Sherman, J. A. (1978). Sex-related differences in mathematics achievement and related factors: A further study. *Journal for Research in Mathematics Education, 9*(3), 189–203.

Friedman, L. (1995). The space factor in mathematics: Gender differences. *Review of Educational Research, 65*(1), 22–50.

Gilligan, C. (1982). *In a different voice: Psychological theory and women's development.* Cambridge, MA: Harvard University Press.

Gordon, H. A. (1990). *Who majors in science? College graduates in science, engineering, or mathematics from the high school class of 1980.* Washington, DC: National Center for Educational Statistics. (ERIC Document Reproduction Service Reprint No. ED 324 197)

Grandy, J. (1987). *Ten-year trends in SAT scores and other characteristics of high school seniors taking the SAT and planning to study mathematics, science, or engineering: Research report.* Princeton, NJ: Educational Testing Service. (ERIC Document Reproduction Service No. ED 289 739)

Grignon, J. R. (1993). Computer experience of Menominee Indian students: Gender differences in coursework and use of software. *Journal of American Indian Education, 32,* 1–15.

Gross, S. (1988, July). *Participation and performance of women and minorities in mathematics: Executive summary.* Rockville, MD: Department of Educational Accountability, Montgomery County Public Schools. (ERIC Document Reproduction Service No. ED 304 515)

Harlen, W. (1985). Girls and primary-school science education: Sexism, stereotypes and remedies. *Prospects, 15,* 541–551.

Hollinger, D. K. (Ed.). (1993). *Single-sex schooling: Perspectives from practice and research* (Vols. 1 & 2). Special report. Washington, DC: Office of Educational Research and Improvement, U.S. Department of Education.

Horizon Research, Inc. (HRI). (1989, August). *Science and mathematics education briefing book.* Chapel Hill, NC: Author.

Howe, A. C. (1982). *Classroom process variables in urban integrated junior high school individualized science programs: Final report.* New York: Syracuse University. (ERIC Document Reproduction Service No. ED 220 283)

Huang, S.Y.L., & Waxman, H. C. (1993). *Comparing Asian- and Anglo-American students' motivation and perception of the learning environment in mathematics.* Paper presented at the annual conference of the National Association for Asian and Pacific American Education, New York. (ERIC Document Reproduction Service No. ED 359 284)

Hyde, J. S., Fennema, E., & Lamon, S. J. (1990). Gender differences in mathematics performance: A meta-analysis. *Psychological Bulletin, 107,* 139–324.

Hyde, J. S., Fennema, E., Ryan, M., Frost, L., & Hopp, C. (1990). Gender comparisons of mathematics attitudes and affect. *Psychology of Women Quarterly, 14,* 299–324.

Irvine, J. J. (1986). Teacher-student interactions: Effects of student race, sex, and grade level. *Journal of Educational Psychology, 78*(1), 14–21.

Johnson, C., & Engelhard, G. (1992). Gender, academic achievement, and preference for cooperative, competitive, and individualistic learning among African-American adolescents. *Journal of Psychology, 126,* 385–392.

Johnson, R. T., & Johnson, D. W. (1987). Cooperative learning and the achievement and socialization crisis in science and mathematics classrooms. In A. B. Champagne & L. E. Horning (Eds.), *Students and science learning: Papers from the 1987 National Forum for School Science.* Washington, DC: American Association for the Advancement of Science.

Johnson, S. (1987). Gender differences in science: Parallels in interest, experience, and performance. *International Journal of Science Education, 9,* 467–481.

Jones, L. R., Mullis, I.V.S., Raizen, S. A., Weiss, I. R., & Weston, E. A. (1992). *The 1990 science report card: NAEP's assessment of fourth, eighth and twelfth graders.* Princeton, NJ: Educational Testing Service.

Jones, M. G., & Wheatley, J. (1990). Gender differences in teacher-student interactions in science classrooms. *Journal of Research in Science Teaching, 27,* 861–874.

Kahle, J. B. (1979, October). An analysis of the minority attitudes toward science from the 1976–77 National Assessment of Science Results. *Attitudes toward science* (Report No. 08-S-02, pp. 72–96). Denver: Education Commission of the States.

Kahle, J. B. (1985). Retention of girls in science: Case studies of secondary teachers. In J. B. Kahle (Ed.), *Women in science: A report from the field* (pp. 49–76). Philadelphia: Falmer Press.

Kahle, J. B. (1990). Real students take chemistry and physics. In K. Tobin, J. B. Kahle, & B. J. Fraser (Eds.), *Windows into science classrooms: Problems associated with higher-level cognitive learning* (pp. 92–134). New York: Falmer Press.

Kahle, J. B., Anderson, A., & Damnjanovic, A. (1991). A comparison of elementary teacher attitudes and skills in teaching science in Australia and the United States. *Research in Science Education, 21,* 208–216.

Kahle, J. B., & Damnjanovic A. (1994). The effect of inquiry activities on elementary students' enjoyment, ease, and confidence in doing science: An analysis by sex and race. *Journal of Women and Minorities in Science and Engineering, 1,* 17–28.

Kahle, J. B., & Danzl-Tauer, L. (1991). The underutilized majority: The participation of women in science. In S. K. Majumdar, L. M. Rosenfeld, P. A. Rubba, E. W. Miller, & R. F. Schmalz (Eds.), *Science education in the United States: Issues, crisis and priorities* (pp. 483–502). Easton, PA: Pennsylvania Academy of Science.

Kahle, J. B., & Lakes, M. K. (1983). The myth of equality in science classrooms. *Journal of Research in Science Teaching, 20*(2), 131–140.

Kahle, J. B., & Meece, J. L. (1994). Girls and science education: A developmental model. In D. Gabel (Ed.), *Handbook of research in science teaching and learning* (pp. 1559–1610). Washington, DC: National Science Teachers' Association.

Kahle, J. B., Parker, L. H., Rennie, L. J., & Riley, D. (1993). Gender differences in science education: Building a model. *Educational Psychologist, 28,* 379–404.

Kahle, J. B., & Rennie, L. J. (1993). Ameliorating gender differences in attitudes about science: A cross-national study. *Journal of Science Education and Technology, 2,* 321–333.

Kelly, A. (Ed.). (1981). *The missing half: Girls and science education.* Manchester, England: Manchester University Press.

Kelly, A. (1985). The construction of masculine science. *British Journal of Sociology, 6,* 133–153.

Kelly, A. (1988). Gender differences in teacher-pupil interactions: A meta-analytical review. *Research in Education, 39,* 1–23.

Khoury, G. A., & Voss, B. E. (1985, April). *Factors influencing high school students' science enrollment patterns: Academic abilities, parental influences, and attitudes towards science.* Paper presented at the Annual Meeting of the National Association for Research in Science Teaching, French Lick Springs, IN. (ERIC Document Reproduction Service No. ED 254 408)

Klein, S. S., Ortman, P. E., Campbell, P., Greenberg, S., Hollingsworth, S., Jacobs, J., Kachuck, B., McClelland, A., Pollard, D., Sadker, D., Sadker, M., Schmuck, P., Scott, E., & Wiggins, J. (1994). Continuing the journey toward gender equity. *Educational Researcher, 23*(8), 13–21.

Kloosterman, P. (1990). Attributions, performance following failure, and motivation in mathematics. In E. Fennema & G. C. Leder (Eds.), *Mathematics and gender* (pp. 96–127). New York: Teachers College Press.

Koehler, M. S. (1990). Classrooms, teachers, and gender differences in mathematics. In E. Fennema & G. C. Leder (Eds.), *Mathematics and gender* (pp. 10–26). New York: Teachers College Press.

Leder, G. C. (1990). Gender differences in mathematics: An overview. In E. Fennema & G. C. Leder (Eds.), *Mathematics and gender* (pp. 10–26). New York: Teacher's College Press.

Leder, G. C. (1990b). Teacher/student interactions in the mathematics classroom: A different prospective. In E. Fennema & G. C. Leder (Eds.), *Mathematics and gender* (pp. 10–26). New York: Teacher's College Press.

Lee, V. E., Marks, H. M., & Byrd, T. (1994). Sexism in single-sex and coeducational secondary school classrooms. *Sociology of Education, 67,* 92–100.

Linn, M.C., & Peterson, A. C. (1983). *Emergence and characterization of gen-der differences in spacial ability: A meta-analysis.* Berkeley: University of California, Adolescent Reasoning Project.

Linn, M. C., & Peterson, A. C. (1985). Facts and assumptions about the nature of sex differences. In S. S. Klein (Ed.), *Handbook for achiev-ing sex equity through education* (pp. 53–77). Baltimore, MD: Johns Hopkins University Press.

McMillan, J. G., & May, M. J. (1979). A study of factors influencing atti-tudes towards science of junior high school students. *Journal of Research in Science Teaching, 15,* 217–222.

Matyas, M. L. (1984, April). *Science career interests, attitudes, abilities, and anx-iety among secondary school students: The effects of gender, race/ethnicity, and school type/location.* Paper presented at the annual meeting of the National Association for Research in Science Teaching, New Orleans, LA. (ERIC Document Reproduction Service No. Ed 251 309)

Meece, J. L., Parsons, J. E., Kaczala, C. M., Goff, S. B., & Futterman, R. (1982). Sex differences in mathematics achievement: Toward a model of academic choice. *Psychological Bulletin, 91,* 324–348.

Meyer, M., & Koehler, M. S. (1990). Internal influences on gender dif-ferences in mathematics. In E. Fennema & G. C. Leder (Eds.), *Math-ematics and gender* (pp. 60–95). New York: Teachers College Press.

Mickelson, R. A. (1989). Why does Jane read and write so well?: The anomaly of women's achievement. *Sociology of Education, 62,* 47–63.

Morse, L. W., & Handley, H. M. (1985). Listening to adolescents: Gender differences in science classrooms. In L. C. Wilkinson & C. B. Mar-rett (Eds.), *Gender influences in classroom interactions* (pp. 37–56). Madison, WI: Academic Press.

Mullis, I.V.S., Dossey, J. A., Owen, E. H., & Phillips, G. W. (1991). *The state of mathematics achievement: NAEP's 1990 assessment of the national and the trial assessment of the states.* (Report no. 21-ST-03). Princeton, NJ: Educational Testing Service.

Mullis, I.V.S., & Jenkins, L. B. (1988). *The science report card: Elements of risk and recovery.* Princeton, NJ: Educational Testing Service.

National Science Foundation. (1992). *Indicators of science and mathematics education.* Arlington, VA: Author.

Nelson-LeGall, S. (1991). The condition of sex equity education: Sex, race and ethnicity. In J. Pfleiderer (Ed.), *Proceedings of the 1991 ETS Invi-tational Conference: Sex equity in education opportunity, achievement and testing* (pp. 91–102). Princeton, NJ: Educational Testing Service.

Noddings, N. (1984). *Caring: A feminine approach to ethics and moral educa-tion.* Berkeley: University of California Press.

Ormerod, M. B., & Wood, C. (1983). A comparative study of three methods of measuring the attitudes to science of 10- to 11-year-old pupils. *European Journal of Science Education, 5,* 77–86.

Ortiz-Franco, L. (1990). Interrelationships of seven mathematical abilities across languages. *Hispanic Journal of Behavioral Sciences, 12,* 299–312.

Parker, L. H. (1985). *Non-sexist science education: An issue of primary concern.* Paper presented at the Science Teachers' Association of Victoria Conference, Monash University, Melbourne, Australia.

Parker, L. H. (1995). *The gender code of school science.* Unpublished doctoral dissertation, Curtin University of Technology, Perth, Australia.

Peterson, P. L., & Fennema, E. (1985). Effective teaching: Student engagement in classroom activities and sex-related differences in learning mathematics. *American Educational Research Journal, 22,* 309–335.

Polina, A., & Gould, L. (1992, November). *Mathematics and science for girls.* Proceedings for a symposium sponsored by the National Coalition of Girls' Schools. Concord, MA: National Coalition of Girls' Schools.

Pollard, D. S. (1989). Defining self concept as a dimension of academic achievement for inner-city youth. In G. L. Berry and J. K. Asamen (Eds.), *Black students: Psychosocial issues and academic achievement* (pp. 69–82). Newbury Park, CA: Sage.

Pollard, D. S. (1993). Gender, achievement, and African-American students' perception of their school experience. *Educational Psychologist, 28,* 341–356.

Rennie, L. J., Parker, L. H., & Hutchinson, P. E. (1985). *The effect of inservice training on teacher attitudes and primary school science classroom climates.* (Research Report No. 12). Perth, AU: University of Western Australia.

Rice, J. K., & Hemmings, A. (1988). Women's colleges and women achievers: An update. *Signs, 23*(6), 34–37.

Rogg, S.R.J. (1990). *Toward the evaluation of the small instructional group in the secondary biology classroom.* Unpublished doctoral dissertation, Purdue University, West Lafayette, IN.

Ross, S. I., & Jackson, J. M. (1991). Teachers' expectations for black males' and black females' academic achievement. *Personality and Social Psychology Bulletin, 17*(1), 78–82.

Sabogal, F., Marin, G., & Otero-Sabogal, R. (1987). Hispanic familism and acculturation: What changes and what doesn't? *Hispanic Journal of Behavioral Sciences, 9,* 397–412.

Sadker, D., & Sadker, M. (1985). Is the OK classroom OK? *Phi Delta Kappan, 66,* 358–361.

Shroyer, M. G., Powell, J. C., & Backe, K. A. (1991, April). *Gender differences: What do kids tell us and what should we do in the curriculum to make a difference?* Paper presented at the annual meeting of the National Association for Research in Science Teaching, Lake Geneva, WI.

Simpson, R. D. (1978). Relating student feelings to achievement in science. In M. B. Rowe (Ed.), *What research says to the science teacher* (Vol. 1, pp. 40–54). Washington, DC: National Science Teachers' Association.

Smail, B. (1985). An attempt to move mountains: The "girls into science and technology" (GIST) project. *Journal of Curriculum Studies, 17,* 351–354.

Smith, D. G. (1990). Women's colleges and coed colleges: Is there a difference for women? *Journal of Higher Education, 61,* 181–197.

Stevenson, H. W., & Stigler, J. W. (1992). *The learning gap.* New York: Summit Books.

Thomas, G. E. (1986). Cultivating the interest of women and minorities in high school mathematics and science. *Science Education, 70*(1), 31–43.

Tobin, K., & Gallagher, J. J. (1987). The role of target students in the science classroom. *Journal of Research in Science Teaching, 24,* 61–75.

Tobin, K., & Garnett, P. (1987). Gender related differences in science activities. *Science Education, 71,* 91–103.

Tyack, D., & Hansot, E. (1988). Sexism in teacher-education texts. *Harvard Educational Review, 50*(1), 36–46.

Valenzuela, A. (1993). Liberal gender role attitudes and academic achievement among Mexican-origin adolescents in two Houston inner-city Catholic schools. *Hispanic Journal of Behavioral Sciences, 15,* 310–323.

Vetter, B. M. (1994a). *Manpower Comments, 31*(7), 30.

Vetter, B. M. (1994b). *Manpower Comments, 31*(3), 20.

von Glasersfeld, E. (1989). Cognition, construction of knowledge, and teaching. *Syntheses, 80,* 121–140.

Wainer, H., & Steinberg, L. S. (1992). Sex differences in performance on the mathematics section of the Scholastic Aptitude Test: A bi-directional validity study. *Harvard Educational Review, 62,* 323–336.

Webb, N. M. (1984). Sex differences in interaction and achievement in cooperative small groups. *Journal of Educational Psychology, 76*(1), 33–44.

Webb, N. M., & Kenderski, C. M. (1985). Gender differences in small-group interaction and achievement in high- and low-achieving classes. In L. C. Wilkinson & C. B. Marrett (Eds.), *Gender-related dif-*

ferences in classroom interactions (pp. 209–236). New York: Academic Press.

Wheatley, G. H. (1991). Constructivist perspectives on science and mathematics learning. *Science Education, 75*(1), 9–21.

Whyte, J. (1986). *Girls into science and technology: The story of a project.* Boston, MA: Routledge & Kegan Paul.

Winerip, M. (1993, November). Study finds boys receive 75 percent of new science scholarships. *The New York Times,* p. B12.

Developing Scientific Talent in Undergraduate Women

Helen S. Astin, Linda J. Sax

By the time women come to college, their interest in science is well below that of men. Among all college freshmen in 1994, only 4 percent of women (versus 18 percent of men) reported plans to major in physical science, mathematics, or engineering (Astin, Korn, Sax, & Mahoney, 1994). Higher education cannot reverse the influence of years of socialization on women's career decisions, so the challenge is to maintain the aspirations of the tiny percentage who have not already turned away, while keeping the door open for women who rediscover science during college.

This chapter deals with the college experience of women considering careers in science. It begins with a brief summary of factors behind women's declining participation in the scientific pipeline and their underrepresentation in science fields. Next, we use data from a national study of undergraduate science education by the Higher Education Research Institute (HERI) (1992) to describe how college affects women's interest in science. We conclude with concrete suggestions for ways institutions can improve their record of attracting and keeping women in the sciences.

Women in Science: What Do We Know from the Literature?

Chapter Three discusses the literature on early preparation in depth. To summarize, girls and boys exhibit relatively equal mathematics and science ability in elementary school, yet girls express less interest in these fields. In junior high, girls and boys still do comparable work in mathematics and science, but girls take fewer of these courses than boys. By senior high, women take far fewer courses in math and science than men. This lack of preparation keeps many women from pursuing scientific fields in college, as they arrive without the prerequisites for college programs (Oakes, 1990a, 1990b; Brush, 1985; Vetter, 1989).

Confidence in Mathematical and Scientific Abilities

Women consistently express lower levels of academic, mathematics, and scientific confidence than men. (Frieze & Hanusa, 1984; Humphreys, 1984; MacCorquodale, 1984; Matyas, 1985a; Sax, 1994a). Ethington (1988) calls math self-confidence the most influential predictor of mathematics test performance, which, in turn, has been linked to women's entry into science fields (see also Matyas, 1985b; Peng & Jaffe, 1979; Ware, Steckler & Lesserman, 1985). Women's lack of self-confidence in mathematics can therefore be seen as a critical barrier to their pursuit of science careers.

It is important to see how women's *perceived* ability (self-concept) relates to their *demonstrated* aptitude. In other words, do women underestimate their mathematics and science potential? Research shows that this is the case. Women tend to express lower opinions of their mathematics and science ability than men even when they perform better than men in science class (DeBoer, 1986) and on tests (Marsh, Smith, & Barnes, 1985; Sax, 1995; Sherman, 1983). Lifelong exposure to cultural messages that women are not cut out for science does much to explain this underestimation (Seymour & Hewitt, 1994). Therefore, besides building scientific and quantitative skills, educators need to make women welcome in science and promote their confidence in the requisite skills.

The type of institution attended can have a significant impact on women's mathematics and science confidence. Women's colleges, for example, have been shown to promote academic and analytical self-confidence, vital for study and success in science (Astin, 1977, 1993). Historically black colleges and universities have also been shown to promote students' academic and scientific self-confidence (Astin, 1993) and to produce significant numbers of science and engineering graduates (Trent & Hill, 1994). These institutions succeed because they understand that some students are inadequately prepared for college-level science, and they provide appropriate support as needed (Trent & Hill, 1994).

Role Models and Mentors

As a result of the underrepresentation of women in scientific careers, women students encounter fewer potential role models than men. One successful woman scientist can serve as a role model to many students, of course, but (as Chapter Seven describes) there is some evidence that singular role models have little influence on students' expectations of their own success.

Women also have fewer opportunities for same-sex mentoring than men. As described by Byrne (1993), mentorship involves actions such as advice and encouragement, recommendations for awards or jobs, or involving students in research and writing—all of which require both a major time commitment and a position of influence on the part of a mentor. Although female students can be mentored by male scientists, research shows that women have more influence than men as mentors for female students (Seymour & Hewitt, 1994; Stake & Noonan, 1985; Wright & Wright, 1987).

The problem, as we said, is that women students are unlikely to meet many women scientists, particularly in the most powerful and well-connected positions. Women in the scientific community tend to be in the lower ranks of position and pay. As discussed elsewhere in this book, women scientists earn less than men at every level (Chapter Two) and are underrepresented in the higher academic ranks (Chapter Eight). Further, women in science are not promoted as fast as men, even after controlling for research productivity (Chapter Eight) or other factors such as field, race, and professional age (National Science Foundation [NSF], 1986). Women also earn less than men and are underrepresented at the higher levels of nonacademic science (Chapter Nine). All these factors reduce the chance for women science students to interact with and be mentored by same-sex leaders in their field.

Parental Influence

Parents play a critical role in influencing women's course of study and career. Chapters Two and Three discuss the tendency of parents to discourage daughters from quantitative fields of study. However, the situation differs for women with highly educated parents; they are more likely to choose a science major in college (Ware, Steckler, & Lesserman, 1985) and to enter sex-atypical careers (Gruca, Ethington, & Pascarella, 1988). Seymour and Hewitt (1994) found that among college science students, women are more influenced than men by parental expectations, but that unless the mother had a professional career, women tended to be most influenced by fathers' expectations and career choices.

Family/Career Interface

Society forces women, more than men, to choose between family and career (Frieze & Hanusa, 1984; Lips, 1992; Peng & Jaffe, 1979; Seymour & Hewitt, 1994). The perception that a science career is incompatible with raising a family turns many women away. For example, Ware and Lee (1988) found that college women who place a high priority on personal life and family responsibilities are less likely than other women to major in science. Seymour and Hewitt (1994) found that among women majoring in science, seniors were much more likely than freshmen or sophomores to express concern over the perceived difficulty of balancing family and a career in science. Interestingly, such perceptions persist despite consistent research findings that marriage and children do *not* have a negative effect on women's science career attainment and productivity, except during child bearing and early child rearing years (Matyas, 1985b).

Science in the College Curriculum

Science teaching practices alienate many students by encouraging competition, reinforcing the notion of science as unconnected to social concerns, and portraying science careers as lonely and excessively demanding (Rosser, 1990; Tobias, 1990). Seymour and Hewitt (1994) report that students in their study noted poor pedagogy and inadequate advising as concerns about science. Students also found faculty to be aloof and indifferent. In general, faculty were seen as unapproachable, preoccupied with research, and lacking motivation to teach well. Although science curriculum and pedagogy may alienate a number of men, Rosser (1990) believes that more women will be discouraged by the non–"female-friendly" teaching they encounter in the sciences.

There is a general consensus among feminist scholars that traditional curricula and pedagogy drive many women from science, but little consensus on what to do to correct the problem. Some institutions have added courses on gender and science, discussing topics such as women's history in science, feminist critiques of science, and inherent bias in theory based only on male research subjects (Rosser, 1990). Outside of such specialized courses, however, science curricula have remained relatively unchanged. Rosser and Davis (Chapter Seven) describe a phased model for developing a curriculum based on a definition of science that includes all of society's diverse groups. Such a curriculum would emphasize practices hypothesized to keep women interested in science, such as student-centered teaching methods and classroom discussions that allow students to explore science as it relates to a broad social and environmental context. However, as Rosser and Davis note, this transformation cannot occur overnight and cannot be forced upon unwilling faculty and students.

A number of institutions have attempted to increase the number of women in science by offering research internships for women, mentoring from women scientists, women's professional and social support networks, and other programs. However, very little is known about how well any of these interventions work. As argued in Chapter Seven, the next critical step is to evaluate existing programs so that effective ones can serve as models for other institutions and ineffective ones can be eliminated.

Research—History and Direction

Forces affecting women's interest in and choice of mathematics and science careers have been reported by numerous investigators using varied samples and data collection techniques. There is a consensus as to the critical variables that predict participation in science: preparation prior to college, self-confidence about scientific work, beliefs about combining work and family, availability of role models, and science pedagogy. Unfortunately, while these issues often emerge in the research on women in science, few studies address them simultaneously. When studying the impact of low self-esteem on the pursuit of a science career, for example, it is very important to control for possible confounding factors such as early preparation and parental education. Further, much of the research on women in science is conducted at a single institution or at a single time. Limiting research to one institution holds all institutional-level variables constant; as a result, the researcher does not know how women's interest in science may be affected by the institution's selectivity, general education program, or percentage of women students and faculty. Similarly, research conducted at one time cannot reveal any causal effects of science curricula or specialized science programs on women's pursuit of science in college.

The need, then, is for longitudinal, multivariate, and multi-institutional data, controlled for precollege factors, to show how the college years affect women's interest in science. To that end, this chapter draws heavily on a unique national study of undergraduate education conducted by the Higher Education Research Institute (HERI) at the University of California, Los Angeles. This chapter summarizes the findings related to women in science; see HERI (1992) for a more complete account of the results. By including a comprehensive set of variables, many institutions, and two separate surveys of the same students, this research makes an important contribution to our understanding of women's experience with science in college.

It is important to note that this study did not disaggregate data by sex and race/ethnicity. While the forces affecting career choices of majority and minority women do differ, most notably in the degree to which minority students are encouraged to pursue science in college (Seymour & Hewitt, 1994), the remainder of this chapter thus examines women as a group, focusing on their gender status only. See Chapter Six for detailed consideration of the factors that differentially affect diverse populations.

College and the Science Pipeline: A National, Longitudinal Study of Undergraduate Science Education

The research summarized in this chapter focuses on a number of salient questions:

- What is the flow of men and women in and out of the science pipeline in college?
- What personal and background characteristics influence the

decision to major in science or to pursue a career in science? How do these factors differ by gender?

- How do institutions, faculty, and student peer groups influence a student's pursuit of science? Do these influences differ by gender?
- How does college affect the development of quantitative skills and mathematical self-concept? Does this differ by gender?
- How do science and nonscience faculty differ? How do female science faculty differ from male science faculty?
- Is women's success in the sciences dependent upon achieving a certain "critical mass" of representation?

To answer these questions, HERI analyzed data primarily from the Cooperative Institutional Research Program (CIRP) 1985 Freshman Survey and 1989 Follow-Up Survey, which are sponsored by HERI and the American Council on Education. The freshman survey, conducted annually since 1966, includes information on students' personal and demographic characteristics, high school experience, and expectations about college, as well as values, life goals, self-concepts, and career aspirations. The 1989 follow-up survey includes information on students' college experience and their perceptions of college, as well as post-tests of many of the items that appeared on the 1985 freshman survey. Additional data, such as enrollment counts, came directly from institutions and from other sources, including the 1989–90 HERI Faculty Survey and the 1989 HERI Registrar's Survey. The final sample includes 27,065 college freshmen at 388 schools who were followed up four years after college entry. Support came from grants by the National Science Foundation (to study undergraduate science education) and the Exxon Education Foundation (to study general education). See HERI (1992) for a complete description of sampling and weighting procedures.

Researchers primarily employed regression analysis, using the Input-Environment-Outcome (I-E-O) framework to assess the impact of various college environments and experiences on student outcomes (Astin, 1991). This model requires control for effects of student input characteristics, such as high school science preparation, parental education, and attitudes and values, to measure the effect of the college environment on cognitive or affective outcomes, such as the choice of a science major and/or career.

Women in Science: Current Data

This section summarizes the results of the HERI research on undergraduate science education. It examines interrelationships among factors presented and discussed in the literature review and provides information and interpretation of how these forces affect students at different types of institutions.

Undergraduate Science Interest

Table 4.1 describes freshman interest in science majors in 1985, as well as how that interest changed by 1989. Men and women had about equal interest in biological science and mathematics/statistics, but there was a moderate difference between their interests in physical science and a large disparity in engineering interests. Four-year comparisons reveal very little change in the numbers of men and women in these science majors, except for the rather large decline in the percentage of men majoring in engineering.

What these figures mask, however, is the high degree of turnover in the sciences. That is, many freshmen who declare one science major will choose another major four years later, and many freshmen with other majors will later switch to any given science major. As shown in Table 4.2, typically less than half of students choosing a science major as freshmen chose that same science major four years later. The highest persistence rates were among engineering men (55.4 percent) and engineering women (47.4 percent). The lowest persistence rates occur for women in the physical sciences (36.4 percent) and men in mathematics/statistics (40.3 percent). These persistence rates are somewhat lower than those reported by Ginorio, Brown, Cook, and Henderson (1994) using single-institution data, but the two studies are consistent.

Do the science students who change majors switch out of science or simply choose a different science or engineering major four years later? Table 4.2 shows that some students transfer *between* science and engineering majors. For example, physical science is

Table 4.1. Four-Year Changes (1985–1989) in Choice of Undergraduate Major Field of Study by Gender.

Field of Study	Women (n=9,519)			Men (n=6,409)		
	1985	1989	1985–1989	1985	1989	1985–1989
Biological science	6.0	5.9	-0.1	5.7	6.9	+1.2
Engineering	4.1	2.6	-1.5	21.3	14.8	-6.5
Math/Statistics	1.8	2.2	+0.4	1.8	2.4	+0.6
Physical science	2.0	2.2	+0.2	4.6	4.7	+0.1

the final major of 5.7 percent of men from biological science majors, 5.6 percent of men from mathematics/statistics, and both women and men from engineering (7.6 percent and 4.6 percent). Final majors in the biological sciences tend to come from the physical sciences (7.8 percent of women and 5.8 percent of men). While women are more likely than men to switch into mathematics (5.3 percent of women physical science majors and 4.4 percent of women engineering majors), men tend to switch into engineering more often than women (9.6 percent of male physical science majors and 6.5 percent of male mathematics/statistics majors).

Science and engineering freshmen also switched to nonscience majors. The social sciences, humanities, and business were all popular choices, although men selected the social sciences and business at slightly higher rates than women, and women selected the humanities at slightly higher rates than men. Psychology and education displayed more profound gender differences, with women switching into these majors more often than men.

What these findings tell us is that attrition statistics include many students who are still in science or engineering, but in new majors. Other apparently lost students are pursuing research in the social sciences or have switched to business or the humanities. Many women, in particular, may have taken their scientific interests and capabilities into fields such as psychology and education. The loss of students may be a detriment to the sciences, but it is smaller than it appears, and it also represents a potential gain for other fields.

Nevertheless, it is important to understand why women leave

Table 4.2. Majors Most Commonly Chosen in 1989 by 1985 Science Majors.

1985 Major	Women	Percent	Men	Percent
Biological sciences	(n=611)		(n=404)	
	Biological sciences	40.6	Biological sciences	49.5
	Psychology	10.8	Social sciences	11.1
	Social sciences	9.0	Humanities	6.4
	Humanities	8.2	Business	5.9
	Education	4.9	Physical sciences	5.7
	Business	4.4	Psychology	3.2
Engineering	(n=407)		(n=1,378)	
	Engineering	47.4	Engineering	55.4
	Business	8.4	Business	9.9
	Physical sciences	7.6	Social sciences	5.2
	Social sciences	5.4	Physical sciences	4.6
	Humanities	5.2	Humanities	3.3
	Math/Statistics	4.4	Computer science	3.2
Math/Statistics	(n=185)		(n=124)	
	Math/Statistics	41.1	Math/Statistics	40.3
	Education	9.2	Business	8.9
	Business	7.6	Social sciences	8.9
	Social sciences	7.0	Engineering	6.5
	Humanities	5.4	Education	5.6
	Psychology	4.3	Physical sciences	5.6
Physical sciences	(n=206)		(n=311)	
	Physical sciences	36.4	Physical sciences	41.5
	Humanities	13.6	Engineering	9.6
	Biological sciences	7.8	Humanities	9.6
	Social sciences	7.8	Social sciences	9.3
	Business	5.3	Biological sciences	5.8
	Math/Statistics	5.3	Business	4.2

science during college. The next section explores the impact of various college environments and experiences on women's persistence in science. Because many of the factors that affect women are similar to those affecting men, some of the findings reviewed in this chapter refer to both sexes. These findings improve our understanding of what it is about science as a curricular and teaching domain that may encourage or discourage students—especially women—from pursuing it.

Factors Promoting Persistence in Undergraduate Science Education

To explore the factors that promote persistence in science, we performed multiple regression analyses utilizing the information we had collected on students as they began college in 1985, on characteristics of institutions these students attended, and on student college experience reported on the 1989 follow-up survey.

Early Preparation

Our research identifies past achievement and ability as the most consistent and important predictors of students' interest in science. High school grades and SAT-Mathematics scores have a significant effect on both men's and women's decision to enter science majors as freshmen, as well as on their ultimate choice of a science career.

The effects of early achievement on college and postcollege scientific work have important implications for education policy. For one thing, they suggest a profound benefit to be derived from raising the level of mathematics competency in the K–12 population. Other findings, reported briefly earlier in this chapter and discussed in Chapters Three and Six, support this conclusion.

Our research has also shown that, independent of ability, men and women with higher levels of mathematics confidence earn higher grades in college, earn higher GRE Quantitative test scores, and are more likely to pursue careers in science. It is therefore disheartening to report that mathematics confidence generally declines in college, and declines more for women than for men (Sax, 1994a). These findings suggest that higher education reinforces the gender gap in mathematics confidence.

However, we did find more encouraging results for mathematics and science majors. Although most students do tend to lose confidence in mathematics at college, women in mathematics and science fields grow more confident. The gender gap in mathematics self-concept persists for the majority of students, but initial gender differences in mathematics confidence among mathematics and science students disappear over the four years. This suggests that women who persist in mathematics and science fields learn to accept (and admit) their high abilities.

Social versus Financial Concern in Career Choice

We also found that students' personal goals play a large role in career choice. For example, among men and women who enter college intending to pursue a scientific career, those who place high priority on raising a family are more likely to leave science. What do students absorb about the effect of marriage and children on scientific careers? Faculty messages about the strong commitment and hard work required by a scientific career, as well as the invisibility of academic women who could serve as role models by successfully combining work and family, may deter students whose goals emphasize family life.

Values and interests have long been found to be predictive of career choices (Super, 1957; Rosenberg, 1957; Kinnane & Gaubinger, 1963; Seymour & Hewitt, 1994). For example, Seymour and Hewitt report that women who persist in science have high intrinsic interest in science and are less materialistic and pragmatic than men in their orientation toward science. Moreover, personal fulfillment counted very high with women who planned to pursue science careers. In our study, we also found that men with extrinsic occupational values, that is, who were motivated by rewards such as business success or money, were less likely to persist in science. For women, the decision to leave science was more likely to stem from a service orientation, such as helping others in difficulty. This finding supports Gilligan's (1982) conclusion that an orientation toward caring strongly influences women's decision making.

Indeed, research indicates that persons in scientific careers are more likely to be motivated by intrinsic interest in ideas and less likely to be interested in either making money or serving others (Holland, 1966). These findings suggest the need for a different representation of careers in science. If we were to show how science serves humanity we might help women integrate their commitment to service with their interest in science.

Role Models

As with previous studies, our research noted the positive impact of role models on career decisions. Men and women are more likely to pursue careers as engineers, research scientists, or science practitioners if one or both parents held such an occupation. We also have some evidence of faculty role modeling: the percentage of women faculty at an institution showed a unique positive impact on women's pursuit of scientific careers. These findings suggest that regardless of factors such as ability or preparation, those students who encounter role models from the scientific community will be more likely to follow up on initial science aspirations.

Faculty

Tobias (1992) and Seymour and Hewitt (1994) have documented how science pedagogy alienates many students from pursuing science in college. HERI research (Milem & Astin, 1994) confirms the finding of science faculty as distant and less interested in students' development. Our data show that faculty in the sciences are much less likely to employ active learning methods in the classroom, such as discussions, cooperative learning techniques, student-selected topics, and student-developed learning activities. Science faculty are more likely to depend on graduate teaching assistants and to prefer lectures to other types of instruction. Further, science faculty are more likely than others to grade on a curve, which promotes competition among students. Women science faculty use these remote and competitive teaching practices somewhat less than men in the field, but much more than women in other fields. For example, women employed extensive lecturing in 79.5 percent of biological sciences classes and 67.2 percent of mathematics/statistics classes, while the average for classes taught by women in all fields was 41.3 percent.

Peers

According to Astin (1993), "The student's peer group is the single most potent source of influence on growth and development during the undergraduate years" (p. 398). For women in science, the peer group is mostly male. Women are surrounded by peers who may take them less seriously, make them feel unwelcome, or even treat them with overt hostility (Seymour & Hewitt, 1994). Whereas Kanter's (1977a, 1977b) theory of tokenism suggests that such behaviors will lead many women to leave science, Seymour and Hewitt found that women did not leave science as a result of the behavior of male peers, which was merely considered annoying.

We addressed this issue in our research by analyzing whether the percentage of women in a major affects women's grades, satisfaction with major, persistence in major, academic self-confidence, mathematical self-confidence, and social self-confidence (Sax, 1994b). Simple correlations indicate that women in male-dominated majors are less satisfied with their major but have higher levels of academic and mathematical self-concept. However, when we run regression analyses and control for student characteristics, we find that the proportion of women in the major has no effect. For example, although women in majors with fewer women express higher levels of mathematical self-confidence, this relationship nearly disappears when we control for the tendency of women who enroll in such majors to have high SAT-M scores and high levels of mathematics confidence when they enter college. In other words, women in majors with lower proportions of women leave college with high levels of mathematics confidence largely because they *enter* college with high levels of mathematics confidence and higher mathematics test scores. Thus the proportion of female peers in a major makes little or no difference to women's development of mathematics confidence.

This type of noneffect is observed for all the achievement, self-concept, and satisfaction outcomes examined in the HERI research on gender composition of majors (Sax, 1994b). Instead, what we might see as effects of gender composition are actually artifacts of self-selection: outcomes seem related to gender composition of a major simply because different types of women are attracted to different majors. Once this bias is controlled, the effects of gender composition disappear. This suggests that when we speak of the importance of having more women in science majors, we cannot assume that an influx of women students per se will improve the environment for other women in the major.

College Experiences

Our research consistently finds that for both women and men, the likelihood of persisting in science depends on the experiences they have in college. Not surprisingly, students who are more focused on course work and on the demands of science are more likely to maintain interest in science than are students with diverse interests or time constraints. These findings generally speak to the time commitment demanded in the sciences.

However, it is important to note that being busy does not necessarily preclude persistence in science. Instead, students' chances of staying in science depend heavily on the *type* of time constraints they face. Activities that keep the student on campus and academically engaged tend to promote retention in the sciences. Students with off-campus jobs are less likely to persist in science careers than those without jobs, while those working on campus are actually more likely to do so. Other activities that appear to strengthen student interest in science are participating in professors' research projects or in independent research, helping faculty teach courses, and tutoring other students. The positive effects of tutoring appear to be especially strong for women.

When we examined the impact of students' interaction with faculty, we found a very interesting pattern of results. Frequent interaction between students and faculty tends to promote student interest in nearly all scientific majors and careers. However, interacting with faculty has a *negative* effect on women's mathematics confidence (Sax, 1994a). This latter finding is particularly disturbing, since it contradicts research describing student-faculty interaction in general, ignoring gender effects, as a positive predictor of self-concept (Astin, 1993; Pascarella, 1985a, 1985b). Seymour and Hewitt's study (1994) supports the findings of our research—that science faculty, most of whom are male, can tend to discourage women from science, downplay women's intellectual capabilities, and make women feel unwelcome in class. These findings suggest that before simply advocating *more* faculty-student interaction, we should focus on the *nature* of the interaction, especially for women students. It is also essential that future studies examine the impact of faculty on women of different racial and ethnic backgrounds and social classes.

Case Studies

To explore the influence of the college environment on science recruitment and persistence, HERI visited five institutions from the sample used in the quantitative analyses. These schools were selected on the basis of strong positive effects (which remained even when all relevant environmental variables were controlled) on attracting and retaining women and students of color in the sciences and encouraging them to pursue science careers. These institutions included Johns Hopkins University (Baltimore, Maryland), Case Western Reserve University (Cleveland, Ohio), Albion College (Albion, Michigan), Santa Clara University (Santa Clara, California), and Georgia Institute of Technology (Atlanta, Georgia). Other institutions did exhibit positive effects, but these five were chosen for closer study because, as a group, they represent a cross-section of higher education.

Observations from the site visits enhanced our understanding of the nurture of students in the sciences and engineering. We believe these five institutions employ practices that others can emulate to increase student retention and recruitment: emphasis on teaching, undergraduate research opportunities, high levels of faculty-student interaction, supportive campus climates, and high priority on undergraduate education.

Emphasis on Teaching

Probably the most significant common factor among the case study institutions is their emphasis on teaching. Even at prestigious research universities such as Johns Hopkins and Case Western Reserve, senior faculty regularly teach undergraduate courses. Many of their students say they were encouraged and inspired by taking introductory courses from world-renowned researchers. At these institutions, faculty do not see teaching as a burden.

High Levels of Faculty-Student Interaction

At all five institutions, faculty were involved with students both in and out of class. Faculty-student interaction includes research, social situations, and intellectual conversation. Faculty encourage students to come to their offices and discuss issues face-to-face. Most of the students we spoke to felt very comfortable approaching professors for advice, jobs, and letters of recommendation. Further, since the faculty/student ratio is favorable at all five institutions, students rarely compete with each other for faculty attention. Unlike the earlier report of negative effects of faculty interaction on women students, the present findings suggest that frequent interaction with faculty helps women when the faculty are student-centered and interested in teaching undergraduates. This suggests that assessing the amount of interaction between students and faculty is not sufficient to explain the effects of interaction unless we know more about faculty values and the nature of the interaction.

Supportive Campus Climate

Science and engineering students feel welcome and at home on all five campuses. We often think of science students as introverted or antisocial, but this was not the case with most of the students we met. Science and engineering majors on these campuses were well respected, and although nonscience students were not interested in changing places with their science classmates, they respected and admired them.

High Value on Undergraduate Education

All five institutions assign a high priority to undergraduate education. Even the research universities, where graduate education is often the focus, considered undergraduates their most important clients. Virtually none of their science or engineering departments use graduate students to teach undergraduate courses. Undergraduates also receive as many opportunities for research experience as graduate students. The typical hierarchy (faculty–graduate students–undergraduates) found at most research universities appears to be absent.

Other Observations

The case studies offer a few other noteworthy findings. First, while innovative teaching methods seem to be well received by students in the sciences, science faculty remain generally hesitant to alter traditional pedagogical styles. Second, peer interaction in the sciences reflects the highly competitive nature of the field. In a sense, the nature of interaction among science students reflects the socialization that occurs within each major—socialization emphasizing independence, achievement, and initiative. Nevertheless, students at the institutions we visited seem to have good rapport with each other and, in general, seem to enjoy their experience with science education.

What Can Institutions Do to Attract More Women to Science?

We offer recommendations for institutional change in three areas: science curriculum and pedagogy, role models, and overcoming early deficiencies in science preparation.

Today, women constitute 55 percent of the undergraduate student body, and women's aspirations for postgraduate study and attainment of the Ph.D. have increased dramatically. Moreover, the national interest requires us to nurture scientific talent and maintain the supply of human resources in the sciences. Women represent a major part of the talent pool, and thus there is a need to identify ways to eradicate barriers that have kept interested women out of science fields.

Science Curriculum and Pedagogy

A study of science education at Hampshire College provides some additional insights (Astin, Milem, Astin, Ries, & Heath, 1991). Unlike most institutions—which lose students from science majors and careers—Hampshire College attracts students into science and develops appreciation for science among students in nonscience fields and careers. They rely on what they call *inquiry learning,* a teaching method designed to help students learn how to ask questions and in turn how to pursue answers. Scientific competence is imparted by taking one topic, say, enzymes, and teaching the quantitative and theoretical concepts of a general biochemistry course through that topic. Students are also encouraged to explore the scientific aspects of topics they choose. For example, a dancer might learn physiology through her interest in how the body works. To enable this kind of learning, the curriculum is not arranged in a sequential fashion; if and when students recognize deficiencies in certain skills and knowledge, they can pursue such learning (Weaver, 1989).

Also, Hampshire College faculty do not use grades to evaluate students' work. We believe that changes in evaluation, especially in introductory science courses, may keep students from dropping out of science early on. The competitive nature of grading on the curve and the attitude that introductory courses are "weeder" courses tend to drive students out of science.

The institutions in the case studies employ some educational practices and philosophies that could be considered by other institutions wishing to improve performance: emphasize teaching and engage senior faculty—rather than graduate students—in teaching undergraduates; encourage faculty-student interaction; create a supportive campus climate for science; and place a high value on undergraduate education, allowing undergraduates to work with faculty on projects and serve as junior apprentices on much the same basis as graduate students.

There is ample evidence that much of the failure to capture student interest in science stems from the way science is taught. Most research has shown how student-centered teaching, active learning, and cooperative learning experiences lead to academic growth (Pascarella & Terenzini, 1991). Impersonal, competitive, and authoritarian teaching practices, on the other hand, drive many students away.

Some ideas for changing these practices derive from work on curricular transformation to bring gender and ethnic perspectives into undergraduate courses. Institutions could help faculty examine current teaching practices, recognize their assumptions about teaching and students, and acquire knowledge about learning styles. Interested faculty could take part in training sessions, paired with a colleague from their department who would serve as mentor. The colleague's role would be to provide feedback about teaching practices. The professor and colleague could conduct periodic interviews with students. In addition, regular seminar discussions could focus on topics of student-centered pedagogy and equity in the classroom. Reviews of empirical information from studies of science education that focused on women and other underrepresented groups could also inform interested faculty. Such an opportunity to learn and examine their own practices might be a beginning toward restructuring the faculty approach.

We have mentioned only some of the possibilities for work involving science faculty. Other ideas and models should be explored as institutions embark on transformation in the sciences. Meanwhile, as Rosser and Davis (Chapter Seven) remind us, we need close evaluations of how different practices and interventions affect student outcomes. Such transformational work will inevitably lead to conversations about pedagogy and course content, as well as hiring and promotion practices.

The Need for Role Models

Role models can be critical agents in women's self-efficacy with respect to career choice (Hackett & Betz, 1981). Although recent research has shown that teaching assistants may have a greater impact than faculty on the career decisions of women science students (Wiegand, Ginorio, & Brown, 1994), women science faculty are undoubtedly essential as role models for women students.

While some complain that there are not enough women for science faculty posts, one could argue that colleges and universities have not done an adequate job of recruiting or finding women. In the past two decades, women increased their representation among science doctorates considerably. Between 1971 and 1992, women went from 3.9 percent to 15.7 percent of doctorates awarded in physical science, mathematics, and engineering and from 16.3 percent to 38.3 percent in the biological sciences (U.S. Department of Education, 1994). But despite these increases, women remain few among faculty in science fields. Higher education has not reached parity among new hires, given the increased availability of women (Milem & Astin, 1993).

Further, women scientists tend to be employed by liberal arts colleges and community colleges. Research universities lag behind in the proportional representation of women in faculty ranks. Besides increasing recruitment, these institutions could also develop visiting scientist programs and appoint women science faculty from neighboring institutions to visiting-scholar slots. The presence of these women will benefit women students seeking female role models and mentors. Visiting-scholar programs would also benefit participating faculty by providing them with a year of the reduced teaching responsibilities typically found in research universities compared to two-year and four-year colleges and with additional resources and support in the form of graduate students to work with them in research, lab assistants, and research colleagues and networks.

Universities often invest resources to bring in a noted male scientist, a Nobel laureate or a member of the National Academy of Sciences. Such resources could also be made available to bring in women from nearby colleges or research institutes. Overall, institutions need to think creatively about increasing the presence of women scientists among their faculty, to benefit those women students who otherwise lack access to role models.

Overcoming Early Deficiencies in Preparation

Colleges and universities need to work with local high schools to improve science preparation, but there are other ways to improve student qualifications. Summer bridge programs have successfully helped minority students develop skills and competencies in a less competitive and pressured environment. Colleges and universities could implement similar summer bridge programs for women who show an interest in mathematics and science but lack adequate preparation. A program of this sort could be designed to include both preparatory courses and reviews of new material, provide role models by bringing women scientists to campus for lectures and discussions, and discuss ways to combine a scientific career with family responsibilities. Some programs of this type are already in operation, and interested institutions could learn from these efforts and reshape programs to fit their own needs and student clientele. There are important benefits to tutoring other students and working with faculty on research projects, and it is essential that institutions design and implement such programs for their students, especially their women students.

In closing, we believe these suggestions require development of mechanisms for sharing information and materials among institutions willing to work on their culture and practices. Our curricular transformation projects involved knowledgeable, committed people, and resources provided by such funding agencies as the Fund for the Improvement of Postsecondary Education and the Ford

Foundation. The National Science Foundation and the Sloan Foundation are two agencies that could become involved in the funding of transformational projects in science education.

Future Research

We have identified a number of variables that play a major role in encouraging women to pursue science; however, there is still a need for more qualitative research into the nature of women's experience as undergraduates in science courses and in majors.

For example, the role of student-faculty interaction in student outcomes needs to be examined more closely. Are faculty supportive or patronizing toward women? We also need to examine how work off or on campus affects academic success. What is the nature of the work and what role do supervisors and peers play in how students perceive their educational experience?

Additionally, in-depth interviews could shed more light on how women shape their expectations about what is possible for them with respect to fields of study and future careers. What role does socialization, college experience, and the structure of opportunity play in the shaping of career expectations?

Finally, we would like to reiterate the need to evaluate the many programs designed to increase the numbers of women in science. As emphasized by Rosser and Davis (Chapter Seven), we must know more about the effectiveness of these interventions, so that time and energy can be spent on those that have proven most successful and diverted from less effective programs. Moreover, we believe that policy makers and educational institutions need to use the information in this sourcebook to create equitable opportunities for women, who will enrich the scientific community with their multiple perspectives and diverse talent.

References

Astin, A. W. (1977). *Four critical years: Effects of College on Beliefs, Attitudes, and Knowledge.* San Francisco: Jossey-Bass.

Astin, A. W. (1991). *Assessment for excellence.* New York: Macmillan.

Astin, A. W. (1993). *What matters in college? "Four critical years" revisited.* San Francisco: Jossey-Bass.

Astin, A. W., Korn, W. S., Sax, L. J., & Mahoney, K. (1994). *The American freshman: National norms for fall 1994.* Los Angeles: Higher Education Research Institute.

Astin, H. S., Milem, J. F., Astin, A. W., Ries, P., & Heath, T. (1991). *The courage and vision to experiment: Hampshire College 1970–1990.* Los Angeles: Higher Education Research Institute.

Brush, L. R. (1985). Cognitive and affective determinants of course preference and plans. In S. F. Chipman, L. R. Brush, & D. M. Wilson (Eds.), *Women and mathematics: Balancing the equation.* Hillsdale, NJ: Erlbaum.

Byrne, E. M. (1993). *Women and science: The snark syndrome.* Washington, DC: Falmer Press.

DeBoer, G. E. (1986). Perceived science ability as a factor in the course selections of men and women in college. *Journal of Research in Science Teaching, 23,* 343–352.

Ethington, C. A. (1988). Differences among women intending to major in quantitative fields of study. *Journal of Educational Research, 81,* 354–359.

Frieze, I. H., & Hanusa, B. H. (1984). Women scientists: Overcoming barriers. *Advancements in Motivation and Achievement, 2,* 139–163.

Gilligan, C. (1982). *In a different voice: Psychological theory and women's development.* Cambridge, MA: Harvard University Press.

Ginorio, A. B., Brown, M. D., Cook, N., & Henderson, R. S. (1994). *Patterns of persistence, switching and attrition among science and engineering majors for women and men students at the University of Washington: 1985–1991.* Final technical report to the Alfred P. Sloan Foundation, University of Colorado, Boulder.

Grandy, J. (1987). *Trends in the selection of science, mathematics, or engineering as major fields of study among top-scoring SAT takers.* Princeton, NJ: Educational Testing Service.

Gruca, J. M., Ethington, C. A., & Pascarella, E. T. (1988). Intergenerational effects of college graduation on career sex atypicality in women. *Research in Higher Education, 29*(2), 99–124.

Hackett, G., and Betz, N. E. (1981). A self-efficacy approach to career development of women. *Journal of Vocational Behavior, 18,* 326–339.

Higher Education Research Institute. (1992). *Undergraduate science education: The impact of different college environments on the educational pipeline in the sciences.* Los Angeles: Author.

Holland, J. L. (1966). *The psychology of vocational choice.* Waltham, MA: Blaisdell.

Humphreys, L. G. (1984). Women with doctorates in science and engineering. *Advances in Motivation and Achievement, 2,* 197–216.

Kanter, R. M. (1977a). *Men and women of the corporation*. New York: Basic Books.

Kanter, R. M. (1977b). Some effects of proportions on group life: Skewed sex ratios and responses to token women. *American Journal of Sociology, 82*, 965–990.

Kinnane, J. F., & Gaubinger, J. R. (1963). Life values and work values. *Journal of Counseling Psychology, 10*, 362–367.

Lips, H. M. (1992). Gender- and science-related attitudes as predictors of college students' academic choices. *Journal of Vocational Behavior, 40*, 62–81.

MacCorquodale, P. (1984). *Self-image, science, and math: Does the image of the "scientist" keep girls and minorities from pursuing science and math?* Washington, DC: National Institute of Education.

Marsh, H. W., Smith, I. D., & Barnes, J. (1985). Multidimensional self-concepts: Relations with sex and academic achievement. *Journal of Educational Psychology, 77*, 581–596.

Matyas, M. L. (1985a). Factors affecting female achievement and interest in science and scientific careers. In J. B. Kahle (Ed.), *Women in science: A report from the field*. Philadelphia: Falmer Press.

Matyas, M. L. (1985b). Obstacles and constraints on women in science: Preparation and participation in the scientific community. In J. B. Kahle (Ed.), *Women in science: A report from the field* (pp. 77–101). Philadelphia: Falmer Press.

Milem, J. F., & Astin, H. S. (1993, March/April). The changing composition of the faculty: What does it really mean for diversity? *Change, 25*(2), 21–27.

Milem, J. F., & Astin, H. S. (1994). *Scientists as teachers: A look at their culture, their roles, and their pedagogy*. Paper presented at the annual meeting of the American Educational Research Association, New Orleans, LA.

National Science Foundation (1986). *Women and minorities in science and engineering*. Arlington, VA: Author.

Oakes, J. (1990a). *Lost talent: The underrepresentation of women, minorities, and disabled persons in science*. Santa Monica, CA: Rand Corporation.

Oakes, J. (1990b). Opportunities, achievement, and choice: Women and minority students in science and mathematics. *Review of Research in Education, 16*, 153–222.

Pascarella, E. T. (1985a). Students' affective development within the college environment. *Journal of Higher Education, 56*, 640–663.

Pascarella, E. T. (1985b). The influence of on-campus living versus commuting to college on intellectual and interpersonal self-confidence. *Journal of College Student Personnel, 26*, 292–299.

Pascarella, E. T., & Terenzini, P. T. (1991). *How college affects students: Findings and insights from twenty years of research.* San Francisco: Jossey-Bass.

Peng, S., & Jaffe, J. (1979). Women who enter male-dominated fields of study in higher education. *American Educational Research Journal, 16,* 285–293.

Rosenberg, M. (1957). *Occupational values.* Glencoe, IL: Free Press.

Rosser, S. V. (1990). *Female-friendly science: Applying women's studies methods and theories to attract students.* New York: Pergamon Press.

Sax, L. J. (1994a). Mathematical self-concept: How college reinforces the gender gap. *Research in Higher Education, 35,* 141–166.

Sax, L. J. (1994b). *The dynamics of tokenism: How college students are affected by the proportion of women in their major.* Unpublished doctoral dissertation, University of California, Los Angeles.

Sax, L. J. (1995). Predicting gender and major-field differences in mathematical self-concept during college. *Journal of Women and Minorities in Science and Engineering, 1*(4), 291–307.

Seymour, E., & Hewitt, N. (1994). *Talking about leaving: Factors contributing to high attrition rates among science, mathematics, and engineering undergraduate majors.* Final report to the Alfred P. Sloan Foundation, University of Colorado, Boulder.

Sherman, J. (1983). Factors predicting girls' and boys' enrollment in college preparatory mathematics. *Psychology of Women Quarterly, 7,* 272–281.

Stake, J. E., & Noonan, M. (1985). The influence of teacher models on the career confidence and motivation of college students. *Sex Roles, 12,* 1023–1031.

Super, D. E. (1957). *The psychology of careers.* New York: Harper.

Tobias, S. (1990). *They're not dumb, they're different—Stalking the second tier.* Tucson, AZ: Research Corporation.

Tobias, S. (1992). *Revitalizing undergraduate science: Why some things work and most don't.* Tucson, AZ: Research Corporation.

Trent, W., & Hill, J. (1994). The contributions of historically black colleges and universities to the production of African American scientists and engineers. In W. Pearson, Jr., & A. Fechter (Eds.), *Who will do science? Educating the next generation.* Baltimore, MD: Johns Hopkins University Press.

U.S. Department of Education. National Center for Education Statistics. (1994). *Digest of education statistics 1992–93.* Washington, DC: U.S. Government Printing Office.

Vetter, B. M. (1989). *Women in science: Progress and problems.* Paper presented at the annual meeting of the American Association for the Advancement of Science, San Francisco, CA.

Ware, N. C., & Lee, V. E. (1988). Sex differences in choice of college science majors. *American Educational Research Journal, 25,* 593–614.

Ware, N. C., Steckler, N. A., & Lesserman, J. (1985). Undergraduate women: Who chooses a science major? *Journal of Higher Education, 56(1),* 73–84.

Weaver, F. (1989). *Promoting inquiry in undergraduate learning: New directions for teaching and learning.* San Francisco: Jossey-Bass.

Wiegand, D., Ginorio, A. B., & Brown, M. D. (1994). *First steps in college science: A comparison of single sex vs. coeducational programs.* Final report to the Women's College Coalition. Seattle: University of Washington.

Wright, C. A., & Wright, S. D. (1987). The role of mentors in the career development of young professionals. *Family Relations, 36,* 204–208.

Chapter Five

The Graduate Experience in the Sciences and Engineering: Rethinking a Gendered Institution

Carol S. Hollenshead, Stacy A. Wenzel,
Barbara B. Lazarus, Indira Nair

This chapter reviews what little is known about the experience of women graduate students in science, mathematics, and engineering (SME). These women work in institutions shaped and codified by white men from privileged backgrounds, who have historically held the vast majority of faculty and student positions. To understand the disparity in participation and persistence between men and women, we review the development and dynamics of the modern role of women in graduate SME programs. We also discuss the structure of institutions, identifying features many women find consistent with their intellectual interests, aspirations, and personal commitments and values, as well as features that often alienate women. Based on this review, we make recommendations for future research and institutional change.

Our discussion involves two broad avenues of exploration. The first focuses on women's entry, persistence, and attachment in graduate school and reviews the relationship of these factors to institutional and programmatic attributes. The second involves the nature of graduate education itself. These inquiries will allow us to identify aspects of graduate institutions that block full participation, and thus they will allow us to develop strategies to facilitate institutional change. (We define *institutional change* as a revision of policies and a restructuring of practices and norms, based on systematic data collection, analysis, synthesis, and evaluation of the existing explicit or implicit standards and codes.) Unfortunately, scholars have conducted little research on the experiences of women in science, mathematics, and engineering graduate education. We find too many gaps in our knowledge along both these lines of investigation. This chapter is intended to offer to the reader a starting point.

The Present Situation

Of the quarter-million full-time science and engineering graduate students working toward doctorates in fall 1991, about a hundred thousand—just over a third—were women. This figure is somewhat misleading: it includes fields ranging from engineering with 13.7 percent women and physics with 24 percent women, to social science with 41.3 percent women, biology with 44.7 percent women, and health sciences with 70 percent women (Vetter, 1994, p. 34). Even this breakdown tells a very partial story. Consider the following percentages of women found among graduate students in various fields (Vetter, pp. 33, 91):

- Engineering: 17.1 percent chemical, 8.1 percent mechanical
- Biological Sciences: 64.8 percent nutrition, 29 percent entomology/parasitology
- Health Sciences: 92.5 percent nursing, 36 percent medicine
- Social Sciences: 65.3 percent psychology, 27.4 percent economics

Although their representation has been rising in all fields since the 1970s, women are not adequately included in most science and engineering graduate programs (Vetter, 1994, p. 34). And the number of women graduate students in science and engineering is only part of the picture. As several observers have noted, the proportion of women receiving degrees shrinks from B.S. to M.S. to Ph.D. (Hornig, 1987; Vetter, pp. 47, 65). In Chapter Two, Vetter confirms that women studying science and engineering are more often in master's than doctoral programs.

We need longitudinal cohort studies to understand the extent to which women succeed after they have entered graduate school, but few such studies exist. Most research has focused on doctoral students—not on students in master's programs where most women are found. Girves and Wemmerus (1988) found evidence suggesting that influences on degree completion differ between master's and doctoral students. Therefore, the little we know about women doctoral students in science and engineering may not tell us much about master's students in these fields.

Our literature review finds a handful of studies examining candidacy and completion rates for cohorts of men and women doctoral students in science and engineering. *Candidacy rates* show what percentage of a cohort of students entering a graduate program at a given time complete requirements for candidacy by a given time. *Completion rates* show what percentage of a cohort gain their doctorate within a given period. The few longitudinal studies available show that women doctoral students in science and engineering are somewhat less likely to complete their degrees and take longer to do so than their male peers.

For example, one study looked at cohorts of doctoral students who enrolled at eight major universities between 1967 and 1976. Of students receiving degrees in natural science, 59 percent of the women completed the doctorate compared to 65 percent of the men. Women in natural science who had prestigious fellowships were not more likely to graduate than women without such funding. In math and physics, women had a longer median time to degree than men (6.8 years versus 5.7 years) at these universities during this time (Bowen & Rudenstine, 1992, pp. 125–126, 132). Another study from a single university finds the median time to doctorate and the completion and candidacy rates for women in biology and health science about the same as for men, varying from cohort to cohort. Data for engineering and physical sciences do suggest gender differences, especially in earlier cohorts. For example, the median candidacy rates for women and men are 39 percent and 63 percent for the 1975–1977 entry cohort and correspondingly 59 percent and 62 percent for 1978–1980; 56 percent and 72 percent for 1981–1983; 59 percent and 72 percent for

1984–1986; and 62 percent and 73 percent for 1987–1989 (Rackham Graduate School, 1994). A third cohort study of three large research universities finds that women in mathematics, physics, computer sciences, economics, and psychology achieve lower rates of candidacy and Ph.D. completion within given time periods. However, the rates differed significantly across the three schools (Zwick, 1991, p. 11).

While there is some evidence to the contrary, most studies suggest that women in science and engineering are less likely to complete degrees than men in those fields or women in other fields. Yet gaps in the data prevent us from understanding at what points women leave SME graduate study. One study of students in an engineering Ph.D. program found that deciding on a thesis topic was a factor that delayed progress toward the degree about equally for men and women. Men were more likely (26.4 percent) than women (18.9 percent) to mention the qualifying exam as a hindrance (Manis, 1993). Where then does the disparity in educational hindrance occur—precandidacy or postcandidacy—and why? We know little. It is difficult to pinpoint the critical times and factors influencing attrition without better information. It is even more difficult to enact change without solid quantitative evidence of completion and candidacy rates. The few institutions cited here that have collected this information found evidence of the need for change. More institutions need to follow their lead and examine their own completion and candidacy rates.

To understand the present reality of women's graduate school participation, we turn our eyes to the past. History points clearly to societal forces and to policies and practices of the higher education community as major causes of women's underrepresentation in science.

Historical Context: How We Got Here

Viewing the present situation in context of the history of women in U.S. higher education adds significant insight. Even privileged women had no access to graduate education until the 1890s (Woody, 1974). After they gained entry to graduate programs, women had to contend with the belief of the day as summarized by Van Hise of Wisconsin in 1908: "It does appear to be a fact that the percentage of women who are willing to work at the same project, six hours a day for three hundred days in a year is much smaller than among men. But this quality is essential for success in research" (Woody, 1974, p. 339).

Despite significant continuing barriers, women made great gains in higher education in the late 1800s and early 1900s. Their proportion of bachelor's and professional degrees increased from 19 percent in 1900 to 40 percent in 1930 (Chamberlain, 1988). By the 1920s, 15 percent of Ph.D.'s were awarded to women (Lomperis, 1990). Women earned 12 percent of the doctorates in science in the 1920s (Vetter, 1984). If women's progress had only continued the trend of the first decades of the twentieth century, we would not be concerned about the issue of graduate participation today.

However, early gains backfired when men, concerned with the "feminization" of higher education (Lomperis, 1990), put caps on female enrollment. Medical schools simply denied access to women, citing economic conditions and overcrowding in the profession (Woody, 1974, p. 347). The situation for women worsened as the twentieth century advanced. During the Depression, the proportion of doctorates awarded to women declined slightly, to 13 percent in 1940 (Chamberlain, 1988). Between 1945 and 1956, the GI Bill and the influx of men returning from war to academia restricted openings for women in higher education. Institutions admitted fewer women to undergraduate programs (Chamberlain, 1988). Graduate programs became increasingly competitive for women not only because the number of applicants grew but also because veterans received preference in admission; in order to study at the graduate level, women had to be far better qualified than men (Hornig, 1984, p. 33). The proportion of Ph.D.'s awarded to women dropped below 10 percent and did not return to 1920 levels until 1972 (Chamberlain, 1988). Thus, it was not women's lack of interest in science that reduced their numbers in the field, but the institutional policies limiting their access to graduate education (Solomon, 1985, p. 190).

With few exceptions, women did not benefit from the financial aid of the GI Bill. Only 3 percent of the millions of veterans who enrolled in colleges and universities in the 1940s were women (Clifford, 1993, p. 138). Further, Hornig (1984) notes that in the 1970s, women graduate students received less public and institutional financial aid than men and were less likely to have research assistantships. This inequity in financial support was justified by many who believed that women in graduate studies were a waste of time and money—they would just go and have babies and not work in their field. Women's higher level of attrition during these years was used to support this argument. It was only in the 1980s that attrition was linked to the amount and type of financial aid women received (Hornig, 1984).

Until the 1970s, there is no record of the numbers of women in engineering. Trescott has noted that until the 1970s women were far less than 1 percent of all practicing engineers. As engineering is primarily a professional undergraduate degree, it is not clear if any of this small number went on to graduate school. We do have a handful of pioneers like Lillian Gilbreth, the "mother of industrial engineering," who did her Ph.D. in psychology. Other early engineers like Kate Gleeson (1865–1933), Bertha Lamme (1869–1954), Emily Roebling (?–1903), and Julia Hall (1859–1925) did have undergraduate engineering degrees; they made contributions to engineering through projects belonging to their husband, father, or brother (Trescott, 1990).

The National Research Council's annual *Survey of Earned Doctorates* allows us to track the gender composition of doctoral output since 1957. The proportion of women in the physical sciences (including engineering) and the life sciences has grown, but not in a linear fashion. In 1960, women represented 2.6 percent of the doctorates in engineering, physics, and mathematics and 8.8 percent in the life sciences; 3.6 percent and 13 percent in 1970; 9 percent and 25.9 percent in 1980; and 12.3 percent and 35.2 percent in 1987. Women's relative progress in these fields comes into clearer focus when their representation in graduate programs is charted for each field. For example, between 1970 and 1986, doctorates awarded to women increased by 2.9 percent in mechanical engineering and by 44.9 percent in health sciences. Most science and engineering fields increased their percentage of women doctorates by around 10 percent or less, well below the average of other academic fields (Lomperis, 1990, pp. 647, 652).

While comparisons across nations can be misleading, the United States trails a number of countries in the integration of women in science. Data for physics show that in Italy, women comprise 21 percent of the doctorates and 23 percent of the faculty; in Hungary, women make up 27 percent of doctorates and 47 percent of the faculty; in Belgium, women are 29 percent of doctorates and 11 percent of faculty; and in the former Soviet Union, 25 percent of doctorates and 30 percent of faculty. Meanwhile, six of Stockholm University's thirteen full professors of cellular and molecular biology are women. At Bosporus University in Turkey, women make up 33 percent of physicists and mathematicians, 66 percent of the chemists, and 20 percent of the engineers ("Comparisons across cultures," 1994).

Graduate Education: Shaped by Assumptions and Norms

An understanding of the problem requires more than an examination of the statistics and demographics of women's participation in graduate school. We need to look at the experience of women's lives and at the underlying philosophy, values, and expectations on which science and engineering graduate institutions operate. Just as in political science, gender implications in science and engineering can be described as the "assumptive backdrop against which research and theorizing . . . has traditionally occurred" (McAdams, 1988, p. 63).

The sciences view themselves as objective intellectual disciplines, and participants like to believe that this quality infuses the institutions where they work and teach. However, the intellectual realm is not purely objective (see, for example, Barnes & Edge, 1982). As Etzkowitz and his colleagues (1992) put it, "Universalism posits openness of science to all with talent but the social structure of science is not gender-neutral" (p. 159). A graduate program has built-in expectations about the type of research to be done and about underlying motivations, desired products, and procedures and constraints to be followed. It has funding policies that help shape the research performed in it, and its structure is based on traditional assumptions about work roles, careers, family support, and productivity. See Merton (1973) for a collection of essays describing the normative structure, reward system, and evaluation processes in science.

These intellectual practices are commonly referred to as *habits of the mind.* In engineering design and in problem solving in the physical sciences, we also speak of a skill called *seeing in the mind's eye*. These two expressions perhaps describe most vividly the experiential components of science and engineering. They give credence to the observation that intellectual endeavors in these areas are not purely objective—as is often claimed—but that habit, practice, and exposure to specific types of activity and context define the repertoire expected of participants. These expectations can in turn alienate, disqualify, or devalue people whose background and experience are different.

We can examine institutional issues at two levels, not totally distinct. One approach is to look at institutions as they are, to see how much of the low participation of women stems from current practices. The other and less common approach begins by examining the realities of women's lives, seeking to identify features of graduate education that are and are not consonant with this reality. Such an inquiry would highlight discrepancies between women's experiences and the dominant paradigms, perhaps yielding insights not otherwise apparent. Donna Shavlik, director of the American Council on Education's Office of Women in Higher Education, asks how institutions of higher education would differ if women ran and designed them. Feminist theorists argue that scholarship should "start thought from women's lives" (Harding, 1993, p. 35), place women "at the center" (Stacey & Thorne, 1985, p. 175), and "locate issues of actual concern to women rather than . . . use women as a comparison group for issues of concern to men" (Reinharz, 1992, p. 68).

We need both approaches in order to identify the important questions and to frame our mode of inquiry. However, the second becomes even more relevant as societal norms and expectations change. We are beginning to develop institutions that don't just accommodate women—almost as a concession—but that incorporate the experiences and goals of women as well as men.

This approach to institutional and disciplinary transformation has a longer history in the humanities and social sciences, where feminist scholarship has seriously examined what "transformations of knowledge" are needed and how to go about effecting them (Minnick, 1990, p. 3). It also seems to fit more easily in these fields, because social sciences allow for behavioral, institutional, and societal variables as legitimate facets of inquiry. By contrast,

natural sciences and engineering—being devoted to physical phenomena—have often denied any connection between their practice and social/political/historical/behavioral influences and have
maintained that gender issues were irrelevant.

The history of science documents the intellectual history of
Western white males from privileged backgrounds, who fashioned
rules and expectations without economic or family constraints.
Their experience led to them to regard interest and perseverance
as all that mattered in participation in the sciences. And from very
early days, their goal was the conquest of nature, not merely its
empirical explanation—see the writings of Francis Bacon (Anderson, 1960; in Keller, 1985). As the scale of work increased, it grew
dependent on funding beyond private resources. This funding usually resulted from priorities of the state—that is, warfare. It is reasonable to ask whether the military focus of the physical sciences,
and engineering especially, has kept women away from these fields
(Rosser, 1990).

We view science and engineering departments and disciplines
as social structures with their own normative values and reward systems. Faculty and policy makers who set the agenda for the
nation's scientific research determine the formal and informal
rules for graduate student life and allocate the resources that students need for success. The formal policies, rules, and canon of
disciplinary knowledge are important, but there is also a crucial
hidden curriculum in any graduate program. The normative information transferred to the professional-in-training is every bit as
important for success as the classroom and laboratory data. Thus
it is useful to view graduate education from the perspective of
social systems and use this perspective to set a course for future
research and change strategy.

Some claim that women tend to avoid the sciences because of
innate biological capabilities and personality factors, and that their
lack of participation thus reflects their own free choices. Others
counter that while men and women differ in some traits, individualistic explanations of career attainment tend to be incomplete.
Those who reject the hunt for fundamental biological causes argue
instead for "a more complex analysis in which an individual's
capacities emerge from a web of interactions between the biological being and the social environment" (Fausto-Sterling, 1992, p.

8). Still others urge a move away from the supply-side psychological perspective that "attributes the causes of women's failure to achieve to internal factors in the women themselves. Such an emphasis ignores external factors which are of major importance in determining how people live their lives" (Frieze, 1978, p. 67).

Ultimately, the individual model fails to explain that men and women overlap in attainment patterns. It locates "at least some of the causes of injuries in the actions of the injured," absolving the system of responsibility for "manufacturing the psychology of their workers" (Kanter, 1977, pp. 262–263). As Harding argues, "Structural obstacles should be the focus here—not the purported biological or personality traits on which the sexist attempts to explain women's lack of equity in science have concentrated" (Harding, 1991, p. 29). Thus, in this inquiry, we focus attention on "changing existing institutional arrangements to accommodate women, instead of changing women to fit into institutional status quo" (Westphal & Sheppard, 1992, p. 186).

Graduate Education: What We Know

We need to look most closely at those institutional arrangements that affect women SME graduate students within their departments. Departmental policies and practices affect the satisfaction and retention of graduate women and the success of their endeavors.

Access and Undergraduate Impact

Very little research has looked at reasons women attend or avoid graduate programs in science and engineering, or at how their prior experience affects their likelihood of success. We understand very little of the impact of different backgrounds on graduate experiences. Private liberal arts colleges continue to be the most productive contributors of students who go on to earn doctorates in science, with women's liberal arts colleges notably successful. Tidball (1986) has found a direct relationship between number of women faculty at an undergraduate institution and number of women students who pursue doctorates. The National Research Council confirms the importance of private liberal arts colleges in educating women who go on to earn science Ph.D.'s. It also points out that the largest number of women Ph.D.'s come from Research I institutions (Frazier-Kouassi et al., 1992, p. 14).

According to preliminary findings from an ongoing study of women in engineering at the University of Michigan (Pipeline project, 1994), women engineering seniors with above-average grades indicated the following reasons for not attending or for hesitating to start graduate studies in engineering (students could select more than one reason):

- 40.3 percent want to pursue more people-oriented fields
- 37.3 percent are unsure what career path to pursue
- 25.4 percent are not interested in academic careers
- 23.9 percent feel they don't need a graduate degree to get a good job
- 23.9 percent are unsure graduate school would improve their opportunity
- 23.9 percent believe they cannot afford graduate education
- 22.4 percent want to do more socially meaningful work

Women may also anticipate the issues they would face once they would become a graduate student and accordingly choose not to apply or attend.

Blatant quotas, such as the systematic exclusion of women from medical school up until the 1970s (Roby, 1973), have finally been abolished. The subtle barriers that remain are harder to see—and thus harder to change. Graduate admission is a highly selective process. Admissions committees consider grades, experience, GRE scores, letters of recommendation, and other factors. Weighting of these components varies from institution to institution. Women graduate students have stronger undergraduate grades than male peers (Roby, 1973), but we know little about women's chances to get research experience as undergraduates or how highly faculty members recommend women compared to men with the same GPAs.

Admissions policies that emphasize the GRE may be biased against women. Hornig (1987) notes that women get higher college grades in engineering, but men get higher GRE quantitative scores. It is unclear whether the gap in scores is due to ability or a difference in course-taking patterns. The gap is decreasing, which makes patterns of enrollment seem a more likely explanation (Hornig, 1987). Gender bias in standardized testing is more heavily debated in regard to the SAT, but it is also a topic of contention for the GRE. A number of recent articles refute the theory of male superiority in spatial tasks, explaining sex differences on mathematics exams as the result not of ability differences but of differences in how men and women deal with strictly timed exams (for example, Goldstein, Haldane, and Michell, 1990).

Funding

The literature documents the positive effect of adequate and consistent funding on graduate school persistence. As described in Chapter Two, there seem to be gender differences in the type of financial support awarded to doctoral students in science and engineering. A study at one research university found that the amount of time women take to earn a degree is related to their satisfaction with the fairness of financial aid awards. Those who saw awards as fair finished more quickly, and some speculate that they probably received adequate financial support themselves (Nerad & Stewart, 1991). Another study at a research university, however, found no significant difference in financial support awarded men and women graduate students in the sciences. Men and women received assistantships and/or fellowships at the same rate (89 percent). Those with these awards were more likely to succeed than those without such support (Berg & Ferber, 1983).

Institutional Environment: Interactions

To understand the experiences of women graduate students in science, we start by examining their interaction with others in their departments, labs, and schools. Interaction with faculty is the most prominent feature of graduate education in science. Students learn the norms or rules of a field by interacting with and observing those more experienced. Moreover, graduate students depend upon faculty for funding and advancement and must function in a patron-client relationship (Etzkowitz et al., 1992, p. 159).

Women graduate students may be at a disadvantage when it comes to interaction with their faculty. According to one study, significantly fewer women than men in science programs said they came to know one or more male faculty members well or that at least one male faculty member treated them as a junior colleague. The implications of this are serious in view of the findings that those who felt that intellectual challenge was important, who were treated as a junior colleague, and who came to know two or more male faculty members well were more likely to finish their degree (Berg & Ferber, 1983). Also, women who make it to faculty ranks are slightly more likely than male peers to have had a mentor along the way (Sand, Parson, & Duane, 1991). Along the same lines, other studies find women graduate students in the sciences to be less satisfied than male peers with the advising and mentoring they received from faculty (Nerad & Stewart, 1991; Manis, 1993; Manis, Frazier-Kouassi, Hollenshead, & Burkam, 1993).

Studies suggest that women benefit from more women science and engineering faculty. In one study, more women (33 percent) than men (20 percent) came to know female faculty well, and more (28 percent to 17 percent) came to feel they had been treated as junior colleagues by at least one female faculty member (Berg & Ferber, 1983). Other studies of graduate students in various fields found that those with women faculty role models considered themselves more career oriented, more confident, more instrumental, and more satisfied with their role (Gilbert, Gallessich & Evans, 1983) and considered the interactions more positively (Schroeder & Mynatt, 1993).

Lack of interaction can hurt women graduate students. So too can the negative interactions found in a number of studies. Clark and Corcoran's interviews (1986) with male and female faculty at the University of Minnesota reveal that faculty sponsorship can have damaging results. For example, they found that some faculty allowed women graduate students access to academic careers and resources but controlled achievement to keep it at medium levels. Some suggest that student-faculty relationships "may perpetuate a male-dominated hierarchical system of authority, competition, and individualism" (Richey, Gabrill, & Blythe, 1988, p. 35). Others have found that in seeking mentorship, they instead find sexual harassment (Paludi, 1990).

Micro-inequities, isolation, and sexual harassment are well-documented influences on women graduate students in science and engineering. Women graduate students in computer science at MIT (1983) pointed out that harassment wasted their time and creative energy while undermining their self-esteem. Men focused undue attention on women's personal lives, sent obscene electronic mail, and expected every woman to represent the views of women in general. A more recent study at another university found that women, especially those in graduate engineering departments with the fewest women, said they were not really discriminated against—but then went on to describe being ignored, getting too much attention, or having to prove themselves in ways similar to the 1983 MIT women (Petrides, 1994).

At another research university, a university-wide survey of graduate students revealed disturbing incidents of harassment. Almost 20 percent of women reported faculty members engaging in sexual teasing or joking and making offensive comments about the bodies or sexuality of women. Around 8 percent of the women reported faculty members giving them suggestive looks or gestures or discussing their bodies or sexuality; 19 percent reported hearing faculty make offensive comments about the bodies or sexuality of women students, staff, or faculty. Male students reported significantly fewer incidences of this type of behavior—and in fact, they may be part of the problem; about 40 percent of women report that other students have directed sexual joking and offensive comments against them and other women (Manis et al., 1993, p. 45).

A third of the women Ph.D. and almost a fifth of the master's engineering students at this university reported being "treated in such a way that they feel ridiculed or humiliated" (Manis, 1993, p. 2). Women engineers are ignored in meetings, but are otherwise highly visible and the focus of unwanted sexual attention. Male peers may doubt women's qualifications until they prove themselves. Some men patronize them and others barrage them with obscene materials. Certainly not all male peers treat them poorly, but even some well-meaning colleagues act in ways that produce a very uncomfortable work environment (Bergvall & Marlor, 1993; Hacker, 1990; MIT, 1983; Ruskus, Williamson, & Kelley, 1993).

Social peers are a key support in the graduate school maze. How do women graduate students get along with peer students? This is an issue of both quality and amount of interaction. As to quality, both women and men engineers noted little warmth, caring, or personal support in their graduate program (Manis, 1993). Others in mathematics and physics talked about the friends in their departments with whom they have parties, play Frisbee, and find a social connectedness (Hollenshead, Soellner-Younce, & Wenzel, 1994). Still others find that no matter what they do as women, they cannot be what others expect a graduate student in science and engineering to be—a man. The MIT women (1983) noted that if a woman is quiet and feminine, her success may be hindered because she is not competitive. If she does not appear quiet or feminine, she is socially ostracized.

Many women graduate students in the sciences feel isolated. One study found that women left mathematics because they lacked social peers (Stage & Maple, 1993). Women in computer science graduate studies (MIT, 1983) noted that they were often ignored in professional settings by peers and faculty. One said, "I even had two people with whom I was trying to have a meeting pull their chairs together and start talking to each other as if they'd forgotten I was in the room" (p. 8). Another summed up the results of this treatment for women graduate students by saying, "I feel like I can never have any friends here, like I can never fit in. I've never felt so isolated in my life" (p. 18).

All too often the scientific workplace ignores the safety and security of women. No amount of protective lab equipment protects women from the dangers of walking to their cars after the midnight shift. One study found that a significant proportion (54 percent) of women graduate students often or sometimes felt unsafe while studying, working, or moving about on campus. In contrast, 88 percent of the men said they almost never felt that way (Manis et al., 1993).

Institutional Environment: Expectations

The normative values held by colleagues and faculty shape both individual action and institutional policy. We note two critical expectations with especially detrimental effects on women. First, unlike fields such as law and medicine, where almost all students earn degrees, science and engineering doctoral programs routinely lose about half the people they admit—both men and women, and both fellowship winners and private students. This situation reveals the norms of faculty responsible for these programs.

In addition, graduate school is structured as if personal and professional roles conflict; indeed as if one can and should put one's personal life on hold. Few institutions have family or dependent care programs for their graduate students. The absence of these programs disproportionately disadvantages women. Home and child care are still largely women's domain (Hochschild, 1989). The expected study, teaching, and laboratory load does not allow time to care for a family. The pace of academic life for graduate students and faculty has been set by men whose wives care for home and children and at times serve as research assistant, editor, and typist (Fowlkes, 1987). We frequently hear women graduate students express frustration that their programs frown on their family responsibilities and expect them to have no real impact on their work—as if someone else is taking care of their homes and children. Interviews with graduate women in science—and those who have left—confirm that "marriage and children are generally viewed by male faculty members as impediments to a scientific career for women" (Etzkowitz et al., 1992, p. 167). When students take time off for childbirth, maternity leave is seen as sick leave; on return, one is expected to go back to normal as if a child requires no lifestyle change.

Stage and Maple (1993) found that one reason women leave mathematics for other fields is because they find that math careers conflict with family goals. Another survey of graduate students found few differences related to parenthood, but parents were more likely than nonparents to mention financial problems that made them consider leaving school. In addition, parents were less likely to describe their departments as welcoming and supportive, though they were also less likely to describe their university environment as alienating. Parents found the university less helpful than did nonparents (Manis et al., 1993).

The Nature of the Discipline

The culture of science promotes competition, and it promotes intellectual inquiry for its own sake rather than for human welfare

(Etzkowitz et al., 1992; Merton, 1973). Many argue that this culture often operates as a deterrent to women (Etzkowitz et al., 1992). The discussion of the existence of a feminine style for doing science continues among women in the sciences and scholars who study the institutions and nature of scientific knowledge. The discussion is actually rather covert, for some women scientists find this topic threatening when it is brought up in the company of their male colleagues (Barinaga, 1993a, 1993b).

Anecdotal evidence predominates, but researchers have begun to examine evidence for (Etzkowitz et al., 1994) and against (see Harriet Zuckerman's comments in Barinaga, 1993a) the emergence of a "female" scientific role (Etzkowitz et al., 1992). Are women less competitive, more cooperative, and different in management style? Do they choose research topics differently? We do not attempt to sort through the debate on these questions. We suggest that rather than label a *woman's way* and a *man's way* of doing science, we recognize that variety in styles should be allowed and encouraged, to make the scientific enterprise more robust by using what Evelyn Fox Keller calls the "full range of human potential" (Barinaga, 1993b). Wilson (1994) argues for this strategy and differentiates it from "survival of the fittest" or an "open door" strategy. The strategy includes creating environments that are hospitable and that foster successful performance and advancement. In addition, the strategy emphasizes transforming organization structures, policies, and practices (Wilson, 1994).

Studies suggest that women are uncomfortable with the standard practices of the science classroom. Chapter Seven cites numerous critiques of the curricula of science and engineering, while Chapter Four points out that faculty in the sciences are less likely to use active learning methods and more likely to depend on lectures and to grade on a curve. While we often associate problems of traditional pedagogy with undergraduate education, graduate students are also affected by teaching practices. In a study of graduate students from all disciplines, fully 82 percent surveyed agreed with the statement, "I would like more cooperative or interactive approaches to learning." While a larger percentage of women than men agreed *strongly* with the statement (46 percent compared to 33 percent), nevertheless, 77 percent of the men also agreed either somewhat or strongly. In response to "the competi-

tive atmosphere at [my university] contributes to feelings of alienation and isolation," 60 percent of the women and 45 percent of
the men agreed. Among Ph.D. students, women in the physical sciences, mathematics, and engineering were less likely than those in
other fields to say they almost always enjoyed their classes. They
were also less likely to say they expressed their views in class (Manis
et al., 1993, pp. 13, 24). In another study, focus groups of graduate students in physics and mathematics revealed that for some,
the poor quality of teaching was their greatest disappointment
(Hollenshead, Soellner-Younce, & Wenzel, 1994).

Intersection of Gender with Race, Sexual Orientation, and Disability

As Beatriz Chu Clewell and Angela Ginorio note in Chapter Six,
very little research has focused on women of color, lesbians, or
women with disabilities in SME graduate programs. They provide
a broad review of the literature on these topics; we highlight a few
additional studies here. The report of the American Association
for the Advancement of Science (AAAS) Conference of Minority
Women Scientists in 1975 noted that, in their graduate studies,
women of color in science faced a double bind, with "the chances
of getting a sponsor whose race and gender prejudices will inter-
fere with the effectiveness of this system of counseling . . . still
much too high" (Malcom, Hall, & Brown, 1976, p. 17). Malcom
(1989, p. 15) writes later that "the isolation (being 'the only')" was
one of the most pressing reasons behind women of color forming
a number of national communication networks.

The Council of Graduate Schools (CGS) task force on minority presence in graduate education has written four volumes on
issues germane to our work. Although none of them focus on
women in graduate training in science, mathematics, and engineering, they contain a number of relevant suggestions and strategies for change and include a study of interventions. The CGS
reports that most of the 394 institutions in their 1992 survey allocate more time to recruitment than retention. The time varies by
institution type, but in all cases is almost embarrassingly small.
While the results are not surprising, they are troubling, and they
underscore the lack of attention to the needs of graduate women

of color. The average time allocated by graduate school staff members for recruitment is 0.23 full-time equivalencies (fte); for retention 0.15 fte. The average time for both activities among large research universities is 0.65 fte; other doctorate-granting institutions, 0.32 fte; master's-granting institutions, 0.23 fte.

With regard to programs targeted to minority students, Matyas and Malcom (1991) report that participation varies greatly by ethnic group. Surveyed programs did good jobs in involving African-American women, but Hispanic and Native American women were less likely to be involved. They also reported that programs for women have not been particularly successful in recruiting women of color into their activities.

Malcom (1992) argues convincingly that to increase the participation of minority students in graduate education we must begin early in the educational process and must give attention to transitions from one educational stage to another and to a wide range of factors that may serve as barriers to participation: "The system of problems that prevents full minority participation in graduate education begins at the front end of the educational pipeline and includes non-educational factors such as health and housing" (Malcom, 1992, p. 45).

Researchers know even less about lesbians in science. As Chapter Six notes, the few studies of lesbians focus on nursing or medicine. We assume that lesbian graduate students in science have special concerns that need to be assessed through research and addressed by institutions. For example, with a great deal of research conducted with the support of various federal defense-related agencies, we wonder about potential discrimination over security clearance. Are questions of sexual orientation commonly asked and are lesbians and gay men considered security risks? Future research should look into this and related issues.

We know of no studies on graduate students with disabilities in the sciences, mathematics, and engineering, let alone on women with disabilities. Matyas and Malcom (1991) note that research universities, doctoral-granting institutions, and comprehensive colleges are more likely than smaller schools to have full-scale disabled student services (DSS) offices. However, they add, "Students with physical disabilities who major in science or engineering may find that the DSS at their institution has not encountered their specific needs before, especially in laboratory courses or when specific technologies or services are required. In general, the offices are willing to try to accommodate each student's needs, but, in many cases, the student will have to put forth considerable effort to prepare the classroom, the professor, and the needed equipment or modifications prior to entry into the specific course" (Matyas & Malcom, 1991, p. 5).

Interventions

Though some dedicated educators are working to improve graduate education for women in science and engineering, there are very few programs targeted to recruit or retain women science and engineering graduate students. Matyas and Malcom (1991) surveyed presidents and chancellors of 276 colleges and universities, directors of almost 400 recruitment/retention programs, and 100 disabled student service offices. They conducted case studies to learn what is currently being done to promote the success of women students in science and engineering. The few interventions that exist are usually located within the graduate school at the university and rely more on administrative support than faculty support. Forty-four percent provide research fellowships, 22 percent give health profession scholarships, 17 percent work to improve graduate recruitment and retention, 9 percent offer TA training, and 9 percent run bridge programs for undergraduates before they go into graduate school. These programs often rely on a single funding source and only half of them have been evaluated for effectiveness. They are seen as time consuming by the faculty—especially women and minority faculty (Matyas & Malcom, 1991).

There are, however, some exemplary programs. For example, Humphreys (1988) describes the electrical engineering and computer science department at the University of California, Berkeley, which has created an affirmative action program. It has also worked with undergraduates and industry to encourage graduate study, provided financial aid and research opportunities for undergraduates, offered a program for students to reenter the computer science field without usual undergraduate backgrounds, assigned faculty mentors to students in an effort to help them move past the master's level, and worked productively with women and minority doctoral candidates as potential faculty recruits.

Transitions are critical. The shifts from high school to college and college to graduate school are natural points for dropping out—and also key points for effective intervention. The University of Michigan's Marian Sarah Parker Scholars program attempts to smooth the transition from engineering B.S. degrees to graduate engineering programs by working with eligible women undergraduates in their junior year. It offers career exploration workshops, intensive group experiences focused on planning for the future, seminars with women researchers, the chance to visit or serve as an intern in research laboratories, and information about graduate school admission and financial aid processes.

Other efforts include formal mentoring programs for women who have begun graduate studies. University-based programs such as the University of Michigan's Women in Science and Engineering and Carnegie Mellon's Associate Provost's Initiatives offer seminars and workshops on writing a dissertation or grant proposals, combining career with family, dealing with harassment, and so forth. Cross-institutional efforts also link women who feel isolated at their own universities. Electronic networks, like the Women in Science and Engineering Network (WISENET), Feminists in Science and Technology (FIST), the Women in Engineering Programs Advocacy Network (WEPAN), and SYSTERS.ACADEME link women around the country. Whether seeking information to aid research progress, discussing ways to deal with sexual harassment, or expressing frustration to others who understand, women graduate students and faculty make good use of the Internet. Newsletters and other methods of communication also provide insider information to women who may not be getting the best advice from their male colleagues and advisers. Professional societies are also getting more involved with issues affecting their women constituents. For example, the physics community—the American Physical Society and the American Association of Physics Teachers—are active in this effort (Franz, 1994).

Yet we know of few attempts to address climate issues and of no serious national effort aimed at institutional change. The Andrew W. Mellon Foundation is bringing humanities and social sciences faculty and deans together to discuss ways to change departmental cultures in those fields. They hope to improve success rates of national fellowship recipients, only about 60 percent of whom earn degrees (Frank, 1994) and who complete their degrees no faster than students in their departments without fellowships. This model for institutional change may be useful for the science and engineering community. A similar conference was held at Carnegie Mellon in October 1995, bringing together panels of academic administrators, faculty, and researchers of women's issues in science and engineering to discuss aspects of institutional change.

Directions for Future Research: What We Need to Know

Despite our understanding of some of the experiences of women graduate students in science and engineering, there are questions that need answers to guide the institutional change process. We outline the key gaps to be filled and recommend a number of research directions to be pursued. With better information, we can improve the effectiveness of future change strategies.

First, as we mention at the beginning of this chapter, we need more complete basic data on women graduate students in science and engineering. We know the completion and candidacy rates and time to degree for a few cohorts of women in science and engineering at a handful of the top research universities. While continued efforts by individual institutions are important, especially to guide their own institutional strategies, we still need a national longitudinal study to look at completion rates of women and men in various fields and institutional types. These data need to be analyzed by race and class as well as gender.

Second, the basic information we do have shows that the branch of science and engineering in which a woman works affects her experience. We need much more information to understand why women do better in some disciplines and subfields than in others. How do women's experiences in physical sciences differ from those in engineering? In mathematics? The biological sciences? In-depth study of successful departments and fields can shed light on how institutions can facilitate the success of all their students.

We know that clues can be found by looking at the historical development of the disciplines and women's participation in them. For example, is the distribution of women across different fields a fairly recent phenomenon or related to historical circumstance? Why, for example, is the participation of women in engineering so different from in medicine? Is it because medicine, though governed by male norms, defines itself as a helping or service profession, while engineers have defined themselves very differently? How recent (or unique to the United States) is the idea that physical sciences are inappropriate for women? The number of women in biological sciences has grown greatly in recent years, and the reason may hold a key to promoting similar improvements in other fields. Is biology a woman's field because it deals with life? Why did computer science, which started out open to women, so quickly become gendered as male?

Third, while disciplines shape departments, departments vary from institution to institution. Some do a better job with women than others. We need to know why. We have some evidence that small departments (Bowen & Rudenstine, 1992) and those that offer collaborative experiences (Anderson, 1993) may benefit science graduate students. However, we do not know whether or how these factors differentially affect women. If small departments are beneficial, just what defines their success? Is it good student-faculty ratios, attitudes in the department, or access to funding and opportunity for research that make the difference? We need cross-institutional studies to answer these questions.

Fourth, far too little is known about patterns of financial aid and their impact by gender and race. Are there differential patterns in the award of aid? How do different types of aid promote or impede student success? Do federal and private fellowship policies provide for part-time support that would allow students to balance education and family responsibilities?

Finally, what are the key influences on persistence, satisfaction, and success in the career of a woman seeking a graduate degree in science or engineering? Today's women graduate students are tomorrow's faculty. However, just as entering graduate school does not mean completing a degree, gaining a faculty position does not necessarily open the way to tenure. Many scholars suggest that faculty success depends in part on a process of accumulating advantage—a process begun in graduate school, perhaps with a good mentor or early chances to publish (see Merton, 1968; Fox, 1995; Clark & Corcoran, 1986). We need more research on how graduate students make the transition to faculty roles. How do they learn to negotiate a starting package? How do they learn strategies for setting up a lab, managing projects, seeking funds efficiently, and so forth? Again, we must reiterate the importance of examining the intersections of race, class, and gender with field of study in this research.

The quality and usefulness of answers found through research depends on the models used to frame the inquiry. As we have discussed, we view the institution as the key influence shaping student experience. In particular, we suggest that research focus on the institution of higher education as well as on the systems essential to the higher education enterprise and on the federal research and scientific funding community.

Research efforts need to recognize the gendered nature of graduate education and the importance of informal socialization processes, and they need to investigate student success accordingly. In addition, we propose that researchers take a student-centered (rather than subject-centered) approach. In a truly student-centered approach, the objective is an individual student's success in the field, subject to the constraints on the total life of that individual. This approach will allow us to see how personal, intellectual, and social factors differ between groups of students and, indeed, to identify the truly relevant contributors that differentiate individuals.

Recommendations for Institutional and Systemic Change

Our review has convinced us that although the questions have not been fully answered, we nevertheless have amassed an enormous amount of data about barriers to women in SME graduate education. Moreover, previous reports have addressed many of the topics covered in this and other chapters and have included recommendations for institutional reform and accountability. (See, for example, Matyas and Malcom, 1991.)

Like Astin and Sax in Chapter Four, we are struck by the way institutions continue to do business as usual in spite of extant data. It is not that we do not know what steps to take toward reform; it appears that either we lack the will or desire to do so or that our institutions are so decentralized that most reform efforts are ineffective. For these reasons we argue for a more systematic approach to change, involving key institutions within and outside higher education.

Linda Wilson, president of Radcliffe College, urges higher education to remove the barriers that impede women in graduate education. "Achieving full access takes, as a very first step, a change in mind-set from gatekeeper to architect" (1994, p. 3). With this thought, we look at the systems that structure the experience of women graduate students in science. We make recommendations to examine the interactions between members of these social structures and to renovate these structures so that they better serve all their participants.

It is obvious that gatekeeping is the norm of SME graduate education today. As evidence of this, one need only look at the dismal 50 percent dropout rate found in most doctoral programs. Others echo Wilson's call for a move away from the weeding-out approach and from wasting the potential of graduate students. "Recognition of the extraordinary amounts of time and effort (as well as money) that many of the brightest students are expected to invest in graduate study heightens still more the feeling that *it is wrong* simply to accept current rates of attrition and present assumptions about how long it should take to earn a doctorate. We need first to understand the factors responsible for current norms. Then we need to see if there are ways to do better [emphasis added]" (Bowen & Rudenstine, 1992, p. 3).

In the following pages, we look at the key institutions that have a direct or indirect impact on graduate students. These include universities and their colleges, departments, faculty members, and graduate students, as well as groups external to higher education that play critical roles in science education, such as government research and funding agencies, professional associations, private funding agencies, and industry.

Assessment

Assessment is an essential ingredient in successful change efforts. As Etzkowitz and colleagues note: "A first step is to become more self-conscious about the social organization of human scientific endeavors. . . . Deconstructing the taken-for-granted gendered dimensions of science allows science to be expanded in at least as many ways as it is currently limited" (1992, p. 177). To enhance women's participation at the graduate level, higher education and key external institutions need to take self-critical looks at their members' individual behavior as well as their collective norms and policies. The following paragraphs describe specific actions desirable for each of the key players to assess their own impact on graduate women in science.

Individual Level

Individual faculty members can review their own graduate students' progress, say, over the last five years. There are numerous questions they can ask themselves, including:

Do my women students progress as well and as rapidly as the men?

Do the women I have advised move into jobs equal to men's after completing the Ph.D.? What have I done to help them secure the best positions?

Do I recognize my students' family responsibilities and concerns?

Have I made clear to the student what priority-setting I expect from her?

Do I share information/resources/social networks as comfortably with women as men?

Have I asked my women students about the climate in the department, and where it could be improved?

Have I spoken up in the department about such issues as sexual harassment, potentially biased financial aid decisions, the need for innovative programs or revised curricula?

Collegial Level

Assessment can also take a collegial form, with faculty members within departments and disciplines discussing the barriers to women and the faculty's effect on them. As a group, they can explore how they impede or enhance the success rates of their graduate students. Department leadership can facilitate such assessments and can draw on the expertise of faculty colleagues in the social sciences.

Institutional Level

Universities must look at their own environments and track records, using the research expertise found in their own backyards. Science and engineering units seldom work with social science units to conduct quantitative and qualitative assessments of academic programs. By doing so, they could examine outcomes at the level of faculty, laboratory, department, school or college, and university. When researchers look at women's experience aggregated over time, patterns emerge in advisory relationships, histories of financial support, and other individual factors. It is in these patterns that gender needs and gender discrimination are more likely to be observable.

All institutions should assess their programs on an ongoing basis and report their findings regularly. Essential data include the following:

- *Completion rates, time to degree, and funding patterns by discipline, race, and gender.* Data should be analyzed and reported by departments as well as at the level of individual advisers and laboratory groups, and it should be correlated with institutional factors such as departmental faculty composition.
- *Exit interviews with all students who leave.* These should be conducted by a third party outside the student's department.
- *Climate surveys, focus groups, and third party assessments of departments.* These should be aimed at assessing the environment.
- *Alumnae and alumni surveys.*
- *Job outcomes of graduates by gender and race.*

Institutions also need to identify where they effectively promote the success and satisfaction of their women science graduate students and alumnae. Descriptive assessment of these "best practices" should document in detail the context within which this success takes place. This can assist others both in and out of the institution to develop similarly successful strategies to fit their own needs.

Extra-Institutional Level

Professional associations set many standards within their disciplines. In this role they need to systematically assess the record of their profession regarding the success of women graduate students. For example, professors and other researchers in physics are currently working through the American Physical Society to learn how gender affects graduate study in selected departments.

Agencies like the National Science Foundation (NSF) and private foundations should assess the impact of their programs by asking, for example, how many fellowship recipients complete their programs and why those who leave do so. They need to evaluate which institutions have good track records in graduating women students and which do not.

Accountability and Rewards

Assessment is only the first step. To make it worth the time and expense, assessment must be linked to increased accountability of individuals and groups for the success and satisfaction of all graduate students, but especially women students. It is through the natural interrelationships between the groups that lines of accountability can be drawn. Accountability must, in turn, be linked with organizational structures that direct rewards toward those who provide the best environments for the graduate education of women students.

Individual Level

Most faculty receive yearly performance reviews. These reviews should include assessment of how faculty interact with and expedite progress of their graduate students, with particular attention to gender issues. The resources needed for success—salary, space, facilities, student support, time off from teaching—should be distributed with strong consideration of how faculty work with graduate women of all races as well as men of color. Faculty who lead innovations and interventions that help graduate women must be explicitly rewarded for this work. Faculty can also be held accountable by funding agencies. As part of the grant application process, faculty could be required to provide information by race and gender about the progress of the graduate students whom they advise and work with.

Collegial Level

The university department is run not so much by hierarchical authority as by collegial control of peers who set the norms (rather than formal rules) by which faculty operate. Faculty in a given department, for example, are often aware of which of their colleagues do not support women students and which colleagues engage in sexual harassment. When collegial norms in a given department change so that faculty peers, for example, do not tolerate harassment, the climate for women in the department changes. If the weed-out norms that accept the loss of half of the students who pass stringent admissions standards were changed by the faculty, for example, this wastage of students would be reduced.

Institutional Level

Rewards within the institution also need to be distributed with attention to the success of women and minority graduate students. Resources such as graduate student fellowships, laboratory equipment and space, research seed monies, and cost-sharing funds could all be powerful tools if used by institutions to reward departments that make progress in gender equity or launch innovative programs.

Extra-Institutional Level

Funding agencies can also hold institutions and investigators responsible for graduate student success. Data on programs and completion rates, time to degree, and allocation of resources such as research assistantships by race, gender, and disability status could be required on all NSF, NIH, or other grant proposals (Matyas & Malcom, 1991). To put teeth in this accountability, funding agencies must require certain levels of performance as requirements for receiving funds. Accreditation agencies could make gender equity in graduate education a critical part of periodic reviews. Professional associations could publish data on enrollments, completion rates, and so forth by institution, race, and gender. To identify student wastage and hold departments accountable, Bowen and Rudenstine (1992, p. 163) offer the following calculation for student-year cost per doctoral degree received (SYC):

$$SYC = \frac{\Sigma \text{ Student Years Invested}}{\text{Number of PhD's Earned}}$$

For a given entering doctoral student cohort, the number of years invested in the doctoral program are summed and then divided by the number of doctorates received by group members. Bowen and Rudenstine note that this measure builds on concepts of completion rate, stages of attrition, and time to degree.

This model should be used to assess outcomes by gender and race. Universities could use a comparison of SYCs by gender as a measure of effectiveness of various graduate programs; funding agencies could make it a requirement in applications.

Action and Innovation

Assessment findings should lead directly to corrective action. For example, if peer harassment is determined to be prevalent, it can be addressed by establishing clear behavioral expectations for students and bringing in teams to conduct training with student groups. If lack of safety is a problem, institutions can develop plans to improve parking, lighting, or escort services.

We commend the attention the National Academies have given to graduate education, as shown by their 1995 report, *Reshaping the Graduate Education of Scientists and Engineers*. They recommend that graduate programs improve students' ability to make career choices by offering a broader range of academic options and providing better information and guidance. On the surface, these are positive steps, and we concur on certain points. For example, women students can benefit if departments are held responsible for shortening students' time to degree to ensure that their educational needs take precedence over faculty needs for research assistants. However, some of the kinds of options and guidance recommended seem likely to promote gender inequity in graduate education. Of primary concern is the Academies' recommendation to steer students into one of three distinct academic options: terminal master's degree, research-oriented Ph.D., and non-research-oriented Ph.D. While each path can lead to important careers, we warn departments to safeguard against disproportionately tracking minorities and women into options one and three.

The Council of Graduate Schools (CGS) task force report (1992) on enhancing the minority presence in graduate schools notes that the nation's universities have "both the responsibility and capability of encouraging, promoting, training, and developing a larger number of scholars of color" (p. 34) and points out that this goal can only be met if it involves the entire university community. We concur with their observation and note that the commitment to enhance the experiences of women in science and engineering also generally requires that

- Trustees and administration develop and regularly monitor and evaluate clear plans with incentives and disincentives.
- Department chairs implement strategies and be held accountable for results.
- Faculty understand their role as the single most important component in student success in graduate school and beyond.
- Mechanisms are developed to evaluate faculty progress.
- Students are involved at each step.

The report recommends a variety of strategies for retention of minority graduate students that reflect themes discussed in this chapter. In brief, they suggest programs that bring students together for formal and informal networking and information sharing and which stress the monitoring of and accountability for student progress. Stronger financial aid is also vital.

Family-Centered Policies

Institutions need to allow for part-time study, modified duties, or leaves for dependent care. They may also need to redefine time lines for degree completion. In any case, expectations of mandatory round-the-clock work and single-minded dedication to graduate study need to be modified to fit the realities of life in the late twentieth century.

Women Faculty

As we have discussed, there is evidence that more women faculty will benefit women graduate students in science. In addition, increased hiring of women will increase career options for women graduate students. Departments must act affirmatively to hire more women in tenured and tenure-track positions. For example, to encourage hiring and to reward initiative, the University of Michigan currently offers departments a program called SHARE

(Special Hiring and Recruitment Effort), which provides funds that enable departments where senior women are underrepresented to upgrade junior faculty positions in order to hire more women into tenured positions. Retention is also critical. In this regard, funding also needs to be allocated for release time for women faculty who do additional service or advising duties. (For additional discussion of women faculty, see Chapters Four and Eight.)

Bridging the Transition to Graduate School

As Malcom (1992) points out, transitions are critical to students' continued participation in the educational pipeline. She suggests that: "Students could be admitted to graduate programs while still undergraduates. They could take specialized courses and participate in undergraduate research and seminars, developing many of the skills desirable in the graduate setting" (p. 44).

Likewise, special graduate fellowship programs could be developed that are awarded to women of all races as well as men of color in fields where they are markedly underrepresented. These fellowships would be awarded in the students' junior year and made contingent upon continued outstanding performance during the remaining undergraduate years.

In addition to bridging the gap between the undergraduate years and graduate school, institutions of higher education should develop new pathways into graduate school. Some programs already prepare students with nonscience bachelor's degrees to enter medical school. Arizona State University successfully tested a program in which returning B.A. students completed M.S. degrees in industrial engineering (Anderson, 1991). Since 1983 the Computer Science Reentry Program at the University of California, Berkeley, has successfully prepared student to enter master's and doctoral programs in computer science and related fields (Sheila Humphreys, personal communication). The models hold promise but have not been replicated. Programs for students who have worked in industry would open the door for people who could bring firsthand knowledge of industrial challenges to their graduate research. We recommend that funding agencies and institutions of higher education work together to create additional model reentry programs.

Graduate Funding Alternatives

Zuckerman and Merton (1973) note that the "master-apprentice relation is central to socialization in the sciences" (p. 521). Graduate students rely on faculty to teach them the knowledge and norms of their discipline and to give them feedback, funding, lab space and equipment, experience, chances to publish and to interact with others in the field, and letters of recommendation. Faculty are equally dependent on students to do the work essential to their own research and publishing. Yet the power differential is clearly skewed. When faculty harbor even subtle gender bias, this skew can demolish student aspirations. Perhaps we should think of changing the nature of this relationship and consider how to balance out the power between faculty and student.

One change that would help avoid this difficulty is to empower graduate women by increasing fellowships and dissertation funding not controlled by faculty. Significant funding from independent national grants for women students would give students greater bargaining power and the freedom to pursue their own research without reliance on support from their adviser's projects. Charles (1992) recommends this approach to promote participation of minority students in graduate education; we regard it as appropriate for women in fields where they are underrepresented as well. "The feasibility of portable funding, similar to the G.I. Bill allowing thousands of military veterans to attain their undergraduate degree from the college or university of their choice, might be explored. This availability of choice could allow graduate students to select institutions, individuals, and/or departments committed to producing minority Ph.D.'s with a track record of actually doing so. This would reduce our reliance on the existing system, which to date has not produced the quality or the numbers needed to sustain even our current level of need or to promote diversity among its members" (p. 71).

The potential risks of a portable funding program may rival the benefits. To ensure that women who receive such funds are not isolated from faculty, facilities, and networks, funders would need to require participating institutions to provide resources and opportunities to students selected as fellowship recipients. Thus, shared responsibility for student support could address the shortage of women graduate students while ensuring that students receiving such awards are not marginalized.

Curriculum and Pedagogy

Institutions need to engage in processes that will bring about curriculum transformation and reduce gender bias in the classroom at the graduate level as well as at the undergraduate level. The issues are much the same as those discussed in Chapter Four, and they need no repetition here.

Degree Completion

Throughout this chapter, we have stressed the low degree completion rates that are accepted as the norm in many disciplines. We challenge institutions to reexamine these rates and reform the practices that perpetuate them. Following the model of the Mellon Foundation in the humanities and social sciences, we encourage funders to join institutions of higher education and undertake serious efforts to improve completion rates. This should include identifying high-quality programs with high completion rates for all students and assessing why they are successful. Funding and rewards need to support programs that promote student success, especially among women of all races and ethnic groups as well as men of color—rather than programs that continue to view graduate education as a gatekeeper that screens out all but the so-called fittest. We recognize the force of the argument that low completion rates may reflect a reaction to the market for Ph.D.'s, but we regard limiting the supply at graduate program admission as a more responsible reaction to low demand.

Women-Centered Institutions

Lazarus and Nair (1991) suggest the development of an engineering institution where the students would be women but the faculty would be mixed, providing both male and female mentors and role models. Such an institution would give women studying engineering the advantages now enjoyed by undergraduate women majoring in science at women's colleges. One could envision an independent Women's Institute for Engineering, but given the realities—and perhaps more important, given the good track record of women's colleges in producing self-confident scholars— it would be more realistic to add an engineering program to an existing women's college. Beyond the value to undergraduates, we are impressed with the potential value of a limited version of this concept for graduate students. Because the relationship between adviser and advisee is critical in graduate education, an entire faculty committed to mentoring women should have dramatic effects on the retention rate, with far fewer women dropping out or having their careers derailed by advisers who prefer to work with men.

As noted earlier, graduate school is not only about mastery of knowledge: it is about creating new knowledge. Self-efficacy at this level means that the student is able to feel the power and legitimacy of the type of knowledge she wants to create, own, and value as her life's work. Graduate research is often narrow in context and topic, and the larger picture of engineering as a socially relevant field with potential for service to society is often lost. Many women express the need to see the usefulness of their work directly, not merely as the contribution of a new piece to the structure of science or engineering. The "tacit centering of knowledge around the lives and experiences of the privileged" (Minnick, 1990, p. 4) and the inflation of these experiences as "universal knowledge" present new obstacles to women and minority students who find themselves outside the privileged circle in terms of experience, norms, and values about education and research issues.

There are obvious financial and logistical difficulties to creating a degree-granting institution. However, setting up a summer research institute for women would be relatively simple, and it would do much to facilitate collaboration by women in the same fields. As a truly modest alternative to a degree-granting institution, a freestanding institute could be located near or sponsored by a major engineering and science university. The purpose of the institute would be to provide an opportunity for women graduate students (at the thesis or dissertation stage), postdoctoral fellows, faculty, and even engineers and scientists from industry to work on their own short-term projects in an environment with a critical mass of women. The institute could provide participants a place to share ideas on research and on the challenges faced by women in engineering and science, for a one-to-three-month period. Such an institute could be the basis for a community of support that could help to sustain women throughout their graduate and faculty careers.

Conclusion

Are these solutions worth serious exploration? Clearly institutions where women are regarded as serious scholars, where women's voices are heard in the classroom and laboratory, and where there is less sex-role stereotyping would and indeed do make a significant difference.

There is much still to learn from research on women's experiences in the advanced study of science and engineering. However, we cannot wait to collect all the data before we improve the situation. From what we do know, we need to devise the best possible change strategy—while we continue to fill in the gaps.

We have offered suggestions for institutional transformation based on what we already know. Some entail incremental improvements on the current assumptions of graduate science education—others entail radical change of institutions and relationships. These suggestions are but a starting point.

Transformation will require individual and institutional commitment and leadership. As Wilson has noted, removing barriers to women "involves transforming organizational structures, policies, and practices so that men and women, both majority and minority, can thrive, work in full partnership with each other, and, at the same time, lead responsible and fulfilling lives in their families and communities. . . . [Such transformation] will require imagination, champions, widespread recognition of the imperatives to change, broad participation, and a solid basis for hope that the benefits of the changes will be broadly distributed" (1994, pp. 1, 11).

References

Anderson, F. H. (Ed.). (1960). *Francis Bacon: The new organon and related writings.* Indianapolis, IN: Bobbs Merrill.

Anderson, M. R. (1991). Graduate career change: Women engineers vs. traditional engineers. In J. Z. Daniels (Ed.), *Women in Engineering conference: A national initiative* (pp. 29–35). West Lafayette, IN: Women in Engineering Programs Advocacy Network.

Anderson, M. S. (1993). *Toward a profile of the highly collaborative graduate program: Effects on the doctoral experience and departmental environment.* Paper presented at the annual meeting of the Association for the Study of Higher Education, Pittsburgh, PA.

Barinaga, M. (1993a). Is there a "female style" in science? *Science, 260,* 384–391.

Barinaga, M. (1993b). Feminists find gender everywhere in science. *Science, 260,* 392–393.

Barnes, B., & Edge, D. (Eds.). (1982). *Science in context: Readings in the sociology of science.* Milton Keynes, England: Open University Press.

Berg, H. M., & Ferber, M. A. (1983). Men and women graduate students: Who succeeds and why? *Journal of Higher Education, 54,* 629–648.

Bergvall, V. L., & Marlor, S. S. (1993, October). *A frozen climate for women? Changing engineering education.* Paper presented at the conference on Reconciling Gender Issues in Higher Education, Burlington, VT.

Bowen, W. G., & Rudenstine, N. (1992). *In pursuit of the Ph.D.* Princeton, NJ: Princeton University Press.

Chamberlain, M. K. (1988). *Women in academe: Progress and prospects* (pp. 5–8). New York: Russell Sage Foundation.

Charles, B. L. (1992). Institutional environment: A critical factor for minorities in the graduate education pipeline. In J. M. Jones, M. E. Goertz, & C. V. Kuh (Eds.), *Minorities in graduate education: Pipeline, policy and practice* (pp.70–75). Princeton, NJ: Educational Testing Service.

Clark, S. M., & Corcoran, M. (1986). Perspectives on the professional socialization of women faculty: A case of accumulative disadvantages? *Journal of Higher Education, 57*(1), 20–43.

Clifford, G. J. (1993). Shaking dangerous questions from the crease: Gender and American higher education. In U.S. Glazer, E. M. Bensimon, & B. K. Townsend (Eds.), *Women in higher education: A feminist perspective* (pp. 135–174). Needham Heights, MA: Ginn Press.

Comparisons across cultures. (1994, March 11). *Science,* pp. 1467–1495.

Council of Graduate Schools (CGS). (1992). *Enhancing the minority presence in graduate education: Models and resources for minority student recruitment and retention* (Vol. 4). Washington, DC: Council of Graduate Schools.

Etzkowitz, H., Kemelgor, C., Neuschatz, M., Uzzi, B., & Alonzo, J. (1992). Athena unbound: Barriers to women in academic science and engineering. *Science and Public Policy, 19*(3), 157–179.

Etzkowitz, H., Kemelgor, C., Neuschatz, M., Uzzi, B., & Alonzo, J. (1994). The paradox of "critical mass" for women in science. *Science, 266,* 51–54.

Fausto-Sterling, A. (1992). *Myths of gender: Biological theories about women and men* (Rev. ed.). New York: Basic Books.

Fowlkes, M. R. (1987). The myth of merit and male professional careers. In N. Gerstel & H. E. Gross (Eds.), *Families and work* (pp. 347–360). Philadelphia: Temple University Press.

Fox, M. F. (1995). Women and higher education: Gender differences in the status of students and scholars. In J. Freeman (Ed.), *Women: A feminist perspective* (5th ed., pp. 220–237). Mountain View, CA: Mayfield.

Frank, M. J. (1994, January 31). Mellon funds U-M-based effort to improve grad education. *The University Record*, p. 5.

Franz, J. (1994). *Improving the climate for women in physics departments.* Unpublished proposal for a national study.

Frazier-Kouassi, S., Malanchuk, O., Shure, P., Burkam, D., Gurin, P., Hollenshead, C., Lewis, D. J., Soellner-Younce, P., Neal, H., & Davis, C. (1992). *Women in mathematics and physics: Inhibitors and enhancers.* Ann Arbor: University of Michigan, Center for the Education of Women, Department of Mathematics, Department of Physics.

Frieze, I. H. (1978). Psychological barriers for women in sciences: Internal and external. In J. A. Ramaley (Ed.), *Covert discrimination and women in the sciences* (pp. 65–95). Boulder, CO: Westview Press.

Gilbert, L. A., Gallessich, J. M., & Evans, S. L. (1983). Sex of faculty role model and students' self-perceptions of competency. *Sex Roles, 9,* 597–607.

Girves, J. E., & Wemmerus, V. (1988). Developing models of graduate student degree progress. *Journal of Higher Education, 59*(2), 163–189.

Goldstein, D., Haldane, D., & Michell, C. (1990). Sex-performances in visual-spatial ability: The role of performance factors. *Memory and Cognition, 18,* 546–550.

Hacker, S. L. (1990). *Doing it the hard way: Investigations of gender and technology.* (D. E. Smith & S. M. Turner, Eds.). Winchester, MA: Unwin Hyman.

Harding, S. (1991). *Whose science? Whose knowledge?: Thinking from women's lives.* Ithaca, NY: Cornell University Press.

Harding, S. (1993). Starting thought from women's lives: Eight resources for maximizing objectivity. In J. S. Glazer, E. M. Bensimon, & B. K. Townsend (Eds.), *Women in higher education: A feminine perspective* (pp. 35–44). Needham Heights, MA: Ginn Press.

Hochschild, A. (1989). *The second shift.* New York: Avon Books.

Hollenshead, C., Soellner-Younce, P., & Wenzel, S. A. (1994). Women graduate students in mathematics and physics: Reflections upon success. *Journal of Women and Minorities in Science and Engineering, 1,* 63–88.

Hornig, L. S. (1984). Women in science and engineering: Why so few? *Technology Review, 87,* 30–41.

Hornig, L. S. (1987). Women graduate students: A literature review and synthesis. In L. S. Dix (Ed.), *Women: Their underrepresentation and career differentials in science and engineering* (pp. 103–122). Washington, DC: National Academy Press.

Humphreys, S. M. (1988, May). One department's response: Women and minorities in the graduate pipeline. *Engineering Education,* pp. 772–774.

Kanter, R. M. (1977). *Men and women of the corporation.* New York: Basic Books.

Keller, E. F. (1985). *Reflections on gender and science.* New Haven, CT: Yale University Press.

Lazarus, B., & Nair, I. (1991). An immodest proposal. *Proceedings of the Women in Engineering Conference: A national initiative* (pp. 157–164). West Lafayette, IN: Women in Engineering Programs Advocacy Network.

Lomperis, A.M.T. (1990). Are women changing the nature of the academic profession? *Journal of Higher Education, 61,* 644–666.

McAdams, D. (1988). Gender implications of the traditional academic conception of the political. In S. H. Aiken (Ed.), *Changing our minds: Feminist transformation of knowledge.* Albany: State University of New York Press.

Malcom, S. M. (1989). Increasing the participation of black women in science and technology. *SAGE, 6*(2), 15–17.

Malcom, S. M. (1992). Unconventional wisdom: Minority students in graduate education. In J. M. Jones, M. E. Goertz, & G. Kuh (Eds.), *Minorities in graduate education: Pipeline policy and practice* (pp. 44–45). Princeton, NJ: Educational Testing Service.

Malcom, S. M., Hall, P. Q., & Brown, J. W. (1976). *The double bind: The price of being a minority woman in science* (AAAS Report No. 76-R-3). Washington, DC: American Association for the Advancement of Science.

Manis, J. (1993). *Engineering student views: Findings from CEW survey of Rackham graduate students.* Unpublished manuscript.

Manis, J., Frazier-Kouassi, S., Hollenshead, C., & Burkam, D. (1993). *A survey of the graduate experience: Sources of satisfaction and dissatisfaction among graduate students at the University of Michigan.* Ann Arbor: University of Michigan Center for the Education of Women.

Matyas, M. L., & Malcom, S. M. (Eds.). (1991). *Investing in human potential: Science and engineering at the crossroads.* Washington, DC: American Association for the Advancement of Science.

Merton, R. K. (1968). The Matthew effect in science. *Science, 159*(3810), 56–63.

Merton, R. K. (1973). *The sociology of science: Theoretical and empirical investigations.* Chicago: University of Chicago Press.

Minnick, E. (1990). *Transforming Knowledge.* Philadelphia: Temple University Press.

MIT Computer Science Female Graduate Students and Research Staff. (1983, February). *Barriers to equality in academia: Women in computer science at MIT.* (Copies available from EECS Graduate Office at MIT, Cambridge, MA, 02139)

National Academy of Sciences. National Academy of Engineering. Institute of Medicine Committee on Science, Engineering, and Public Policy. (1995). *Reshaping the graduate education of scientists and engineers.* Washington, DC: National Academy Press.

Nerad, M., & Stewart, C. L. (1991). *Assessing doctoral student experience: Gender and departmental climate.* Paper presented at the annual conference of the Association for Institutional Research, San Francisco, CA.

Paludi, M. A. (1990). Preface. In M. A. Paludi (Ed.), *Ivory power: Sexual harassment on campus.* Albany: State University of New York Press.

Petrides, L. A. (1994, November). *A study of the gendered construction of the engineering academic context in graduate school.* Presented at the 1994 annual meeting of the Association for the Study of Higher Education, Tucson, AZ.

Pipeline project. (1994). [Preliminary findings on cohort 1 from "Education and career plans of women in engineering" survey, University of Michigan Center for the Education of Women]. Unpublished data.

Rackham Graduate School. (1994, April). *Doctoral cohort study: Update 1994* (Preliminary draft report). Horace H. Rackham School of Graduate Studies, University of Michigan.

Reinharz, S. (1992). *Feminist methods in social research.* New York: Oxford University Press.

Richey, C. A., Gabrill, E. D., & Blythe, B. J. (1988). Mentor relationships among women in academe. *AFFILIA, 3*(1), 34–47.

Roby, P. (1973). Institutional barriers to women students in higher education. In A. S. Rossi & A. Calderwook (Eds.), *Academic women on the move* (pp. 37–56). New York: Russell Sage Foundation.

Rosser, S. V. (1990). *Female-friendly science: Applying women's studies methods and theories to attract students.* New York: Pergamon Press.

Ruskus, J., Williamson, C. L., & Kelley, F. A. (1993, April). *From a woman's point of view: Barriers and facilitators to success in science and engineering.* Paper presented at the 1993 American Educational Research Association annual meeting, Atlanta, GA.

Sand, R. G., Parson, L. A., & Duane, J. (1991). Faculty mentoring faculty in a public university. *Journal of Higher Education, 62*(2), 174–193.

Schroeder, D. S., & Mynatt, C. R. (1993). Female graduate students' perceptions of their interactions with male and female major professors. *Journal of Higher Education, 64,* 555–573.

Solomon, B. M. (1985). *In the company of educated women.* New Haven, CT: Yale University Press.

Stacey, J., & Thorne, B. (April 1985). The missing feminist revolution in sociology. *Social Problems, 32*(4), 173–188.

Stage, F. K., & Maple, S. (1993, November). *Dropping out of the mathematics/ science pipeline: Narratives of women doctoral candidates.* Paper presented at the annual meeting of the Association for the Study of Higher Education, Pittsburgh, PA.

Tidball, E. M. (1986). Baccalaureate origins of recent natural science doctorates. *Journal of Higher Education, 57,* 606–620.

Trescott, M. M. (1990). Women in the intellectual development of engineering. In G. Kass-Simon & P. Farnes (Eds.), *Women of science: Righting the record* (pp. 147–187). Bloomington: Indiana University Press.

Vetter, B. M. (1984). Changing patterns of recruitment and employment. In V. B. Haas & C. C. Perrucci (Eds.), *Women in scientific and engineering professions* (pp. 59–74). Ann Arbor: University of Michigan Press.

Vetter, B. M. (Ed.). (1994). *Professional women and minorities: A total human resource data compendium* (11th ed.). Washington, DC: Commission on Professionals in Science and Technology.

Westphal, S., & Sheppard, C. (1992). Breaking the barriers: Women, knowledge and equality in the university. *New Approaches to Employee Management: Fairness in Employee Selection, 1,* 185–202.

Wilson, L. (1994, March). Reform, renewal, and resilience: Educating our aspirations and changing our ways. *Communicator.* Washington, DC: Council of Graduate Schools.

Woody, T. (1974). *A history of women's education in the United States.* New York: Octogon Books.

Zuckerman, H., & Merton, R. K. (1973). Age, aging, and age structure in science. In R. K. Merton (Ed.), *The sociology of science: Theoretical and empirical investigations* (pp. 497–559). Chicago: University of Chicago Press.

Zwick, R. (1991). *Differences in graduate school attainment patterns across academic programs and demographic groups* (Research Rep. No. 143). Princeton, NJ: Educational Testing Service.

Chapter Six

Examining Women's Progress in the Sciences from the Perspective of Diversity

Beatriz Chu Clewell, Angela B. Ginorio

Research studies often fail to address multiple equity areas, and their findings are prone to misinterpretation as a result. Campbell (1989), MacCorquodale (1988), McDowell (1990), and other observers have written eloquently about this problem. Grant and Sleeter (1986) reviewed a ten-year sample of education literature from four journals to determine the degree to which race, social class, and gender were considered. They found very few papers examining the interaction of these status groups, and they warned that attending only to racial status oversimplifies the conclusions and may help perpetuate gender and class biases. McDowell reviewed seventy-three papers published between 1980 and 1986 on educational research in science, cognition, and education and found that 68 percent did not consider race, class, or gender in their analysis. None of the studies included class alone or in combination with race or gender in their analyses. In a summary of research on sex and ethnic differences in mathematics and science for students in Grades 4 through 8, Lockheed, Thorpe, Brooks-Gunn, Casserly, and McAloon (1985) found thirty-one studies addressing gender and sixteen addressing ethnicity, but only six addressing the two factors simultaneously.

At the college level, there are so few ethnic minority science students that review by both ethnicity and gender is very rare. For example, even though the number of ethnic minority students planning graduate work has grown significantly, Grandy (1992) reported that of the 121,982 people taking the Graduate Record Examination (GRE) in December 1990, only 1,063 were ethnic minorities (.9 of 1 percent). Despite the size of this sample, a seventy-two-cell table of ethnicity (six categories) by gender (two categories) by field (six categories) winds up with forty-five cells filled with one-digit numbers—including five with zeroes (p. 8)! The problems reported with data on black college students by the Howard University Institute for the Study of Educational Policy in 1976 are still true today for all ethnic minority students.

This chapter's reference list is extensive, but had we cited only studies that address any two issues together (for example, ethnicity and gender or disability and gender) we would have had a very short list. It should also be noted that many of these papers are what have been viewed as nonmainstream sources: research reports and special issues or articles in journals on ethnic minorities and/or women. The authors have prepared a description of studies involving interaction among issues, and interested readers can obtain copies by writing to Angela B. Ginorio at the University of Washington.

This chapter focuses on populations underrepresented in SME fields. The K–12 section includes only reports with information on American Indians, African Americans, and Latino/as. The rest of the chapter also includes information on Asian Americans, disabled students, and lesbians. (The Asian- American pattern of participation in SME fields is different from that of other ethnic minorities, but at the college level it exhibits variations affected by gender.) Thus we report on a limited selection of studies, and we include references to other groups (for example, white women) only to provide a context for the experiences of women of color, women with disabilities, and lesbians. We discuss class issues when they were noted in the literature—which is to say, not as frequently as we suspect they were operating.

Only recently have SME programs begun to address the needs of the physically disabled. Disabled persons have not had full access to science in high school, higher education, or careers (Ricker, 1978; Lucky, 1989). Opening science to the physically disabled involves more than widening doors and providing alternatives to stairs; it also involves making a commitment to the basic right of disabled students to learn and to receive encouragement and opportunities that will lead to science-related careers (Ricker, 1978).

While studying the status of ethnic minorities, women, and the disabled may be difficult, it is far easier than studying populations not protected by antidiscrimination laws, such as lesbians and gays. In the latter case, no numbers are kept by any institution. We have only the results of a few specialized studies, plus some extrapolations from general surveys of the population. Lesbians face different issues from those confronted by heterosexual women of color or disabled women. There is evidence of homophobia in the academic (Governor's Commission on Gay and Lesbian Youth, 1993) and scientific communities (Tinmouth & Hamwi, 1994). Because visible factors do not make lesbians' sexual minority status obvious, disclosure of their sexual orientation becomes an issue of prominence. Fear of the repercussions of coming out contributes to the difficulties faced by lesbian scientists, engineers, and mathematicians.

Although deep structural issues shape the experience of diverse populations in our society, we begin our review at the individual level, so as to understand and sort what we know about individuals before tackling the complexities of the sociocultural level. Our analysis follows the educational ladder, going from the early years (K–3) to middle school (4–8) and high school (9–12) and concluding with the undergraduate and graduate levels and a very brief overview of postgraduate employment. The chapter closes with a discussion of directions for further research.

Lower Ladder (Grades K–12)

As indicated earlier, the focus here is on racial/ethnic groups underrepresented in mathematics and science: African Americans, Latino/as, and American Indians. From this point on, the term *women and girls of color* will refer to members of these groups.

Early Years (K–3)

Few studies have analyzed education in early life. This is unfortunate, because the first years seem especially important. After third grade, data show great consistency in children's performance from one year to the next, leaving much less room for intervention (Entwisle, Alexander, Cadigan, & Pallas, 1986). Even less is known of the early antecedents of mathematics or science achievement for girls of color or girls with disabilities. Data from the National Assessment for Education Progress (NAEP) begin to document results by race/ethnicity and gender at the fourth grade. (Except for recent mathematics and science assessment results, presented later in this chapter, the NAEP does not provide disaggregation of data by gender within racial/ethnic subgroups.)

However, we did identify a few studies for this age group that focus on race, social class, and sometimes gender differences in early mathematics education. Some looked at student perception of and preparation for mathematics up to the point of school entry. Another focused on how social factors shape the attainment of children as they begin their academic careers. Other studies examined student progress and achievement during the first years of schooling as well as factors influencing that progress.

Three studies investigated race, social class, and gender differences in mathematics readiness at the time of school entry, mostly concluding that differences are small (Entwisle & Alexander, 1990; Tizard, Blatchford, Burke, Farquhar, & Plewis, 1988). "Basic mathematical thought develops in a robust manner among lower- and middle-class children, black and white" (Ginsberg & Russell, 1981, p. 56). (Although not mentioned in the quote, Ginsburg and Russell found very few gender differences for any of the groups studied.) The Entwisle and Alexander study found that African-American and white students had equivalent scores in computational and verbal skills on the California Achievement Test at the start of first grade, but there was a significant difference of about one-quarter of a standard deviation favoring white students in mathematics concepts (reasoning skills). Tizard and her colleagues had similar findings in their 1988 study of black and white British preschoolers (Tizard, Blatchford, Burke, Farquhar, & Plewis). Black boys outperformed girls in mathematics reasoning, but there was no significant difference between white boys and girls. Boys of the two races also performed similarly. Furthermore, the authors felt that the significant difference seen for black boys over girls was due to sampling fluctuations, as it did not show up in subsequent scores for this sample. Entwisle and Alexander also found that all groups scored higher if their parents expected them to do well, that unlike white parents, African-American parents did not have higher expectations of boys than girls or perceive boys as having more ability in mathematics, that socioeconomic factors were an important influence on mathematics skills for all groups, and that family configuration (mother-father, mother-other, and mother only) did not affect mathematics scores for children of either sex or race at this age.

Once students enter school, what influences their success in mathematics? Researchers have studied effects of student and parent expectations and of parent socialization on success in the early years of schooling. One tracking study was conducted in two Baltimore schools—one with white, middle-class enrollment and the other with mixed-race, lower-class enrollment—from the first through third grades (Entwisle & Baker, 1983). The study sought to answer the question of whether socializing forces that shape mathematical performance along stereotypic sex-role lines are present long before junior high. The researchers found that experience in these early grades does differ by gender. Although their arithmetic marks or general aptitude were not higher than those of girls, boys developed higher expectations for performing well in mathematics, apparently in response to differential expectations held by their parents. The link between parent and child expectations was considerably weaker in the lower-class school; also, parents whose children attended the lower-class school expected more from girls in arithmetic than they did from boys. Thus the tendency for boys to be overly optimistic or for girls to be overly pessimistic about their arithmetic performance was not as strong in the lower-class school as it was in the middle-class school.

Given that students of both genders and races start out with similar mathematics achievement, what accounts for their differential performance as they progress through school? One longitudinal study tracked a sample of black and white first graders for twenty-four months and found that by the end of the period, blacks—both girls and boys—were about half a standard deviation behind, despite roughly equal starting scores (Entwisle & Alexander, 1992). The most important factors affecting this change were differences in socioeconomic status, followed by segregation. Over the two-year period, students in integrated schools showed about the same gains in mathematics skills, while segregated schools tended to penalize blacks, especially poor ones. The overall difference between racial groups could be traced mainly to the performance of segregated youngsters. Once again, family configuration was not related to achievement levels. Poor children of both races and genders consistently lost ground in the summer, but tended to perform at similar levels or better than their wealthier peers in the winter when school was in session.

Another study of British working-class children traced their progress in infant school (Blatchford, Burke, Farquahar, Plewis, & Tizard, 1985). Results showed few differences in literacy and numeracy between black and white five-year-olds entering school, although girls had higher test scores than boys. Test score variation could be attributed mainly to teaching at home and mothers' educational achievement. By the end of the third grade, white boys had the highest scores, girls of both races performed at similar levels, and black boys scored the lowest. A follow-up study of this cohort (Plewis, 1991) noted that white children of both sexes had higher mathematics scores than black children by the end of junior school, at age eleven.

In an attempt to relate income, gender, age, and level of cognitive development to selected domain-specific skills, Stokes (1990) tested African-American students ages five to eight. She found ability to solve mathematics problems correlated significantly with level of cognitive development, but not with gender. The study also suggested that age is more important to success in addition, subtraction, and algorithm problems and less important to success in measurement and word problems, while the opposite is true for cognitive level (which is relatively uncorrelated with age).

Middle School (Grades 4–8)

The middle school years have been identified as the most crucial for the mathematics/science talent pool. According to Berryman

(1983), after eighth grade, more people leave the pool than enter it. It is in middle school that girls, especially girls of color, must develop skills and maintain attitudes to carry them through high school courses in mathematics and science. What do we know about the achievement and experiences of girls of color during the middle school period? What are some of the factors that influence their performance and persistence on the mathematics/science ladder?

Achievement and Performance

At this point in the research on girls of color, it is difficult to say which of their intersecting statuses is the most powerful influence on their performance and participation in mathematics and science. When we also consider class, socioeconomic status (SES), disability, language minority status, and sexual preference, the complexity of the problem becomes obvious and overwhelming.

Mathematics

Research on white students suggests that mathematics performance diverges between girls and boys by eighth or ninth grade, almost always favoring boys (Armstrong, 1981; Fennema, 1980; Fennema & Carpenter, 1981; Fox, Brody, & Tobin, 1985; Moore & Smith, 1987). Ethnic and racial differences on standardized tests are larger and appear much earlier than gender differences (Dossey, Mullis, Lindquist, & Chambers, 1988; Gross, 1988; Reyes & Stanic, 1988). NAEP mathematics scores have shown large differences favoring white students beginning at the fourth-grade level in 1973, 1978, 1982, 1986, 1990, and 1992 (Dossey et al., 1988; Mullis, Dossey, Owens, & Phillips, 1993).

In addition, Gross (1988, 1989) suggests that students who fall below standard performance for a grade level are unlikely to catch up; this is especially true for African-American and Latino students. By age nine, for example, African Americans performed well below the NAEP mathematics average, and the difference increased with age (Holmes, 1980; Matthews, 1983). In past NAEP mathematics assessments, students of color made greater gains than white students—though their scores were still well below the national average (Dossey et al., 1988; Matthews, Carpenter, Lindquist, & Silver, 1984). More recently, however, white students have gained more than most minorities, while still lagging behind gains of Asian-American/Pacific Islander students (Mullis et al., 1993).

There is less evidence of gender differences in mathematics performance among students of color. Jones (1987) found that both African-American and white women scored lower than men at all levels of mathematics. Moore and Smith (1987) reported that the largest differences in favor of boys were among white and Latino students, and the smallest were among African-American students. Nelson (1978) reported no gender differences in mathematics achievement among African-American fifth graders but she did find that eleventh-grade boys had higher scores than girls. This suggests achievement patterns for African-American males and females similar to those noted for white students. Results from the most recent NAEP mathematics assessments (1990 and 1992) for Grades 4, 8, and 12 (displayed in Table 6.1) again show similar patterns of achievement for white and African-American male and female students at each grade level, with males either equal to or slightly ahead of females. The results for Latino students in 1992, however, show females outperforming males at all three grade levels, in marked difference from the 1990 assessment. Although it is too early to tell, it might be interesting to follow this development to see if it is the beginning of a trend.

In a study of the relationship of race, class, and gender to mathematics achievement among fifth, eighth, and eleventh graders, Kohr and his colleagues (1989) observed differences across grade levels for SES and race, but not for gender, with white students scoring higher than African-American students. Achievement also varied directly with SES level, with higher-SES students having higher achievement than lower-SES students.

Science

The performance gap between men and women, and between white and Asian-American students as compared to their African-American, Latino, and Native American counterparts, persists in the 1990 NAEP science assessment (Jones, Mullis, Raizen, Weiss, & Weston, 1992). As shown in Table 6.2, boys outperformed girls in all racial/ethnic groups, especially at higher ages and levels of proficiency. NAEP data show an advantage for boys in physical sciences

**Table 6.1. Average Mathematics Proficiency Levels by Race/
Ethnicity and Gender, Grades 4, 8, and 12, 1990 and 1992.**

	1990 Average proficiency	*1992 Average proficiency*
Grade 4		
White Male	221 (1.4)	228 (1.0)
White Female	220 (1.3)	225 (1.3)
Black Male	189 (2.1)	192 (1.6)
Black Female	190 (2.5)	191 (1.6)
Hispanic Male	198 (3.1)	200 (1.6)
Hispanic Female	198 (2.3)	201 (1.7)
Grade 8		
White Male	271 (1.2)	277 (1.2)
White Female	269 (1.3)	277 (1.1)
Black Male	238 (3.2)	237 (1.9)
Black Female	238 (3.3)	237 (1.5)
Hispanic Male	245 (2.6)	246 (1.7)
Hispanic Female	242 (3.4)	247 (1.9)
Grade 12		
White Male	303 (1.5)	307 (1.0)
White Female	298 (1.4)	303 (1.0)
Black Male	272 (2.4)	277 (2.3)
Black Female	264 (2.5)	273 (1.8)
Hispanic Male	280 (3.3)	281 (3.4)
Hispanic Female	272 (3.7)	285 (2.5)

Proficiency levels for grade 4 are as follows: Advanced, 280; Proficient, 248;
Basic, 211. For grade 8: Advanced, 331; Proficient, 294; Basic, 256. For grade
12: Advanced, 366; Proficient, 334; Basic, 287.

Source: Adapted from Mullis, Dossey, Owen, and Phillips, 1993.

at Grade 3 that increased at Grades 8 and 12, but data were not disaggregated by sex within racial/ethnic categories (Jones et al.).

Course Enrollment/Participation

Students in Grades 4 through 8 rarely have a choice about taking
mathematics and science classes, as the general curriculum usually

Table 6.2. Distribution of Students and Average Science Proficiency by Race/Ethnicity and Gender.

	Percentage of students	Average proficiency
Grade 4		
White Male	36 (0.7)	243 (1.3)
White Female	34 (0.7)	241 (1.1)
Black Male	7 (0.3)	205 (1.8)
Black Female	8 (0.4)	206 (1.8)
Hispanic Male	6 (0.2)	213 (1.6)
Hispanic Female	5 (0.2)	211 (1.9)
Grade 8		
White Male	36 (0.8)	274 (1.8)
White Female	35 (0.7)	271 (1.4)
Black Male	7 (0.3)	232 (2.9)
Black Female	8 (0.3)	230 (2.1)
Hispanic Male	5 (0.2)	243 (3.0)
Hispanic Female	5 (0.2)	239 (2.5)
Grade 12		
White Male	36 (0.8)	307 (1.5)
White Female	37 (0.7)	298 (1.3)
Black Male	6 (0.4)	261 (2.7)
Black Female	8 (0.4)	253 (2.9)
Hispanic Male	4 (0.3)	2781 (3.1)
Hispanic Female	4 (0.3)	268 (3.5)

Levels of science proficiency are as follows: Level 200—Understands simple scientific principles; Level 250—Applies general scientific information; Level 300—Analyzes scientific procedures and data; Level 350—Integrates specialized scientific information.

Source: Jones, Mullis, Raizen, Weiss, & Weston, 1992, p. 12.

includes these subjects (Lockheed et al., 1985). Thus there is little variation due to gender or race/ethnicity at the middle school level, though schools show substantial differences in the amount and quality of mathematics and science instruction. However, participation in related activities does differ. By age nine, sex and ethnic differences in other science activities are already apparent

(Kahle & Lakes, 1983). From 1976–77, NAEP data on science attitudes showed that nine- and thirteen-year-old girls consistently had less exposure than boys. Furthermore, the 1977–1986 trend analysis of NAEP responses continued to reflect differential experiences based on gender. White students had more science experiences than African-American students, and the difference increased with age. Johnson (1981) studied the extent of extracurricular mathematics activities undertaken by a small sample of African-American youth in Grades 7 and 8. He found no sex differences; all reported low participation. A study of 1981–82 NAEP data nevertheless revealed that African-American girls at ages nine and thirteen had conducted the fewest science experiments (Hueftle, Rakow, & Welch, 1983), and the 1990 NAEP science assessment shows this trend continuing for thirteen-year-old African-American girls, who were the most likely to respond that they had never done a science experiment.

Factors Affecting Performance and Participation

It is clear that females and males in racial/ethnic categories are much more similar to each other than to students in other categories. Obviously, race/ethnicity is much more important than gender in this matter. A study of Chicano, white, and African-American adolescents by Creswell and Houston (1980) confirms that ethnicity was the primary source of variance in performance.

However, there are some differences in performance, achievement, and participation rates between girls of color and their male counterparts. There are also differences between girls of color and white girls. To study these factors, it is useful to classify them as *learner-related* and *environmental* variables.

Learner-Related Variables

Variables such as attitudes, perceptions, and learning styles depend on factors each student brings to the learning process.

Attitudes and Perceptions

Students' performance and participation in mathematics and science seem to depend on enjoyment of the subjects, perceptions of the subjects as useful to themselves and/or as the domain of white males, and confidence in their own abilities. Although this has been shown to be true for white girls and women (Fennema & Sherman, 1978; Jones et al., 1992; Sherman, 1980), it is unclear whether such a relationship exists between attitudes and achievement for girls and women of color. Research on white women and girls has also documented a decline in attitudes toward mathematics and science that begins in middle school and escalates through high school (Fennema & Sherman, 1978; Jones et al., 1992; Mullis & Jenkins, 1988; Schreiber, 1984). By high school, boys' attitudes toward mathematics are substantially more positive than girls' (Dossey et al., 1988; Fennema & Sherman, 1978) even though girls' attitudes are as positive as those of boys in elementary school (Dossey et al., 1988; Matthews, 1984). A similar trend occurs for science (Jones et al., 1992; Schreiber, 1984). Furthermore, males who report liking science demonstrate higher science proficiency than females who report liking science (Jones et al., 1992).

Interestingly, NAEP data on science preference show greater disparities between males and females age thirteen and older than among racial/ethnic categories, although all students show declining preference for both mathematics and science after Grade 4 (Jones et al., 1992; Dossey et al., 1988). James and Smith (1985) attempted to find out when alienation from science occurs, and they concluded that the greatest decline was between Grades 6 and 7. This held true for the whole population as well as for female and African-American students. African Americans started out well ahead in science subject preference, but by the later grades were at or below the population; females ranked at or below the total population and the African-American population across all grade levels. This study did not disaggregate data by race and gender.

Yong (1992) found no gender differences in attitude toward mathematics and science among gifted African-American middle school students—but did find significant gender differences in attitudes toward success in mathematics and perception of the subject as a male domain. Girls tended to anticipate positive consequences as a result of success in mathematics more than boys did. Further, girls were less likely than boys to perceive mathematics as a male domain.

A study of African-American students in Grades 5 and 11 concluded that few sex differences existed in mathematics attitudes, but that those differences favored males (Nelson, 1978). Fifth graders showed no sex differences in achievement, but eleventh-grade males had higher achievement scores than females. The study also found significant relationships between mathematics achievement and attitudes for fifth-grade males and eleventh-grade females. Creswell and Exezidis (1982) reported that African-American and Mexican-American adolescent women had more positive attitudes toward mathematics than did their male counterparts and that the attitudes of African Americans were more positive than those of Mexican Americans. Data from the 1992 NAEP mathematics assessment show few sex differences among nine-year-olds in liking for mathematics.

In a study of attitudes toward science, Rakow (1985) found that sex appeared to be a better predictor of the attitudes of nine-year-olds than ethnicity. Males of all the groups studied—whites, African Americans, and Latinos—had much more positive attitudes than did females, with Hispanic females having the least positive attitudes. For thirteen-year-olds, the pattern was repeated. This study was based on 1981–82 NAEP data. NAEP data from 1990 show that for nine-year-old white and African-American students, girls are less likely than boys to answer yes when asked, Do you like science? whereas Latina girls are more likely than boys to agree. For thirteen-year-olds, boys of all three groups are more likely to respond that they like science than are girls. The pattern reappears for seventeen-year-olds, but the percentages of white and African-American women liking science have declined, whereas those for white men and Latinos of both sexes have increased slightly.

Overall, students' liking of math and science declines from elementary to high school. Thirteen-year-olds show a sharp drop in preference for mathematics, and seventeen-year-olds show a further drop. Except for Latino nine-year-olds, boys of all groups like mathematics better than do girls. Latino and African-American students of both sexes surpass their white counterparts in mathematics preference. In science, the gap between boys and girls increases sharply after age thirteen, while preference for science, though declining, is fairly similar across racial/ethnic lines. For all three age levels, white boys show greater preference for science than white girls. However, African-American students show little gender difference for nine- and thirteen-year-olds; the gap increases sharply (favoring boys) at seventeen. Latina girls start out liking science more than boys at nine, but after thirteen, boys show a greater preference.

Stereotypes about mathematics and science are part of the middle school intellectual environment. Both girls and boys begin to view mathematics as masculine by Grade 6 or 7 (Erickson, 1987), but this view is more likely to be held by boys than by girls (Armstrong, 1981; Brush, 1980; Eccles (Parsons) et al., 1983; Fennema & Sherman, 1977, 1978; Fox, 1981; Kahle & Lakes, 1983; Kelly, 1978; Sherman, 1980). Students of all groups also absorb racial stereotypes of mathematics and science as white fields (Hall, 1981; Kenschaft, 1981). It seems, however, that like white girls and women, girls and women of color are less likely than their male counterparts to consider science and mathematics as male domains. MacCorquodale (1980) found that white and Mexican-American women in her study were less biased than their male counterparts and thought that science was just as appropriate for women as for men. Yong (1992) concluded that the gifted African-American middle school girls in her study were less likely to perceive mathematics as a male domain than their gifted male counterparts.

The importance and usefulness students ascribe to science and mathematics, and the self-confidence they feel in working with these subjects, affect their attitudes. As they progress in high school, girls see mathematics as diminishing in usefulness to women and increasing in usefulness to men (Boswell & Katz, 1980; Fennema & Sherman, 1978). African-American students of both sexes have misperceptions about science, have fewer scientific experiences, find science less useful out of school, are less aware of scientific methods and how scientists work, and are less confident of the ability of science to solve problems (Kahle, 1982). MacCorquodale (1980) found that whereas white and Mexican-American women and men shared positive attitudes toward science, white women and Mexican-American men perceived it as most important for an understanding of the world. Mexican-American women rated science as less important than did either white women or white and Mexican-American men.

A study of African-American eighth graders in an inner-city school found that although there were no sex differences in mathematics and science achievement, boys scored higher than girls on science self-concept. Further, boys were significantly more likely than girls to choose a science-related occupation over a non-science-related occupation (Jacobowitz, 1983). Rhone (1989), on the other hand, found mathematical self-concept to be a significant predictor of adolescent African-American girls' and boys' mathematics achievement and problem-solving ability. In a study of achievement, self-efficacy, anxiety, and attributions in mathematics among African-American junior high school students, Lewellyn (1990) found females outperforming males in mathematics achievement but found no gender differences for mathematics anxiety, self-efficacy, or attributions. (This study also noted that greater self-efficacy for both boys and girls was achieved in the eighth grade, suggesting a possible developmental trend. Ninth graders in the same study also used ability attributions more than seventh or eighth graders.) Hart and Stanic (1989) found sex differences in mathematics self-confidence reversed for white and African-American seventh graders. Among whites in this study, boys scored higher than girls on the Fennema & Sherman confidence scale, but among African Americans, girls scored higher than boys. Furthermore, African-American girls showed more confidence than any of the other three groups.

Although most research has associated positive attitude with increased participation and performance, this may not be true for people of color. Several studies have shown that African-American and Latino students have positive attitudes toward mathematics and science equalling or exceeding those of white students, but still have lower achievement levels in these subjects (Gross, 1988; James & Smith, 1985; Kahle, 1982; Matthews, 1984; Rakow, 1985; Walker & Rakow, 1985). The association does seem to apply to gender, however, as studies reveal that men have more positive attitudes and also achieve at higher levels (Kahle & Lakes, 1983; Mullis & Jenkins, 1988; Rakow, 1985; Schibeci, 1984; Schreiber, 1984; Simpson & Oliver, 1985; Walker & Rakow, 1985).

Marrett (1986) has suggested that for students of color the relationship between attitude, involvement, and achievement is complex and that, at least for African Americans, forces other than attitude shape participation in mathematics and science. The relationship may be even more complex for girls and women of color. The most recent NAEP assessments show that African-American and Latina girls and women differ from their white counterparts in preference for science (1992) and mathematics (1990). For all groups, males seem to surpass females in liking for mathematics. A larger percentage of African-American and Latino males and females responded that they liked mathematics than did their white counterparts of either sex. Science preference shows little gender difference among African Americans and Latinos; the difference between white males and females is much larger, favoring males. There is some evidence that African-American adolescent girls show more liking for science and greater mathematics self-confidence than do their white sisters or African-American and white males. A burning question is whether or not, for women and girls of each of the underrepresented groups, attitude toward mathematics and science is related to achievement. This is definitely an area where more research is needed.

Attitudes that influence course taking in high school are present at middle grades. Some girls are already avoiding science electives, and some African-American and Latino students say science is optional without recognizing the effect of this belief on their educational and occupational choices (MacCorquodale, 1980). Nevertheless, MacCorquodale found no significant sex or ethnic differences in attitudes toward science courses among Mexican-American and white eighth graders. In attempting to identify the determinants of middle school students' intentions to enroll in a high school science course, Crawley and Coe (1990) found that the relative contributions of attitudes and social pressures to the prediction of intention vary according to students' gender, race/ethnicity, general ability, and science ability, but the authors provide no data on race and gender interactions. They found that the major determinant of males' attitudes toward enrolling in science is the perceived difficulty of science vis-à-vis other elective subjects, whereas for females, the major determinant is interest in learning new information. Minority students value the opportunity to do "fun" experiments, and this is the major determinant for them.

Learning Styles

Researchers have begun to address female and male *learning styles,* that is, basic differences in the way people process knowledge (Belenky, Clinchy, Goldberger, & Tarule, 1986; Gilligan, 1982). Parallel research on people of color is grouped around various racial and ethnic groups, with most studies looking at African-American learning styles. Some studies have suggested that African-American culture is more affective and cognitively united than the prevailing European tradition of universal facts and knowledge (Hale-Benson, 1984; U.S. Congress, 1988). Ramirez and Castaneda (1974) examined the ways Mexican-American children's learning styles differed from those of white children by applying the psychological concepts of field dependence and field independence. There is, however, no research on the learning styles of girls of color and the ways in which sex and race or ethnicity interact to influence learning.

Research on learner characteristics and their relationship to mathematics and science focuses on locus of control/learned helplessness, cognitive skills, cognitive abilities, persistence and independence, language background, and spatial visualization skills. These factors have all been cited as influencing differential achievement in mathematics and science for women and people of color. For a review of research on these topics, see Clewell and Anderson, 1991.

Environmental Variables

Variables such as schools, teachers, parents, peers, and society as a whole also affect students' learning experiences.

School-Related Factors

Teacher expectations and encouragement may affect student attitudes and achievement. Chapter Three discusses extensive research showing that teachers treat girls and boys differently throughout K–12 education and interact more with and have higher expectations of boys.

Matthews (1984) found that teachers may have strong positive effects on mathematics attitudes of students of color. Students of color indicated that they were encouraged and assisted by teachers who worked with them, gave them extra help, explained things carefully, and provided encouragement (Matthews, 1981; Treisman, 1982). Teachers' expectations of achievement potential were lower for students of color (Olstad, Juarez, Davenport, & Haury, 1981). Gross (1988) found that high-achieving African-American students must prove themselves to the teacher each time they enter a new math class. And Beane (1985) suggested that teachers tend to see students of color as low achievers and white students as high achievers even when performance is the same. Hall, Howe, Merkel, and Lederman (1986) support this finding, reporting that teachers in desegregated junior high school science classes rated the ability of whites higher than that of African Americans with similar achievement scores. In the same study, teachers also expressed the belief that African-American girls made the most effort and their male counterparts the least effort. Irvine (1985) found that a girl's race affected the amount of feedback she received from the teacher, with white girls receiving the least classroom feedback of any type, although girls overall received less feedback than boys.

Students of color developed the best mathematics attitudes and performance on reasoning tasks when teachers showed positive attitudes toward students, felt comfortable with the mathematics curriculum, and interacted positively with students during mathematics instruction (Pulos, Stage, & Karplus, 1982). Schools that raised African-American students' mathematics achievement on normative and criterion-referenced tests all offered a safe and orderly environment, a clear school mission, high expectations for students, time on task, and frequent monitoring of student progress (Engman, 1986).

Balanced and comprehensive illustrations in science and mathematics texts may help girls of color to develop positive attitudes toward these subjects and to see themselves as science professionals. Studies in the 1970s and early 1980s revealed that textbooks contained a stereotyped view of women and minorities and perpetuated the common view of mathematics and science as white male domains. More recent studies have found that contemporary texts are much less sexist and racist than those of two decades ago (García, Harrison, & Torres, 1990), although representation of women and people of color in careers requiring knowledge of advanced mathematics is less than adequate. Powell and García (1985) found that recent elementary textbooks do show students of color performing science activities, but that the majority of adults shown in science-related occupations are white. There is no research on the effect of textbooks on the mathematics and science attitudes of girls of color.

Instructional techniques and strategies may have differing success with various groups of students. Erickson, Gall, Gersten, and Grace (1987) looked at whether instruction differentially affected the achievement of boys and girls in basic algebra. They found that boys' achievement was most affected by classroom management and teacher presentation, whereas girls showed lower achievement with increased quizzing, more guided practice, and higher-level cognitive questions. This finding suggests that girls may have greater difficulty performing under stress. Cooperative learning situations in this class enhanced girls' achievement. A very different pattern emerged in an intermediate algebra class, however, where active questioning, guided practice, and assistance resulted in greater gains for girls than for boys.

Mathematics is customarily taught in a manner inappropriate to the needs of many people of color, as shown by research on American Indians (Green, Brown, & Long, 1978), Latinos (Valverde, 1984), and African Americans (Beane, 1985). Among others, Lockheed and Gorman (1987) have suggested adjusting teaching strategies and curricula to the cultural milieu of students in a class. Cohen, Intili, and DeAvila (1982) studied the relationship of social status and cooperative interaction to learning in a hands-on experimental program for bilingual elementary classes. This study showed a clear relationship between status (social rankings in which it is usually believed that it is better to be in the high than in the low state) and peer interaction, with higher-status children interacting more. A higher degree of task-related peer interaction, in turn, led to higher achievement. There is also some evidence favoring inquiry learning over traditional approaches for middle school students generally and for girls in particular (see Clewell, Anderson, & Thorpe, 1992, for a review of these studies). While few studies have examined the relationship of instructional approach to the achievement of students of color, there is evidence that middle school African-American and Latino students experience positive effects from hands-on inquiry activities (Cohen & DeAvila, 1983). This study also reported higher achievement for a bilingual, mostly Hispanic group of students in a cooperative inquiry program, compared to control classes with a competitive structure.

Activity-based classroom science programs have been cited as successful with students of color. Reynolds (1991) studied the effects of an experiment-based physical science program on the content knowledge and process skills of African-American, Latino, and white urban fourth to eighth graders. Results showed significant impact on process skills but not on content skills. Further, white and Latino students benefited from the program, whereas African-American students did not. Girls did better than boys, net of other factors (such as race or grade level).

A partial explanation for the low performance of students of color in mathematics has been underrepresentation in high school mathematics courses, which results from the cumulative effects of years of education. By the time critical decisions are being made regarding high school class placement, as many as one-third to one-half of African-American and Latino students have fallen so far behind as to be ineligible to take higher-level mathematics courses in the future (Gross, 1988).

There are very few studies on the influences of peers on girls' attitude toward mathematics and science, and we found none on such peer influences among students of color, let alone girls of color. Talton and Simpson (1985) found that children's views become more and more homogeneous, with similarity reaching a peak at the ninth grade. Girls have a strong conflict between liking science and desiring popularity, especially with boys (Schreiber, 1984), which may explain why girls in single-sex schools express more positive attitudes toward science than those in mixed schools (Kelly, 1981). Kelly and Smail (1986) found that boys often show stronger sex-role stereotypes than girls, which tends to support this finding.

Home and Societal Factors

Parents' expectations regarding children's success in certain subjects are a potent influence on performance and attitudes in those subjects. Parsons, Adler, and Kaczala (1982) found that parents' perceptions of their children's math aptitudes favored sons over daughters despite the similarity of boys' and girls' actual performance. (Andrews reported similar findings in 1989.) Additionally, these sex-stereotyped parental beliefs were critical to the children's own achievement self-concepts. Rhone (1989) found that parental expectation was a strong predictor of African-American seventh and eighth graders' mathematics achievement and problem-solving ability.

Kahle (1983) and Schreiber (1984) reported that parents of middle school girls had low expectations of their performance in science. This did not hold true for African Americans, however, who were the most supportive of the four groups—Latino, Asian American, African American, and white—studied by Andrews (1989). Asian-American and Latino parents in this study were more likely to see mathematics as a male domain than either African-American or white parents. A more recent study found parental influences on African-American girls to be more similar to such influences on white boys than other groups (Maple & Stage, 1991).

Family background and parental influence affect both attitude and achievement of mathematics students (Tsai & Walberg, 1983). As MacCorquodale (1988) noted, Mexican-American parents were more supportive of children than were white parents but lacked the experience and information necessary to assist in children's education. NAEP data suggest a correlation between home support for and involvement in students' learning, parental education level, and proficiency in various science subject areas (Dossey et al., 1988; Mullis & Jenkins, 1988). This relationship was tested by items on the mathematics and science assessments that collected data on parental education, home assistance with homework and projects, participation in science-related projects, number and kinds of reading material in the home, and television viewing habits. Mullis and Jenkins interpret NAEP results as suggesting that African-American and Latino students from lower-SES homes are disadvantaged by differences in parental education levels and access to reading materials in the home.

The exposure of students to role models in science has been linked to a corresponding improvement in attitudes. Because few scientists are women of color, girls of color see much less of role models than other students. Smith and Erb (1986) demonstrated a connection between increasing exposure to female role models—by having women scientists visit classrooms to talk about their careers or by giving students information about women who have made important contributions to science, for example—and changes in early adolescents' attitudes toward women scientists.

The study found that both boys' and girls' attitudes toward women scientists improved after exposure to the role models. Although this study did not disaggregate data by race, some researchers have suggested that the lack of diverse role models in science may lead students of color to view science as a white male domain (Beane, 1985; Malcom, 1990; Marrett, 1986).

High School (Grades 9–12)

This section discusses mathematics and science achievement of women of color in high school, including their course-taking patterns, intended undergraduate majors, and career plans.

Achievement and Performance in Mathematics and Science

On the 1992 NAEP mathematics assessment, African-American and Latina girls continue to show lower proficiency and achievement levels than white girls at Grade 12. African-American and white girls lag even further behind their male counterparts than in middle school. For Latino students, however, just the opposite is the case: Latina girls outperform boys, and their gender gap has also increased from that of middle school (Mullis et al., 1993).

The NAEP 1990 science assessment lists African-American and Latina girls at all grade levels with lower average proficiency than their white counterparts. In each racial/ethnic category, males outperform females, with the differences widening sharply at Grade 12 (Jones et al., 1992). Using data from the 1990 NAEP science assessment, Bruschi and Anderson (1994) found that by age seventeen, males consistently outperformed females in all racial/ethnic groups in all content areas except natural sciences. (White males outperformed white females in this area as well.)

School-Related Factors Affecting Achievement and Performance

Teachers are an important influence on students of color. In a study of role-model effects in high school, Evans (1992) did not find evidence of a gender-based effect. He did find, however, that African-American teachers induced a nearly 19 percent increase in the achievement of African-American students whose mothers lacked a college education; the effect appeared to be equally strong with male or female students or teachers.

Research shows that students of color have less exposure to mathematics and science activities and experiences in high school than whites, and there is some evidence of gender differences favoring males in exposure to these activities. Rakow and Walker (1985) found that seventeen-year-old white students reported more science participation than did African-American or Latino students. Of this group, Latina women reported the least science experience.

There is also some evidence that girls of color have less access to computers than their male counterparts. Grignon (1993) reported significant gender differences in the application of software and course taking among eighth and twelfth grade Menominee Indian students. In Grade 12, the differences occurred in the use of software; girls spent less time using games and graphics than did boys in the same grade. Girls also were enrolled at a significantly lesser rate in classes offering sophisticated graphics programs. Also, more boys than girls enrolled in computer science classes.

Two studies on at-risk girls of color reveal interesting findings. One was designed to determine the effectiveness of supplementary computer-assisted algebra materials on achievement levels and attitudes of urban minority students who had failed a semester of basic algebra (Mickens, 1991). This study found that students receiving computer-assisted instruction (CAI) had greater academic achievement than students in the control group and that the achievement level was greater for female students than for male students. Furthermore, students of both sexes in the experimental group indicated that they perceived their teachers to have a high expectation for their success. In another study of a remedial mathematics course for at-risk high school students using CAI and computer-adaptive testing (CAT), Signer (1991) found that African-American female students exhibited greater self-confidence toward computer use than was found in other studies that examined gender.

Course Enrollment and Participation

Course enrollment also has an effect; students who have taken advanced mathematics and science courses tend to have higher achievement levels. Traditionally, females and students of color enroll in fewer optional or advanced courses in mathematics than white male students (Fennema, 1984; Marrett, 1981). Vanfossen (1984) investigated the gender gap between the sophomore and senior years and concluded that women took fewer mathematics courses than men and that differential performance was due to gender differences in enrollment in advanced mathematics courses. This echoes the general underrepresentation of students of color in high school mathematics courses (Gross, 1988). Davis (1986, 1989) found that regardless of race/ethnicity, higher levels of mathematics achievement correlated with enrollment in advanced mathematics courses. Anick, Carpenter, and Smith (1981) found that African-American students averaged about one year less high school mathematics than was the norm for all students. Sells (1980) studied high school course patterns and found that African-American women were the least prepared of all students in mathematics, while white men were the most prepared. A later study, however, found that African-American women took more advanced mathematics courses in high school than did African-American men (Matthews, 1984).

NAEP data from the 1982 mathematics assessment also revealed that course experiences varied not only between African-American and white students but also from school to school. African-American students in racially segregated schools took more mathematics courses than those in integrated schools, but achievement in segregated schools was lower (Davis, 1986, 1989).

Lee and Ware (1986) set out to identify the point at which high school students, especially girls, were most likely to leave the college prep mathematics sequence, and to find predictors of persistence. They found that girls tended to drop out of the less advanced courses in the college prep mathematics sequence at a greater rate than boys, but the proportion of girls making the transition to advanced levels was slightly higher than that of boys. The early leakage, however, diminished the pool of female advanced mathematics students. The study also found a direct positive relationship—stronger for boys than girls—between social class and persistence in mathematics. When SES was held constant, African-American females were more likely to persist in mathematics even though, in general, the proportion of minority students decreases with each increasingly advanced course.

African-American students enroll in fewer than three years of high school science and tend to avoid advanced science courses, and those who are college bound are much more likely than their white peers to report no courses in the biological or physical science areas (Anderson, 1989). In fact, Anderson and Pearson (1988) found that more than half of high-ability African-American students who eventually left science had not completed an advanced mathematics or science course in high school.

Rakow and Walker (1985) suggest that the underrepresentation of Latino students in advanced high school science courses may be due to their absence from college prep programs. Data from the 1990 NAEP science assessment show a direct relationship between high school science course taking and average proficiency, with more course work in each content area being related to higher proficiency in that area and to higher overall proficiency (Jones et al., 1992). Data from this assessment show that more males than females had taken a year or more of physics, and more white and Asian-American/Pacific Islander students had taken one year or more of this subject than had their African-American, Latino, and American Indian counterparts (Jones et al.).

There is some evidence that the gender gap in course taking has begun to narrow, though differences favoring boys persist for the more advanced courses. Data from the 1993 SAT Student Descriptive Questionnaire (SDQ) show few gender differences in years of study of mathematics and natural sciences for African-American, American Indian, Latin American, Mexican-American, and Puerto Rican students. What differences there were occurred for the last three racial/ethnic groups. In terms of course-taking patterns, a larger proportion of females consistently studied biology, chemistry, and space/earth science/geology. For physics, more males took courses than females, except among African Americans, where 56 percent of the course takers were female, and Latin Americans and Puerto Ricans, where there was an even split between males and females. Females surpassed males in all groups in science honors course participation.

For mathematics, the pattern is similar: females of almost all underrepresented groups surpass males in algebra, geometry, trigonometry, and precalculus. Among American Indians, slightly more males than females take trigonometry and precalculus. For calculus, American Indian, Latino, and Mexican-American males surpass their female counterparts in course taking. Puerto Ricans are evenly split, and African-American females surpass males 58 percent to 42 percent. With the exception of American Indians, females once again outnumber males in the taking of honors courses. For African Americans, the difference in favor of females is very large (63 percent versus 37 percent).

Comparison of 1988 and 1993 SDQ data confirmed that females of all underrepresented groups are taking more courses at all levels of mathematics and science. In 1988, the crucial filter in mathematics was precalculus; that is, more males than females in all groups except African Americans took precalculus. By 1993, females formed the majority of precalculus students among African Americans, Latin Americans, Mexican Americans, and Puerto Ricans. The critical filter is now calculus. The gap also narrowed in physics for all groups between 1988 and 1993.

Career Interests and Aspirations

Relatively few women of color are mathematical scientists, but among women of color, African Americans are most likely to have earned a bachelor's degree in mathematics (National Science Foundation [NSF], 1994). Studies report that African-American interest in scientific careers is lower among women than among men of similar achievement levels (Jacobowitz, 1983), and African-American men and white women have a greater level of participation in hard science careers than African-American women (NSF, 1994).

In 1993, female SAT takers of all underrepresented groups surpassed male SAT takers of those groups in plans to major in the biological sciences. Here again, the difference for African Americans was very large—63 percent versus 37 percent. For engineering, just the opposite was true for every group, with a much larger proportion of males than females among prospective majors. This was also true for physics, but the differences were not as large. For mathematics, American Indian, Latin American, and Mexican-American males outnumbered females, but female African-American and Puerto Rican students outnumbered males.

A number of studies have investigated influences on women's choices of majors and careers in scientific fields (Berryman, 1983;

Ethington & Wolfle, 1988; Ware & Lee, 1988). Many girls forfeit the opportunity to pursue a mathematics career because by the time they enter junior high they have not developed adequate interest in mathematics and thus fail to enroll in the courses required for quantitative majors in college (Berryman, 1983). A study of factors affecting the attitudes of African-American and female middle school students toward science and science-related careers found that across both races and both sexes, the major factor affecting science-related career decisions appeared to be personal contact with a scientist (Hill, Pettus, & Hedin, 1990). The study also found that African-American females scored higher than white females on a self-image subscale. On a relevance-of-science subscale, African-American males who knew a scientist outscored their female counterparts, while the opposite was true for white students; on this subscale, African-American females who did not know scientists outscored their male counterparts, while the opposite was true for white students. These findings suggest differences between African-American and white females regarding traditional gender roles, with the African Americans being less influenced by tradition. The study concluded that sex differences in the pursuit of science careers are primarily based on interest in these careers established by the time children reach middle school.

Ethington and Wolfle (1988) found that the number of math and science courses taken in high school was the most important factor in determining women's choice of a quantitative major. Maple and Stage (1991) echoed this finding, concluding that number of math and science courses completed through the senior year of high school was one of three variables with significant direct effects on African-American females' choice of major field. (The other two were sophomore choice of major and math attitudes.) Steinkamp and Maehr (1984) found females' orientation toward these fields to be higher than males' in disadvantaged communities, but lower in upper-middle-class communities. Dunteman, Wisenbaker, and Taylor (1979) found that for African Americans, higher family SES increased the likelihood of selecting a science major; indeed, after background measures were controlled, African Americans revealed a higher probability of majoring in science than did whites. Berryman (1983) reported ethnic/socioeconomic interactive effects on the selection of a quantitative major. Ethington and

Wolfle (1988) did not find interactive effects for race and SES but did find that both variables had significant effects. Their study revealed that for African-American and white women with equal measures on other variables, African-American women were more likely to select a quantitative field, supporting other research that found that sex rather than race is a major factor in the underrepresentation of minority women in the sciences.

Krist (1993), in one of the few studies to examine the motivation of high-ability African-American women making educational and career choices in mathematics and science, tested the utility of the academic choice model of achievement developed by Eccles-Parsons and her colleagues (1983; see also Meece, Parsons, Kaczala, Goff, & Futterman, 1982). The study supported the model, which is based on expectancy-value theory, and confirmed that achievement behavior for this population also involved choices made by the individual, influenced by cultural norms and socialization experiences. The study also found that gifted African-American women had higher self-esteem and confidence than their white counterparts and that they expected to succeed in traditionally male-dominant fields. Other findings included early interest in mathematics and science, with middle school a critical period for the decision. Extended families, particularly mothers and grandmothers, encouraged and helped the women in the study; friends, mentors, and the community affected their aspirations and expectations more strongly than did their school experiences; and they were affected more often by racial stereotyping than sex-role stereotyping.

Undergraduate College Experience

The 1989 fall survey of entering freshmen conducted by the Cooperative Institutional Research Program (CIRP) shows that the number planning careers as engineers and scientific researchers is very small (Astin, 1990). (Only 8.3 percent of blacks and 8.9 percent of whites chose engineering, and 0.8 percent of blacks and 1.7 percent of whites chose research.) The situation is equally dismal at historically black colleges, where only two retain any significant SME education enrollment (Clark, 1985).

In spite of increased enrollment rates, minority students are less likely to graduate than white students. When data on degree completion by ethnic minority group members is disaggregated by gender, some interesting patterns appear. During the four years expected to complete a bachelor's degree, Asian-American, Hispanic, and American Indian women leave in higher proportions than same-ethnicity men. While more African-American men than women leave (over 50 percent versus 40 percent), when considering the data on women alone, black women have the highest attrition rate at about 40 percent (NSF, 1994).

Data originally generated by Chipman and Thomas in 1984 (cited in Garrison, 1987) show that in all natural sciences, Latino, Asian-American, and white males earn more degrees than females, while among African Americans that is true only in engineering and physical sciences (Durán, 1987). More recent data (NSF, 1994) confirm earlier results (Durán, 1987) that among ethnic minorities, only black women earn more degrees overall than men. When these data are viewed as a percentage change in degrees earned and disaggregated by race, Asian-American, American Indian, and Hispanic women all show a greater percentage change in degrees earned across all science fields when compared to men of those groups. Black women exhibit a positive percentage change in all fields except social sciences. However, for some time now, the number of SME baccalaureate degrees earned by males has been decreasing, thus making the small increase in degrees awarded to women appear larger than it is.

Individual Factors

The structure of college education is very different from that in most high schools, so as college students advance in their education, their attitudes grow increasingly different from those of high school seniors. The pursuit of a major in college combined with increasing maturity will solidify students' vocational interests and aptitudes into achieved skills and career decisions. While high school academic preparation influences college success, its effects can be mediated by a number of factors, including gender and ethnic group as well as motivation and use of learning strategies.

Achievement

Among 1987 first-year college students, high school grade point average (GPA)—the prevailing measure of performance in U.S.

education—was highest among students planning SME majors, regardless of gender (NSF, 1990). First-year ethnic minority college students are often underprepared and overconfident (Seymour & Hewitt, 1994). No doubt many first-year students share this problem—high dropout rates plague all groups of freshmen. However, larger proportions of minority students tend to withdraw (National Research Council, 1994). Looking back on their first year in college, even successful seniors recalled how hard it had been to go from the top of their high school class to the bottom of their college class (Hewitt & Seymour, 1991). The most consistent finding for ethnic students in the sciences (other than Asian Americans) was that they had higher GPAs than nonscience ethnic students but lower than white students (Nettles, 1987). Asian Americans reported higher first-year GPAs in college than whites or Latino/as, who had very similar self-reported GPAs (NSF, 1990). While self-reporting is not an entirely accurate measure of actual GPA, this finding is interesting because a higher self-report reflects not only actual GPA but also student self-concept.

In a study of an organic chemistry course, García, Yu, and Coppola (1993) reported that motivation was correlated with achievement for Asian-American, African-American, and Latino/a students and that all ethnic students had higher levels of extrinsic motivation than white students.

Self-confidence/Self-concept

In a study of Asian-American and white Westinghouse Talent Search winners, Campbell (1991) reported that the first three variables to emerge from a stepwise discriminant analysis were mathematics self-concept, science self-concept, and general self-concept. Men had higher levels on all three than women, and Asian-American women had higher levels than white women in mathematics self-concept. Asian-American men were likeliest to choose a technical major, followed by white men and Asian-American women almost equally, with white women having the lowest likelihood of pursuing a technical career.

Black freshmen's academic self-concept, as measured by the CIRP survey since 1971, is lower than that of whites (Astin, 1990), and they acknowledged a greater need for remediation than did their white classmates. They also expected to do as well in their classes as whites did. But other aspects of freshman self-concept, such as social self-confidence, drive to achieve, and popularity, are higher in black students than in white students. This drive to achieve may explain the finding that a higher proportion of black GRE takers from 1979 to 1983 aspired to the Ph.D. than did whites. Higher aspirations also characterized Mexican-American test takers, especially women (Astin, 1990; Brown, 1995). However, aspirations did not translate into graduation patterns, even for the most able students (Brown, 1995).

Home and Cultural Factors

Most cultural influences on college performance are hard to assess with quantitative measures. A study of Asian-American students showed that regression equations derived for white students, which used language as a variable to predict freshman academic success, underpredicted scores of Chinese and other Asian-American students who said English was not their best language, but overpredicted scores of Filipinos, Japanese, and other Asian-Americans who said English was their best language (Stanley & Abe, 1988). In addition, other factors may mediate the effects of language on performance. For example, bilingual skills in Spanish and English had positive effects on mathematics and verbal SAT scores among Latino/as, but only if accompanied by high SES (Durán, 1987).

Culture and family structure affect the choices college students make and the opportunities open to them. In some instances, parents, peers, and other social groupings apply direct pressure. Other influences show up in student choices, such as the reasons stated for choosing a major. And still other cultural and familial influences are evident as prejudices and expectations held by parents, classmates, and teachers.

Parental Influence

Parental influence occurs directly through personal encouragement, as well as indirectly through parental levels of education, SES (Astin, 1982; Hill et al., 1990), and occupation. Parents are often cited as very important influences on decisions about attending or staying in college and choosing a major.

The NSF report *Women and Minorities in Science and Engineering* (1990) notes that about equal numbers of males and females report having parents with a bachelor's degree or higher. When disaggregated by ethnicity, however, striking differences occur, with whites having the largest number of college-educated parents and Latino/as the smallest. This report did not list educational attainment of American Indian parents of college students, but Garrison (1987) cites an American Council on Education report that indicates higher degree completion rates for American Indians than for African Americans or Latino/as.

Campbell (1991) reported that parents' educational level emerged as a variable in his study of outstanding Asian-American and white students. The fathers of Asian Americans had higher levels of education than fathers of whites, and the mothers of Asian-American male students had lower levels of education than mothers of white males but levels similar to those of mothers of white females. Thus, while the mother's education had a moderate loading on the discriminant function, this result could be due to a ceiling effect on the father's education—all the fathers were reasonably well educated. Rayman and Brett (1993) reported that the Asian-American pre-med and life sciences majors in their Wellesley College sample were more likely than white students to have fathers who were medical doctors. It should be noted that these studies have samples so highly selective that they are not easily generalizable to the population as a whole. It is entirely possible that a confound of SES and/or generation may be operating in them.

In a study of first-year students enrolled in introductory chemistry and in single-sex or coeducational science enrichment programs, ethnic women (almost all Asian Americans) reported that mothers were a significant influence in their decision to pursue a science major, even though the women most committed to science were the ones to report the lowest level of maternal influence (Wiegand, Ginorio, & Brown, 1994). These young women reported that their mothers gave them emotional support, but not necessarily support specific to the careers that they were pursuing. While other research (Hewitt & Seymour, 1992) indicated that parents had significant impact on Asian-American students' choice of majors, it is possible that the influence of mothers of Asian women on their daughters' choice of and or success in science may be mediated by factors such as educational level of the fathers and/or the related SES of the family.

Among Chicano/as (Chacón, Cohen, Camarena, González, & Stover, 1983), parents encouraged both females and males to pursue higher education, but males were more likely to report very high support, which was more likely to be from mothers rather than fathers. On the other hand, in his pathbreaking study of the patterns of success of minorities in science and engineering, Rodríguez (1993) found that for Latino and African-American males, family encouragement was the most important personal variable, a situation that among females was true only for American Indian nonpersisters. He also reported that if a Latina reported *explicit* discouragement from science or engineering from a parent, it was usually from the father.

Latino/a and white students indicated that having relatives and friends in technical fields influenced their own decision to pursue similar studies (Mestre & Robinson, 1983). However, this influence was more prevalent among white students, who were more likely than Latino/a students to have parents in technical fields. Even though Latino/as said that family encouragement was very important in their persistence in science and engineering, only 13 percent of the ethnic minority students in the qualitative section of Rodríguez's (1993) study mentioned their parents as role models for the pursuit of science or engineering. This finding is reasonable, given that most of the latter group were first-generation college students.

On the other hand, fathers' support seems to be important for African-American women, especially for those choosing careers in science (Cobb, 1989; Holden, 1992). There are a number of reports by ethnic professionals in science fields acknowledging their parents' encouragement—and at times, demands—as vital to their success (Cobb; Sands, 1993; Sims, 1992a). These studies show that parental influence is mediated by other familial factors.

Cultural Influences

Students bring cultural values with them into college, where they find that both college and science have cultures of their own. Successful students adapt to these new cultures, a process made easier if what they bring is similar to what they find. The culture of science is intimately bound to the character traits Western society associates with scientists, which are for the most part those associated with white males—desire for personal power, prestige, and authority; competition for possessions, resources, and personnel; absolute confidence in self and in the knowledge to be produced (Namenwirth, 1988).

Seymour and Hewitt (1994) interviewed 88 ethnic minority students and 335 white students on seven campuses and explored the cultural values students brought with them into college. The ethnic minority students' sense of obligation to serve their community and family turned out to vary from that of the white students both in intensity and in extent of what community and family encompassed. Many students found their values in conflict with the culture of the science major. The demands of the major made it difficult for those students who saw community and family obligations as part of their student role to juggle all their responsibilities; this was especially true of inner-city blacks, Latinos, and reservation American Indians who felt the pull of family very strongly.

The commitment to that same community served as an incentive for a number of students to stay with SME. In the words of a black female science major: "Take the Black community for example. There are few presentations of academic excellence. So, we feel we are supposed to do well and if we don't do well, it's kind of devastating. 'Cause it's not just yourself you're representing, it's the whole community" (Seymour & Hewitt, 1994, p. 451). Faced with the conflicting values of community and science, some students draw strength from the conflict to persist; others, unwilling to further compromise their own family and community values in favor of those prevailing in the culture of the scientific community, switch out of science.

Tobias (1990) speaks of students who leave science as rejecting "the culture of competition" in favor of "the culture of competence" (p. 74) because they prefer majors in which they feel intrinsically motivated rather than driven by the next test or getting into graduate or medical school. Both of Tobias's cultures are individualistic. Ethnic minority students who feel uncomfortable with the culture of competition may find a culture of competence only in the context of a "culture of meaningful community."

School-Related Factors

Students who reach college still need the kind of experiences and support that facilitated their success up to that point—and the attrition rate makes it clear that many students have lost that support. Affirming and positive experiences are important to the success of all students, and they are especially important for individuals who differ from their college norm. Thus historically black colleges and universities and single-sex colleges offer more opportunities to maintain a supportive climate for their students.

According to Seymour and Hewitt (1994), ethnic minority students encounter four areas of difficulty that white students do not face:

- Ethnic cultural values and socialization
- Internalization of stereotypes
- Ethnic isolation and perceptions of racism
- Inadequate minority program support

These issues are similar to those confronted by women in nontraditional majors, as becomes evident when the list is changed to read as follows:

- Feminine gender role and socialization
- Internalization of stereotypes
- Sense of isolation and perceptions of sexism
- Inadequate program support for women

The first three list items result from the clash between campus and student cultures where students of color or women are in the minority. Thus, it is necessary to deal with the stereotypes held by the majority culture in order to understand the experiences of nonmajority students. And for women of color, the burden is double. As Hammonds puts it: "I'm always Black and female. I can't say 'well, that was just a sexist remark' without wondering would he have made the same sexist remark to a white woman" (Sands, 1993, p. 248). Lesbians and disabled women could say the same thing.

Kind of College Attended

In their review of the characteristics of institutions that affect career choice and development, Pascarella and Terenzini (1991) reported that, when controlling for all other factors, attending a predominantly black college had a significant effect on black women's occupational status. They explained this by citing Thomas (1984), who found that black women were much more likely to major in biological, natural, or technical sciences at black colleges. Pascarella and Terenzini interpret this finding to mean that black colleges may encourage women to enroll in high-status majors, including SME majors.

However, other sources indicate that coeducational black colleges may be less encouraging than women-only black colleges (Sands, 1993). Students in historically black colleges do show more evidence of academic and intellectual development. However, Fleming reported that black women students in black schools were less assertive than black women in white schools even though they were better off intellectually (Bradley, 1990).

The experiences that promote success may be difficult to attain in the institutions that educate the majority of U.S. college graduates. Some large coeducational institutions provide small, single-sex class experiences organized around ethnicity or gender. We know of only one study that shows the usefulness of such a program, especially for ethnic women (Wiegand, Ginorio, & Brown, 1994). Women participating in the program took introductory chemistry in a large mixed lecture, but had single-sex laboratory sessions with female teaching and research assistants. Sixty-nine percent of the women in the single-sex program intended to continue in science at the end of the year. By comparison, only 50 percent of the women in a coeducational enrichment program in the same chemistry course and 47 percent of those in a control group planned to stay in science. Among ethnic women, the persistence rates were 87 percent of the single-sex, 57 percent of the coeducational enrichment, and 54 percent of the control; corresponding figures for white women were 45 percent, 42 percent, and 41 percent.

Little is known about ethnic women students at community colleges. Astin (cited in Garrison, 1987) and Vélez (1985) note that students who start their education at two-year institutions are less likely to graduate than students at four-year institutions. In their five-college study of Chicano higher education in California, Chacón et al. (1983) reported that those Chicano/as attending community colleges were more likely than Chicano/as attending four-year colleges and universities to experience academic difficulties and to be making slow progress. In spite of this, community colleges play a very important role in Chicano education; more than half of the Chicano/as who enroll in college do so at the community college level (Thomas, 1986). Chicanas choose community college for the same financial reasons as other students, and also because it may offer the best option to satisfy expectations for family involvement (Meléndez & Petrovich, 1989).

Financial Aid

Three of the seven major findings of Porter's study (1989) of persistence using the *High School and Beyond* data concern SES and financial needs. He reported that while SES and academic ability influence persistence, financial aid does too: 90 percent of students receiving grants in the first year were still enrolled in the second semester compared to 75 percent of those who did not receive grants, regardless of ethnicity.

Astin's (1990) analysis of data for black freshmen showed how the changing patterns of financial aid have affected blacks. A higher proportion of black freshmen than white freshmen receive financial aid. Blacks also receive more types and larger amounts of aid. Lane (1990) shows that fully a third of the minority students relied on grants and scholarships, compared to a quarter of the white students, and that financing is more of a problem for women than for men. In 1987, 16 percent of women freshmen intending to major in science and engineering indicated that financing their education was of major concern, as opposed to 11 percent of the men. Ethnic minority students' heavier dependence on financial aid means that any changes in aid policies, especially at the federal level, will have a greater effect on them than on other students. Thus, the shift to loans for undergraduate financial aid makes it more difficult and risky for these students to consider graduate school, if this means further debt. Not surprisingly, students who could go to school full time without holding down a job were more likely to succeed (Chacón et al., 1983).

Teacher Behavior and Courses

Teachers who encourage students promote success (Cobb, 1989; Massey, 1992; Sands, 1993), but negative experiences with advisers or teachers can be very discouraging for students (Rodríguez, 1993; Sands, 1993; Seymour & Hewitt, 1994). In a survey of disabled scientists, many recalled being denied participation in laboratory activities by their teachers as one of the important barriers to their progress in scientific training (Lucky, 1989). In 1994, the Carolinas and Ohio Science Education Network reported that African-American women ascribed greater importance than white women to the race and gender of the faculty (5.10 vs. 3.64 on a scale of 7, where 7 is "very important") (cited in Association of American Colleges and Universities, 1994).

The "chilly climate" series of the Association of American Colleges and Universities gives many examples of ways teachers can create a welcoming climate for women in the classroom and also in the lab and field and other learning environments. Two series publications focus on the impact of teacher behavior on ethnic minority women: *Black Women in Academe: Issues and Strategies* (Moses, 1989), and *Hispanic Women: Making Their Presence on Campus Less Tenuous* (Nieves-Squires, 1991), and two focus on women in science or medicine: *Warming the Climate for Women in Academic Science* (Ginorio, 1995) and *Improving the Climate for Women in Medical Schools and Teaching Hospitals* (Ehrhart & Sandler, 1990). Collins and Matyas (1985) also address minority issues and teacher behavior. Seymour (1992) found that 30 percent of students who switched out of science majors reported that poor teaching had contributed directly to their decision. However, she also found that many students interpreted teaching quality more in terms of personal attributes and pedagogical style than transmission of content. Women were more critical of the teaching than were men and placed more emphasis on the affective aspects of education. Poor teaching is a less important reason for leaving SME for ethnic minority switchers (21 percent, ranked ninth) than for white switchers (42 percent, ranked second) (Seymour & Hewitt, 1994). See Rosser (1990, and Chapter Seven in this volume) and Tobias (1990) for extensive treatments of pedagogy.

Peer Influences

Interactions with peers can provide a sense of integration in the campus or department as well as access to valuable information and support. Treisman (1992) found that white and Asian-American students study in groups, but black students study alone. Faculty advisers working with blacks have also noted this and advised the students to form study groups of their own (Sims, 1992b). Believing that the difference in grades between the groups was partly attributable to their ways of studying, Treisman designed programs to address this isolation without stigmatizing the students involved. It should be noted that blacks are rare in SME majors, making it difficult to form study groups composed of blacks only, and that black students are not usually invited into study groups of other racial/ethnic backgrounds (Pearson, personal communication, 1994).

Students with strong peer relationships are more likely to have high GPAs (Nettles, Thoeny, & Gosman, 1986). Chicano/a students who met with at least two other peers on a weekly basis were more likely to graduate (Chacón et al., 1983). Both white and black students were more likely to do well as members of the racial majority of their campus, an experience whites find more readily available than blacks. Latino/as and American Indians are the numerical majority in only a handful of colleges.

Peers can also provide negative experiences. Blacks found support from other black students in failure but ostracism in success, while the opposite was true for Asian Americans, who lost their very tight support group organized around studying a common discipline when they switched out of science (Seymour & Hewitt, 1994). Some successful black students report concern with being seen as selling out or turning white (Suskind, 1994). The fear of losing connection to their community is a potent impediment for many ethnic minority students.

Women also reported lack of peer support. Hammonds (Sands, 1993) was surprised by the opposition she experienced because of her commitment to science over social aspects of her life—such as dating. "I expected opposition from White people, and I expected that to be because I was a Black person, but I never expected opposition because I was a woman" (p. 242). It may be this kind of peer pressure that accounted for Fleming's finding that female students in historically black colleges show less assertiveness as seniors than as freshmen. Fleming attributes this to women's conditioning to try to please the men around them (Bradley, 1990).

Further, ethnic minority students attending white-majority colleges were likely to report feeling undermined by the belief among white peers that their presence resulted from affirmative action rather than their own performance. When white students expressed open racial hostility, it was directed at students they considered undeserving of financial aid, presumed to have been allocated exclusively by affirmative action (Seymour & Hewitt, 1994). Interestingly, racial hostility by white students was more pronounced in campuses where ethnic minority students were more than a token presence, yet the students of color in such campuses reported less overt discrimination than did students of color in colleges where they were a very small minority. The larger number of students of color may have created a sense of support that shielded these students from the brunt of the overt discrimination or created a sense of security that made the experience less salient for them than for students who were more isolated.

Role Models and Mentors

The literature often cites the benefits of role models and mentors (Adams, 1993; Moses, 1989). There is much discussion, however, about the need for similarity between role model and student, or mentor and student. Evidence points to the need for similar role models (Byrne, 1993; Thomas, 1984, as cited in Garrison, 1987) but not similar mentors.

Byrne argues that role models are useful because they break the stereotype and thus prove that it can be done, not because they provide inspiration. Further, she argues that most students see a lone role model as aberrant—what they need is a critical mass of models. The presence of many role models is one of the reasons for the disproportionately high percentage of black scientists still produced by historically black colleges, even though most have minimal technical resources (Culotta, 1992a; Pearson & Pearson, 1985; Sands, 1993). Similarly, the presence of large numbers of female teachers as role models is considered to be the crucial factor in the success of women's colleges in producing disproportionately high numbers of women who go on to achieve prominence in scientific careers (Pascarella & Terenzini, 1991; Tidball, 1989). For 90 percent of black students and 98 percent of whites, the most influential person in their choice of career in college was of the same race (Thomas, 1984, as cited in Garrison, 1987).

Hill et al. (1990) developed the Science Career Predictor Scale (SCPS) to assess seven factors affecting science career choice. A sample of 187 students from a historically black university took the SCPS. The most important factor turned out to be personal knowledge of a scientist. Given the results from this sample and a larger sample of high school students, Hill, Pettus, and Hedin concluded that while historical discrimination factors may be diminishing, role models remain of paramount importance to individual career choices.

Byrne (1993), arguing from the perspective of mentors of different genders, supported the effectiveness and efficiency of mentors of either sex. In their literature review, Pascarella and Terenzini (1991) note that studies point to same-sex role models and mentors being more beneficial to women than to men students, but the effects in some of these studies were not strong.

Looking back on their college careers, successful scientists recalled people who made a difference for them in moments that could have meant the end of their scientific careers, at points when they were shocked (Massey, 1992), angry (Sands, 1993, p. 241), despairing (Ginorio, 1993), or excited (King, 1989). Most of the support came from professors, and invariably, except for students at historically black colleges, these mentors were not of the students' own race (Holden, 1992).

Graduate School

Just as the number of students in science decreases at every step of the educational ladder (Massey, 1992), so does the amount of research available. The numbers of ethnic minority students who consider graduate school are so small that a breakdown by both ethnicity and gender is very rare. When translated to numbers, a clearer image emerges of what we mean by *small:*

- In 1992, a total of 15,706 doctorates were awarded in science and engineering; only 306 of those went to blacks (NSF, 1994).
- There are only 780 American Indians with Ph.D.'s in science and engineering today (Levy, 1992).
- The first black woman ever to earn a Ph.D. in chemical engineering received her degree in 1979 (from MIT).

- The University of California system, which has a high proportion of Latino/as, in 1980–81 awarded only 19 Ph.D.'s to Latino/as and only two of those went to women (Hayes-Bautista, Schink, & Chapa, 1988).
- Only twelve universities have awarded more than five Ph.D.'s in mathematics and computer science to ethnic minorities (excluding Asian Americans) in the decade from 1983–1992 (Ginorio, 1994).

State institutions produced the most Latino, Asian-American, and American Indian Ph.D. graduates, with the University of California, Berkeley, among the top five for these groups (Culotta & Gibbons, 1992). The pattern for African Americans is different, with two historically black colleges and three private institutions among the top five.

Individual Factors

Even at the graduate level, ethnicity and gender are related to individual factors such as age of decision to pursue SME or to achievement measures such as the GRE. Not surprisingly, some of the contributing factors to success stem from a supportive climate in college.

Knowledge of Careers

Many of today's working scientists knew little about careers in science when they were in primary school. And some learned of the possibility only in college (King, 1989). In a study of entomologists, 36 percent of the respondents mentioned K-12 school teachers as most influential in stimulating interest in science, with another 30 percent mentioning parents or relatives. Ethnic minorities were almost out of high school (average age of 18 years) before they decided to follow a science career, while whites made that decision by age 14.7 years. The later this choice is made, the less time there is to adequately prepare for college (G. Pearson, 1992a).

Most students decided to pursue entomology (as opposed to science in general) in college. Women and ethnic minorities chose this path at age twenty-three, almost two years later than white males (G. Pearson, 1992a). Sixty percent of the students mentioned professors whose excitement about the field of entomology and knowledge of it facilitated the choice, indicating the importance of contact with faculty as a source of career options.

Among ethnic minority students with a bachelor's degree in science, mathematics, or engineering, the switch out of those fields occurs when going to graduate school. The lack of career opportunities was a factor in opting out of science, particularly for Latino/as (Grandy, 1992).

Among disabled professionals, one-third reported that they did not get career information on the same basis as nondisabled students. Many also reported being counseled to enter careers other than science (Lucky, 1989).

Achievement and Skills

GRE scores predict graduate school performance as well as high school GPA does for college. Durán (1987) reported that across all fields, including the humanities and social sciences, Asian Americans and whites consistently earned higher GRE scores than other groups. Grandy (1992) noted that black male students who opted out of science at the graduate level had lower quantitative GRE scores than those who stayed. For black females, on the other hand, low GRE scores were related to dislike of courses but not to switching (Grandy, 1992).

On the other hand, in a study of 4,257 graduate students at three universities, Zwick (1991) found that GRE scores and college GPA were almost entirely unrelated to candidacy or graduation at the Ph.D. level. Women had lower candidacy and graduation rates than males, and ethnic minorities had lower candidacy and graduation rates than whites. Surprisingly, rates were higher in quantitative departments than in humanities or the social sciences. Zwick postulated that among graduate students in very selective universities, personality and availability of support (social as well as financial) were more important factors in candidacy and graduation than were academic predictors.

Ethnic minority women who had succeeded in entering or completing a SME graduate program reported that interpersonal relations caused more difficulty than such structural barriers as recruitment practices, faculty composition, tutorial and counseling support, and receipt of teaching or research assistantships.

Problem factors included isolation, racism, sexism, being racially or ethnically identifiable, and faculty and student relationships (Brown, 1995).

In a study of pharmacy students, Bandalos and Sedlacek (1988) found that while the same cognitive variables predicted the success of black and Asian students, they did so in different orders. The Pharmacy College Admission Test (PCAT) comprehension score and the required prepharmacy GPA predicted black student success, while for Asians a third factor was added: if they attended a state or community college their scores were higher than if they attended out-of-state (and presumedly more competitive) institutions. In addition, Bandalos and Sedlacek tested the effect of noncognitive variables by adding them to the regression equations, and they found only one that significantly increased the predictive score: understanding and dealing with racism. This quantitative outcome supports other qualitative observations (Hewitt & Seymour, 1991; Moses, 1989; Sands, 1993; Seymour & Hewitt, 1994) of the impact that racism can have on student success.

Home and Cultural Factors

The disjunction between the world in their community of origin and the world they enter through the practice of science is a source of both strength and distress for many ethnic minority students. An African-American graduate student coming to grips with how her work can coexist with her community (Culotta, 1992b) faces similar struggles as a half-Mohawk veterinarian specializing in environmental toxicology (Levy, 1992): the bridging of two world cultures. This bridging is a lifelong challenge that starts as early as high school (Fordham & Ogbu, 1986; Suskind, 1994), continues in college, and persists through professional life. The importance of this experience of biculturalism is often underestimated, especially for first-generation college students.

At the graduate level, parental, family, and community influence seems to be indirect. Black scientists are likely to have fathers who are professionals or managers (Pearson, 1982, 1986). On the other hand, for a small sample of low-SES Latinas who achieved Ph.D., J.D., or M.D. degrees the biggest success factor was the support of the whole family *and* the strong role models their mothers provided (Gándara, 1982). Access to family, friends, and large populations of people from their own racial/ethnic group was an important consideration for ethnic minority students choosing a graduate program (Brown, 1995).

School Factors

There are many rules for succeeding in graduate school, but "One is not presented a list of the rules, it's up to one to divine the rules" (Etzkowitz, Kemelgor, Neuschatz, Uzzi, & Alonzo, 1992, p. 165). Given that the majority of ethnic minority students are first-generation college graduates (Brown, 1988, Table 3.5) and that most of these students did not find mentors in college, divining the rules of graduate school is likely to be a more arduous task for them than for white students.

Social Rejection and Isolation

For ethnic minority women, isolation was compounded by visibility: identifiable women were more likely to report racist attitudes and behaviors in their schools than nonidentifiable women. The women described white students as indifferent at best and reported that ethnic minority men often treated women as intellectual inferiors (Brown, 1995).

G. Pearson (1992b) reported that ethnic minority graduate students in entomology were significantly less likely to interact with classmates than were whites. This isolation prevented valuable feedback about strengths and weaknesses (W. Pearson, 1987). It is not known how much isolation results from discrimination rather than choice, but students in Brown's sample (1995) could not form collaborative study relationships with white students. To the degree that discrimination does cause ethnic minority student isolation, the Bandalos and Sedlacek (1988) report of the predictive value for success in pharmacy of ability to understand and address racism should come as no surprise.

At science meetings, as in graduate school, ethnic minorities tend to lack a critical mass, and the ethnic minority student is usually the lone black or brown face in the crowd. Ethnic minorities often have to be more assertive than whites when meeting people or making connections (Culotta, 1992b).

Ethnic minority students were not the only ones reporting discrimination in graduate school. Although surveys at an eastern medical school found that nearly eight out of ten students stated that homosexuals are "no different from anyone else" (Tinmouth & Hamwi, 1994), there seemed to be less acceptance of lesbians than of gays. In a study of U.S. psychiatry programs that asked lesbians and gays about peers or support groups, issues of disclosure, and perceptions of their sexual orientation, the women had more negative experiences than gays in fourteen of the twenty-six inquiries (Townsend, Wallick, & Cambre, 1993). The report concluded that lesbians felt all the stressors that affect women in medical school, plus others related to their lesbianism. Regarding general program support for lesbians and gays, the same study found that more men said their programs affirmed their sexuality, while more women felt stigmatized.

Groups working with problems of gender discrimination are not always helpful for lesbians. For example, support services for women at the University of Chicago Pritzker School of Medicine centered on timing of marriage and other issues predicated on a heterosexual standard (Tinmouth & Hamwi, 1994). In a study of lesbian and gay medical students, all seventy-two respondents expressed a desire for a support group at their school (Townsend et al., 1991). But among gay and lesbian students and residents of U.S. psychiatry programs (Townsend et al., 1993), interest in formal support groups decreased as training progressed.

Faculty and Courses

"More than any other group, Black women believed that race was the deciding factor in how they were treated by faculty and other students" (Brown, 1995, p. 33). Ethnic minority women were the most dissatisfied with faculty-student relationships and very few had true mentors. In class, both male and female ethnic minority students felt lack of acceptance (52 percent and 45 percent, respectively). Echoing Hammonds (Sands, 1993), these women also had a hard time distinguishing racist from sexist behaviors in classrooms.

For lesbians, we have data only from medical settings. Homophobic comments on medical wards had deleterious effects on gay and lesbian medical students. Tinmouth and Hamwi (1994) reported offensive statements by faculty in the context of training. These statements maintained stereotypes among heterosexual students and were devastating to lesbians and gays who had to hear them, increasing their sense of isolation and invisibility.

Lesbians in medical schools have expressed dissatisfaction about the curricula on homosexuality. A study of all 126 U.S. medical schools found an average of three hours and twenty-six minutes spent on the topic of homosexuality (Wallick, Cambre, & Townsend, 1992). The limited amount of time for this topic—and some of the teaching strategies used to convey the information—potentially trivialized the topic's importance for both faculty and students.

Lesbians, like heterosexual women, have fewer opportunities to establish mentoring relationships. As a result, lesbians may be less secure in the academic hierarchy, having few female and even fewer lesbian role models.

Financial Needs

It was not surprising to find that many ethnic minority students, with loans dating back to their first year in college, opted not to go to graduate school when offered a paying job (Pearson, 1987). Others who began graduate school stopped with a master's degree, given the cyclical nature of employment in the sciences (Schwartz, 1993) and the competitive salaries for master's graduates in some fields (Nettles, 1987).

Graduate students with less financial support took longer to complete their degrees than those with ample support, and ethnic minority women took longer to complete the Ph.D. than men regardless of level of support (Brown, 1995). Based on data from 1985 Ph.D. recipients, Leggon (1987) suggested that the differing time for degree completion by students from various ethnic groups was tied to sources of student support. According to an NSF report, less than one-third of American Indians had university-based financial support and less than one-sixth had federal support in 1990 (Levy, 1992). Brown (1988) argued that the decline of Ph.D.'s attained by blacks from 1976 to 1986 was related to a dramatic decline in federal financial aid, which seemed to affect black men more negatively than black women.

Postgraduate Employment

U.S. employment figures for 1986 reveal that at least 11 percent of female scientists and engineers are women of color (NSF, 1990). This is not the place to do justice to the information on ethnic minority postgraduate employment; for that, the reader is referred to *Increasing Minority Faculty: An Elusive Goal* (Brown, 1988) and to *Women, Minorities and Persons with Disabilities in Science and Engineering: 1994* from NSF. The only aspect of postgraduate employment included in this chapter concerns barriers to career satisfaction and success.

In a survey of minority women in science, respondents reported encountering disapproval and resentment. This included perceptions of special privileges and advantages afforded by affirmative action (Hall, 1981). Resentment and prejudice of colleagues and co-workers may result in passing over black women for training or job opportunities. When they are called upon, it is often to offer the "black woman's point of view" rather than their own opinions (Hall, 1981). Anthropologists have labeled this type of request "a cultural tax." According to Collins and Matyas (1985, p. 121), black women scientists are faced with the role of public relations officers, "trying to dispel unfounded myths about their own abilities." Discrimination that focuses on the automatic questioning of the competence of an individual on the basis of racial/ethnic identity and/or gender diminishes the level of personal satisfaction (Amaro, Russo, & Johnson, 1987).

In a study of executive positions in twenty-five academic institutions (Haro, 1992), a search committee did not consider women and minority finalists for a university presidency because it was uncertain how these candidates would "interact with well-to-do white alumni and donors, and the intercollegiate athletic team benefactors" (p. 12). Haro also reported responses indicating suspicion of minority finalists for executive academic positions, referring to finalists of color as "affirmative action products" (p. 21).

Asian Americans also encounter barriers in the sciences. Although they appear to be strongly represented in the scientific arena, the NSF reports that the number of Asian Americans in the upper echelons of science and technology does not parallel their presence as scientists (Miller, 1992). Asian Americans in the middle ranks are underpaid (Brown, 1988), and Alice Huang, New York University Dean for Science, has said: "There is no question that a glass ceiling exists for Asian-American scientists. I've experienced it. And the elite institutions are the worst" (Miller, p. 1224). Miller adds that most explanations of the barriers to Asian-American career advancement make internal attributions rather than external or racially motivated ones. These internal attributions include difficulties in communication due to poor mastery of the English language; cultural differences such as lack of assertiveness; or work values that focus on scholarship over social interactions.

Lesbians and gays face open discrimination. Forty percent of physicians responding to a survey said they would not continue to refer patients to a gay or lesbian colleague; 40 percent would discourage gay men and lesbians from becoming psychiatrists or pediatricians; and about one-third would not admit a qualified, openly gay or lesbian applicant to medical school (Matthews, Booth, & Turner, 1986). However, one "out" lesbian professor remarked that male colleagues were prepared to respect her talents because "they don't really think of me as a woman, so it's not so weird that I can do science" (Mukerjee, 1995).

The issues of dual careers and caretaking responsibilities affect all women. In a study of scientists leaving careers, the only difference in reasons reported by males and females related to family concerns (Ginorio, Barnett, & Keefer, 1995), although this was not listed as the most important reason. Lesbians find this a particularly difficult topic to approach with their advisers or with potential employers (Feminists in Science and Technology, electronic discussion group, 1994).

The congruence of values in science and individual cultural values raises another issue related to career satisfaction. Native American scientists have found that science and technology often directly oppose and threaten traditional Native American ways of life (Levy, 1992), and the resolution of such conflicts is not always satisfactory. However, if the resolution involves changes in science values rather than in individual values, this discrepancy also provides an opportunity for unique contributions by Native American scientists in many fields.

Implications for Future Research

The body of research on girls and women of color in mathematics and science suggests that this subgroup, while sharing many factors with white women, is also affected by racial/ethnic status. The following section outlines possibilities for further research into the attitudes, achievement/performance, course taking, and career aspirations of women of color.

As can be seen from the studies summarized at the beginning of this chapter, research on the causes of underrepresentation of white women and girls in mathematics and science is not generalizable to women and girls of color. Neither is research conducted on girls or women of one race/ethnicity or social class generalizable to those of other races/ethnicities or social classes. The majority of research on girls and women of color has been conducted on African-American girls and women, followed by Latinas; there is practically no research on American Indian girls and women. Research is needed to address the different populations of ethnic minority students and, in some cases, subpopulations. As the Asian-American and Latino populations diversify in terms of countries of origin, the umbrella terms that have been traditionally used become less accurate. To a lesser extent, the African-American population is also diversifying with influx from Latin America and Africa. Research is also needed on the effect of social class, gender, race/ethnicity, disability status, and sexual orientation as well as the interaction of all these statuses on differential performance, course taking, and career choice for girls and women of color by each racial/ethnic group, for lesbians, and for disabled girls and women. Such research should address the following areas:

- *K-3 experiences.* What is the effect of parental influence, school-related factors, and varying levels of cognitive development on girls' mathematics achievement?
- *Relationship of attitudes to achievement for diverse populations of girls and women.* Is there such a relationship, and if so, does it vary by race/ethnicity and social class? What factors affect these attitudes?
- *Predictive power of GPA and tests.* What are the reasons for the differential predictive power of GPA and various tests

on the educational outcomes of girls and women of color, especially for college education? Are other, noncognitive predictors necessary?

- *Differential performance of girls and women in mathematics and science, particularly physical sciences and higher-level mathematics.* What are some of the reasons performance differs? Do reasons vary by race/ethnicity and SES? Why does girls' performance in mathematics and science decline as they progress up the ladder? How do top-scoring girls compare to top-scoring boys in their racial/ethnic groups?
- *Course taking in mathematics and science.* What are reasons for differential course-taking patterns? Do these vary by race/ethnicity and SES? Why have course-taking patterns for girls changed in the last five years?
- *Choice of major in college.* What factors affect choice of college major for women of color? Do these factors differ according to race/ethnicity and SES?
- *Career choice.* What are reasons for gender differences in career choice? Do these vary according to race/ethnicity, disability, and SES?
- *Parental expectations of daughters' participation in mathematics/ science.* How do parental attitudes and levels of support differ among various racial/ethnic groups and socioeconomic levels? What is the effect of parental support and attitudes on daughters' performance and participation in mathematics and science among various racial/ethnic groups? Are both parents equally influential on their daughters' participation?
- *Teacher influence.* Do teachers treat girls and women differently? Does treatment vary by race/ethnicity and social class? What is the effect of differential treatment? Are women more aware of or responsive to teacher attitudes and behaviors?
- *Peer influence.* What is the effect of peer pressure on girls' and women's attitudes, participation, and achievement in mathematics and science? How important are same-ethnicity and same-sex study groups to the success of undergraduate women?
- *Counseling.* What is the role of counseling in excluding girls and women of color from higher-level mathematics and science courses as well as from careers in mathematics and science?

- *Instructional strategies.* What learning/cognitive styles are represented among girls of various racial/ethnic groups? What relationship do these have to achievement and performance in mathematics and science? What instructional strategies are most effective for addressing these learning/cognitive styles?
- *Access to computers.* What access do girls and women of color have to computers and how does this access affect their achievement in mathematics? The effectiveness of computer-assisted instruction in mathematics, especially for at-risk African-American adolescents, needs further investigation.
- *Role models.* How effective are role models in enhancing attitudes, achievement, and career aspirations of girls in diverse populations? Are same-sex, same-ethnicity role models needed? What combination of role model characteristics is most effective?
- *Mentors.* How effective are male mentors to women of color? Is the effect different if the mentor is of the same ethnicity? What characteristics help mentors succeed with students? What is the best match between mentor and student characteristics? What are the key skills needed by mentors working with girls and women of color, lesbians, and disabled girls and women?
- *Meaningful community.* What is the optimum relationship between members of the community of origin, including the extended family, and the student? How important are same-ethnicity and same-sex peers to the success of graduate women? What role, if any, does electronic communication play in the creation of a sense of meaningful community? What constitutes a meaningful community for lesbians and disabled girls and women?

Issues in Conducting Research on Girls and Women of Color, Lesbians, and Disabled Girls and Women

This chapter has discussed the dearth of studies integrating race, social class, and gender or considering disability status and sexual orientation and has urged the necessity of such research. At present, the collection and reporting of national data hinders this research. For example, NAEP math and science reports are disaggregated by sex within racial/ethnic categories only for data on proficiency levels. The NAEP collects the gender and racial/ethnic data needed to disaggregate all its reports, but it does not do so.

Social class or socioeconomic status are even more difficult to report. Proxy characteristics such as parents' education and occupation and family income can be used to determine SES, but such information is difficult to obtain and, when self-reported, of questionable reliability. Further, the greater the disaggregation by various characteristics, the smaller the sample size of the population being studied.

The failure of research studies and national data bases to disaggregate data by race/ethnicity and gender may be due to the tendency of researchers and policy makers to ignore people of color, but the sheer difficulty of working with such small numbers may also be a factor. When the numbers of people of color are too small for quantitative methods, qualitative data as well as case studies can provide different lenses to explore issues for groups with small populations in a given setting. Information about students contextualized by information on their institution, faculty, and peers could provide data useful in generating explanations or challenging established explanations.

It is reassuring, nevertheless, that there have been changes in data reporting to include disaggregation by race/ethnicity and gender within racial/ethnic categories. For an example of this, see the recent NSF publication *Women, Minorities, and Persons with Disabilities in Science and Engineering: 1994.*

Doing research is one issue; publishing and disseminating it is another. Three factors make information on ethnic minorities hard to find: it is rarely gathered; when it is gathered, sample sizes are often too small for standard statistical analysis; and when it is analyzed, it tends to appear in research reports and not in official journals (Ginorio, 1993). *The Journal of Women and Minorities in Science and Engineering* provides an easily identifiable outlet for research on women of color. But science and education journals also need to include this information if it is to reach the audience that needs to find out about it.

Given projected demographic changes, an increasingly larger proportion of the population will belong to groups currently underrepresented in mathematics and science fields; half of the individuals in these groups will be women and girls. Given this dramatic shift, it is no longer feasible, appropriate, or just to conduct research solely on white subjects and use the findings of this research to make policy decisions for the entire populace.

References

Adams, H. G. (1993). *Focusing on campus milieu: A guide for enhancing the graduate school climate.* Notre Dame, IN: National Consortium for Graduate Degrees for Minorities in Engineering and Science, Inc. (GEM).

Alper, S. (1993). Extended school year programs: A community-driven curriculum model. *Mental Retardation, 31*(3), 163–170.

Amaro, H., Russo, N., & Johnson, R. (1987). Family and work predictors of psychological well-being among Hispanic women professionals. *Psychology of Women Quarterly, 11,* 505–521.

Anderson, B. T. (1989). Black participation and performance in high school science. In W. Pearson, Jr., & H. K. Bechtel (Eds.), *Blacks, science, and American education* (pp. 43–58). New Brunswick and London: Rutgers University Press.

Anderson, B. T., & Pearson, W., Jr. (1988, November). *Understanding the underrepresentation of blacks in American science: Why capable blacks do not persist in their pursuit of scientific careers.* Paper presented at the joint conference of the Society for the Studies of Science (4S) and the European Association for the Study of Science and Technology (EEAST), Amsterdam.

Andrews, J. V. (1989, April). *Attitudes and beliefs about mathematics: Do parents, students, teachers, counselors and principals agree?* Paper presented at the annual meeting of the American Educational Research Association, San Francisco, CA.

Anick, C. M., Carpenter, T. P., & Smith, C. (1981). Minorities and mathematics: Results from the national assessment of educational progress. *Mathematics Teacher, 74,* 560–566.

Armstrong, J. M. (1981). Achievement and participation of women in mathematics: Results of two national surveys. *Journal for Research in Mathematics Education, 12,* 356–372.

Association of American Colleges and Universities. (1994). On campus with women. *25*(1), 1–2.

Astin, A. W. (1982). *Minorities in American higher education.* San Francisco: Jossey-Bass.

Astin, A. W. (1990). *The black undergraduate: Current status and trends in the characteristics of freshmen.* Research report. Los Angeles: Higher Education Research Institute.

Bandalos, D. L., & Sedlacek, W. E. (1988). *Predicting success of pharmacy students using traditional and nontraditional measures by race* (Research Report No. 7–88). College Park: University of Maryland, Counseling Center.

Beane, D. B. (1985). *Mathematics and science: Critical filters for the future of minority students.* Washington, DC: American University, Mid-Atlantic Center for Race Equity.

Belenky, M. F., Clinchy, B. M., Goldberger, N. R., & Tarule, J. M. (1986). *Women's ways of knowing: The development of self, voice, and mind.* New York: Basic Books.

Berryman, S. E. (1983). *Who will do science? Minority and Female Attainment of Science and Mathematics Degrees.* New York: Rockefeller Foundation.

Blatchford, P., Burke, J., Farquhar, C., Plewis, I., & Tizard, B. (1985). Educational achievement in the infant school: The influence of ethnic origin, gender and home on entry skills. *Educational Research, 27*(1), 52–60.

Boswell, S. L., & Katz, P. A. (1980). *Nice girls don't study mathematics.* Washington, DC: National Institute of Education. (ERIC Document Reproduction Service No. ED 188 888)

Bradley, M. (1990, April 30). Fleming advocates black student leadership. *Barnard Bulletin,* pp. 8–9, 12.

Brown, S. V. (1988). *Increasing minority faculty: An elusive goal.* Princeton, NJ: Educational Testing Service.

Brown, S. V. (1995). *The early career preparation of minorities for academic careers in science and engineering: How well are we doing?* Princeton, NJ: Educational Testing Service.

Bruschi, B. A., & Anderson, B. T. (1994, February). *Gender and ethnic differences in science achievement of nine-, thirteen-, and seventeen-year old students.* Paper presented at the annual meeting of the Eastern Educational Research Association, Sarasota, FL.

Brush, L. (1980). *Encouraging girls in mathematics: The problem and the solution.* Cambridge, MA: Abt Books.

Byrne, E. M. (1993). *Women and science: The snark syndrome.* Washington, DC: Falmer Press.

Campbell, J. R. (1991). The roots of gender inequity in technical areas. *Journal of Research in Science Teaching, 28,* 251–264.

Campbell, P. B. (1989). So what do we do with the poor, non-white female? Issues of gender, race, and social class in mathematics and equity. *Peabody Journal of Education, 95,* 112.

Chacón, M. A., Cohen, E., Camarena, M. M., González, J. T., & Stover, S. (1983). Chicanas in California postsecondary education. *La Red/The Net,* 65(Suppl.9), 2–22.

Clark, J. V. (1985). The status of science and mathematics in historically black colleges and universities. *Science Education, 69,* 673–679.

Clewell, B. C., & Anderson, B. T. (1991). *Women of color in mathematics, science and engineering: A review of the literature.* Washington, DC: Center for Women Policy Studies.

Clewell, B. C., Anderson, B. T., & Thorpe, M. (1992). *Breaking the barriers: Helping female and minority students succeed in mathematics and science.* San Francisco: Jossey-Bass.

Cobb, J. P. (1989). A life in science: research and service. *SAGE, 6*(2), 39–43.

Cohen, E. G., & DeAvila, E. A. (1983). *Learning to think in math and science: Improving local education for minority children.* Final report to the Walter S. Johnson Foundation. Stanford, CA: Stanford University School of Education.

Cohen, E. G., Intili, J., & DeAvila, E. A. (1982). *Learning science in bilingual classrooms: Interaction and social status.* Stanford, CA: Stanford University Center for Educational Research.

Collins, M., & Matyas, M. L. (1985). Minority women: Conquering both sexism and racism. In J. B. Kahle (Ed.), *Women in science: A report from the field* (pp. 102–123). Philadelphia: Falmer Press.

Crawley, F. E., III, & Coe, A. S. (1990). Determinants of middle school students' intention to enroll in a high school science course: An application of the theory of reasoned action. *Journal of Research in Science Teaching, 27,* 461–476.

Creswell, J. L., & Exezidis, R. H. (1982). Research brief: Sex and ethnic differences in mathematics achievement of black and Mexican American adolescents. *Texas Tech Journal of Education, 9,* 219–222.

Creswell, J. L., & Houston, G. M. (1980). *Sex related differences in mathematics achievement in black, Chicano and Anglo adolescents.* Houston, TX: University of Houston. (ERIC Document Reproduction Service No. ED 198 079)

Culotta, E. (1992a). Black colleges cultivate scientists. *Science, 258,* 1216–1218.

Culotta, E. (1992b). Scientists of the future: Jumping high hurdles. *Science, 258,* 1209–1213.

Culotta, E., & Gibbons, A. (Eds.). (1992). Minorities in science: The pipeline problem. *Science, 258,* 1180.

Davis, J. D. (1986). *The effect of mathematics course enrollment on racial/ethnic differences in secondary school mathematics achievement* (NAEP Report 86-EMC). Princeton, NJ: Educational Testing Service.

Davis, J. D. (1989). The mathematics education of black high school students. In W. Pearson, Jr., & H. K. Bechtel (Eds.), *Blacks, science, and American education* (pp. 23–42). New Brunswick and London: Rutgers Press.

Dossey, J. A., Mullis, I.V.S., Lindquist, M. M., & Chambers, D. L. (1988). *The mathematics report card: Are we measuring up? Trends and achievement based on the 1986 national assessment* (Report No. 17-M-01). Princeton, NJ: Educational Testing Service.

Dunteman, G. H., Wisenbaker, J., & Taylor, M. E. (1979). *Race and sex differences in college science program participation* (NSF No. SED-7–18728). Arlington, VA: National Science Foundation.

Durán, R. P. (1987). Hispanics' precollege and undergraduate education: Implications for science and engineering studies. In L. S. Dix (Ed.), *Minorities: Their underrepresentation and career differentials in science and engineering* (pp. 73–128). Washington, DC: National Academy Press.

Eccles (Parsons), J., Adler, T. F., Futterman, R., Goff, S., Kaczala, C., Meece, J. L., & Midgely, C. (1983). Expectancies, values and academic behaviors. In J. T. Spence (Ed.), *Achievement and achievement motives: Psychological and sociological motives* (pp. 75–146). New York: W. H. Freeman.

Ehrhart, J. K., & Sandler, B. R. (1990, May). *Rx for success: Improving the climate for women in medical schools and teaching hospitals.* Research report. Washington, DC: Association of American Colleges.

Engman, L. R. (1986). School effectiveness characteristics associated with minority student mathematics achievement. *Dissertation Abstracts International, 47,* sec. 3, 813A. (University Microfilms No. DA86-07170).

Entwisle, D. R., & Alexander, K. L. (1990). Beginning school math competence: Minority and majority comparisons. *Child Development, 61,* 454–471.

Entwisle, D. R., & Alexander, K. L. (1992). Summer setback: Race, poverty, school composition, and mathematics achievement in the first two years of school. *American Sociological Review, 57,* 72–84.

Entwisle, D. R., & Baker, D. P. (1983). Gender and young children's expectations for performance in arithmetic. *Developmental Psychology, 19,* 200–209.

Entwisle, D. R., Alexander, K. L., Cadigan, D., & Pallas, A. (1986). The schooling process in first grade: Two samples a decade apart. *American Educational Research Journal, 23*(4), 587–613.

Erickson, D. K. (1987). *A review of research on the effect of mathematics teachers' classroom behavior on girls' and boys' learning, attitudes, and participation in mathematics.* Paper presented at the American Education Research Association Special Interest Group on Research on Women in Education Conference, Portland, OR.

Erickson, D. K., Gall, M. D., Gersten, R., & Grace, D. P. (1987, April). *The differential effects of teacher behavior on girls' and boys' achievement, attitudes and future coursework plans in high school algebra classes.* Paper presented at the annual meeting of the American Educational Research Association, Washington, DC.

Ethington, C. A., & Wolfle, L. M. (1988). Women's selection of quantitative undergraduate fields of study: Direct and indirect influences. *American Educational Research Journal 25*(2), 157–175.

Etzkowitz, H., Kemelgor, C., Neuschatz, M., Uzzi, B., & Alonzo, J. (1992). Athena unbound: barriers to women in academic science and engineering. *Science and Public Policy, 19*(3), 157–179.

Evans, M. O. (1992, Summer). An estimate of race and gender role-model effects in teaching high school. *Journal of Economic Education,* 209–217.

Fennema, E. (1980). Sex-related differences in mathematics achievement: Where and why. In L. H. Fox, L. Brody, & D. Tobin (Eds.), *Women and the mathematical mystique* (pp. 76–93). Baltimore, MD: Johns Hopkins University Press.

Fennema, E. (1984). Girls, women, and mathematics: An overview. In E. Fennema & J. Ayer (Eds.), *Women and education: Equity or equality* (pp. 137–164). Berkeley, CA: McCutchan.

Fennema, E., & Carpenter, T. P. (1981). Sex related differences in mathematics: Results from the national assessment. *Mathematics Teacher, 74,* 554–559.

Fennema, E., & Sherman, J. A. (1977). Sex-related differences in mathematics achievement, spatial visualization and affective factors. *American Educational Research Journal, 14*(1), 51–71.

Fennema, E., & Sherman, J. A. (1978). Sex related differences in mathematics achievement and related factors: A further study. *Journal for Research in Mathematics Education, 9*(3), 189–203.

Fordham, S., & Ogbu, J. (1986). Black students' school success: Coping with the burden of acting white. *The Urban Review, 18,* 176–206.

Fox, L. H. (1981). *The problem of women and mathematics.* New York: Ford Foundation.

Fox, L. H., Brody, L., & Tobin, D. (1985). The impact of early intervention programs upon course taking and attitudes in high school. In S. F. Chipman, L. R. Brush, & D. M. Wilson (Eds.), *Women and mathematics: Balancing the equation* (pp. 249–274). Hillsdale, NJ: Erlbaum.

Gándara, P. (1982). Passing through the eye of the needle: High-achieving Chicanas. *Hispanic Journal of Behavioral Sciences, 4*(2), 167–179.

García, J., Harrison, N. R., & Torres, J. L. (1990). The portrayal of females and minorities in selected elementary mathematics series. *School Science and Mathematics, 90*(1), 1–12.

García, T., Yu, S. L., & Coppola, B. P. (1993). *Women and minorities in science: Motivational and cognitive correlates of achievement.* Ann Arbor: University of Michigan.

Garrison, H. H. (1987). Undergraduate science and engineering education for blacks and Native Americans. In L. S. Dix (Ed.), *Minorities: Their underrepresentation and career differentials in science and engineering* (pp. 39–65). Washington, DC: National Academy Press.

Gilligan, C. (1982). *In a different voice: Psychological theory and women's development.* Cambridge, MA: Harvard University Press.

Ginorio, A. B. (1993). Feminism and ethnicity. *FOCUS: Newsletter of the Society for the Psychological Study of Ethnic Minority Issues, 7*(1), 3–4.

Ginorio, A. B. (1995). *Warming the climate for women in academic science.* Washington, DC: Association of American Colleges and Universities.

Ginorio, A. B., Barnett, N., & Keefer, J. (1995). *Survey of career change for scientists.* Unpublished manuscript, University of Washington, Seattle.

Ginorio, A. B. & Marshall, T. (1994). [Analysis of National Research Council data on ethnic minority Phds and graduate students]. Unpublished raw data.

Ginsberg, H. P., & Russell, R. L. (1981). Social class and racial influences on early mathematical thinking. *Monographs of the Society for Research in Child Development, 46*(6, Serial No. 193).

Gore, D., & Roumagoux, D. (1983). Wait-time as a variable in sex-related differences during fourth-grade mathematics instruction. *Journal of Educational Research, 76,* 273–275.

Governor's Commission on Gay and Lesbian Youth. (1993, July). *Making colleges and universities safe for gay and lesbian students.* Boston, MA: Author.

Grandy, J. (1992). *Graduate enrollment decisions of undergraduate science and engineering majors: A survey of GRE test takers* (Research Rep. 92–51). Princeton, NJ: Educational Testing Service.

Grant, C. A., & Sleeter, C. E. (1986). Race, class, and gender in education research: An argument for integrative analysis. *Review of Educational Research, 56*(2), 195–211.

Green, R., Brown, J. W., & Long, R. (1978). *Report and recommendations: Conference on mathematics in American Indian education.* Washington, DC: Educational Foundation of America and American Association for the Advancement of Science.

Grignon, J. R. (1993). Computer experience of Menominee Indian students: Gender differences in coursework and use of software. *Journal of American Indian Education, 32,* 1–15.

Gross, S. (1988). *Participation and performance of women and minorities in mathematics: Vol. 1. Findings by gender and racial/ethnic group.* Rockville, MD: Montgomery County Public Schools, Carver Educational Services Center.

Gross, S. (1989, March). *Early mathematics performance and achievement: The beginning of a downward spiral for blacks and Hispanics.* Paper presented at the annual meeting of the American Educational Research Association, San Francisco, CA.

Hale-Benson, J. E. (1984). *Black children: Their roots, culture, and learning styles* (Rev. ed.). Baltimore, MD: Johns Hopkins University Press.

Hall, P. (1981). *Problems and solutions in education, employment and personal choice of minority women in science.* Washington, DC: American Association for the Advancement of Science.

Hall, R. M., & Sandler, B. R. (1982). *The classroom climate: A chilly one for women.* Washington, DC: Association of American Colleges.

Hall, V. C., Howe, A., Merkel, S., & Lederman, N. (1986). Behavior, motivation, and achievement in desegregated junior high school science classes. *Journal of Educational Psychology, 78*(2), 108–115.

Haro, R. P. (1992). *Women in higher education: Barriers against women and minorities.* Salinas, CA: San Jose State University.

Hart, L. E., & Stanic, G.M.A. (1989, March). *Attitudes and achievement-related behaviors of middle school mathematics students: Views through four lenses.* Paper presented at the annual meeting of the American Educational Research Association, San Francisco, CA.

Hayes-Bautista, D. E., Schink, W. O., & Chapa, J. (1988). The burden of support: Young Latinos in an aging society. Stanford, CA: Stanford University Press.

Hewitt, N. M., & Seymour, E. (1991). *Factors contributing to high attrition rates among science, mathematics, and engineering undergraduate majors.* Research report. Boulder: University of Colorado, Bureau of Sociological Research, Ethnography and Assessment Research.

Hewitt, N. M., & Seymour, E. (1992, February). A long, discouraging climb. *Prism: Journal of the American Society for Engineering Education,* pp. 24–28.

Hill, O. W., Pettus, W. C., & Hedin, B. A. (1990). Three studies of factors affecting the attitudes of blacks and females toward the pursuit of science and science-related careers. *Journal of Research in Science Teaching, 27,* 289–314.

Holden, C. (1992). Minority survivors tell their tales. *Science, 258,* 1204–1206.

Holmes, B. J. (1980). *Black students' performance in the national assessments of science and mathematics* (No. SY-SM-50). Princeton, NJ: Educational Testing Service.

Howe, A. C., & Shayer, M. (1981). Sex-related differences on a task of volume and density. *Journal of Research in Science Teaching, 18*(2), 169–175.

Hueftle, S. J., Rakow, S. J., & Welch, W. W. (1983). *Images of science: A summary of results from the 1981–82 national assessment in science.* Minneapolis: Minnesota Research and Evaluation Center.

Irvine, J. J. (1985). Teacher communication patterns are related to the race and sex of the student. *Journal of Educational Research, 78*(6), 338–345.

Jacobowitz, T. J. (1983). Relationship of sex, achievement, and science self-concept to the science career preferences of black students. *Journal of Research in Science Teaching, 20,* 621–628.

James, R. K., & Smith, S. (1985). Alienation of students from science in grades 4–12. *Science Education, 69*(1), 39–45.

Johnson, R. C. (1981). *Psychosocial influences on the math attitudes and interests of black junior high school students.* St. Louis, MO: Institute of Black Studies.

Jones, L. R., Mullis, I.V.S., Raizen, S. A., Weiss, I. R., & Weston, E. A. (1992). *The 1990 science report card: NAEP'S assessment of fourth, eighth, and twelfth graders.* Washington, DC: National Center for Education Statistics.

Jones, L. V. (1987). The influence on mathematics test scores, by ethnicity and sex, of prior achievement and high school mathematics courses. *Journal for Research in Mathematics Education, 18*(3), 180–186.

Kahle, J. B. (1982). Can positive minority attitudes lead to achievement gains in science? Analysis of the 1977 National Assessment of Educational Progress, Attitudes Toward Science. *Science Education, 66,* 539–546.

Kahle, J. B. (1983). *The disadvantaged majority: Science education for women.* Burlington, NC: Carolina Biological Supply Company.

Kahle, J. B., & Lakes, M. K. (1983). The myth of equality in science classrooms. *Journal of Research in Science Teaching, 20*(2), 131–140.

Kelly, A. (1978). *Girls and science.* Stockholm: Almquist and Wilksell International.

Kelly, A. (Ed.). (1981). *The missing half: Girls and science education.* Manchester, England: Manchester University Press.

Kelly, A., & Smail, B. (1986). Sex stereotypes and attitudes to science among eleven-year-old children. *British Journal of Educational Psychology, 56,* 158–168.

Kenschaft, P. C. (1981). Black women in mathematics. *American Mathematical Monthly, 88,* 592–604.

King, R. C. (1989). Becoming a scientist: An important career decision. *SAGE: A Scholarly Journal on Black Women, 6*(2), 47–50.

Kohr, R. L., Masters, J. R., Coldiron, J. F., Blust, R. S., & Skiffington, E. W. (1989). The relationship of race, class, and gender with mathematics achievement for fifth-, eighth-, and eleventh-grade students in Pennsylvania schools. *Peabody Journal of Education, 66*(2), 147–171.

Krist, P. S. (1993). *Educational and career choices in math and science for high ability African American women.* Unpublished doctoral dissertation, University of North Carolina, Chapel Hill.

Lane, M. J. (1990). Women and minorities in science and engineering. Arlington, VA: National Science Foundation.

Lee, V. E., & Ware, N. C. (1986, April). *When and why girls "leak" out of high school mathematics: A closer look.* Paper presented at the annual meeting of the American Educational Research Association, San Francisco, CA.

Leggon, C. B. (1987). Minority underrepresentation in science and engineering graduate education and careers: A critique. In L. S. Dix (Ed.). *Minorities: Their underrepresentation and career differentials in science and engineering* (pp. 151–158). Washington, DC: National Academy Press.

Levy, D. (1992). Bridging tribal, technological worlds. *Science, 258,* 1231.

Lewellyn, R. J. (1990). Gender differences in achievement, self-efficacy, anxiety, and attributions in mathematics among primarily black junior high school students. *Dissertation Abstracts International, 50,* sec. 7, 1989A. (University Microfilms No. AAC89–22339).

Lockheed, M. E., & Gorman, K. S. (1987). Sociocultural factors affecting science learning and attitude. In A. B. Champagne & L. E. Hornig (Eds.), *This year in school science, 1987: Students and science learning* (pp. 41–66). Washington, DC: American Association for the Advancement of Science.

Lockheed, M. E., Thorpe, M., Brooks-Gunn, J., Casserly, P., & McAloon, A. (1985). *Sex and ethnic differences in middle school mathematics, science and computer science: What do we know?* Princeton, NJ: Educational Testing Service.

Lucky, L. F. (1989). Boosting science careers for the physically handicapped student. *Quarterly Journal of the Florida Academy of Sciences, 52*(3), 145–153.

MacCorquodale, P. (1980). *Psycho-social influences on the accomplishments of Mexican-American students.* Paper presented at the meeting of the American Association of School Administrators, Chicago, IL. (ERIC Document Reproduction Service No. ED 200 355)

MacCorquodale, P. (1988). Mexican-American women and mathematics: Participation, aspirations, and achievement. In R. R. Cocking & J.

P. Mestre (Eds.), *Linguistic and cultural influences on learning mathematics* (pp. 137–160). Hillsdale, NJ: Erlbaum.

McDowell, C. L. (1990). The unseen world: Race, class, and gender analysis in science education research. *The Journal of Negro Education, 59,* 273–291.

Malcom, S. M. (1990). Reclaiming our past. *The Journal of Negro Education, 59*(3), 246–259.

Maple, S. A., & Stage, F. K. (1991). Influences on the choice of math/science major by gender and ethnicity. *American Educational Research Journal, 28*(1), 37–60.

Marrett, C. B. (1981). *Patterns of enrollment in high school mathematics and science.* Madison: Wisconsin Research and Development Center.

Marrett, C. B. (1986, April). *Minority females in precollege mathematics: Towards a research agenda.* Paper presented at the annual meeting of the American Educational Research Association, San Francisco, CA.

Massey, W. E. (1992). A success story among decades of disappointment. *Science, 258,* 1177–1179.

Matthews, W. (1981). Black females and mathematics: Barricade or bridge? *Journal of Social and Behavioral Science, 27,* 88–92.

Matthews, W. (1983). *Influences on the learning and participation of minorities in mathematics.* Madison: Wisconsin Center for Education Research.

Matthews, W. (1984). Influences on the learning and participation of minorities in mathematics. *Journal for Research in Mathematics Education, 15*(2), 84–95.

Matthews, W., Booth, M. W., & Turner, J. D. (1986). Physicians' attitudes toward homosexuality: Survey of a California county medical society. *West J Med, 144,* 10–111.

Matthews, W., Carpenter, T. P., Lindquist, M. M., & Silver, E. A. (1984). The third national assessment: Minorities and mathematics. *Journal for Research in Mathematics Education, 15*(2), 165–171.

Meece, J. L., Parsons, J. E., Kaczala, C. M., Goff, S. B., & Futterman, R. (1982). Sex differences in mathematics achievement: Toward a model of academic choice. *Psychological Bulletin, 91,* 324–348.

Meléndez, S., & Petrovich, J. (1989). Hispanic women students in higher education: Meeting the challenge of diversity. In C. S. Pearson, D. Shavlik, & J. Touchton (Eds.). *Educating the majority: Women challenge tradition in higher education* (pp. 57–68). Washington, DC: American Council of Education/Macmillan Series on Higher Education.

Mestre, J. P., & Robinson, H. (1983). Academic, socioeconomic, and motivational differences of Hispanic college students enrolled in technical programs. *Vocational Guidance Quarterly, 31,* 187–194.

Mickens, M. (1991). Effects of supplementary computer-assisted instruction on basic algebra 1 and basic algebra 2 achievement levels of mathematics at-risk minority students (low-achieving). *Dissertation Abstracts International, 53,* sec. 3, 704A. (University Microfilms No. AAD92–15127).

Miller, S. K. (1992). Asian Americans bump against glass ceilings. *Science, 258,* 1224–1228.

Moore, E.G.J., & Smith, A. W. (1987). Sex and ethnic group differences in mathematics achievement: Results from the national longitudinal study. *Journal for Research in Mathematics Education, 18*(1), 25–36.

Moses, Y. T. (1989). *Black women in academe: Issues and strategies.* Washington, DC: Association of American Colleges.

Mukerjee, M. (1995). Coming out in the sciences. *Scientific American, 272,*(4), 24.

Mullis, I.V.S., Dossey, J. A., Owen, E. H., & Phillips, G. W. (1993). *Mathematics report card for the nation and the states* (NAEP Report No. 23-STO2). Princeton, NJ: Educational Testing Service.

Mullis, I.V.S., & Jenkins, L. B. (1988). *The science report card: Trends and achievement based on the 1986 national assessment* (Report No. 17-S-01). Princeton, NJ: Educational Testing Service.

Namenwirth, M. (1988). Science seen through a feminist prism. In R. Bleier (Ed.), *Feminist approaches to science* (pp. 18–41). Elmsford, NY: Pergamon Press.

National Science Foundation. (1990). *Women and minorities in science and engineering* (NSF Publication No. 90–301). Arlington, VA: Author.

National Science Foundation. (1994). *Women, minorities, and persons with disabilities in science and engineering.* (NSF Report No. 94–333). Arlington, VA: Author.

Nelson, R. E. (1978). *Sex differences in mathematics attitudes and related factors among Afro-American students.* Knoxville: University of Tennessee.

Nettles, M. T. (1987). Baccalaureate-level production of scientists and engineers: A critique. In L. S. Dix (Ed.), *Minorities: Their underrepresentation and career differentials in science and engineering* (pp. 67–72). Washington, DC: National Academy Press.

Nettles, M. T., Thoeny, A. R., & Gosman, E. J. (1986). Comparative and predictive analyses of black and white students' college achievement and experiences. *Journal of Higher Education, 57,* 289–318.

Nieves-Squires, S. (1991). *Hispanic women: Making their presence on campus less tenuous.* Research report. Washington, DC: Association of American Colleges.

Olstad, R. G., Juarez, J. R., Davenport, L. J., & Haury, D. L. (1981). *Inhibitors to achievement in science and mathematics by ethnic minorities.*

Seattle: University of Washington. (ERIC Document Reproduction Service No. ED 223 404)

Parsons, J. E., Adler, T. F., & Kaczala, C. M. (1982). Socialization of achievement attitudes and beliefs: Parental influences. *Child Development, 53,* 310–321.

Pascarella, E. T., & Terenzini, P. T. (1991). *How college affects students: Findings and insights from twenty years of research.* San Francisco: Jossey-Bass.

Pearson, G. A. (1992a). A funny thing happened on the way to graduate school: Race, gender, and entomology career choice. *American Entomologist, 38*(2), 80–83.

Pearson, G. A. (1992b). Gender, race, nationality, and the graduate student entomology experience. *American Entomologist, 38,* 103–114.

Pearson, W., Jr. (1982). The social origins of black American doctorates in the sciences. *Sociological Spectrum, 2,* 13–29.

Pearson, W., Jr. (1986). Black American participation in American science: Winning some battles but losing the war. *Journal of Educational Equity and Leadership, 6*(1), 45–49.

Pearson, W., Jr. (1987). The graduate education and careers of underrepresented minorities in science and engineering. In L. S. Dix (Ed.), *Minorities: Their underrepresentation and career differentials in science and engineering* (pp. 133–150). Washington, DC: National Academy Press.

Pearson, W., Jr., & Pearson, L. C. (1985). Baccalaureate origins of Black American scientists: A cohort analysis. *Journal of Negro Education, 54*(1), 24–34.

Plewis, I. (1991). Pupils' progress in reading and mathematics during primary school: Associations with ethnic group and sex. *Educational Research, 33*(2), 133–140.

Porter, O. F. (1989). *Undergraduate completion and persistence at four-year colleges and universities: Completers, persisters, stopouts, and dropouts.* Research report. Washington, DC: National Institute of Independent Colleges and Universities.

Powell, R., & García, J. (1985). Portrayal of minorities and women in selected elementary science series. *Journal of Research in Science Teaching, 22,* 519–533.

Pulos, S., Stage, E. K., & Karplus, R. (1982). Setting effects in mathematical reasoning of early adolescents: Findings from three urban schools. *Journal of Early Adolescence, 2*(1), 39–59.

Rakow, S. J. (1985). Minority students in science. *Urban Education, 20*(1), 103–113.

Rakow, S. J., & Walker, C. L. (1985). The status of Hispanic American students in science: Achievement and exposure. *Science Education, 69,* 557–565.

Ramirez, M., & Castaneda, A. (1974). *Cultural democracy: Bicognitive development and education.* New York: Academic Press.

Rayman, P., & Brett, B. (1993). *Pathways for women in the sciences.* Wellesley, MA: Wellesley College Center for Research on Women.

Reyes, L. H., & Stanic, G.M.A. (1988). Race, sex, socioeconomic status, and mathematics. *Journal for Research in Mathematics Education, 19*(1), 26–43.

Reynolds, A. J. (1991). Effects of an experiment-based physical science program on cognitive outcomes. *Journal of Educational Research, 84*(5), 296–302.

Rhone, L. M. (1989). Relations between parental expectation, mathematics ability, mathematics anxiety, achievement on mathematics word problems, and overall mathematics achievement in black adolescents. *Dissertation Abstracts International, 50,* sec. 12, 3902A. (University Microfilms No. AAD90–04317).

Ricker, K. S. (1978). Science and the physically handicapped. *Viewpoints in Teaching and Learning, 55,* 67–76.

Rodríguez, C. M. (1993). *Minorities in science and engineering: Patterns for success.* Unpublished doctoral dissertation, University of Arizona.

Rosser, S. V. (1990). *Female-friendly science: Applying women's studies methods and theories to attract students.* New York: Pergamon Press.

Sadker, D., & Sadker, M. (1985). Sexism in the schoolroom of the 80's. *Psychology Today, 19*(3), 54–57.

Sands, A. (1993). Never meant to survive: A black woman's journey. In S. Harding (Ed.), *The "racial" economy of science* (pp. 239–258). Bloomington and Indianapolis: Indiana University Press.

Schibeci, R. A. (1984). Selecting appropriate attitudinal objectives for school science. *Science Education, 67,* 595–603.

Schreiber, D. A. (1984). *Factors affecting female attitude formation toward science: Specific reference to 12–14 year old female adolescents and their affective orientation toward middle school science.* Master's thesis, University of Cincinnati, Cincinnati, OH. (ERIC Document Reproduction Service No. ED 256 617)

Schwartz, B. B. (1993). *Breaking the mold: Expanding the horizons for physics students (and the responsibility of the physics community).* Unpublished manuscript. Brooklyn College, City University of New York.

Sells, L. W. (1980). The mathematics filter and the education of women and minorities. In L. H. Fox & D. Tobin (Eds.), *Women and the mathematical mystique* (pp. 66–75). Baltimore, MD: Johns Hopkins University Press.

Seymour, E. (1992). Undergraduate problems with teaching and advising in SME majors: Explaining gender differences in attrition rates. *Journal of College Science Teaching, 11*(5), 284–292.

Seymour, E., & Hewitt, N. M. (1994). *Talking about leaving: Factors contributing to high attrition rates among science, mathematics, and engineering undergraduate majors.* Final report to the Alfred P. Sloan Foundation on an ethnographic inquiry at seven institutions, University of Colorado, Boulder.

Sherman, J. (1980). *Women and mathematics: Summary of research from 1977–1979 NIE Grant.* Final report. Madison: Women's Research Institute of Wisconsin, Inc. (ERIC Document Reproduction Service No. ED 182 162)

Signer, B. R. (1991). CAI and at-risk minority urban high school students. *Journal of Research on Computing in Education, 24*(2), 189–203.

Simpson, R. D., & Oliver, J. S. (1985). Attitude toward science and achievement motivation profiles of male and female science students in grades six through ten. *Science Education, 69*, 511–526.

Sims, C. (1992a). From inner-city L.A. to Yale engineering. *Science, 258,* 1232.

Sims, C. (1992b). What went wrong: Why programs failed. *Science, 258,* 1185–1187.

Smith, W. S., & Erb, T. O. (1986). Effect of women science career role models on early adolescents' attitudes toward scientists and women in science. *Journal of Research in Science Teaching, 23*, 667–676.

Stanley, S., & Abe, J. (1988). *Predictors of academic achievement among Asian American and white students* (College Board Report No. 88–11). New York: College Entrance Examination Board.

Steinkamp, M. W., & Maehr, M. L. (1984). Gender differences in motivational orientations toward achievement in school science: A quantitative synthesis. *American Educational Research Journal, 21*, 39–59.

Stokes, A. (1990). Relationships among level of cognitive development, gender, chronological age, and mathematics achievement. *Journal of Negro Education, 59*, 299–315.

Suskind, R. (1994, September 22). Class struggle: Poor, black and smart, an inner-city teen tries to survive M.I.T. *Wall Street Journal*, pp. A1(W), A1(E), col 1.

Talton, E. L., & Simpson, R. D. (1985). Relationships between peer and individual attitudes toward science among adolescent students. *Science Education, 69*(1), 19–24.

Thomas, G. E. (1984). *Black college students and factors influencing their major field choice.* Atlanta, GA: Southern Education Foundation.

Thomas, G. E. (1986). *The access and success of blacks and Hispanics in U.S. graduate and professional education.* (Available from National Research Council, Office of Scientific and Engineering Personnel, 2101 Constitution Ave. NW, Washington, DC 20418)

Tidball, E. M. (1989). Women's colleges: Exceptional conditions, not exceptional talent, produce high achievers. In G. S. Pearson, J. G. Touchton, & D. L. Shavlik (Eds.), *Educating the majority.* New York: Macmillan.

Tinmouth, J., & Hamwi, G. (1994). The experience of gay and lesbian students in medical school. *Journal of the American Medical Association, 271,* 714–715.

Tizard, B., Blatchford, P., Burke, J., Farquhar, C., & Plewis, I. (1988). *Young children at school in the inner city.* Hillsdale, NJ: Erlbaum.

Tobias, S. (1990). *They're not dumb, they're different: Stalking the second tier.* Tucson, AZ: Research Corporation.

Townsend, M. H., Wallick, M. M., & Cambre, K. M. (1991). Support services for homosexual students at U.S. medical schools. *Academic Medicine, 66*(6), 361–363.

Townsend, M. H., Wallick, M. M., & Cambre, K. M. (1993). Gay and lesbian issues in residency training at U.S. psychiatry programs. *Academic Psychiatry, 17*(2), 67–72.

Treisman, P. U. (1982). *Helping minority students to excel in university-level mathematics and science courses.* Unpublished manuscript, University of California Professional Development Program, Berkeley.

Treisman, P. U. (1992). Studying students studying calculus: A look at the lives of minority mathematics students in college. *College Mathematics Journal, 23,* 362–372.

Tsai, S., & Walberg, H. J. (1983). Mathematics achievement and attitude productivity in junior high school. *Journal of Educational Research, 76,* 267–272.

U.S. Congress. Office of Technology Assessment. (1988, December). *Elementary and secondary education for science and engineering: A technical memorandum* (OTA-TM-SET-41). Washington, DC: U.S. Government Printing Office.

Valverde, L. A. (1984). Underachievement and underrepresentation of Hispanics in mathematics and mathematics-related careers. *Journal for Research in Mathematics Education, 15*(2), 123–133.

Vanfossen, B. E. (1984, August). *Sex differences in mathematics performance: Continuing evidence.* Paper presented to Sociologists for Women in Society session, American Sociological Association.

Vélez, W. (1985). Finishing college: The effects of college type. *Sociology of Education, 58,* 191–200.

Walker, C. L., & Rakow, S. J. (1985). The status of Hispanic American students in science: Attitudes. *Hispanic Journal of Behavioral Sciences, 7,* 225–245.

Wallick, M. M., Cambre, K. M., & Townsend, M. H. (1992). How the topic of homosexuality is taught at U.S. medical school. *Academic Medicine, 67,* 601–603. Washington, DC: National Academy Press.

Ware, N. C., & Lee, V. E. (1988). Sex differences in choice of college science majors. *American Educational Research Journal, 25,* 593–614.

Wiegand, D., Ginorio, A. B., & Brown, M. D. (1994, October). *First steps in college science: A comparison of single sex versus coeducational programs.* Final report to the Women's College Coalition. Seattle: University of Washington.

Yong, F. I. (1992). Mathematics and science attitudes of African-American middle grade students identified as gifted: Gender and grade differences. *Roeper Review, 14*(3), 136–140.

Zwick, R. (1991). *Differences in graduate school attainment patterns across academic programs and demographic groups* (Research Rep. No. 143). Princeton, NJ: Educational Testing Service.

Chapter Seven

Program and Curricular Interventions

Cinda-Sue Davis, Sue V. Rosser

Over the past two decades, there has been an increasing national awareness, even urgency, about the underrepresentation of women in science, mathematics, engineering, and other technical fields. Women now make up over half the undergraduate population in this country, yet, as described in Chapter Two, their presence in technical fields still lags behind. Advocates for equitable representation initially argued that it was only right and just that females have an equal opportunity for careers in science, mathematics, and engineering (SME). Now another argument has been added: in an increasingly technological world, the United States can ill afford to lose the contributions of half its brainpower.

Equity and national self-interest justify a significant investment of time and resources to encourage, recruit, and retain girls and women in SME fields. In 1993, the federal government spent $2.2 billion on 290 programs in science, mathematics, engineering, and technology. Of this amount, 42 percent went to graduate education, 35 percent to elementary and secondary education, 20 percent to undergraduate education, and 3 percent to public understanding of science. Funding went for organizational reform, comprehensive programs, student support, curriculum improvement, faculty enhancement, and other activities. Eleven percent (or $236 million) supported programs that targeted underrepresented groups such as women, minorities, or persons with disabilities. Support for women in SME accounted for 22 percent of the $236 million (National Science Foundation, 1993).

Obviously, investment in SME education is substantial. The question remains, however, whether this investment is making any difference. Is the overall scientific literacy of the population increasing? Are any more underrepresented individuals pursuing SME degrees and careers? This chapter examines two areas of core funding with direct impact on students, namely curriculum and programmatic intervention.

While we know from Chapter Two that some gains have been made in some fields, we do not know how much is due to effective intervention in recruiting and retaining women, and how much to other factors. Which interventions are the most effective, particularly at the undergraduate and graduate level? What evaluation has been done of the myriad of intervention programs and/or curricular reforms? What would a female-friendly SME curriculum look like? This chapter will address these issues by attempting to identify effective intervention and curricular efforts while also identifying gaps in the evaluation literature.

Programmatic Interventions and Evaluations

The past two decades have seen a slow but steady proliferation of campus women-in-science and women-in-engineering initiatives. Matyas and Malcom (1991) identified over three hundred programs dedicated to SME interventions at U.S. colleges and universities. Of these, 51 percent were for minority students (naturally including women of color), while 10 percent were for female undergraduate students. Most of these were women-in-engineering programs, although some, like the programs at Dartmouth, Douglass College, and the University of Michigan, focus on women's issues in science and engineering. A 1991 survey by the Women in Engineering Program Advocates Network (WEPAN) found that thirty-one institutions of higher education had formal women-in-engineering programs (Brainard, 1993). Due to extensive regional training programs offered to individuals at the college and university level by WEPAN, the number of such programs is likely to increase in the immediate future.

Evaluation is critical to any intervention program or curricular innovation. Without evaluation, it is impossible to tell whether an intervention or curriculum has achieved the desired goal or objective. Good evaluation has several important outcomes, as documented in an excellent book entitled *Evaluating Intervention Programs* (Davis & Humphreys, 1985). These outcomes include the following:

- Evaluation gives you knowledge.
- Evaluation helps you plan.
- Evaluation results help shape policy.
- Evaluation helps you document achievement.
- Evaluation helps you attract funds.
- Evaluation helps identify successful innovations.
- Evaluation identifies the best and propagates it.
- Evaluation educates the public.

Evaluation can take many forms: *formative,* to help manage the program more effectively, and *summative,* to report on program quality and merit. Evaluation can be both *quantitative,* using questionnaires, enrollment and graduate data, grades, and so on; and *qualitative,* using focus groups or interviews. Combining these methods is particularly effective. It is beyond the scope of this chapter to describe evaluation methods in detail, but the references cite several excellent sources (see, for example, Udinsky, Osterlind, & Lynch, 1981; Fitz-Gibbon & Morris, 1987; Rossi & Freeman, 1989; Patton, 1990; Berk & Rossi, 1990).

Statistics on the Evaluation of Intervention Programs

Of the federally funded core programs, 20 percent have been evaluated, 32 percent have been monitored (that is, statistics have been collected and reviewed), and 48 percent have been neither evaluated nor monitored. In 1993, funding for evaluation ($8 million) constituted less than one-half of 1 percent of core funding for SME education (Expert Panel . . . , 1993). Matyas and Malcom (1991) found that fewer than half of the intervention programs at U.S. colleges and universities had done *any* kind of evaluation of their activities. Obviously, there is an enormous lack of evaluation data upon which to build programmatic interventions.

Types of Interventions

Intervention programs take many forms. Some focus on engineering, like those at Purdue University or the University of Washington, while others combine science, mathematics, and engineering, as at the University of Michigan or Dartmouth College. Some focus on recruitment at the K–12 level, others on college-age students; most combine the two approaches. Intervention techniques are equally varied. Most programs incorporate traditional tools: career workshops, mentoring, one-on-one counseling, internships, role models, and publicity brochures and posters. Some, like the University of Michigan Women in Science and Engineering (WISE) Program, combine these techniques with advocacy and research on women's issues, both within the institution and nationally.

Evaluation of these program components is spotty at best. Professional networks such as WEPAN and the Association for Women in Science (AWIS) report that some programs do some form of evaluation. Seldom, however, does this evaluation involve long-term studies of effect. Very few programs use random assignment so that effect can be reliably assessed. Most evaluations are formative, looking only at participants, with no controls. Summative evaluations are rare. For summaries of programmatic efforts with evaluations, see Stage, 1992; Matyas and Dix, 1992; and Sherry and Dix, 1992.

Evaluations are most often used in-house, to improve the next program. Results seldom appear in peer review journals, and computerized library searches turn up almost nothing about them. This section summarizes various interventions and the extent of the evaluation that can be determined. Insofar as possible, we report only programs at the undergraduate or graduate level that have been evaluated. This further restricts the data available, since most of the meager literature is at the K–12 level.

Research Internships

Research internships are traditional for recruiting and retaining students in science and engineering, both in high school and at college/university. The University of Michigan (Sloat & DeLoughry, 1985) and the University of Alberta, Canada (Armour, 1987) have sponsored high school women as interns since 1984. The National Science Foundation (NSF) has sponsored undergraduate internships, on and off, for at least the last thirty-five years. Most recently, the NSF sponsored the Research Experience for Undergraduates (REU) program, which funds students in science and engineering by providing money either directly to sites, usually university or college departments, which in turn sponsor students, or through supplements to research grants whereby principal investigators select and sponsor students (National Science Foundation [NSF], 1990).

At the college level, freshman or sophomore internships can recruit students, especially women and minorities, to science and engineering majors. Institutions where students select majors at the end of the second year or the start of the third year typically use this approach. Examples of such programs are the Research Internship Program at Dartmouth or the Undergraduate Research Opportunity Program at Michigan. Both of these programs are too new to have sufficient data for analysis, but preliminary results at Dartmouth are positive. As reported by Muller (1993), "Of the women students who undertook research internships during the project's first year, 60 percent have declared a major in science. Of those who participated in the project in other ways, 43 percent declared a science major. Of those women students who initially expressed an interest in pursuing a science major but did not participate in the project, only 22 percent declared a science major" (p. 43). The next set of data to be collected will be graduation rates and majors of these women.

The Undergraduate Research Opportunity Program (UROP) at the University of Michigan is studying how research partnerships between faculty and freshmen or sophomores affect retention rates and quality of educational experience. This study targets four hundred or more students per year, of whom a significant number will be at risk of attrition from science. UROP students are chosen from lower division undergraduate students, with an emphasis on women interested in the sciences. A cohort of these students will be tracked while in the program and for five years thereafter, to assess academic progress and changes in attitudes, especially attitudes about identification with college. Appropriate control groups will be used in the study (Gregerman, personal communication, 1994).

When offered at the junior or senior year, undergraduate research internships can encourage and motivate students to pursue graduate degrees. The NSF REU program addresses this issue, as does the Pipeline Program developed by University of Michigan WISE staff. The NSF reported that 80 percent of REU students indicated increased interest in science and engineering as a result of their participation. A larger proportion of students planned to attend graduate school in science or engineering after REU involvement than before. After participation, female students were more likely than males to have indicated that "learning about the nature of the job of a researcher" and "the basics of the scientific method" were very important to them (NSF, 1990, p. 8).

The Michigan Pipeline Program is designed to encourage high-achieving women engineering students to consider graduate degrees in the field. The program combines research internships for juniors with career workshops, graduate school orientation workshops, and small counseling sessions called "Planning Your Future" groups. Formative and summative evaluations with non-participating male controls are still being analyzed, but preliminary data indicate some interesting gender differences. Pipeline participants seem to have had less direct personal encouragement about graduate work in engineering from faculty members, and perhaps generally from others in their environment, than have their male peers. In addition, women express less confidence in their academic ability than men, despite identical GPAs. Women show more interest than men in working on a research team with faculty or graduate students. Lastly, women are less comfortable challenging other students in class. All of this preliminary data strongly suggests the need for a program such as Pipeline (Davis & Hollenshead, 1993).

It is important to note that few of these programs use random assignment. It can be argued that participating students are highly committed to science or engineering before they join, and that such programs are therefore not really increasing overall numbers of students recruited or retained in science.

Role Models

Many if not all programs also work on providing role models. Workshops feature professional women scientists and engineers, both from academia and industry. Lectureship series with visiting women faculty members are common. Indeed, one of the factors often cited as fostering future scientists at women's colleges is the abundance of women role models among the faculty. Tidball (1980) argues, "The more adult women of accomplishment present in the environment, the more likely are women students to proceed to their own post-college accomplishments" (p. 515). This study was done with women faculty and students in the natural sciences.

However, little is actually known about the effectiveness of role models. What must a role model do to influence students to pursue scientific studies and careers? Is it sufficient to participate in a two-hour workshop on careers in science, or must there be more sustained interaction such as teaching a course or working together on a project? In the latter case, is it still role modeling or is it mentoring? Must the role model necessarily be female? How senior (or junior) must a role model be? Much more research is needed on role models, with appropriate controls.

The University of Queensland's Women in Science and Technology in Australia (UQ WISTA) project sampled ten major institutions, finding no evidence that mere numbers of women faculty or staff increased the numbers of undergraduate women in a field (Byrne, 1993). To date, this is the only comprehensive study on the subject, and it strongly suggests that mere role modeling, as opposed to mentoring, is not effective. Byrne goes on to outline several implications of this research. If the effectiveness of role models is accepted on faith but is not valid, the already limited time of the very busy women who are continually asked to appear before groups of students is likely to be wasted. Men, feeling they cannot be appropriate role models, will not bother to assist girls and women to pursue careers in nontraditional areas. Lastly, time and money spent on inspirational video and television programs featuring women scientists might better be invested in other interventions.

Living-Learning Communities

The best-known residential community for women in science and engineering is Bunting-Cobb, at Douglass College, the women's college of Rutgers. This residence hall holds one hundred women; it has undergraduate and graduate student living space, counselors, on-site computers, and recreation facilities. A similar program, the Women in Science and Engineering Residential Program

(WISE-RP), has been developed over the past year at the University of Michigan. Although the two institutions have very different academic environments, the principles of creating a living-learning community are essentially the same. These consist of providing a small, supportive academic and social community, complete with study groups, career and academic workshops, cohort grouping of first-year classes, and counseling.

Both programs have extensive evaluations in place, both formative and summative, with appropriate controls. The Michigan study uses quantitative and qualitative methodology. It is still too early to judge the impact of these activities, but a preliminary report from the Michigan study finds that the three main sample groups (WISE-RP women, other women, and men, all with comparable math SAT scores and interest in science, mathematics, or engineering studies) differed significantly in how they responded to a pre-survey. WISE-RP and control women are more likely than men to say they prefer to work with a study group and to talk with members of that group if they encounter academic difficulty. Women are more confident than men of success in their chosen field. Men and WISE-RP women have more confidence in their mathematics ability than control women. Women are more likely to say that discrimination is a problem that could discourage them from technical careers. Friends in their field of choice, supportive study groups, tutoring, smaller classes, and lack of anonymity are benefits of a residential program that are more important for WISE-RP women than for control women or men (Wenzel & Manis, 1994).

Mentoring Programs

The value of an advanced graduate student or faculty member who takes a special interest in nurturing the intellectual and professional potential of a student cannot be underestimated. Mentors are believed to be even more critical for women students, who perceive themselves as minorities in the physical sciences, some fields of mathematics, and engineering.

Several institutions have incorporated various aspects of mentoring. The University of Washington and Rutgers-Douglass have implemented similar programs that match freshman women with older, more experienced women students (advanced undergraduates or graduate students) with the intention of developing a mentoring relationship. Others have developed mentoring programs for students with faculty members (University of California, Berkeley) or with professionals (University of Washington).

The Association for Women in Science (AWIS) has undertaken an ambitious program called "The Mentoring Project" (Bird & Didion, 1993). AWIS chapters conduct a wide variety of activities that promote formation of mentoring relationships. These include the following:

- Periodic receptions or luncheons with guest speakers
- Chapter meetings and seminars
- Workshops on mentoring and other topics
- Funding of travel for students to attend scientific meetings
- Other activities that foster the development of mentoring relationships, such as scientific poster sessions
- One-on-one mentoring and small-group discussion meetings

This project includes extensive evaluation, assessing the various mentoring methods to determine how effective they are in reaching students and influencing career decisions. Ongoing formative evaluations identify activities most worthwhile for each chapter. It would be desirable to compare graduation rates and graduate degrees of AWIS participants versus women (and men) not in the program, but most institutions do not collect this type of data. Instead, qualitative information will be collected from participants in an effort to determine why individuals chose to pursue or to refrain from pursuing professional interests in science, mathematics, or engineering (Bird & Didion, 1993).

The effectiveness of mentoring programs can depend on the institution. A program developed by Brooklyn College as part of the Eureka Program met with limited success (Miller & Silver, 1993). On a commuter campus, students with outside jobs often find it very difficult to take part in program offerings. Only 4 percent of Eureka participants found the faculty mentor program very helpful. Often, faculty overtures met with no response.

Professional and Social Support

Women in science often miss out on the traditionally all-male social networks. They thus miss the exchange of information and resources, and they also miss whatever advantages or privileges may derive from network membership.

Living-learning communities and interventions such as the Pipeline Program attempt to create alternative support networks for women in science. Other interventions designed for the same purpose include social gatherings or orientations at which women can meet and see others with similar goals and interests. Several universities have compiled directories of women in various fields or of local women in the sciences, or maintain current files on campus or national organizations for women in these fields.

Comprehensive Programs

Most university or college women-in-science and women-in-engineering programs use combinations or variations of the interventions we have described. For example, over its fifteen-year history, the University of Michigan WISE Program has offered career workshops, undergraduate internships, a living-learning program for first and second year undergraduate women, a women scientist lecture series (for role modeling), social support groups, and a pipeline program to encourage undergraduate women to pursue graduate degrees, among others.

Most university programs do some evaluation, either of individual interventions (generally in a formative manner) or of entry and graduation rates of female students. The University of Washington, for example, obtains student feedback through annual surveys and individual interviews and assesses the effectiveness of each of the primary programs and services. The faculty and the corporate advisory board each conduct separate formal evaluations (Brainard, 1993). Michigan, Purdue, and Penn State conduct similar evaluations.

Many institutions use national trends in female enrollment and degrees to assess program success. Alternatively, they look for increases in female enrollment and graduation rates at their own campuses to track effectiveness. Although the statistics are vital, far too few institutions look at graduation rates by both discipline and gender. And even such graduation rates are not enough on their own—without formative and summative evaluations and appropriate controls, it is dangerous to attribute increases in female participation and graduation directly to programmatic interventions.

Many factors—new freshman curricula, new and inspirational professors, improvements in high school mathematics preparedness—can all increase student participation in science or engineering. It is also important to determine whether programs draw new students into the scientific pipeline or merely reshuffle students already in it. If an engineering program simply persuades women planning engineering careers to choose one university over another, there is no overall gain in the number of women pursuing engineering degrees. It is imperative that women-in-science and women-in-engineering programs address these issues—and have the financial support and staff to do so.

Undergraduate Curriculum Reform

Of the less than 10 percent of programs that do focus on women (Matyas & Malcom, 1991), virtually none consider the impact of classroom activities on recruitment and retention. A growing body of research documents the need to change the way science is taught at the undergraduate level to make it more appealing to students, regardless of gender (Astin & Astin, 1993; Astin, Green, Korn, & Riggs, 1991; Green, 1989a, 1989b; Seymour & Hewitt, 1994). For example, the latest Cooperative Institutional Research Program (CIRP) report (Astin & Astin, 1993) reveals that 40 percent of freshmen interested in science, mathematics, and engineering (SME) change their plans before they graduate. Other studies document that the highest risk of SME switching (35 percent) occurs between the first and second years (NSF, 1990).

In response to these and other studies (Tobias, 1990, 1992; Seymour & Hewitt, 1994; Astin & Astin, 1993) relating SME attrition to problems with undergraduate pedagogy and curriculum, government agencies (NSF, 1989; National Research Council [NRC], 1993; Neale et al., 1991) and private foundations (Oakes, 1990; Strenta, Elliott, Matier, Scott, & Adair, 1993; Tobias, 1992) have emphasized—and poured funding into—curricular reform. New freshman engineering courses, tailored physics sequences for engineering, Chemistry in Context, and guided design calculus (NSF, 1991–1993) exemplify some of the large-scale curricular reforms funded at the undergraduate level. Hands-on laboratory experiences, collaborative learning, emphasis on practical applications, and group work (Project Kaleidoscope, 1994) have been implemented in an attempt to improve retention of all students.

Although some studies have explored relative gender differences in SME retention (Seymour & Hewitt, 1994; Astin & Astin, 1993; Strenta et al., 1993), very few reforms have focused on women. For example, the NSF's *Undergraduate Course and Curriculum Development Program 1991 Summary* reveals that in 1991 two out of 88 new awards focused on women as a specific target population; in 1992 the figure was five out of 110 new awards, and in 1993 it was six out of 82 new awards.

In an attempt to increase the presence of women in most areas of science, mathematics, and engineering, the NSF set up the Program for Women and Girls in its Division of Human Resource Development, with three initiatives to involve and retain women in the pipeline from kindergarten through the faculty level. However, only twenty-two of forty-three Model Projects funded between 1988 and 1993 (NSF, 1994) targeted the undergraduate level and above; of those twenty-two, only eleven might be said to center on pedagogy, curriculum, or classroom climate, by applying the most liberal definitions of those terms. Of the eleven Experimental Projects proposals (first funded in fiscal 1994), only three focus on the undergraduate classroom or have a major classroom component. Similarly, of the twenty projects funded by the Women's Educational Equity Act Programs in 1993, five targeted postsecondary women (Women's Educational Equity Act [WEEA], 1993). Of those five, only one had a faculty development component designed to make upper division instructors aware of the needs of women students and to introduce collaborative learning and gender neutrality, and that was not the primary focus of the project. In sum, most of the curriculum reform efforts in science, mathematics, and engineering have not focused on women, and most of the efforts centered on women in science have not focused on curriculum or classroom issues.

In contrast, a growing body of research in education (Harding, 1985; Kahle, 1985; Astin & Astin, 1993), sociology (Seymour & Hewitt, 1994), and women's studies (Rosser, 1990, 1993b; Fausto-Sterling, 1992) documents the need for new science pedagogy and curriculum to appeal to women. Women's studies scholars have noted that science as it is currently taught and practiced may reflect a masculine approach to the world that tends to exclude women (Keller, 1985; Harding, 1986). This critique has been developed most extensively for biology (Bleier, 1984; Birke, 1986; Fausto-Sterling, 1992; Hubbard, 1990; Rosser, 1986, 1990), leading scholars to examine curricular content and pedagogy in that field. Very recently, scholars have begun to expand the critique to physics (Barad, 1995), geology (Richardson, Sutton, & Cercone, 1995), mathematics (Campbell & Campbell-Wright, 1995), computer science (Eastman, 1995), engineering (Hynes, 1995), and chemistry (Harris, 1995). Because physical science and engineering faculty have only just begun to consider the impact of gender and the implications of new scholarship on women for their disciplines and classrooms, their efforts will need considerable development to reach the level of work done in the early 1980s on the biological sciences.

Faculty have evolved new approaches to teaching and expanded the curriculum to include new and more "female-friendly" material (Rosser, 1990). Some curriculum reform projects consider research from women's studies, or a women's studies scholar may be brought in to discuss curricular content or pedagogy. However, most projects pay little attention to findings from women's or ethnic studies, which might be useful in attracting women and people of color to science. For example, the Ford Foundation report on the incorporation of ethnic minority women into the curriculum noted that even after a curriculum transformation project, ten of twelve courses still had less than 10 percent of content focusing on women of color. One had 10 percent and one had 20 percent (Ginorio, Butler, Conte, & Schmitz, 1993). That report also described science faculty as claiming less familiarity with ethnic studies scholarship in their fields than did scholars in other disciplines. This may be particularly unfortunate, since, as Seymour and Hewitt (1994) conclude, "There are substantial numbers of students who could be retained in SEM majors if appropriate structural and cultural changes are made" (p. 521).

Transformation in Curricular Content: A Model

A few projects funded by the NSF (Rosser & Kelly, 1994; Ross & Rosser, 1994) do apply approaches and curricular content from women's studies as their primary means of involving and retaining women in science. They build on the twenty-five years of women's studies scholarship and experience with curriculum transformation projects that have enabled faculty to develop models (McIntosh, 1984; Schuster & Van Dyne, 1984) charting the phases through which changes occur in a variety of disciplines in diverse institutions. The Rosser and Kelly (1994) and Ross and Rosser (1994) projects apply a similar phase model and pedagogical techniques for the sciences. This model suggests a progression through which faculty and institutions may move to build a curriculum more inclusive of people of color and of women (Rosser, 1993b).

Phase I: Absence of Women Is Not Noted

Many physical science, math, and engineering (and some life science) curricula are in this phase. That is, faculty and students are unaware of the lack of women in theoretical and decision-making positions in the scientific establishment or of the absence of women in the curriculum. They assume that since science is objective, gender does not influence either who becomes a scientist or the results produced. Many scientists hold that science is "manless" as well as "womanless"—they are unaware of or openly reject the idea that gender might influence theories, data collection, subjects chosen for experimentation, or questions asked. Many scientists in the behavioral and biological sciences have moved beyond this stage to acknowledge the influence of gender and to evolve strategies incorporating it in appropriate ways in their classrooms.

Phase II: Recognition That Science Has a Masculine Perspective

Recent publicity from the government and professional societies has made most scientists aware that women are underrepresented in all natural science fields, particularly at the theoretical and decision-making levels (Vetter, 1992). Some scientists, influenced by scholarship in women's studies, philosophy and history of science, and psychology have begun to recognize that gender may influence science. Fee (1982) and Keller (1982) have suggested that the absence of women from decision making has produced a science that views the world from a male perspective and is, therefore, womanless. The failure of scientists to recognize this bias has perpetuated the idea of the objectivity of science. Errors such as extrapolating data collected on males to all members (both male and female) of a species (Rosser, 1993a); using the male body as the norm for defining a disease such as AIDS, which has different symptoms in males and females (Rosser, 1991; Marte & Anastos, 1990); and funding extensive research into cardiovascular disease in men while vastly underfunding research into breast cancer in women (Rinzler, 1993) exemplify the influence of the masculine perspective in biological and health care research.

Phase III: Identification of Barriers to Women in Science

Many indicators suggest that the U.S. scientific establishment is currently in this phase. The studies of attempts to attract more women into science and math illustrate this phase. Virtually every federal funding agency (NSF, 1992; Pinn & LaRosa, 1992), professional society, and foundation (American Chemical Society [ACS], 1983; Vetter, 1992; NRC, 1991) involved with science and science funding have issued studies and reports documenting the lack of women in science and the barriers that may have led to this dearth.

Phase IV: Search for Women Scientists and Their Unique Contributions

Historians of science, spurred on by the work of feminists in history, have recovered the names and contributions of the lost women of science, such as Rosalind Franklin, whose fundamental (but widely undervalued) work on the x-ray crystallography of DNA led to the theoretical speculation of the double helical nature of the molecule by Watson and Crick (Watson, 1969; Sayre, 1975). Ellen Swallow provides another excellent example: her groundbreaking work in water, air, and food purity; sanitation; and industrial waste disposal began the science of ecology, but it was reclassified as home economics mainly because it was done by a woman (Hynes, 1984, 1989). Using history to show that women have been successful in traditional science is important in that it documents the excellent scientific work women have done despite extreme barriers and obstacles and thus establishes science as both natural and appropriate for women.

Phase V: Analyzing Science Done by Feminists/Women

Uncovering women scientists and their contributions offers an opportunity to examine differences between their work and that of men. Because of the scarcity of women scientists and their need to conform to standards set largely by their male peers, few studies compare the work of women and men in science (Keller, 1983; Harding, 1991; Morell, 1993). Science courses rarely cite these studies, but history or philosophy of science or women's studies courses may do so. Recent work suggests possible differences between men and women in distance between scientist and subject, in the use of females as experimental subjects, and in the effect of language in conceptualizing theories.

For example, Barbara McClintock was an achieving scientist who was not a feminist. However, in her approach to the study of maize, she revealed a shortening of the distance between observer and object and a consideration of the complex interaction between the organism and its environment. Her statement upon receiving the Nobel Prize was, "It might seem unfair to reward a person for having so much pleasure over the years, asking the maize plant to solve specific problems and then watching its responses" (Keller, 1984, p. 44). Her words suggest a closer, more intimate relationship with her research subject than typically expressed by the male scientist. One does not normally associate "a feeling for the organism" (Keller, 1983, p. 197) with the rational, masculine approach to science. McClintock also set aside the predominant hierarchical theory of genetic DNA as the Master Molecule controlling gene action and focused on the interaction between the organism and its environment as the locus of control.

Use of female experimental subjects may lead to models that come closer to functioning, complex biological systems. Hoffman (1982) questions the use of male rats or primates as subjects now that new blood measurement techniques have revealed episodic rather than steady hormone secretion patterns in both sexes. She suggests that the rhythmic cycle of hormone secretion as also portrayed in the cycling female appears to be a more accurate model for the secretion of most hormones.

Women in primate research have begun to challenge the language used to describe primate behavior and the patriarchal assumption inherent in the search for dominance hierarchies in primate groups. For example, Lancaster (1975) describes a single-male troop as follows: "For a female, males are a resource in her environment which she may use to further the survival of herself and her offspring. If environmental conditions are such that the male role can be minimal, a one-male group is likely. Only one male is necessary for a group of females if his only role is to impregnate them" (p. 34). Her work points out the androcentric bias of primate behavior theories, which describe a single-male group as a harem and its behavior as dominance and subordination. The situation would sound quite different if a theorist used a gynocentric term such as *stud*—which reveals the importance of gender-neutral language such as that suggested by Lancaster.

Phase VI: Science Redefined and Reconstructed to Include Us All

The ultimate goal of the phase model is the production of a more complete account of the knowledge base. This enhanced curriculum, including information about people of color and women, should in turn draw individuals from those groups to the study of science. Obviously this comprehensive picture of reality has not yet been fully developed. Most curricular reform documents state phase VI as an overarching goal (American Association for the Advancement of Science [AAAS], 1990; Project Kaleidoscope, 1994). Part of the scientific community remains in phases I and II, but it is probably fair to place the scientific establishment as a whole between phases III and IV, identifying barriers unique to women in science and searching for unique contributions of women scientists in an attempt to overcome barriers. Only tiny hints of phase V, in which the unique approaches of women scientists reveal new information, have begun to emerge. No institution of higher education, no entire department, and possibly no complete course has reached phase VI, a truly evenhanded view of science.

Pedagogical Techniques

Research in women's studies, ethnic studies, sociology, and science education offers suggestions for pedagogy to make SME more attractive to a diverse group of students. Although evolved to attract men of color, women, and others underrepresented in the pool of scientists, these techniques have been shown to be as successful—or more so—for white males (Rosser & Kelly, 1994). Seymour and Hewitt (1994) state the argument somewhat differently:

It is also clear from our data that the most effective way to improve retention among women and students of color, and to build their numbers over the longer-term, is to improve the quality of the learning experience for all students—including those who wish to study science and mathematics as part of their overall education. Though faculty sometimes like to begin a program of reform with discussions about curriculum structure and content, this is unlikely to improve retention unless it is part of a parallel, and iterative, discussion of how best to present these materials so as to secure maximum student comprehension, application, and knowledge transfer, and how to give students meaningful feedback on their academic performances [p. 523].

Undertake fewer military-based experiments and more experiments on problems of social concern. As discussed in Chapter Five, most women prefer problems and learning techniques that do not involve guns, violence, and war. Some women avoid SME studies because they are disturbed by the ways technology has been used against the environment and against human beings. Most girls and young women are neither adamant nor articulate about these feelings. However, many are uncomfortable with experiments that appear to hurt animals for no reason or that seem to apply only to calculating bomb trajectories. On the other hand, they are also attracted to science for its usefulness, particularly to help people (Harding, 1985; Astin & Astin, 1993).

A laboratory exercise common in introductory biology, with which more female than male students express discomfort, involves killing a frog by pithing its brain. One wonders if this exercise is traditional, as Halpin (1989) points out, precisely because it serves as an initiation rite and discourages students with too much empathy with animals from majoring in biology. This exercise may also pose problems for students from certain ethnic groups. For example, in some Native American tribes, the frog is a sacred animal; requiring such students to pith a frog may violate their religious beliefs (Greer, 1992). Since introductory biology serves as the gateway course for other science studies, including chemistry and physics, negative or problematic experiences here may keep students from further work in science.

In designing ways to teach problem-solving skills, it may be advisable to use some examples and problems from traditionally female fields such as home economics or nursing. Although defined as nonscience, primarily because of their association with women (Ehrenreich & English, 1978; Hynes, 1984), many approaches used in these fields are scientific. Familiar terms, equipment, and subjects will let female students concentrate on what problems really ask, without being put off by ignorance of transformers, trajectories, or other traditionally male subjects.

Investigate problems of holistic, global scope, using interactive methods. Gilligan (1982) suggests that adolescent girls approach problem solving from the perspective of interdependence and relationship rather than from the hierarchical, reductionist viewpoint favored by most adolescent boys. In addition, among college freshmen, the average female scores higher than the average male on the Perry scale (Perry, 1970) of student development. This means that she can deal with complex problems and ambiguity, while he is more comfortable with problems having one correct or concrete answer. Thus, females are more likely to feel comfortable with class assignments if they understand the relationship of the immediate problem or experiment to a larger problem to which this solution may contribute. The high attrition of women from science majors after the first course despite good grades (Matyas, 1985) may be explained partially by the way introductory courses tend to take the limited, one-true-answer approach comfortable for college freshmen.

Most instructors emphasize that scientists must be objective about their subject of study. This is seen as necessary to establish rigor and to school students in the difference between approaches used in the sciences and those used in the humanities and social sciences. Feminist critics (Haraway, 1978; Keller, 1982) and practicing scientists (Bleier, 1984; Hubbard, 1990) have pointed out that the portrayal of the scientist as distant from the object of study masks the creative interaction many scientists have with their experimental subjects. Because girls and women consider relationships to be an important part of problems, emphasis on a relationship with the object of study may attract females to study science, and absence of relationship may discourage them (Sax, 1994; Seymour & Hewitt, 1994).

Expand the kinds of observations employed in scientific research. Female students often convince themselves they are not scientific because they do not see or are not interested in observing the things required by assigned experiments. Since most scientific investigations have been undertaken by males, this difference in vision of what is interesting and important is not surprising. Accurate perceptions of reality are more likely when scientists with diverse backgrounds and outlooks observe a phenomenon. Because women often have different expectations from men, they may note different factors in their observations. This example may explain why female primatologists (Fossey, 1983; Goodall, 1971; Hrdy, 1977, 1979, 1984) saw new data such as female-female interaction when observing primate behaviors. This data, which male primatologists had not considered, led to substantial changes in the theories of subordinance and domination as the major interactive modes of primate behavior. Women students may see new data that could make a valuable contribution to scientific experiments and thus advance scientific knowledge.

Increase the numbers of observations and remain longer in the observational stage of the scientific method. As described in Chapter Two, girls at ages nine, thirteen, and seventeen have significantly less science experience than boys of comparable ages, and the disparity persists through high school. Girls and young women who lack laboratory experience are apt to feel apprehensive about using equipment and instruments in data gathering. Some research on the decreasing numbers of women majoring in computer science suggests that dislike of spending so much time with computer hardware may partially account for the decreased interest of women in the field (Gries & Marsh, 1992).

Several studies show that programs that involve and retain women in equipment-oriented fields such as engineering have a special component for remedial hands-on experience (Daniels & LeBold, 1982; Nair & Majetich, 1995). Young women feel more comfortable and successful in the laboratory when they do more hands-on work during a lengthened data-gathering stage. In a coeducational class, it is essential that females have female laboratory partners. Male-female partnerships frequently result in the male working with the equipment while the female writes down the observations. Her clerical skills may improve, but she gains no experience with equipment for her next SME course.

Incorporate and validate women's experiences in the class discussion or laboratory exercise. Most people, regardless of learning style, are interested in phenomena and situations with which they have had personal experience. Beginning the course or individual lesson with examples and equipment with which students are more likely to be familiar may reduce their anxiety. Often the context of a problem can be switched from one that is male gender–role typed to one that is female gender-role typed, or gender neutral. Many textbooks—particularly those in mathematics—have attempted to change problems to make them more inclusive of females' experiences; textbooks in physics unfortunately demonstrate few such changes (Barad, 1995).

Include women scientists who have made important discoveries. Curricula must be modified to integrate work done by women into the discussion of important scientific experiments. Students should hear of the nine women who succeeded in the traditional science establishment and won the Nobel Prize. In some cases, just mentioning the first name of the experimenters—for example, referring to Alfred Hershey and Martha Chase when discussing the finding that DNA was the genetic component in bacteriophage (Taylor, 1965)—will break the documented stereotype held by students (Chambers, 1983; Kahle, 1990) that scientists are males.

It may be crucial to convey to students that although the scientific hierarchy is set up so that one person heads the laboratory and usually wins the prize, much of the work leading to an important discovery is done by teams of people, many of whom are women. Emphasizing the lives of ordinary women in science, who have not won prizes or achieved fame, may be particularly useful in building the confidence of young women that they too can be scientists. Some recent research (Fort, 1993) suggests that women may feel inadequate for science careers when the only role models they see are famous women in the field.

Teach science with less competitive and more interdisciplinary methods. While males may thrive on competing to see who can finish a problem first, many females prefer and perform better in situations where everyone wins. Chapters Three, Four, Five, and Six all discuss ways cooperative classroom and laboratory methods make mathematics and science more attractive to females.

Converting introductory courses from the weed-out model to one that lays a foundation for future study has successfully retained more students in chemistry (Mills, 1993) and mathematics (Davis,

1993). Weed-out teaching is unlikely to appeal even to very able female students (Seymour & Hewitt, 1994). Women, who tend to be well socialized to heed overt and covert messages suggesting they are not welcome (Kahle, 1988), may respond particularly badly to weed-out instruction and particularly well to foundation building (Seymour & Hewitt).

Interest in relationships and interdependence leads female students to be more attracted to science and its methods when they perceive its usefulness in other disciplines. Mills College, a small liberal arts college for women, capitalized on this idea by emphasizing interdisciplinary courses stressing applications of mathematics to sociology, economics, and chemistry (Blum & Givant, 1982). They also developed a five-year dual degree program that permits the students to earn bachelor's degrees in both liberal arts and engineering (Blum & Givant).

Discuss the role of scientist as one facet to integrate into students' lives. Chapters Four, Five, and Six present extensive research establishing that most women worry about combining a scientific career and family life. It is clear that the issue of the compatibility between career and family must be addressed if larger numbers of young women are to be attracted to science. Role models of successful and ordinary women scientists from a variety of backgrounds can best address this issue (Fort, 1993). Including these women as part of the curricular content, for example to present seminars on their research, suggests to both male and female students that women scientists exist and that they reflect a variety of ages, sizes, races, and lifestyles.

Put increased effort into communications techniques and ethics. Technical terminology is frightening and inaccessible to many people in our society, particularly females (Bentley, 1985). In addition, Hall and Sandler (1982) provide evidence that female speech patterns and other verbal and nonverbal communication methods lead faculty and others to devalue women's answers and theories. New approaches for communicating scientific information may aid in attracting women to science while opening the door for a new appreciation and valuing of the ideas of females in science. It may be necessary to restructure the science curriculum to emphasize communication skills. A survey of engineering seniors at Purdue University (Daniels & LeBold, 1982) discovered that

female students were more apt than males to emphasize education goals stressing general education and communication skills.
The same study also revealed that women placed great value on
goals involving high ethical standards, and such goals need to be
built into science curricula—now almost silent on the subject.

*Discuss the practical uses of scientific discoveries to help students see
science in its social context.* The tremendous usefulness of science for
improving people's lives is a very persuasive argument to attract
women to science. The social benefits of science and technology
seem to be overwhelmingly important to females (Sax, 1994).
Harding (1985) shows that females who choose to study science do
so because of the social implications of the problems science can
solve. When asked to develop a technology such as a prosthesis to
help a disabled elderly person, for example, boys and girls took different approaches: boys viewed the problem in terms of producing an apparatus; girls considered the problem in its social context
or environment (Grant, 1982).

Numerous studies (Harding, 1985; Kahle, 1985; Rosser, 1993b;
Hynes, 1995) have noted that females are attracted to science when
they can perceive its social usefulness for human beings. For example, the chemistry department at Fort Lewis College in Colorado
changed its curriculum to include more real-world content, which
seemed to reach the female students (Mills, 1993).

Combine qualitative and quantitative methods in data gathering.
Some females suggest that their lack of interest in science comes
in part from their perception that the quantitative methods of science do not allow them to report nonquantitative observations,
thereby restricting the questions to those they find less interesting.
Textbooks, laboratory exercises, and views of scientific research
propagated by the media all reinforce these perceptions. In their
efforts to teach the objectivity of science and the steps of the scientific method, very few instructors and curricular materials manage to convey the creative and intuitive insights that are crucial to
most scientific discoveries.

*Encourage exposure of biases permeating theories and conclusions
drawn from experimental observation.* Data collected from programs
attempting to recruit and retain minorities in science have been
interpreted to show that minorities of both sexes may be repelled
from science for some of the same reasons as white women

(George, 1982; Matyas & Malcom, 1991). In addition, racism among scientists, both overt and covert, and the use of scientific theories to justify racism are additional powerful deterrents.

Reading *Black Apollo of Science: The Life of Ernest Everett Just* (Manning, 1983) can sensitize students to the discrimination and alienation felt by African-American male scientists. Comparing Manning's work and the black critiques of science with feminist critiques will help to elucidate the separate but overlapping biases contributed by race and gender (Fee, 1986; Harding, 1993).

As discussed in Chapter Six, women of color face double barriers posed by racism and sexism. We need more research into particular curricular and pedagogical techniques that might help attract and retain minority women, including complex analyses recognizing the intersection of class, race, and gender as factors affecting each individual in the classroom.

Cautionary Conclusions

Surveys indicate that some of the new scholarship on women's and ethnic studies and many of the pedagogical improvements advocated by women's studies have made their way into mainstream science education (Project Kaleidoscope, 1994; AAAS, 1993). Collaborative learning in groups, emphasis on practical applications, integration of the history of science, and placing science in a more holistic and social context represent the cornerstones of good teaching.

Typically, mainstream science education fails to acknowledge the origin of these improvements in women's studies. In some ways this is understandable and appropriate. Other science education reform movements such as Science, Technology, and Society (STS) and undergraduate curriculum reform (Tobias, 1992) have urged some of the same steps without a focus on gender. Some NSF projects with goals of using women's studies pedagogy and curriculum to attract and retain women in science (Rosser & Kelly, 1994; Ross & Rosser, 1994) have documented that these methods may be more effective in attracting and retaining white men than the groups targeted by the project.

However, an unfortunate consequence can arise when the connection with women's studies is severed as ideas move into the mainstream. The crucial research on the role of gender and gender dynamics that causes a technique to attract and retain women in science may be lost to practitioners, and the technique may lose its effectiveness as a result. Consider the case of collaborative or group work: small group work is currently popular in science and mathematics classes, and some faculty undertake it without understanding the connection to research in gender and race dynamics necessary to make group work succeed for women and men of color in nontraditional areas for them. For example, a faculty member might divide a physics class consisting of five females and twenty males into five groups, placing one female in each group in an effort to promote gender equity. Far from promoting equity, such a division ignores findings documenting the tendency of lone women to drop out of science study groups (Light, 1990). Even if the faculty member had read about the significance of racial groupings (Treisman, 1992) for encouraging success for African-American and Hispanic students in study groups, he or she might remain ignorant of the importance of gender composition and dynamics. Connecting this faculty member with the research from women's studies and gender dynamics in group communication would be helpful in making these study groups work for women.

Similarly, some changes advocated as female friendly, such as focusing on practical applications, discussing the history of science, and placing science in its social context, may lose their appeal unless they include serious curriculum updates on gender and race. For example, experiments using the seventy-kilogram white male as the prototype for chemical or drug effects do have practical applications, but they do little to illustrate the relevance of science to women or students of color. Benefits and side effects may well differ by gender or race, and the course needs to acknowledge the possibility, if nothing else, to keep the attention of the entire class. Likewise, if Western European white males are the only mathematicians discussed, students who never see anyone of their gender or race portrayed may conclude they have nothing to contribute to the field, no matter how much time the course spends on the history of mathematics. And hydrology courses can deal with the social effects of water resource policies in third world countries and still not seem female friendly unless they consider the impact on women's lives in terms of distances walked each day to obtain water. Simply adding a few practical applications or a bit of history, without rethinking the structure and perspective from which a course is taught, may result in cosmetic changes that fail to create the environment needed to involve and retain more women in science.

As scientists who are teachers struggle to find inclusive curriculum and pedagogy, they must continue to study and focus on gender and race and seek to identify action that encourages or discourages women in overt and covert ways. Some may view the tight job market and shrinking resources for basic science research as an excuse to discourage women and minorities from science and to ignore the potential influence of gender on the practice of science. However, encouraging women to drop out of science when their grades surpass the men who continue seems especially shortsighted at this time when our country needs the best brain power possible to compete in our increasingly technological world.

References

American Association for the Advancement of Science. (1990). *Science for all Americans.* Washington, DC: Author.

American Association for the Advancement of Science. (1993). *Benchmarks for science literacy.* New York: Oxford University Press.

American Chemical Society. (1983). Medalist's study charts women chemists' role. *Chemistry and Engineering, 14,* 53.

Armour, M. (1987). *Women into science, engineering, and technology: Strategies for change at the University of Alberta.* Contributions to the third Girls and Science and Technology (GASAT) conference, Ann Arbor, MI.

Arnold, K. (1987). *Retaining high-achieving women in science and engineering.* Paper presented at the Conference on Women in Science and Engineering, University of Michigan, Ann Arbor.

Astin, A. W., & Astin, H. S. (1993). *Undergraduate science education: The impact of different college environments on the educational pipeline in the sciences.* Los Angeles: Higher Education Research Institute.

Astin, A. W., Green, K. C., Korn, W. S., & Riggs, E. R. (1991). *The American freshman: Twenty-year trends, 1966–1985.* Los Angeles: Higher Education Research Institute.

Barad, K. (1995). A feminist approach to teaching quantum physics. In S. V. Rosser (Ed.), *Teaching the majority* (pp. 43–75). New York: Teachers College Press.

Bentley, D. (1985). *Men may understand the words, but do they know the music? Some cries de coeur in science education* (Supplementary contributions to the third Girls and Science and Technology conference; pp. 160–168). London: University of London, Chelsea College.

Berk, R. A., & Rossi, P. H. (1990). *Thinking about program evaluation.* Newbury Park, CA: Sage.

Bird, S., & Didion, C. J. (1993). Returning women science students: A mentoring project of the Association for Women in Science. *Initiatives, 55*(3), 3–11.

Birke, L. (1986). *Women, feminism, and biology: The feminist challenge.* New York: Methuen.

Bleier, R. (1984). *Science and gender: A critique of biology and its theories on women.* Elmsford, NY: Pergamon Press.

Blum, L., & Givant, S. (1982). Increasing the participation of college women in mathematics-related fields. In S. Humphreys (Ed.), *Women and minorities in science* (pp. 119–138). Boulder, CO: Westview.

Brainard, S. G. (1993). Student ownership: The key of successful programs. *Initiatives, 55*(3), 23–30.

Browne, M. W. (1994, February 20). Cold war's end clouds research as openings in science dwindle. *The New York Times*, pp. A1, A11.

Byrne, E. M. (1993). *Women and science: The snark syndrome.* Washington, DC: Falmer Press.

Campbell, M. A., & Campbell-Wright, R. (1995). Toward a feminist algebra. In S. V. Rosser (Ed.), *Teaching the majority* (pp. 127–159). New York: Teachers College Press.

Chambers, D. (1983). Stereotypic images of the scientist: The draw-a-scientist test. *Science Education, 76*, 475–476.

Daniels, J., & LeBold, W. (1982). Women in engineering: A dynamic approach. In S. Humphreys (Ed.), *Women and minorities in science* (AAAS Selected Symposia Series; pp. 139–163). Boulder: Westview.

Davis, B. G., & Humphreys, S. (1985). *Evaluating intervention programs: Applications from women's programs in math and science.* New York: Teachers College Press.

Davis, C. (1993). Stepping beyond the campus. *Science, 260,* 414.

Davis, C., & Hollenshead, C. (1993). Marian Sarah Parker Scholars: A pipeline program for undergraduate women in engineering. In *Contributions to the Seventh International Gender and Science and Technology (GASAT)Conference* (pp. 721–729). Waterloo, Ontario, Canada.

Eastman, C. (1995). Accommodating diversity in computer science education. In S. V. Rosser (Ed.), *Teaching the majority* (pp. 160–168). New York: Teachers College Press.

Ehrenreich, B., & English, D. (1978). *For her own good: 150 years of the experts' advice to women.* Garden City: Anchor.

Expert Panel for the Review of Federal Education Programs in Science, Mathematics, Engineering and Technology. (1993). *The federal investment in science, mathematics, engineering and technology education: Where now? What next?* Arlington, VA: National Science Foundation.

Fausto-Sterling, A. (1992). *Myths of gender: Biological theories about women and men* (Rev. ed.). New York: Basic Books.

Fee, E. (1982). A feminist critique of scientific objectivity. *Science for the People, 14*(4), 8.

Fee, E. (1986). Critiques of modern science: The relationship of feminism to other radical epistemologies. In R. Bleier (Ed.), *Feminist approaches to science* (pp. 42–565). Elmsford, NY: Pergamon Press.

Fitz-Gibbon, C. T., & Morris, L. L. (1987). *How to design a program evaluation.* Newbury Park, CA: Sage.

Fort, D. (Ed.). (1993). *A hand up: Women mentoring women in science.* Washington, DC: Association for Women in Science.

Fossey, D. (1983). *Gorillas in the mist.* Boston: Houghton Mifflin.

Gardner, A. L. (1986). *Effectiveness of strategies to encourage participation and retention of precollege and college women in science.* Doctoral dissertation, Purdue University, West Lafayette, IN.

George, Y. (1982). Affirmative action programs that work. In S. Humphreys (Ed.), *Women and minorities in science* (AAAS Selected Symposia Series; pp. 87–98). Boulder, CO: Westview.

Gilligan, C. (1982). *In a different voice: Psychological theory and women's development.* Cambridge, MA: Harvard University Press.

Ginorio, A. B., Butler, J., Conte, C., & Schmitz, B. (1993). *Incorporating American ethnic minority women into the curriculum: An evaluation of curriculum change projects. January 1989–December 1992.* Seattle: University of Washington.

Goodall, J. (1971). *In the shadow of man.* Boston: Houghton Mifflin.

Grant, M. (1982). Prized projects. *Studies in Design Education, Craft and Technology, 15,* 1.

Green, K. C. (1989a). A profile of undergraduates in the sciences. *The American Scientist, 78,* 475–480.

Green, K. C. (1989b). *An exploration of the nature and quality of undergraduate education in science, mathematics and engineering.* [Keynote address to the Wingspread Conference of the Sigma Xi National Advisory Group, Racine, WI].

Greer, S. (1992, Spring). Science: It's not just a white man's thing. *Winds of Change,* pp. 12–18.

Gries, D., & Marsh, D. (1992). The 1989–90 Taulbee Survey. *Communications of the American Council on Mathematics, 35*(1), 133–143.

Hall, R. M., & Sandler, B. R. (1982). *The classroom climate: A chilly one for women*. Washington, DC: Association of American Colleges.

Halpin, Z. (1989). Scientific objectivity and the concept of "the other." *Women's Studies International Forum, 12,* 285–294.

Haraway, D. (1978). Animal sociology and a natural economy of the body politic. *Signs, 4*(1), 21–60.

Harding, J. (1985). Values, cognitive style and the curriculum. *Contributions to the third Girls and Science and Technology Conference.* London: University of London, Chelsea College.

Harding, S. (1986). *The science question in feminism*. Ithaca, NY: Cornell University Press.

Harding, S. (1991). *Whose science? Whose knowledge?* Ithaca, NY: Cornell University Press.

Harding, S. (1993). *Racial economy of science.* Bloomington: Indiana University Press.

Harris, H. (1995). The Clare Boothe Luce Program for Women in Science at Creighton University. In S. V. Rosser (Ed.), *Teaching the majority* (pp. 98–110). New York: Teachers College Press.

Hoffman, J. (1982). Biorhythms in human reproduction: The not so steady states. *Signs, 7,* 829–844.

Hrdy, S. (1977). The langurs of Abu: Female and male strategies of reproduction. Cambridge, MA: Harvard University Press.

Hrdy, S. (1979). Infanticide among animals: A review, classification and examination of the implications for the reproductive strategies of females. *Ethnology and Sociobiology, 1,* 3–40.

Hrdy, S. (1984). Introduction: Female reproductive strategies. In M. Small (Ed.), *Female primates: Studies by women primatologists* (pp. 1–14). New York: Alan Liss.

Hubbard, R. (1990). *The politics of women's biology.* New Brunswick, NJ: Rutgers University Press.

Hynes, P. (1984, November/December). Women working: A field report. *Technology Review,* p. 38.

Hynes, P. (1989). *The recurring silent spring.* Elmsford, NY: Pergamon Press.

Hynes, P. (1995). No classroom is an island. In S. V. Rosser (Ed.), *Teaching the majority* (pp. 211–219). New York: Teachers College Press.

Kahle, J. B. (Ed.). (1985). *Women in science.* Philadelphia: Falmer Press.

Kahle, J. B. (1988). Recruitment and retention of women in college science majors. *Journal of College Science Teaching, 17*(5), 1–5.

Kahle, J. B. (1990). [Draw a Mathematician Test.] Unpublished data.

Keller, E. F. (1982). Feminism and science. *Signs, 7,* 589–602.

Keller, E. F. (1983). *A feeling for the organism.* San Francisco: Freeman.

Keller, E. F. (1984, November). Women and basic research: Respecting the unexpected. *Technology Review,* pp. 44–47.

Keller, E. F. (1985). *Reflections on gender and science.* New Haven, CT: Yale University Press.

Lancaster, J. (1975). *Primate behavior and the emergence of human culture.* Troy, MO: Holt, Rinehart & Winston.

Light, R. (1990). *Explorations with students and faculty about teaching, learning, and student life.* Cambridge, MA: Harvard University Press.

McIntosh, P. (1984). The study of women: Processes of personal and curricular re-vision. *Forum for Liberal Education, 6*(5), 2–4.

Manning, K. (1983). *Black Apollo of science.* Oxford, England: Oxford University Press.

Marte, C., & Anastos, K. (1990). Women—the missing persons in the AIDS epidemic. Part II. *Health/PAC Bulletin 20*(1), 11–23.

Matyas, M. L. (1985). Obstacles and constraints on women in science: Preparation and participation in the scientific community. In J. B. Kahle (Ed.), *Women in science: A report from the field* (pp. 77–101). Philadelphia: Falmer Press.

Matyas, M. L., & Dix, L. S. (1992). Promoting undergraduate studies in science and engineering. In M. L. Matyas & L. S. Dix (Eds.), *Science and engineering programs: On target for women?* (pp. 67–98). Washington, DC: National Academy Press.

Matyas, M. L., & Malcom, S. M. (1991). *Investing in human potential: Science and engineering at the crossroads.* Washington, DC: American Association for the Advancement of Science.

Miller, A., & Silver, C. B. (1993). The limits of intervention: Lessons from Eureka, a program to retain students in science and math-related majors. *Initiatives, 55*(2), 21–29.

Mills, J. (1993). Shedding chemistry's uncool image. *Science, 260,* 413.

Morell, V. (1993). Called "trimates," three bold women shaped their field. *Science, 260,* 420–425.

Muller, C. B. (1993). The Women in Science Project at Dartmouth. *Initiatives, 55*(3), 39–47.

Nair, I., & Majetich, S. (1995). Physics and engineering in the classroom. In S. V. Rosser (Ed.), *Teaching the majority* (pp. 25–42). New York: Teachers College Press.

National Research Council. (1991). *Women in science and engineering: Increasing their numbers in the 1990s: A statement on policy and strategy.* Washington, DC: National Academy Press.

National Research Council. National Committee on Science Education Standards and Assessments. (1993). *National science education standards working papers: An enhanced sampler.* Washington, DC: Author.

National Science Foundation. (1989). *Report on the NSF disciplinary workshops on undergraduate education.* Arlington, VA: Author.

National Science Foundation. (1990). *National Science Foundation's Research Experiences for Undergraduates (REU) Program: An assessment of the first three years* (NSF 90–58). Arlington, VA: Author.

National Science Foundation. (1991–1993). *Undergraduate Course and Curriculum Development Program Summary.* [Annual reports]. Arlington, VA: Author.

National Science Foundation. (1992). *Women and minorities in science and engineering: An update.* (NSF 92–903). Arlington, VA: Author.

National Science Foundation. (1991). *Survey on retention at higher education institutions.* Arlington, VA: Author.

National Science Foundation. (1993). *The federal investment in science, mathematics, engineering, and technology education: Where now? What next?* Arlington, VA: Author.

Neale, A., Gerhart, J. B., Hobbie, R. K., McDermott, L. C., Romer, R., & Thomas, B. R. (1991). The undergraduate physics major. *American Journal of Physics, 59,* 106–111.

Oakes, J. (1990). *Lost talent: The underrepresentation of women, minorities, and disabled persons in science.* Santa Monica, CA: Rand Corporation.

Patton, M. Q. (1990). *Qualitative evaluation and research methods* (2d ed.). Newbury Park, CA: Sage.

Perry, W. (1970). *Forms of intellectual and ethical development in the college years.* Troy, MO: Holt, Rinehart & Winston.

Pinn, V. W., & LaRosa, J. (1992). *Overview: Office of Research on Women's Health* (pp. 1–10). Washington, DC: National Institutes of Health.

Project Kaleidoscope. (1991). *Volume I. What works: Building natural science communities.* Washington, DC: Independent Colleges Office.

Project Kaleidoscope. (1992). *Volume II. What works: Resources for reform.* Washington, DC: Independent Colleges Office.

Project Kaleidoscope. (1994). *Project Kaleidoscope Phase II: What works: Focusing on the future.* Washington, DC: Independent Colleges Office.

Richardson, D., Sutton, C., & Cercone, K. (1995). Female-friendly geoscience: Eight techniques for reaching the majority. In S. V. Rosser (Ed.), *Teaching the majority* (pp. 183–192). New York: Teachers College Press.

Rinzler, C. A. (1993). *Estrogen and breast cancer.* New York: Macmillan.

Ross, J., & Rosser, S. V. (1994, January). *Science and diversity: Two systemic approaches to curriculum changes.* Presentation at the annual meeting of the National Association for Science, Technology, and Society, Arlington, VA.

Rosser, S. V. (1986). *Teaching science and health from a feminist perspective: A practical guide.* Elmsford, NY: Pergamon Press.

Rosser, S. V. (1990). *Female-friendly science: Applying women's studies methods and theories to attract students.* Elmsford, NY: Pergamon Press.

Rosser, S. V. (1991). AIDS and women. *AIDS Education and Prevention, 3*(3), 230–240.

Rosser, S. V. (1993a). Gender bias in clinical research and the difference it makes. *Applied Clinical Trials, 2*(1), 44–52.

Rosser, S. V. (1993b). Female friendly science: Including women in curricular content and pedagogy in science. *The Journal of General Education, 42*(3), 191–220.

Rosser, S. V., & Kelly, B. (1994). From hostile exclusion to friendly inclusion: USC System Model Project for the transformation of science and math teaching to reach women in varied campus settings. *Journal of Women and Minorities in Science and Engineering, 1*(1), 29–44.

Rossi, P. H., & Freeman, H. E. (1989). *Evaluation: A systematic approach* (4th ed.). Newbury Park, CA: Sage.

Sax, L. J. (1994). Retaining tomorrow's scientists: Exploring the factors that keep male and female college students interested in science careers. *Journal of Women and Minorities in Science and Engineering, 1*(1), 45–62.

Sayre, A. (1975). *Rosalind Franklin and DNA: A vivid view of what it is like to be a gifted woman in an especially male profession.* New York: W. W. Norton.

Schuster, M., & Van Dyne, S. (1984). Placing women in the liberal arts: Stages of curriculum transformation. *Harvard Educational Review, 54,* 413–428.

Seymour, E., & Hewitt, N. M. (1994). *Talking about leaving: Factors contributing to high attrition rates among science, mathematics and engineering undergraduate majors.* Final report to the Alfred P. Sloan Foundation on an ethnographic inquiry at seven institutions, University of Colorado, Boulder.

Sherry, J., & Dix, L. S. (1992). Promoting graduate and postdoctoral studies in science and engineering. In M. L. Matyas & L. S. Dix (Eds.), *Science and engineering programs: On target for women?* (pp. 67–98). Washington, DC: National Academy Press.

Sloat, B. F., & DeLoughry, C. M. (1985). *Summer internships in the science for high school women.* Ann Arbor: University of Michigan, Center for the Education of Women.

Stage, E. (1992). Interventions defined, implemented, and evaluated. In

M. L. Matyas & L. S. Dix (Eds.), *Science and engineering programs: On target for women?* (pp. 15–26). Washington, DC: National Academy Press.

Strenta, C., Elliott, R., Matier, M., Scott, J., & Adair, R. (1993). *Choosing and leaving science in highly selective institutions: General factors and the question of gender.* Report to the Alfred P. Sloan Foundation, University of Colorado, Boulder.

Taylor, J. (1965). *Selected papers on molecular genetics.* New York: Academic Press.

Tidball, E. M. (1980). Women's colleges and women achievers revisited. *Signs, 5*(3), 504–517.

Tobias, S. (1990). *They're not dumb. They're different: Stalking the second tier.* Tucson, AZ: Research Corporation.

Tobias, S. (1992). *Revitalizing undergraduate science: Why some things work and most don't.* Tucson, AZ: Research Corporation.

Treisman, P. U. (1992). Studying students studying calculus: A look at the lives of minority mathematics students in college. *College Mathematics Journal, 23,* 362–372.

Udinsky, B. F., Osterlind, S. J., & Lynch, S. W. (1981). *Evaluation resource handbook: Gathering, analyzing, reporting data.* San Diego, CA.

Vetter, B. M. (1992). *What is holding up the glass ceiling? Barriers to women in the science and engineering workforce* (Occasional Paper 92–3). Washington, DC: Commission on Professionals in Science and Technology.

Watson, J. D. (1969). *The double helix.* New York: Atheneum.

Wenzel, S., & Manis, J. (1994). Unpublished data.

Women's Educational Equity Act. (1993, November). *Women's Educational Equity Act program abstracts.* Washington, DC: Author.

Chapter Eight

Women, Academia, and Careers in Science and Engineering

Mary Frank Fox

Scientists and engineers work across sectors—education, industry, federal government and the military, nonprofits, hospitals, and state and local government. However, 51 percent of doctoral-level women in science and engineering (SME) were employed in educational institutions as of 1991, and the vast preponderance of them (95 percent) were in higher education—academia. This is also true for doctoral-level men in SME, though their proportion (46 percent) in educational institutions is somewhat smaller. Table 8.1 details the breakout of doctoral SME employment. The smaller proportion of men in education owes principally to their higher concentration in engineering, which is more likely than other fields to be practiced in nonacademic, industrial settings. Because so few academic women in SME fields are in engineering, this chapter sometimes refers to "women in science" rather than "science and engineering."

Note: I thank Susan Mitchell and Dan Pasquini of the Survey of Doctoral Recipients for providing data, and Angela Ginorio for helpful comments on this chapter.

Table 8.1. Employed Doctoral Scientists and Engineers, by Sector and Sex, 1991.

Sector	n	Percentage of total	Men	Women
Educational institutions	206,255	47.2	46.2	51.4
Industry/Self-employed	157,256	36.0	37.5	29.1
Federal govt. and military	29,729	6.8	7.2	5.3
Nonprofit organizations	15,848	3.6	3.3	4.9
Hospitals/Clinics	13,901	3.2	2.6	5.5
State and local government	10,357	2.4	2.3	2.6
Total employed[a]	437,206	100.0	100.0	100.0

[a]Includes those who did not report employment sector.

Source: National Science Foundation/Science Resources Studies, 1991.
Survey of doctoral recipients (unpublished data).

Assessment of women's scientific careers in academia is essential to analysis of women and science, since for a number of reasons academia has been central to science, and vice versa. Science and higher education evolved as reciprocal developments in the United States. Science played a major role in transforming the nineteenth-century college into the modern university, and it still shapes the characteristics of the university.

From the mid-nineteenth century on, science acted to break up the generalist, classical college tradition, which, based largely upon religion, prepared young men for the ministry, law, or government service. After the Civil War, three factors affected higher education: the Morrill Land-Grant Act of 1862 (supporting the proliferation of research universities); the establishment of experimental stations for agricultural research; and the development of new, specialized academic programs at Johns Hopkins and elsewhere, based on the German university. All three helped introduce specialized curriculum, lectures, seminars, and independent work. Eventually, this new education largely replaced the classical education of canonical literature and philosophy, and pedagogy emphasizing drill and recitation (Fallon, 1980; Montgomery, 1994; Wolfle, 1972).

Science also paved the way for graduate education across fields. The first U.S. doctorate was in science, awarded by the Sheffield

School of Scientific Study at Yale in 1861. In the next twenty years, fourteen of the twenty doctorates awarded in the country were in science (Wolfle, 1972, p. 89). Generalist natural sciences gradually gave way to botany, zoology, and geology, and natural philosophy gave way to chemistry and physics. This led to increasing special-ization in graduate education throughout the university and to hiring based on specialized qualifications (Wolfle, 1972, p. 87). As graduate work spread to other fields, the proportion of doctoral degrees awarded in the sciences declined, although the number of science degrees increased. Between 1911 and 1945, the physical and natural sciences accounted for 45 percent of doctorates awarded (Wolfle, 1972, p. 89).

In like manner, sciences led the way in securing federal sup-port for research and training. This partnership of higher educa-tion and the government began in agricultural colleges, spread to other sciences, and filtered down through the university. The flow was not passive. Scientists did not merely set the pattern for other fields; they played leading roles in establishing the pace and were important participants in developing the new federal agencies for the arts and humanities. The line of development created in science extended first to psychology, then serially to the social sci-ences, humanities, and the arts (Wolfle, 1972, p. 91).

With specialization, federal support for research, and winning of autonomy in research—forces largely related to developments of science—the university became decentralized, even fragmented. Power in appointments and control of research funds moved from central administration to departments. Such decentralization came to define the complex university, which continues to dominate higher education in the United States.

None of this happened without conflict and opposition (Mont-gomery, 1994), and tension and ambivalence in higher education still reflect the history of strain between teaching and research in particular (Fox, 1992b, pp. 301–302). However, from the mid-nine-teenth century onward, higher education did transform from the generalist curriculum, and scientists were largely responsible for the characteristic features of the modern university. Accordingly, within higher education and for the public support underlying it, science became a model (albeit frequently faltering) of research expertise, a standard for research training and apprenticeship, and often a gauge of national resourcefulness, power, and prestige. Although discussion of science and nationalism is well beyond the scope of this chapter, the relationship is clear (see, for example, Montgomery, 1994) and points to the stake of the state in science and, by implication, in gender and scientific careers.

Women's attainments in academic careers are crucial to—and telling of—their status in science. Women with academic careers have already survived barriers of selection (self-selection and selection by institutions) in science; they have moved through the proverbial pipeline; they have completed doctoral degrees and earned credentials for professional work. Nonetheless, the highest career attainments generally elude this select group of women. What is happening to them? What status and level of research performance do they reach in academic science? What are the barriers to their success?

Status refers to occupational location, rank, and rewards, and *performance* in academic science refers to research productivity. Status and performance together constitute *career attainments*. In academic science, women and men have different locations (fields, institutional types), rank and promotion, and rewards. Women's research productivity, both cause and effect of their status, lags behind men's. Gender profoundly affects academic careers in science. In this chapter, I present evidence of comparative career attainments, assess the ways organizational and individual factors account for women's lower attainments, and propose an analysis of women's limited success.

Women's Career Attainments in Academic Science

Fields

In 1991, 20 percent of the doctoral-level scientists and engineers in four-year colleges and universities were women. (The proportion was about the same for all educational institutions, including two-year colleges and precollege settings.) Women's distribution across fields is highly uneven, as shown in Table 8.2. In 1991, 87 percent of SME women in four-year colleges and universities were in three sets of fields—life sciences, psychology, and social science. Men were at least twice as likely as women to be in the physical sciences and mathematics, and six times more likely to be in engineering. The disparity was greatest in engineering, with 14 percent of the men and 2.4 percent of the women faculty in 1991.

The distribution of women and men by field is not well understood (Zuckerman, 1991). It remains unclear how much the difference owes to preferences and how much to pressures to stay out of (or move into) certain fields—and variations in women's status in science and engineering are an important consideration.

Institutional Types

The data shown in Table 8.3 cover broad classifications; the university category, for example, is aggregated across types of universities (except medical schools), and the data are not separated by field. What they do show is that in 1987, the most recent year for which we have such data, 70 percent of the men and only 57 percent of the women were in universities other than medical schools. Women were more apt than men to be in medical schools—21

Table 8.2. Doctoral Scientists and Engineers Employed in Four-Year Colleges and Universities, by Field and Sex, 1991.

Field	Percentage female	n	Men	Women
Physical scientists	7.8	27,716	16.3	5.7
Mathematical scientists	8.6	13,832	8.1	3.1
Computer specialists	13.3	2,453	1.4	0.9
Environmental scientists	11.7	5,370	3.0	1.7
Life scientists	26.2	59,915	28.2	40.8
Psychologists	35.8	21,395	8.7	20.0
Social scientists	23.4	41,859	20.4	25.5
Engineers	4.1	22,777	14.0	2.4
Total employed[a]	19.7	195,317	100.0	100.0

[a]Entries may not add to totals due to rounding.

Source: National Science Foundation/Science Resources Studies, 1991. Survey of doctoral recipients (unpublished data).

percent versus 13 percent. This may reflect the concentration of women in life sciences and the frequent placement of microbiology programs in medical colleges; it may also reflect numbers of low-ranking, off-track positions (instructorships, lectureships) in those settings. Few SME scientists were in precollege settings, but it is notable that women were three times more likely than men to be in these lower- prestige institutions.

The distribution of women and men in universities, which must be considered in combination with their ranks, is an important indicator because it is in universities that time, equipment, research facilities, and graduate student research assistants are located. Such human and material resources provide ways and means for research performance.

Rank and Promotion

In academia, ranks are clearly and fairly uniformly specified as professorial levels. In considering rank, we need to look at the *distribution* of women and of men by rank—that is, the proportion of women and of men who hold levels of positions in science and engineering. But it is also necessary to consider women as a *proportion* of faculty at each rank, because this reflects women's presence relative to men and the availability of women at higher ranks to influence teaching and research. Thus, while a given depart-

Table 8.3. Doctoral Scientists and Engineers Employed in Academia, by Type of Institution and Sex, 1987.

Type of Academic Institution	Percentage female	n	Men	Women
Pre-college	41	4,019	1.3	4.0
Two-year college	23	5,226	2.2	2.9
Four-year college	20	31,693	13.7	15.5
Medical school	27	31,711	12.5	20.7
Other university	16	153,154	70.3	57.0
Total Academia[a]	19	225,803	100.0	100.0

[a]Percentages may not add to 100 due to rounding.

Source: National Research Council, 1991, Table 6.

ment may have three women, one at each professorial level, the proportion of total faculty that women represent at each rank may be a more important indicator of their status in the department.

Looking at the distributions of women and men by rank shown in Table 8.4, we find inequalities at the upper and lower ranks: most notably, in 1991, 42 percent of the men and 16 percent of the women were full professors, while 37 percent of the women and 22 percent of the men were at the level of assistant professor or lower. Excluding "no report" and "does not apply" data, the differences increase somewhat: 48 percent of the men and 21 percent of the women are full professors and 47 percent of the women and 25 percent of the men are assistant professors or below.

Considering the proportions of women compared to men at each rank, the patterns of gender disparity are dramatic (Table 8.5). Across SME fields, the higher the rank, the lower the proportion of women. As of 1991, women were 29 percent of the assistant professors, 21 percent of the associate professors, and 9 percent of the full professors in SME fields. While a general pattern of lower proportions of women at higher ranks holds across the fields, certain fields possess a greater proportion of women at high ranks than other fields. Just as women were concentrated in three fields—life science, psychology, and social science—so we find higher proportions of women at each rank in these fields than

Table 8.4. Doctoral Scientists and Engineers Employed in Four-Year Colleges and Universitites by Rank and Sex, 1991.

Rank	Percentage female	n	Men	Women
Full professor	8.7	71,780	42.0	16.2
Associate professor	20.9	46,474	23.4	25.2
Assistant professor	29.1	36,270	16.4	27.4
Instructor/Lecturer	43.0	4,158	1.5	4.6
Other faculty	26.1	7,685	3.6	5.2
Total[a]	19.7	195,317		

[a]Percentages do not add to 100 because total includes "does not apply" and "no report" responses.

Source: Vetter, 1994, Table 5–1.

Table 8.5. Doctoral Scientists and Engineers in Four-Year Colleges and Universities, by Field and Rank, 1991.

Field	Total[a]	Full professor	Associate professor	Assistant professor
Physical scientists	27,716	11,098	4,193	3,447
Percent women	*7.9*	*2.9*	*9.0*	*15.6*
Mathematical scientists	13,832	5,827	4,407	2,328
Percent women	*8.6*	*4.6*	*10.2*	*14.8*
Computer specialists	2,453	362	807	1,064
Percent women	*13.3*	*8.0*	*11.4*	*15.7*
Environmental scientists	5,370	1,890	1,395	728
Percent women	*11.8*	*5.6*	*6.8*	*23.4*
Life scientists	59,915	18,965	12,996	12,225
Percent women	*26.2*	*10.7*	*27.2*	*35.9*
Psychologists	21,395	7,695	5,200	3,987
Percent women	*35.8*	*20.5*	*33.4*	*46.5*
Social scientists	41,859	16,368	12,298	8,478
Percent women	*23.4*	*11.2*	*26.3*	*32.1*
Engineers	22,777	9,575	5,178	4,013
Percent women	*4.1*	*1.0*	*3.9*	*9.4*
Total, all fields	195,317	71,780	46,474	36,270
Percent women	*19.7*	*8.7*	*20.9*	*29.1*

[a]Total includes instructor/lecturer, other faculty, "does not apply," and "no report."

Source: Vetter (Ed.), 1994, Table 5–1.

in others. In life sciences, psychology, and social sciences, as of 1991, women were 36 percent, 47 percent, and 32 percent, respectively, of the assistant professors, and 27 percent, 33 percent, and 26 percent of the associate professors.

However, for every field except psychology, the proportion of women at the rank of full professor is meager. In half the categories—physical, mathematical, and environmental sciences, and engineering—women are 6 percent or fewer of the full professors. Only in psychology are women more than 11 percent of the full professors. Despite the number of women with doctorates earned in the 1970s and the 1980s and the passage of years for these women to mature in professional time, the proportion of women who are full professors has not kept pace with the growth of the supply of women with doctorates. In 1973, women were 4 percent of the full professors in SME fields; in 1987 that proportion was 7 percent; and in 1991, it was still just 9 percent (also see Gibbons, 1992).

Chemistry, for example, exhibits a notable discrepancy between the number of women with doctorates and that of women faculty at *any* rank (Chamberlain, 1988, p. 214). At doctoral-granting institutions, between 1985 and 1990 women went from 11 percent to 18 percent of assistant professors, from 9 percent to 13 percent of associate professors, and from 3 percent to 4 percent of full professors (Roscher, 1990, pp. 72–73). Consider these proportions against the growth in women's share of doctoral degrees in chemistry—7.7 percent in 1970, 11 percent in 1975, 17 percent in 1980, 20 percent in 1985 and 25 percent in 1990 (Roscher, 1990, Table 1.1; National Center for Education Statistics, 1993, Table 240)—and the maturation of the cohorts over the period. Even allowing for up to ten years between receipt of doctorate and the rank of associate professor and fifteen years from doctorate to full professorship, women's degrees are not translating into expected rank over time. Such discrepancies also occur in mathematics (American Statistical Association, 1993, p. 4; Vetter, 1992, pp. 37–38) and indeed, across fields in higher education (University of Wisconsin, 1991, p. ix).

The reported data on patterns of gender and rank (Table 8.5) and those on discrepancy between availability of women with doctorates and rank over time do not control for research productivity. Studies that do, however, indicate that rank may be the area of greatest disparity in the status of women and men in academic science. Accordingly, Cole (1979) found that for scientists at each level of productivity in his classification, women were less likely than men to receive promotions. This held with controls for prestige.

Among a sample of biochemists who received doctorates between 1956 and 1967 and who held faculty positions in graduate departments at some point in their careers, Long, Allison, and McGinnis (1993) found notable sex differences in advancement in rank. Controlling for both numbers of articles and citations to articles (as well as other variables including marriage and parenthood), promotion rates from assistant to associate to full professor are lower and slower for women. Further, although being in a prestigious department delays promotion for both sexes, the negative effect is stronger for women. Finally, a small group of women with highest levels of productivity have high probabilities of promotion to full professor, but the majority of women are less likely than *comparable* men to be promoted to this rank. Long and his colleagues conclude that "particularistic factors" are operating and that "women are expected to meet higher standards for promotion" (p. 720).

Likewise, among pairs of women and men matched on year of doctorate, field of study, institution awarding doctorate, and race, but not research productivity, Ahern and Scott (1981) found large and pervasive sex differences in rank among natural, physical, and biological scientists. Ten to nineteen years past the doctorate, men were 50 percent more likely than women to have been promoted to full professor. Among younger matched pairs, men were more likely than women to have been promoted to associate professor, independent of marital status, parenthood, or whether their work orientation was primarily research or teaching.

In addition, a study of recipients of prestigious postdoctoral fellowships between 1955 and 1986 reports that, controlling for years since doctorate, field, and fellowship, the predicted academic rank of women is one-third lower than that of men (Sonnert, 1990). However, in this study, the disadvantage for women was in physical sciences, mathematics, and engineering; women biologists progressed through academic ranks at rates similar to men. This highlights the issue of differences by discipline.

Salary

Because salary has both symbolic and material value, it is an indicator of women's status in academia as in other occupations and professions (Fox, 1981). The earnings of women compared to men in academic science thus merit scrutiny.

This, however, is easier said than done. The National Science Foundation (1992) document on women and minorities in science and engineering does not list specific salary data on academic scientists. Such data as one can find come from various professional societies and, as such, are not standardized with controls for length of contract (nine-month versus twelve-month), type of department (doctoral or nondoctoral granting), rank, years in rank, or sex. Without control for sex, data are not applicable for this chapter. For salary data that are separated by sex, nonuniformity of the other controls makes comparison difficult across fields. What we are able to discern from the available data, for chemistry, pharmacy, physics, and psychology only, is this: 1) Without controls for rank, as for pharmacy (Commission on Professionals in Science and Technology [CPST], 1993, Table 263), women earn 77 percent to 84 percent of what men earn (which is about the same ratio found among doctoral-level scientists across fields and employment sections, academic and nonacademic, without controls for rank [Fox, 1995a]). 2) In chemistry and physics, fields in which data do control for rank, the gender gap in salaries is greater for full professors than for associates or assistants (CPST, 1993, Tables 237, 242). 3) In psychology, with controls not only for rank but for time in rank, we find that full-time faculty salaries in doctoral-granting departments are close to parity for men and women (CPST, 1993, Table 251). This may be an effect of the control variables and/or this particular field, which has the largest proportions of SME women compared to men, both overall and at higher ranks (see Table 8.5).

Research Productivity

The term *research productivity* actually refers to *outcomes* of research—in basic science, publications. Publication productivity is not strictly equivalent to research productivity, but the one is an indicator of the other. No guarantee exists that a big producer of publications makes a significant contribution or a given nonpublisher makes no contribution, but in the aggregate the correlation is high between quantity of publications and scientific impact, assessed through awards and citations (see Blume & Sinclair, 1973; Cole & Cole, 1973; Gaston, 1978).

In analysis of women's SME careers, publication productivity is important for two reasons. First, publication is an important social process of science because it is through publication that research findings are communicated and verified and priority of work is established (Fox, 1983). Second, and accordingly, until we understand productivity differences, we cannot adequately assess other sex differences in location, rank, and rewards. National data on field, rank, and salary do not present gender comparisons on productivity or controls for productivity, so we must refer to more limited samples, as in previous discussions of promotion.

What do we know about the publication productivity of women compared to men? As described in Fox (1995a), samples indicate that women publish less than men in SME fields. Over a twelve-year period, Cole (1979) found that across chemistry, biology, psychology, and sociology, the median number of papers published was 8 for men and 3 for women. Among a sample of scientists in six fields who were matched for year of Ph.D. and doctoral department, Cole and Zuckerman (1984) report that women publish half as much as men—6.4 compared to 11.2 papers.

Between fields and disciplines, levels of sex differences in publication vary. Among psychologists, men are significantly more productive than women, publishing 1.7 compared to .7 papers in a three-year period (Helmreich, Spence, Beane, Lucker, & Matthews, 1980). Women ecologists publish about 47 percent as many papers as men (Primack & O'Leary, 1989). For chemists, Reskin (1978) reports slighter differences that suggest "a true but small sex difference between the populations" of the field (p. 1236). Likewise, in my national sample of social scientists in four fields (economics, sociology, political science, and psychology), the sex difference in mean number of articles published in a three-year period is modest (but statistically significant)—2.25 for women compared to 2.5 for men. Considering timing, Long and his colleagues (1993) report that although male and female biochemists begin careers in graduate departments with similar levels of productivity, by the sixth year of their appointments men have significantly more publications. Ward and Grant (1995) report recent convergence in men's and women's publication rates, but the convergence is mainly outside of natural, biological, and physical sciences.

However, while women and men in science publish at different rates, the distribution for both is strongly, positively skewed: low, even null, performance is most frequent, and high, or even moderate, performance is rare. That is, most of the papers come from a few scientists, while the majority publish little.

Factors Accounting for Women's Career Attainments

The first set of indicators discussed (rank, institutional location, salary), together with research performance, constitute career attainments in science. The two are connected, and the lower success of women in science and engineering refers to both status and performance. Thus, the following explanations of women's attainments refer to both.

Individual Factors

In explaining career outcomes in science, personal factors play a part (Fox, 1983). But such individual factors do not exist in a social vacuum. For example, we find no direct relationship between productivity and measured creative ability or intelligence in science (Andrews, 1976; Cole & Cole, 1967). Further, although women's attainments in science are lower than men's, their measured ability (IQ) is higher. Among chemistry, biology, psychology, and sociology Ph.D.'s, women have slightly higher IQs than men (Cole, 1979, p. 61); and for departments of varying ranks, there is less variation in average IQ for women than for men (Cole, 1979, p. 159). Data on IQ may not be adequate indicators of intelligence or ability, but to the extent that they capture differences, they indicate that, if anything, women in science are a more select intellectual group than men.

For women employed in academia in SME fields, educational levels attained are not a variable—almost all have doctorates, and this chapter focuses on that group. The attainment of the doctoral degree is virtually uniform for both academic women and men in the data presented in this chapter and does not, by itself, account for women's depressed status. Educational levels are certainly requisite for professional participation and essential for women's employment in academic science. But as the data on rank and promotion presented earlier indicate, assumptions and beliefs about women's growing access to education resulting in career parity with men are faulty. Further, women without educational credentials are generally at a greater disadvantage than men, whatever their occupation (Featherman, 1980). Thus, women do not get equitable rewards for education, and if they lack education, their disadvantage is even greater (Fox, 1981; see also Vaughter, Ginorio, & Trilling, 1977).

For science as for other fields, the relationship between women's education and status is complex—not a simple, linear progression of more education and more social and economic opportunity. It is not clear whether women's gains in education lead or follow changes in their economic, social, and political roles (Fox, 1995b). And increased levels of education have not resulted "as a matter of course" in progress in other areas (Schwager, 1987, p. 335). This has been true throughout women's history of education. Accounts of the Renaissance and Reformation periods, for example, cast doubt on the notion that increased access to literacy and higher learning resulted in greater equality for women (Prentice, 1981, pp. 46–47). The idea of education, by itself, as emblematic of progress for women is questionable.

One might ask, then, are women and men in science receiving degrees from different types of institutions? Are women's degrees incomparable to men's, and from lower-ranking institutions? With some variation by discipline, women and men are about as apt to have degrees from top-ranking institutions (National Research Council, 1983). The greatest difference is in mathematics, where 46 percent of the men and 37 percent of the women have Ph.D.'s from departments rated as strong or distinguished. Women in physics were somewhat less likely to have graduated from a top-ranking department, and women in psychology and microbiology were more likely to have done so (National Research Council, 1983). For my national sample of social scientists, I find insignificant differences in the ratings of institutions from which women and men obtained their doctoral degrees; that is true for each of the four major fields considered: economics, psychology, political science, and sociology. Thus, across scientific fields, the general pattern is one of similarity in doctoral origins of women and men.

Likewise, gender differences are small in certain indicators of financial support for graduate training, measured as percentages of women compared to men who held research or teaching assistantships in graduate school (National Research Council, 1979, 1983). However, these data do not specify the quality or character of assistantships and graduate training (see Hornig, 1987). These factors may, in turn, indicate differing opportunities for women and men to join research groups, to collaborate, and to gain access to the scientific enterprise. The clue to education and career outcomes may lie in such organizational matters, discussed below.

Much has been said of the impact of marriage and children on women's attainments in science. The mythology of science (Bruer, 1984) has it that good scientists are either men with wives or women without husbands and children. Yet the evidence contradicts this conventional wisdom. Almost all married professional women—including scientists—are married to other professionals. In contrast, only some men are in such marriages. The difference reflects norms of hypergamy for women, which prescribe that women should marry at their own social and economic level or higher, as women do not confer social and household status on men but rather derive household status from their spouses. Professional men, being able to confer social status on a wife and household, can marry at more variable social levels. The questions here for women in science are then: Are women scientists constrained geographically in their jobs and job mobility, since they have to take into account their husbands' as well as their own jobs? Does marriage affect their status in science? Relatedly, do marriage and motherhood, with their presumed demands on women's time and resources, take a toll on their research productivity?

Marwell, Rosenfeld, and Spilerman (1979) look at issues of location, marriage, and careers for academic women in general (rather than just for women in science). They find that women are located disproportionately in large, urban areas. This, they argue, reflects women's need to settle in areas with more opportunities for two-career households. However, Marwell and his colleagues did not find that geographic constraints affected women's academic rank; they found no connection between location and academic rank for women.

Other data indicate that while marriage negatively affects rank and salary of academic women, the effects are insignificant except in the case of salary for women in research universities (Ahern & Scott, 1981, Tables 6.1, 6.5, 6.9, and 6.13). Long and his colleagues' analyses of biochemists (1993) indicate for women (and men) a positive effect of marriage on odds of being promoted from assistant to associate professor; for promotion to level of full professor, marriage had no effect in their sample.

Further, married women publish as much as unmarried women, or more. This has been found across scientific and non-scientific fields (Astin & Davis, 1985); in physical, biological, and social sciences (Cole & Zuckerman, 1987); in social sciences (Fox, 1994); and in psychology (Helmreich et al., 1980). Moreover, among various samples of scientists (and scholars in other fields), children had either no effect on women's productivity (Cole & Zuckerman, 1987; Helmreich et al.); a slightly negative, non-significant effect (Reskin, 1978); or a positive effect (Astin & Davis, 1985; Fox & Faver, 1985; Fox, 1994).

Thus, while the perception may persist that marriage and motherhood govern women's performance in science, the data indicate otherwise. First, single women and childless women do either no better or more poorly than women with husbands and children. Second, sex differences in productivity persist with controls for marital status (Fox, 1994). However, these data describe only those women with careers in science, who have survived a demanding process of scrutiny, selection, and evaluation. Family demands may take their toll along the way, driving numbers of women out of scientific careers and thus out of the data bases under consideration (see Long, 1987). We can not say that family status has no effect on women in science. It may have a number of consequences. But among women with scientific careers, the consequences are not negative for their rank or their research productivity.

Organizational and Environmental Factors

In explaining the status and performance of women in academic science and engineering, we must look also to features of the organizations where they study and work—the signals, priorities, and alliances of their organizational environments—and at the features of the larger communities of their fields.

Organizational settings are important to the attainments of women—and men—across occupations. But they are especially important in science and engineering. Why? Science and engineering are performed within organizational policies; they involve the cooperation of persons and groups and require human and material resources. In scope and complexity, scientific and engineering work relies very heavily on facilities, funds, apparatus, and teamwork (Fox, 1991). Further, scientists and engineers work in a larger community and environment that can boost or hinder status and performance. Researchers must continually shape, test, and update their work, and this takes place interactively with others in the field (Fox, 1991). In these ways, science and engineering are more social than are the arts and humanities. Compared to humanities, they are more likely to be performed in teams than solo, to require funding for staff and equipment, and to be more interdependent enterprises (Fox, 1992b).

What are the consequences of these social features of the workplace and the field for women's careers in academic science and engineering? Conditions have improved since the end of the nineteenth century, when the appointment of mathematician Sonya Kovalevsky as professor at the University of Stockholm was greeted with the reaction: "as decidedly as two and two makes four, what a monstrosity is a woman who is a professor of mathematics, and how unnecessary, injurious, and out of place she is" (Mozans, 1913/ 1974, p. 163). Yet academia and academic science and engineering continue to be a male milieu, in which men share traditions, understandings, and styles of competition, barter, and success, and in which women are more likely to be outsiders. In consequence, women are more apt than men to be shut out of professional opportunities and services (Fox, 1995b, p. 232).

As indicators of the situation, I find in my national survey of social scientists that in both B.A.- and Ph.D.-granting units, women report significantly less interaction with and recognition from faculty than do men. In M.A. and Ph.D. departments, women rank available resources significantly lower than men do, and in Ph.D. departments, women report significantly higher undergraduate teaching loads. Interaction, reported resources, and teaching loads—elements of the departmental, organizational setting—are important factors because they correlate with productivity levels in the same sample.

Women's roles in professional meetings indicate that they are less likely than men to be in professional networks. Women are relatively well represented in life sciences—41 percent of all doctoral-level women in academic science and engineering are in the life sciences, and 37 percent of the doctorates in life sciences are now awarded to women. At professional meetings, women biologists contribute presentations in about the same proportion in which they are represented in the membership of the associations. However, as prestigious invited speakers, women are often underrepresented (Glenn, Monroe, & Lamont, 1993). At the large meetings of the American Institute of Biological Sciences in 1989, none of the symposia organizers and only 6 percent of the invited speakers were women. In contrast, half the speakers in the category of contributed papers were women (Glenn et al., 1993). For symposia of the Ecological Society of America, when women were involved as organizers, women made up 23 percent of invited speakers. For symposia organized by men only, the proportion of invited women speakers was 7 percent (Gurevitch, 1988).

These matters of networks and participation are important because, as emphasized, science is a social process. Active researchers gain information—and standing—relevant to their work through meetings, face-to-face interactions, sharing of preprints, and other means that allow them to generate ideas, engage interest, and evaluate work. For example, in her account of physicists at the Stanford Linear Accelerator Center, Traweek (1988) makes a case for "what is accomplished by physicists by talking" (p. 117). Talking, she says, is the way physicists evaluate their peers and their work and persuade others to support their own work. And within the workplace, "talking is the way to get something done, to win computer or beamtime for one's group" (p. 118). It is also the way graduate students or post-docs are placed or acquired. Access to these processes governs the possibility not simply to participate in a social circle but, more fundamentally, to do research, publish, be cited—to show the marks of status and performance in science (Fox, 1991).

In graduate education, organizational factors are also important to understanding—and modifying—women's participation and performance. Aggregate data on funding, assistantships, and financial aid fail to address the dynamics of graduate education as they may affect the attainments of women. We need to know more about matters of inclusion and exclusion in research and research groups, the nuances of training, and evaluative practices as they operate for women. (These are the subject of my current study, *Women in Science and Engineering: Improving Participation and Performance in Doctoral Education,* supported by the NSF.) Of course, male students do not have open and uniform access to opportunities in graduate education. But in advising, informal communication, and other processes that promote significant participation and performance, I hypothesize that men fare better.

Why Such Limited Success for Women?

Ability is not an explanation for women's attainments in science. Neither is educational level. And although marriage and motherhood may have many consequences for women in science, married women and women with children publish as much or more than single women and women without children, and marriage does not have negative consequences for women's academic rank.

The attainments of women in SME are not a simple function of their individual characteristics. Rather, they are a consequence also of the characteristics and practices of the environments in which they are educated and in which they work. To understand the career attainments of women in SME, we must consider the features of their workplaces and their scientific communities. This means attention to the location of women and men in different types of institutions and settings (as well as fields). Further, the same *type* of setting (institution, field), indeed the same *specific setting* (a given department), does not necessarily operate uniformly for women and for men. Collegial opportunities and rewards often turn out to be different.

In analysis of the social organization of science, there is also the matter of gender and cognitive authority. Some hold that scientific research has no gender, that research questions, methods, and inferences are neither masculine or feminine. Others maintain that gender shapes the meaning of science—the ways questions are framed, data are interpreted, and knowledge and applications are created. In this sense, then, scientific findings are more than an expression of objective inquiry, more even than reflections of the social and political processes that are the focus of this chapter. Rather, they are also the result of connections between "mind, nature, and masculinity" (Fox, 1986). This view is best represented by Keller (1985), who characterizes science as inherently masculine in explanations and causal theories, and as steeped both in paradigms of domination and control and in a schism between objectivity and subjectivity. To the extent that this is true, cognitive authority interacts with (even permeates) the organizational factors discussed here, and further influences their impact on women's scientific careers.

Policy and Prospects

What then are the implications for attempts to improve the attainments of women in science and engineering? Programs and policies attributing women's status to shortcomings of attitude, motivation, or other individual characteristics will seek to correct such "personal deficits" and enhance performance. But it is not enough to improve women's human capital—their educational level, years of experience and seniority, or work attitudes. Rather, one must also look to the contexts in which women study and work. Just as explanations of career attainment must take account of the features of both workplaces and scientific communities, so too, programs or policies for improvement of women's careers must attend to enabling and disabling organizational processes. These include matters such as character and quality of graduate education, placement of junior faculty in research projects, range and scope of collaborative opportunities, access to professional networks, and administrative favors bestowed or withheld.

Is the solution intractable? As Vetter points out in Chapter Two, barriers to women's careers would change "if employers wanted them changed, if the government wanted them changed, if academic administrators or faculties wanted them changed," no matter how entrenched the patterns. Those with the means to effect change could have brought it about but have not been moved to do so—and may have been disinclined to do so.

Even those who care about the career attainments of women in science—both women and men—have been reluctant to apply the harsh light of political analysis. Yet it is fundamental to the study of social organization that within existing social structures, some groups benefit and some do not. In science and engineering, men are more likely to benefit and women are not. Most men do not consciously oppose equality for women (Kluegel & Smith, 1986), and only a small subset makes the rules that protect gender-related benefits. However, as Reskin noted in her analysis of sex differences in employment outcomes across occupations, white men have had an incentive to preserve their advantaged positions and they do so by establishing means to distribute valued resources in their favor (1988, p. 61). Applied to science and engineering, then, this means that any explanation of career attainments is incomplete if it ignores men's incentive to preserve the advantages of prestigious institutional location, rank and promotion, and access to research resources.

Improved career attainments for women in SME depend on an understanding of individual factors and contextual factors of the workplace and scientific communities as they account for status and performance. But they also rest upon recognition that there are beneficiaries of current arrangements and distributions of resources and that there are incentives to preserve those arrangements. Gender equity may thus hinge upon political means: monitoring, reporting, sanctioning, and enforcement by regulatory agencies of institutions that receive federal grants and awards. Such means do make a difference; for an account of women's career advancement in engineering firms with and without federal contracts (and corresponding affirmative action requirements), see McIlwee and Robinson (1992). The use of political means in turn implies confronting political realities such as the tendency to regard gender bias within institutions as less invidious than bias based on other characteristics, a view that stems in part from enduring beliefs about gender stratification as a natural and necessary part of the social order. Ultimately, the approach proposed here will require direct political action on issues affecting the employment status of women.

References

Ahern, N., & Scott, E. (1981). *Career outcomes in a matched sample of men and women Ph.D.s.* Washington, DC: National Academy Press.

American Statistical Association. (1993). Women PhDs continue to face hurdles to employment in doctoral-granting institutions. *Amstat News, 204,* 1, 4.

Andrews, F. (1976). Creative process. In D. Pelz & F. Andrews, *Scientists in organizations.* Ann Arbor, MI: Institute for Social Research.

Astin, H. S., & Davis, D. E. (1985). Research productivity across the career- and life-cycle. In M. F. Fox (Ed.), *Scholarly writing and publishing: Issues, problems, and solutions* (pp. 147–160). Boulder, CO: Westview Press.

Blume, S. S., & Sinclair, R. (1973). Chemists in British universities: A study of the reward system in science. *American Sociological Review, 38,* 126–138.

Bruer, J. (1984). Women in science: Toward equitable participation. *Science, Technology, and Human Values, 9,* 3–7.

Chamberlain, M. K. (1988). *Women in academe: Progress and prospects.* New York: Russell Sage Foundation.

Cole, J. R. (1979). *Fair science: Women in the scientific community.* New York: Free Press.

Cole, J. R., & Cole, S. (1967). Scientific output and recognition. *American Sociological Review, 32,* 391–403.

Cole, J., & Cole, S. (1973). *Social stratification in science.* Chicago: University of Chicago Press.

Cole, J., & Zuckerman, H. (1984). The productivity puzzle: Persistence and change in patterns of publication among men and women scientists. In P. Maehr & M. W. Steinkamp (Eds.), *Women in science* (pp. 217–256). Greenwich, CT: JAI Press.

Cole, J., & Zuckerman, H. (1987). Marriage, motherhood, and research performance in science. *Scientific American, 255,* 119–125.

Commission on Professionals in Science and Technology. (1993). *Salaries of engineers, scientists, and technicians.* Washington, DC: Author.

Fallon, D. (1980). *The German university.* Boulder: Colorado Associated University Press.

Featherman, D. (1980). School and occupational careers. In O. G. Brimm & J. Kagan (Eds.), *Constancy and change in human development* (pp. 675–738). Cambridge, MA: Harvard University Press.

Fox, M. F. (1981). Sex, salary, and achievement: Reward-dualism in academia. *Sociology of Education, 54,* 71–84.

Fox, M. F. (1983). Publication productivity among scientists: A critical review. *Social Studies of Science, 13,* 285–305.

Fox, M. F. (1986). Mind, nature, and masculinity. *Contemporary Sociology, 15,* 197–199.

Fox, M. F. (1991). Gender, environmental milieu, and productivity in science. In H. Zuckerman, J. Cole, & J. Bruer (Eds.), *The outer circle:*

Women in the scientific community (pp. 188–204). New York: W. W. Norton.

Fox, M. F. (1992a). Research productivity and the environmental context. In T. Whiston & R. Geiger (Eds.), *Higher education: The United Kingdom and the United States* (pp. 103–111). Buckingham, England: Society for Research into Higher Education/Open University Press.

Fox, M. F. (1992b). Research, teaching, and publication productivity: Mutuality versus competition in academia. *Sociology of Education, 65,* 293–305.

Fox, M. F. (1994, February). *Gender and research productivity: The role of background and family status characteristics.* Paper presented at the meeting of the American Association for the Advancement of Science, San Francisco, CA.

Fox, M. F. (1995a). Women and scientific careers. In S. Jasanoff, J. Markle, J. Petersen, & T. Pinch (Eds.), *Handbook of science and technology studies* (pp. 205–223). Newbury Park, CA: Sage.

Fox, M. F. (1995b). Women and higher education: Gender differences in the status of students and scholars. In J. Freeman (Ed.), *Women: A feminist perspective* (5th ed.; pp. 220–237). Mountain View, CA: Mayfield.

Fox, M. F., & Faver, C. (1985). Men, women, and publication productivity. *The Sociological Quarterly, 26,* 537–549.

Gaston, J. (1978). *The reward system in British and American science.* New York: Wiley.

Gibbons, A. (1992). Key issue: Tenure. *Science, 255,* 1386.

Glenn, M., Monroe, D., & Lamont, J. (1993). Pathways to the podium: Women organizing, women speaking. In D. Fort (Ed.), *A hand up: Women mentoring women in science* (pp. 226–232). Washington, DC: Association for Women in Science.

Gurevitch, J. (1988). Differences in the proportion of women to men invited to give seminars: Is the old boy still kicking? *Bulletin of the Ecological Society of America, 69,* 155–160.

Helmreich, R., Spence, J., Beane, W., Lucker, G. W., & Matthews, K. (1980). Making it in academic psychology: Demographic and personality correlates of attainment. *Journal of Personality and Social Psychology, 39,* 896–908.

Hornig, L. S. (1987). Women graduate students: A literature review and synthesis. In L. S. Dix (Ed.), *Women: Their underrepresentation and career differentials in science and engineering* (pp. 103–122). Washington, DC: National Research Council.

Keller, E. F. (1985). *Reflections on gender and science.* New Haven, CT: Yale University Press.

Kluegel, J., & Smith, E. (1986). *Beliefs about inequality: Americans' view of what is and what ought to be.* New York: Aldine.

Long, J. S. (1987). Discussion: Problems and prospects for research on sex differences. In L. S. Dix (Ed.), *Women: Their underrepresentation and career differentials in science and engineering* (pp. 157–169). Washington, DC: National Academy Press.

Long, J. S., Allison, P. D., & McGinnis, R. (1993). Rank advancement in academic careers: Sex differences and the effects of productivity. *American Sociological Review, 58,* 703–722.

McIlwee, J., & Robinson, J. G. (1992). *Women in engineering.* Albany: State University of New York Press.

Marwell, G., Rosenfeld, R., & Spilerman, S. (1979). Geographic constraints on women's careers in academia. *Science, 205,* 1225–1231.

Montgomery, S. L. (1994). *Minds for the making: The role of science in American education, 1750–1990.* New York: Guilford Press.

Mozans, H. J. (1974). *Woman in science.* Cambridge, MA: MIT Press. (Original work published by D. Appleton and Company, 1913).

National Center for Education Statistics. (1993). *Digest of education statistics, 1993.* Washington, DC: U.S. Department of Education.

National Research Council. Committee on the Education and Employment of Women in Science and Engineering. (1979). *Climbing the academic ladder: Doctoral women scientists in academe.* Washington, DC: National Academy Press.

National Research Council. Committee on the Education and Employment of Women in Science and Engineering. (1983). *Climbing the ladder: An update on the status of doctoral women scientists and engineers.* Washington, DC: National Academy Press.

National Research Council. (1991). *Women in science and engineering: Increasing their numbers in the 1990s.* Washington, DC: National Academy Press.

National Science Foundation. (1992). *Women and minorities in science and engineering: An update.* Arlington, VA: Author.

Prentice, A. (1981). Towards a feminist history of women and education. In D. Jones, N. Sheehan, R. Stamp, & N. McDonald (Eds.), *Monographs in education* (Vol. 5). Manitoba, Canada: University of Manitoba.

Primack, R. B., & O'Leary, V. E. (1989). Research productivity of men and women ecologists: A longitudinal study of former graduate students. *Bulletin of the Ecological Society of America, 70,* 7–12.

Reskin, B. (1978). Scientific productivity, sex, and location in the institution of science. *American Journal of Sociology, 83,* 1235–1243.

Reskin, B. (1988). Bringing the men back in: Sex differentiation and the devaluation of women's work. *Gender and Society, 2,* 58–81.

Roscher, N. M. (1990). *Women chemists 1990.* Washington, DC: American Chemical Society.

Schwager, S. (1987). Educating women in America. *Signs, 12,* 333–372.

Sonnert, G. (1990, August). *Careers of women and men postdoctoral fellows in the sciences.* Paper presented at American Sociological Association meeting.

Traweek, S. (1988). *Beamtimes and lifetimes: The world of high energy physicists.* Cambridge, MA: Harvard University Press.

University of Wisconsin, Office of Equal Opportunity Programs and Policy Studies. (1991). *Retaining and promoting women and minority faculty members: Problems and possibilities.* Madison, WI: Author.

Vaughter, R. M., Ginorio, A. B., & Trilling, B. A. (1977). The failure of trait theories to predict success. *Signs, 2,* 664–674.

Vetter, B. M. (1992). Ferment: Yes, Progress: Maybe, Change: Slow. *Mosaic, 23,* 34–41.

Vetter, B. M. (Ed.). (1994). *Professional women and minorities: A total human resource data compendium* (11th ed.). Washington, DC: Commission on Professionals in Science and Technology.

Ward, K., & Grant, L. (1995). Gender and academic publishing. In J. Smart (Ed.), *Higher education: Handbook of theory and research* (Vol. 11), 175–215. New York: Agathon.

Wolfle, D. (1972). *The home of science.* New York: McGraw-Hill.

Zuckerman, H. (1991). The careers of men and women scientists: A review of current research. In H. Zuckerman, J. R. Cole, & J. T. Bruer (Eds.), *The outer circle: Women in the scientific community* (pp. 27–56). New York: W. W. Norton.

Chapter Nine

Women Scientists in Industry

Paula M. Rayman, Jennifer S. Jackson

"Women in science: why so few?" asked Alice Rossi three decades ago (Rossi, 1965). This chapter builds on her work and a similar study of the National Research Council (1994), seeking to break new ground by offering a multilens perspective on equity for women in science. While one lens focuses on institutional barriers, another focuses on the larger economic forces that shape current industrial policy.

Two other questions—Science by whom? and Science for whom?—deserve center stage in the gender equity debate. At a recent National Academy of Sciences meeting preparing for the United Nations Fourth World Conference on Women in Beijing, women from the United States and third world nations discussed the importance and difficulty of opening doors for women at all levels of scientific practice—from grassroots efforts to Big Science. Participants noted the need to consider women in varying occupations and settings, not just those seeking first-rate professional jobs. They also sought to identify whose interests science serves. They felt it was critical to look at science from a standpoint of sustainable development, because women shoulder primary responsibility for the next generation and for general caregiving.

This chapter begins with a problem definition, followed by a discussion of the current status of women in industry, with information on numbers, rank, pay equity, and labor segregation. We then examine research on barriers women find in the industrial sector and review theories that attempt to explain inequity patterns. Then we present three brief case studies that trace pathways for women in a traditional field (medicine), a nontraditional field (chemistry), and an emerging field (computer science), seeking to identify both universal and unique factors.

Problem Definition

The work of investigating the problem of "Why so few?" rests on a definitional terrain that still needs to be settled. Most data on scientific occupations are for academia rather than industry, and the few studies of industry generally do not disaggregate data by sex. There are also problems with the commonly used definition of the scientific and engineering (S/E) work force. This definition includes the social sciences and psychology—historically both more open to women than engineering and other science fields and less likely to lead to industrial employment. In addition, at least three other definition issues complicate the discussion.

First, there is no consensus on what constitutes a science occupation. This dilemma became apparent at a recent advisory board meeting of the Pathways for Women in the Sciences project. (The authors have served as this project's director and research associate, respectively.) To see who had survived in science and who had left, we asked attendees—all scientists themselves, from a variety of disciplines—to pick out the scientists from an alumnae survey of science and mathematics majors. However, there was little agreement around the table, even among those in the same field. Some thought a high school chemistry teacher was a scientist, while others did not, and there was similar disagreement over a pharmaceutical company sales representative, a hospital administrator, and an upper-level manager in a computer company.

Second, research tends to look at Ph.D.'s and exclude jobs requiring lesser degrees. The question of professional versus technical or applied positions generated a heated discussion of what is meant by a scientific labor force. Do we wish to open jobs at all skill levels, or to concentrate on the more professional careers?

Third, research rarely looks at differences between the public sector and the private sector. Are government laboratories more friendly to women than those in private industry? And how can we categorize quasi-public enterprises or public/private initiatives? These initiatives not only cross the public/private boundaries but also cross academic/industrial divisions, with an increasing number of research universities forming partnerships with industry to establish joint research endeavors.

Recent Statistics on Women in Industrial Science

What are the current realities for women entering nonacademic science occupations? Research shows that women at all degree levels are less likely than men to work in business, industry, and government. This discrepancy implies that nonacademic science must offer conditions less congenial than those in academia, and statistics on rank, pay equity, labor segregation, and employment of minority women bear out this assumption. Though some companies do seek to recruit and retain women in science, the numbers demonstrate a need for a greater commitment.

The Overall Picture

In 1991, women made up 18.8 percent of all employed doctoral scientists and engineers as defined by the Commission on Professionals in Science and Technology. The definition includes computer scientists, life scientists, physical scientists, mathematicians, computer specialists, psychologists, social scientists, and all engineers. Women with Ph.D.'s comprised only 15.2 percent of all those employed in business and industry compared to 20.5 percent of those in education. At lower degree levels, more women work in industry, but they continue to enter at slower rates than men. Of those receiving master's degrees in science and engineering in 1988, 38.2 percent of the women were employed in business and industry in 1990, compared to 57.8 percent of the men. For 1988 bachelor's degree recipients, 53.3 percent of the women held positions in industry by 1990, compared to 67.6 percent of the men (Vetter, 1994).

Federal government attempts to recruit women appear more successful. At the master's and bachelor's degree levels, more women than men of the class of 1988 worked for the government in 1990 (12.2 percent versus 8.0 percent at master's level, and 4.2

percent versus 2.6 percent at bachelor's level). However, women are only 14.8 percent of the scientists employed by the government (Vetter, 1994). The federal government is the third-largest employer of all doctoral scientists and engineers, but only the fourth-largest employer of women in that category (National Science Foundation [NSF], 1990).

Rank

Women in government and industry tend to start out in the lower ranks—and remain there (Zuckerman, Cole, & Bruer, 1991). When asked where she stood in relation to her male colleagues, one respondent to a Pathways survey of women working in science occupations said, "They're the bosses; I'm the grunt." Another was upset that women always did the "grunge work" in her lab. In government and industry, management responsibility serves as an indicator of success. Table 9.1 shows that beyond the bachelor's level, female scientists are less likely to be primarily involved in management.

The difference in management responsibility was greatest in aeronautical/astronomical engineering (68 percent of men versus 25 percent of women) and physical science (60 percent of men versus 40 percent of women). The difference in other R&D fields ranged from 1 percent to 9 percent. In government, male scientists and engineers are more than twice as likely to be supervisors or managers (29.5 percent of men versus 12.6 percent of women) (National Research Council, 1992). Even women who achieve some managerial responsibility may reach a point where they can

Table 9.1. Distribution of Women in Non-Academic Science Occupations.

Degree Level	Research and development	Management
All employed Ph.D.'s	15.1%	10.3%
Received master's in 1988, employed in 1990	23.6%	18.7%
Received bachelor's in 1988, employed in 1990	10.9%	17.9%

Source: Vetter (1994).

go no further. As a respondent to the Pathways survey noted, "The 'glass ceiling' is in full force here—there are very few women above my level in the company."

Pay Equity

One environmental engineer interviewed in the Pathways survey stated that although she is advancing rapidly, she continues to earn less than men with comparable degrees. Overall, women scientists and engineers earn 75 percent as much as men. The difference is smaller among engineers, where women's salaries are 86 percent of men's (NSF, 1990). Women in industry with a bachelor's degree in chemistry, physics, or chemical engineering earn the same salaries or more than men with the same degree. At the Ph.D. level, however, men start with higher salaries in the same three fields (Babco, 1990). In the federal government, female scientists and engineers earn 90.1 percent of the average male salary (Vetter, 1989).

There are a number of possible explanations for these discrepancies, including differential starting salaries and variances in promotion, on-the-job training, and mentoring. Some of the difference can be explained by noting that men, on average, have more experience than women, but this difference does not justify the entire gap in wages (National Research Council, 1992; Zuckerman et al., 1991). The National Science Foundation found that about half the salary gap between male and female doctorates persists after standardizing for field, race, years of experience, and sector of employment (1986). One woman answering the Pathways survey commented that she makes only one-third the salary of her male supervisor though she has the same amount of experience. Further analysis is needed to determine which explanations are primary or how they interact, so that appropriate strategies for redress can be implemented.

Labor Segregation

Large numbers of both men and women work in life sciences, but women tend to concentrate in psychology and the social sciences and men in engineering and physical sciences (National Science

Board [NSB], 1991). Many jobs in industry require knowledge in the hard sciences; thus there are simply fewer qualified women. However, female scientists and engineers with the qualifications for industrial work are more than twice as likely to be unemployed as men (NSF, 1990). In addition, those with jobs are often under-utilized (National Research Council, 1992). One woman with a Ph.D. in physics states, "I have more credentials and education compared to men in the same job category."

Also, many women stop with bachelor's degrees in science and engineering (National Research Council, 1992). The termination of their education also hinders them when vying for jobs requiring high-level technical knowledge. As one Pathways respondent stated, "All of us in 'non-graduate degree' research jobs are in the same boat. . . . Although I have seen some male bias, it is more a 'degree' biased field."

Minority Women in Nonacademic Science and Engineering

Chapter Six discusses the overall picture on minority employment, but it is important to note here that opportunities for women of color in science and engineering appear to be even more limited than for white women. Among women doctoral scientists, white women make up 84 percent of those employed in business and industry, followed by Asian-American women at 14.1 percent. African-American, Hispanic, and Native American women collectively hold only 2.8 percent of all doctoral positions in business and industry. The numbers are much the same for women working in the federal government, although Asian-American women occupy only 7 percent of all positions (Vetter, 1994).

Barriers: The Chilly Industrial Climate

The often-cited barriers women meet in today's work force—sexual discrimination and harassment, lack of family-friendly policies, pay inequity—are universal; scientific industries are far from immune. The following section reviews current research on these issues as they affect women scientists and engineers in the industrial sector. We will also be concerned with special difficulties for women who work in the sciences.

Access

The significant and persistent underrepresentation of women in science reflects the convergence of social, historical, and economic factors. Until the nineteenth century, the "doing of science" was located in the domestic sphere, where men and women often worked together in family units. However, science became institutionalized in the mid- to late nineteenth century. As described by Abir-Am and Outram (1987), "Women remained fixed in what had been in the nineteenth century a situation typical for both sexes while men in science moved on to a quite different one: in the twentieth century, small-scale, deeply personalized patronage came to be replaced by Big Science" (p. 4).

Women's studies research has investigated how the separation of the domestic and public spheres, the new definition of family life, and the identification of women with domestic roles launched the modern gender classification that exaggerates differences between females and males and promotes sex inequality (Matthaei, 1982; Kessler-Harris, 1990; Reskin & Padavic, 1994).

Except perhaps for the life sciences, modern science has become a male domain. Only a minority of jobs are advertised. Instead, access to work has been tied to traditional or old-boy networks, which serve to ensure the re-creation of self—that is, to recruit people who resemble those already in place. These networks are built on personal contacts from school and industry, and thus they effectively exclude women. Even with affirmative action and other equal opportunity measures, the network-access highway to jobs in science is largely invisible and subtle, and it remains an effective barrier to women's representation.

The Committee on Women in Science and Engineering report (National Research Council, 1994) refers to the *model applicant* concept prevalent in industry. Companies maintain a stereotyped notion of the ideal candidate who will fit comfortably into the existing group. Women, especially older women, lesbian women, and women of color, are excluded as not matching the group's picture of itself.

In terms of women's access to jobs in scientific industries, it is useful to review relevant laws. Prior to 1964, the U.S. government primarily reduced women's access to jobs in science industries through protectionist policies. These protective laws were meant to shield women and children from danger, but they had the effect of keeping women out of jobs, including many science industries. Title VII of the 1964 Civil Rights Act outlawed job discrimination on the basis of sex in firms employing fifteen or more people. The Act created the Equal Employment Opportunities Commission (EEOC) to administer Title VII—but the EEOC is part of the executive branch, and its implementation has varied with each presidential administration.

In later years, regulations required firms with federal government contracts, including military defense industries, to engage in affirmative action: "An affirmative action program must include an analysis of areas within which the contractor is deficient in the utilization of minority groups and women" (U.S. General Services Administration, 1990).

As Reskin and Padavic note, recommended affirmative action procedures included replacing customary recruitment methods and training and promoting protected groups (1994). The enforcement of federal contractor guidelines has been uneven but has expanded women's access to scientific occupations.

Chilly Climate

A number of factors contribute to the well-named chilly climate of the workplace for women: pay inequity, sex discrimination and harassment, and regressive work-family policies. Again, while these factors influence most jobs in the United States, they have particular characteristics in the science industries.

Pay Inequity

As stated earlier, women scientists and engineers earn only about 75 percent as much as men. The discrepancy is smaller for master's recipients (84 percent) and Ph.D.'s with one year or less of experience (88 percent). There is almost no research on racial/ethnic variations among women. One good cross-racial study from a national census sample reported a 5 percent wage gap between Asian-American and white scientists and engineers, while African Americans trailed whites by as much as 15 percent (Tang, 1993). Salaries also vary by field. For example, the average salaries of women exceed those of men in civil, industrial, and materials engineering as well as in social sciences.

In the industrialized world, jobs regarded as female pay lower wages than jobs regarded as male. Women at the lower levels in science industries reflect this pay inequity. However, even women who work in so-called male jobs (engineering, for example) usually make less than their male counterparts. The U.S. Equal Pay Act of 1963 requires that employers pay workers in different jobs of comparable worth at the same rate—that is, jobs involving comparable skills and responsibility should command equal salaries. An Institute for Women's Policy Research report (1993) on pay equity estimated that the gender pay gap would be cut by one-third if women were properly compensated for their work.

Sex Discrimination and Sexual Harassment

Generally, science industries mirror other workplaces in our society in that they maintain and often promote sex discrimination. This takes a number of forms, including segregation, promotion and retention differentiation, and harassment.

Sex Segregation. Sex segregation refers to a division of labor in which men and women perform different tasks. It can be compounded by racial/ethnic segregation so that women of color are clustered in particular jobs. In the sciences, sex segregation occurs in a number of ways:

Soft versus hard science. Women are clustered in the life sciences, also known as the soft sciences, rather than the physical or hard sciences. Women of color may experience other forms of labor segregation. For example, African-American women are more likely to be found in medicine and engineering than chemistry or physics.

Subfield segregation. Within fields, there is further segregation. For example, in medicine, women are clustered in pediatrics, gynecology, and family practice. In engineering, women tend to be clustered in material and civil subfields. In general, women are concentrated in the lower-paying scientific subfields, which also tend to carry less status.

Subfield segregation poses at least two significant research and policy aspects. First, a women may self-select for certain subfields.

A recent study finds that women were more likely than men "to want to work in areas involving contact with people but they were less keen on research that was defense funded or involved animal experimentation" (O'Driscoll & Anderson, 1994). However, if women choose certain fields, the question of volition remains—are other subfields closed or hostile to women? Second, the status and pay of various subfields reflect the higher value assigned those labeled male versus those labeled female. How society evaluates fields and subfields is a critical policy matter.

Sex discrimination also affects promotion and retention within a profession. Even in predominantly female subfields,males tend to be in the higher-status, higher-paid positions. If we look at internal labor markets, which indicate patterns of mobility, women in science rarely move beyond middle management. As in other corporate settings (as well as academia), women do not break through the glass ceiling. Indeed, certain cohorts of women find themselves consigned to the industrial basement, far below any management ceiling.

Sexual Harassment.   Courts identify two types of sexual harassment: "One is the quid pro quo in which a supervisor demands sexual acts from a worker as a job condition or promises work-related benefits in exchange for sexual acts . . . [and] the other is the 'hostile work environment' in which a pattern of sexual language, lewd pinups or sexual advances makes a worker so uncomfortable that it is difficult for her or him to do the job" (Reskin & Padavic, 1994, pp. 130–131).

Sexual harassment laws make employers responsible for creating harassment-free workplaces. At present, the lower courts are interpreting the law on a case-by-case basis, as Supreme Court decisions have left room for debate.

Research shows that women in nontraditional fields are more likely to encounter sexual harassment on the job (Reskin & Padavic, 1994; National Research Council, 1994). We need more investigation to understand how and why this harassment occurs. The Pathways Project found that women in all fields of science reported relatively high rates of harassment both in graduate school and at the workplace. In fact, women in medicine (which has a critical mass of females), reported the highest rates of discrimination and harassment in a survey that was done across science fields. According to the most recent Pathways Project data, while 40 percent of those in all science fields reported having experienced sexual harassment at work or in graduate school, 55 percent of those in medicine reported such experiences (Rayman & Brett, 1993). Another researcher interviewed fifty women in the natural sciences and engineering and found little harassment but rather more subtle forms of discrimination, including lack of respect and miscommunication (Preston, 1993).

Family and Work Issues

The difficulty of balancing family and employment demands has been well documented across occupations (Hartmann, 1974; Baxandall, Gordon, & Reverby, 1976; Beechey, 1987; Beneria & Stimpson, 1987). Family issues include sick leave for dependent care—children, elders, spouses—and differential responsibility for household tasks such as home maintenance, food shopping and cooking, clothing, and family activities. As noted in *Out to Work* (Kessler-Harris, 1982), paid employment has meant that most women shoulder double burdens, becoming increasingly responsible for overall household income while retaining primary responsibility for family needs.

Until recently, we had no studies of the family work experiences of women scientists, including those in industry. New research raises some interesting points. For example, Preston (1993) compared retention of male and female scientists and reported that women were 72 times more likely than men to quit for family reasons. Preston goes on to say that "only 31 percent of the women who left the labor force for family reasons before 1989 had returned by 1989." Thus, many female scientists and engineers who left are perhaps permanently lost to science.

The Pathways Project provides supporting documentation. The project studied the cohort of women who earned mathematics or science degrees from 1983 to 1991, conducting a survival analysis to see who persisted in science occupations. (See Willett & Singer, 1988, for a discussion of survival analysis.) Of those women who changed from science to nonscience careers, the major reason cited was "family concerns." The women did not see a way to continue in science and meet the needs of their families. A profile of a young woman mathematician reflects the tension between work and family values. She responded to the Pathways survey by writing of her desire for a full-time mathematics career while simultaneously believing women with preschool children should only work part time. Her future hopes present a conflict requiring resolution (Rayman & Brett, 1993).

A quality that may be more prevalent in scientific fields than in most other professions is the sense that doing science, especially first-rate science, demands more than a normal full-time commitment. Early writings on the sociology of science spoke of the heavy demands involved with scientific discovery, where competition and total devotion were necessary to be in the forefront of discovery (Merton, 1957, 1973). This all-consuming commitment is a major impediment to a balanced life—unless one has a wife or paid help at home to take care of family duties.

A number of studies help us look more closely at the time issue. Schor's groundbreaking analysis provides a disturbing general picture of the "Alice in Wonderland" phenomenon: people are working longer hours, running harder just to stay in place financially. "If present trends continue, by the end of the century, Americans will be spending as much time at their jobs as they did in the nineteen twenties" (1992, p. 1). In *Falling Behind While Getting Ahead*, a study of dual-income couples where both spouses were scientists, males and females each reported an average work week of sixty-five to seventy-five hours (Rayman & Burbage, 1990). Meanwhile, Preston reports that both her male and female subjects agreed that women take on most household tasks, with married women doing roughly 65 percent of the chores (1993).

Both the Pathways Project and the Preston study also found that female scientists are more likely than male scientists to move to a new location to satisfy a spouse's career. For women, this may also mean sacrificing their own career options. *Falling Behind* confirmed that women who resigned to follow a partner or husband often failed to find another upwardly mobile career position, taking a lesser job in the new location. They suffered loss of pay, loss of prestige, and loss of opportunity to make a contribution in their field.

Finally, as we examine work and family issues, we note that full-time jobs offering flexible hours or job-sharing options are rare. Preston found that while 95 percent of her male sample were working full time, only 70 percent of the women were; conversely almost 14 percent of the women were working part-time compared to only 1 percent of the men. Part-time jobs include marginal teaching appointments in academic science and part-time lab and research assistantships or lower-level administration posts in industry. To really do science—conduct full experiments, influence topics for research, write and publish findings, influence R&D decisions—a full-time commitment is necessary.

Yet, as recent U.S. Department of Labor statistics show, an increasing percentage of jobs fall into the *contingency* category. Contingency workers—also termed disposable workers, flex force workers, or simply temporary workers—number nearly thirty-four million or nearly one out of four employed people (Carre, 1992). There are no studies that focus on contingency work in science, engineering, and technology, but the trend to create a two-tier work force is no doubt present in these sectors. The new economic order, which may be as disruptive as the industrial revolution a century ago, is forming a bifurcated labor force in which a core of essential, highly skilled workers is supplemented by contingency workers.

What does the rise of contingency work mean for women in nonacademic science occupations? Most studies examining women's employment in the sciences have focused on highly skilled jobs, usually requiring postgraduate degrees and at least a college diploma. A major issue for this category of workers has been the glass ceiling, which refers to the inability of women to move into senior management. However, far less attention has been aimed at lower-skilled positions in science and technological industries. While the Workforce 2000 report predicts that two out of three new workers entering the labor force will be women, and many of them will be minority women, we know little about their pathways in science-related jobs (U.S. Department of Labor, 1986). For these women, discussion of the "muddy basement" where they get stuck in low-paid, low-skilled jobs may be more appropriate than the glass ceiling debate.

For both the highly skilled and the lower-skilled women in science and technology, the expansion of contingency work will pose questions. While a contingency work force provides employers with flexibility and a supposed competitive advantage in the global economy, workers are left to carve out uncertain paths, usually without health insurance, pensions, or vacation time. This form of work is especially problematic for women who are single heads of household or in a household where no one has health coverage. Contingency workers also miss the training and career advancement options available to full-time employees.

At the same time, some women like more flexible schedules for paid work, largely to do unpaid dependent care. The new technologies, including home computers, fax machines, and modems, make it possible to do complex and well-paid work at home. However, home work has its own difficulties; it isolates people from other workers, offers few options for advancement, and interferes with the sense of being a part of a working community.

Explaining Occupational Gender Inequity

A number of theoretical perspectives—including those from psychology, sociology, and economics—inform the discussion of gender inequity at work. Of particular import for this chapter are the *human capital theory* from mainstream economics, the *gender schematic framework* of psychologist Sandra Bem, and the *organizational approach* of sociologist Rosabeth Kanter.

Human capital theorists assume that labor markets operate in a value-free manner. Skill and experience determine each worker's human capital. If employees or employers invest in education and training, for example, workers' human capital can be augmented. If women are not doing as well as men in terms of pay levels, promotions, and other criteria, this theory attributes the difference to women being less productive than men. Becker (1957) notes that human capital theorists believe women's attachment to family limits their investment in work and thus lowers their productivity. Women can be seen as choosing family over work and thus as responsible for their occupational inequity.

Bem (1993) conceptualizes culturally defined gender schema that hold that gender inequity is enacted and promoted by social institutions, practices, and discourse. For example, our androcentrism defines male experience as the universal and better experience, against which women are judged as other and inferior. Various aspects of society converge and reinforce each other, creating a feedback loop. Families and schools, for instance, channel girls into life choices that connect with occupational pathways different from those of boys. Individuals absorb cultural norms that make it difficult to go against the stream. This view of socialization maintains that while some gender differences are fixed (who bears children, for example), most result from the cultural bias that one sex is better than the other. The hierarchical arrangement is systematized in all our society's institutions, including the world of work.

Fifteen years ago, *Men and Women of the Corporation* (Kanter, 1977) suggested that being the majority or minority in a firm created different patterns of interaction and opportunity. "Quite apart from the content of particular jobs and their location in the hierarchy, the culture of corporate administration and the experiences of men in it were influenced by this fact of numerical dominance, by the fact that the men were the many" (p. 206). Kanter went on to discuss the consequences of being a token woman in a male work setting: isolation, stereotyping, and increased visibility and self-consciousness. Thus women (and other underrepresented groups) in nontraditional settings face separateness coupled with increased scrutiny, resulting in lots of attention but little support.

Kanter's work is relevant for women in most mid- and upper-level scientific circles where males clearly dominate. Women scientists, from Kanter's view, face the problem of assimilating into male culture while still being expected to act like females. A question that deserves further research is how Kanter's work applies to different fields. For example, though there are clear critical masses of women in the life sciences, research suggests that discrimination persists there. As recent Pathways Project findings confirm, women in medicine are more likely to experience sexual harassment at graduate school and at work than women in other fields. Numbers alone may be a necessary but insufficient strategy for creating an equitable climate.

The occasional breaks in the glass ceiling may not be significant, as women in senior positions seem to do little to improve the general workplace climate. Kanter (1977) notes that senior women often see advantages in "dissociating themselves from others of their category" and, aware of their differences from the dominant group, "pretend that the differences do not exist, or have no implications" (p. 239). Very few, if any, workplaces fully incorporate a female-friendly environment.

Case Study I—Women Physicians

The field of medicine presents an interesting case in the history of women in scientific professions. In earliest times, when medicine was "purely and primitively empirical," a great number of women practiced it (Farnes, 1990, p. 269). The beginning of the Renaissance, however, marked the launching of medicine as a scientific profession. Not surprisingly, women disappeared at professional levels. Fighting both formal and informal discrimination, women began to bounce back around the beginning of the present century. During this time, women such as Florence Sabin, Dorothy Reed, and Alice Hamilton made contributions to medical science that are still recognized today. In addition to their scientific contributions, these women worked to change social conditions detrimental to health. They fought to improve working conditions, advocated for midwifery, and taught child nutrition (Farnes, 1990).

In the years since the time of these pioneer women doctors, women have slowly but steadily approached critical mass in the medical profession. In 1992, 20.4 percent of all physicians in the United States were women, roughly similar to the 1988 level and up 2.5 percent from 1990. While these numbers may still seem a bit small, women made up over 36 percent of all individuals receiving medical degrees in 1992, and 38 percent in 1993 (Vetter, 1994). Women are entering medicine at increasingly higher rates, largely due to the elimination of the formal discrimination that used to discourage women from applying to medical school and to bar them from certain positions. The numbers might lead one to conclude that women are nearing a position of equality in this traditionally male-dominated field.

However, despite the number of women in the medical profession, they are still vastly underrepresented in higher-level positions of authority. Rarely can a woman be found as chief of staff at a large hospital, dean of a medical school, or head of a medical research lab. In short, a glass ceiling remains omnipresent in medicine, barring women from top positions. Lorber attributes this occurrence to what she calls the Salieri phenomenon: "a combination of faint

praise and subtle denigration of their abilities to lead which dele-
gitimates women physicians' bids to compete for positions of great
authority. The reason men are so reluctant to allow women into the
inner circles . . . is their fear that if too many women become leaders, the profession will 'tip' and become women's work—and men
will lose prestige, income and authority" (Lorber, 1993, p. 153). The
name comes from Salieri, the court composer in Peter Shaffer's play
Amadeus (1980), who takes advantage of Mozart's lack of social
knowledge to block his advancement as a composer.

As Lorber describes it, the Salieri phenomenon operates by let-
ting women in but keeping them in their place. The literature provides insight into how this phenomenon may work by pointing to
three areas that help keep women out of the top positions in medicine. These include family responsibilities, job segregation, and
sexist attitudes and behaviors.

One Pathways respondent, when asked how her career compared to that of her male colleagues, stated she felt "restricted due
to the possibility of marriage and children." Her words echo what
can be found in much of the literature. A woman who wants or has
children is automatically seen as being less serious about her work
regardless of the amount of time and effort she exerts, which may
well equal or exceed her male colleagues' investment (Grant,
Simpson, & Rong, 1990). Women, particularly married women,
are prejudged by the possibility that they will have children rather
than by how dedicated they are to their career. One woman physician reported that she was "given the most hassle" when she
became pregnant as a resident even when she was able to continue
at a pace comparable to the other residents. Another told her
mother's story: "My biggest role model has always been my mother.
She handled a full-time career (including being one of the top
researchers in her specialty) and a family. Ironically, she went into
research because she could not find a job in private practice,
because she had three young children at home and was 'unreli-
able.' There are more women in medicine now but some of those
attitudes still persist."

In addition to the perceived conflict between work and family
roles, women lose bargaining power by working in medical subfields
with less influence, money, and prestige. Vetter (1994) found that
the largest number of women are clustered in primary care (21.7

percent), pediatrics (13.6 percent), and obstetrics/gynecology (8.6 percent). She described a striking display of labor segregation in the field of medicine, with the proportion of women declining to 4.2 percent in general surgery and 3.6 percent in radiology/ diagnostics and pathology. As power, money, prestige, and competition increase, the number of women in a given subfield drops sharply. Physicians from our Pathways sample were aware of this inverse relationship. "I find women (including myself) entering the low paying, long hour career of primary care medic. I find more men enter the high paying, long hour specialties, such as cardio surgery (increased pressure and competition)."

Some evidence indicates that women may be informally tracked into these less powerful fields. As one physician put it, "there are still many 'road blocks' for women in medicine, especially in the specialties." Regardless, as women continue to stay away from the more competitive, high-prestige subfields, they decrease their ability to compete for high-level positions.

Finally, women are limited by sexist attitudes and behavior persisting in the profession. In a survey of recent medical school graduates, Cohen, Woodward, and Ferrier (1988) found that women worry most that sexist attitudes/behavior and being taken less seriously than men will hinder their careers. Another study found that as more women enter medicine and become stronger competition, they receive less support from male peers and immediate supervisors (Grant, 1988). As one physician noted, men "are able to get things done quicker without being questioned about why it is being done." Lorber argues that sexism is at the root of inequality in medicine: "What is in actuality structured and institutionalized sexism is often transformed into women's seemingly free choice to limit their ambitions, not work too many hours and put their families before their professions" (1993, p. 162). She goes on to note that women stay out of powerful positions, not because they are less ambitious or place their families first but because the existing structure of the medical profession can be used to their detriment.

Whether one subscribes to Lorber's views or not, the fact remains that women hold almost no high-level medical positions. They therefore have almost no part in decisions about research priorities, medical school curricula, or policies for the field. As medicine becomes more bureaucratized and women fail to occupy high positions in HMOs, hospitals, insurance companies, and the government, Lorber predicts the situation will grow even worse: "Women will be in positions where they will have discretion and autonomy in their treatment of patients but where they do not control the budgets, allocate resources or determine the overall directions for the organizations for which they work. The need for reliable, hard-working, non-rebellious, professionally satisfied rank-and-file professional employees will be neatly solved, as will the problem of what to do about increasing numbers of women physicians" (1993, p. 163).

Though Lorber paints a rather frightening picture, the current climate offers evidence for the idea that critical mass does not mean equality for women in medicine. Female physicians must break through the glass ceiling before their interests are truly represented in the field.

Case Study II—Women and Chemistry

Chemistry, like biology, finds its origins in the ancient fields of medical cookery and alchemy. Women played important roles in both fields. The word chemistry is said to derive from the Egyptian word for black earth—*Khem*—and is thus linked to the goddess Isis who ruled the Egyptian delta. Early representations of the field depicted a female form, and illustrations show males and females doing experiments together in laboratories. "Famous women such as Cleopatra and Maria the Jewess were models for practicing alchemists, inventing the first chemical symbols, providing recipes for reactions and producing useful laboratory equipment" (Miller, 1989).

The products of early chemistry tended to be for women: dyes, cleaning substances, perfumes, and cosmetics. The good cook, according to historian Londa Schiebinger, was an empirical chemist, and the art of preparing food was seen as a branch of chemistry. Moreover, medical cookery centered in the kitchen rather than the pharmacy, and it emphasized disease prevention.

By the mid 1700s, medicine became increasingly separated from cookery, laboratories were housed in the academy rather than the home, and women were pushed out of the mainstream of the chemical profession: "Domestic cooking and nutrition devolved into the nonmedical duties of the wife and mother, while the professional preparation of food became the preserve of the male chef" (Schiebinger, 1989). During this period of transition, women such as Marie Lavoisier, wife of the "founder of modern chemistry," often assisted male relatives (Miller, 1989). By the end of the nineteenth century, as more women became active in modern chemistry, some still did their work at the kitchen table, while others entered single-sex schools to earn degrees.

The twentieth century has found women to be a minority in chemistry and, as in medicine, clustered in particular subfields. According to the 1988 National Science Foundation survey, only 18 percent of chemists employed in the United States are women (Amato, 1992). Miller (1989) noted that women tend to congregate in certain subfields, including research in radioactivity (Marie Curie and her daughter, Irene Joliot-Curie) and crystallography (Dorothy Crowfoot Hodgkin and Rosalind Franklin).

Today, industry employs six out of ten chemists. The 1990 American Chemical Association report on women chemists (Roscher, 1990) states: "Women are more likely to be employed in the pharmaceutical industry and in non-manufacturing and less likely to be employed in specialty chemicals industry" (p. 28). The difference is nearly double, according to the report—only 12.5 percent in specialty chemicals, but 21.9 percent in pharmaceuticals and 22.5 percent in nonmanufacturing jobs. The "clustering" of women chemists in industrial settings is one aspect of the differences between males and females (p. 11). There are also issues of age, degree attainment, and promotion. The American Chemical Society reported that women chemists in its 1990 survey are younger than men at each level; 40 percent of women with bachelor's degrees are under thirty years old, versus 19 percent of the men. While this marks an increase in the number of women with degrees in chemistry, women remain less likely to have advanced degrees—39 percent of the women have doctorates compared to 63 percent of the men. In terms of the glass ceiling, only one out of fourteen women have managerial positions compared to one in five men. The report notes that women are considerably less likely to hold positions in R&D management or in general industrial management (p. 49).

This inability to rise up the corporate structure has a ripple effect in the salary comparison between male and female chemists.

Although beginning salaries in industry are comparable for men and women, the American Chemical Society reports that female chemists earn, on average, only 88 percent of male salaries, even with controls for age, experience, and degree (Roscher, 1990).

Perspectives differ on women's prospects in chemistry. Mary Good, former president of the American Chemical Society and a senior vice president of Allied Signal Inc., thinks that gender discrimination is now a minor issue and that the challenge for a woman is to become a first-rate chemist (Amato, 1992). Responses from two women chemists in industry back up her view. One is a respondent to the Pathways for Women in the Sciences survey in 1991. Earning her doctorate in 1989, she is now an environmental toxicologist at a major chemical corporation: "My work is interesting, challenging. There are few female environmental toxicologists. My opportunities are as good or better because I am a female, in general. On the whole, the company I work for is very male oriented but the particular department I am part of is 50:50 male:female and our opportunities are equal."

Another woman chemist also feels things have changed for the better: "My first industry convention was a shocking revelation. I was one of three women in attendance. Today, industry gatherings have a more equal representation. . . . Change is slow, but the changes are positive" (Roscher, 1990, p. 59). There is some evidence that women prefer environmental fields where they can make a difference in ecological problems. Carl Bauer, director of personal resources for Dow Chemical, says that women are attracted to chemical engineering in greater numbers today in order to find "real solutions" (Shannon, 1992).

However, other women chemists employed in industry comment on the difficulties of moving ahead, often citing the limits of their educational backgrounds or the stresses of trying to combine work and family. One says, "The most frustrating obstacle I have found in my employment is the lack of advancement into managerial positions of non-Ph.D. employees. Time, ability and proven work skills alone are not enough. Since I am a working mother in a household where two incomes are required, it is frustrating to be held back when additional schooling is unlikely" (Roscher, 1990, p. 52). A Pathways respondent who worked as a technician at a major chemical corporation before returning to school to finish her Ph.D. reported, "Sometimes you really have to go the extra mile to prove you are 'equally capable' of doing the job. You must conduct yourself professionally at all times, while male colleagues can be lazy, immature or sexually suggestive. If you show a momentary weakness, it will not be overlooked."

The American Chemical Society report of the 1990 study suggests that the chemical industry has little interest in issues involving part-time work, flex time, or dependency care. However, there has been some movement. Eastman Kodak, for example, has instituted some family-friendly policies. The lack of a universal family work policy clearly has an impact on women in the world of industrial chemistry.

Another economic reality that currently affects options for women chemists is the restructuring of chemistry companies. In recent years, worldwide recession and cutbacks involved with company reengineering have caused the large chemistry companies to greatly reduce their work force. According to a survey of major industries, 53 percent of the larger chemical, drug, and rubber companies planned to lay off workers in 1993 (Moffat, 1993). The layoffs have resulted in a speedup for those still on the job, in the R&D sector as well as in manufacturing.

A question facing all chemists is where new jobs will come from. The biotechnology, communications, materials, and transport industries offer some possibilities. For example, the search is on for lightweight materials to replace traditional ones for use in transportation. For women chemists, the challenge will be to engineer new attachments to chemical industries while creating less discriminatory and more friendly environments.

Case Study III—Women and Computers

"I've been lucky to work for very progressive and young companies. The computer industry is very young, people who work there are very forward thinking and very different." This statement, from an engineer being interviewed for a Wellesley College course on women in science, offers a framework for the way many people think of the computer industry. It is young and forward thinking, a field where women have fewer worries about sexual discrimination and pay equity. Is this an accurate assessment for all women employed in the computer industry?

Despite its youth, the history of the computer industry mirrors that of other scientific disciplines. Women were there in the beginning, primarily in software development. Though much of this female contribution is undocumented, some women stand out. Ada Lovelace, for example, was responsible for introducing the binary system. As the field advanced and achieved higher status, however, women lost ground. For women, the professionalization of the computer industry led to exclusion (Perry & Greber, 1990).

It seems likely that the few women who entered the computer profession in its infancy faced some of the same barriers as women in other scientific professions. Their representation has grown steadily, however, to a point where women now comprise 29.6 percent of systems analysts/computer scientists and 33.3 percent of all programmers (Vetter, 1994). With increasing numbers of women in a young field, it is easy to believe that the computer industry provides a female-friendly environment. This hypothesis is confirmed by some of the respondents from the Pathways Project.

One senior analyst in a financial software company wrote: "There are an overwhelming number of men in computers, yet less sexism than in other fields, I think. Maybe it's because the field is younger or maybe it's that we're all just introverted and weird with a be-different and let-be-different attitude." A software engineer also relates her positive experience in the field: "Male colleagues are great to have around, they create a challenge and make good mentors."

Other respondents could not echo these sentiments, however. One analyst stated, "The anti-female, anti-human chill in scientific circles is too much to pay for a prestigious career." The discrepancy between the first two statements and the third poses an interesting question. What factors cause such dramatic differences in satisfaction within the computer industry?

Upon closer observation, statistics show that computer-related occupations tend to be highly sex segregated. Though increasing numbers of women occupy high-paying, prestigious jobs as analysts and programmers, they amount to somewhat less than a third of the work force, well short of equity. At the same time, large clusters of women can be found in low-paying, low-status jobs as operators (63.6 percent) and data entry keyers (84.9 percent) (Vetter, 1994). Strober and Arnold's study of 1970 and 1980 U.S. Census samples confirmed that this has been the trend in the computer industry for the last twenty years. They also found that women earned less than men in the three occupations studied, even when age and education level were held constant (1987). Despite positive reports from some women, these findings demonstrate the presence of gender inequity within the computer industry, a finding not so different from other science occupations.

Other issues may impede a woman's entrance and progress in the computer industry. Spertus (1991) suggests that traditional stereotypes continue to operate against women in computer-related occupations. "In our society, males and females are regarded very differently. Assertiveness, confidence and high achievement are considered consistent with masculinity but not femininity. In addition to the stigma associated with success in general, technical fields are considered particularly unattractive for females. These factors can influence a girl not to pursue an interest in mathematics or engineering and they can sabotage a woman's career because either she acts feminine and is not taken seriously or she acts masculine and is met with disapprobation" (p. 15).

These double standards leave some women in highly technical fields walking a very fine line. One survey respondent said she is not taken seriously because she is attractive. With her appearance serving as a symbol for her femininity, her colleagues see her as a show piece. A software engineer regrets that she is not as aggressive as her male colleagues, saying, "I tend to fall back because I don't 'toot my own horn.'" These statements confirm the idea that traditional stereotypes continue to operate against women in the computer industry. To be successful, a woman must take on enough masculine qualities to be taken seriously, for which she runs the risk of being judged as aggressive or hostile. Hacker (1981) has suggested that these judgments are part of a "culture of engineering." This culture "includes an extension of the profession's formal objectification and control of the natural world to an informal objectification of women" (Strober & Arnold, 1987, p. 173).

Women may also feel somewhat isolated from men in the industry as a result of their work style. Turkle notes that boys and girls relate to computers in characteristic ways. "Girls tend to be soft masters, while the hard masters are overwhelmingly male. At Austen, girls are trying to forge relationships with the computer that bypass objectivity altogether. They tend to see computational objects as sensuous and tactile and relate to the computer's formal system not as a set of unforgiving 'rules,' but as a language for communicating with, negotiating with a behaving psychological entity" (1984, pp. 108–109). The majority of those in high-ranking, creative jobs are male—hard masters. A woman's soft-master approach to computational problem solving may lead to feelings of isolation when working on a predominantly male team or under a male supervisor. However, some women have discovered how to turn their difference in approach into a positive work experience. "I feel that I am more theoretical than my male colleagues and that this ability is well appreciated" (Pathways respondent, programmer/analyst). "I take a more 'human' view [than male co-workers]; spending time thinking about how to best teach non-computer specialists in a language they can understand" (Pathways respondent, software specialist). The success of these women lies in realizing that their soft approach, though in the minority, can be a useful tool in the field of computer science.

Finally, the introduction and spread of network technology has transformed the structure of work itself. Perry and Greber address the impact of automation at nonmanagement levels, where many women work: "As more offices use computer networks instead of personal computers, the possibilities for monitoring increase. Network file access tends to be organized hierarchically; supervisors can read their employees' documents and memos before employees have finished them—but not vice versa. . . . Workers themselves may feel that such surveillance is dehumanizing and degrading, reducing their already limited control over their work environment and increasing their stress" (1990, p. 79). In addition, as discussed earlier, the computer has also made it possible to move work into the home. Home work appeals to many women, but it carries a price. "Out" workers tend to be paid by the piece and to earn less, get no benefits, and have decreased bargaining power (Perry & Greber, 1990). The computer is an essential tool for expediting and simplifying tasks, but great care must be taken to ensure that the benefits of new technology outweigh the expense to those using it.

Though Pathways respondents report some positive experiences in the computer industry, sex segregation and unequal pay remain common. In addition, sexism, objectification, and differing work styles continue to block women from entrance and progress. While the computer industry does offer some stories of hope, it can not be held up as a model for other scientific disciplines.

Implications for Research and Policy

Nonacademic science still poses barriers to equality for women. Since Alice Rossi's 1965 essay, women have made numerical gains in the sciences. But opportunities are limited, especially in the physical sciences. And even in areas with more promise, such as the emerging field of computer science and the medical and life sciences, women continue to face hard realities of sexual discrimination and harassment.

The question Science by whom? leaves us with an uneven picture at best. We need more data. Thus far, research has disproportionately focused on women in academia. A definition of women in science must be wider in scope and include a wide range of workplaces, from manufacturing, industrial, and high technology settings to private and public laboratories, communication centers, and development/think tanks.

Once we have such data, the next step will require further disaggregation, both of new and preexisting data. Creating an accurate picture is dependent on breakdowns by race/ethnicity, industrial classification, age, marital status, and family status. In what ways, for example, is race more significant than age in determining occupational status in a science field?

Moreover, we need data on all women working in nonacademic science and engineering, from the muddy bottom to beyond the glass ceiling. Unlike academia, industry and government employ women at all degree and skill levels. If investigations focus on a Ph.D.-level research and development manager and ignore the fifty bachelor's-level technicians working under her, we are not working toward creating a truly equitable climate.

As we design new research on women and minorities in science, we need both more longitudinal and more thorough work. Lotte Bailyn of MIT suggested at the CURIES conference on women in science held at Wellesley College, May 1994, that research should focus on micro studies of nonacademic science workplaces. This case-study approach requires significant time and resources and should be interdisciplinary (that is, combine sociological, economic, and psychological perspectives). With this method, investigators would study individual companies, look at workplace environments, interview working scientists, and assess which programs and policies benefit the women (and men) employed there.

One research firm is doing research of this kind. Working directly with major corporations, they assess the utilization and impact of company policies on parental leave, sexual harassment, mentoring, child care, and flexible work arrangements (Catalyst, 1992). At the present time, such research groups must rely on the willingness of each corporation to allow an inside look.

The public policy implications of this situation include the need for regulations requiring both public and private sector employers to periodically report practices regarding pay equity, sexual discrimination and harassment, and work-family policies. They also include the necessity for consistent enforcement of laws against sexual discrimination and harassment, whose implementation has been inconsistent and often nonexistent. This is an issue facing women across occupational categories.

Scientists increasingly face the reality of job insecurity, contingency/part-time work without benefits, and enormous strains on the family-work balance. In addition to the difficulties that the new economic order raises for workers in general in our society, women scientists face the particular difficulties of nonregular work hours (such as weekends and nights in labs) that have consequences for safety as well as dependent care. And women scientists face the still dominant ideal that to be a good scientist one must be wedded to the field. This is fine if the scientist has a spouse (or resources to hire a spouse substitute) to keep the home fires burning, but few women have this option.

On the other question—Science for whom?—there has been much discussion, largely in feminist circles. However, there may be a creative connection between the two questions that would help us respond to both. For example, at a recent meeting organized by the National Academy of Science to plan for the 1995 Women and Development conference in Beijing, women from the third world joined women from North America in seeking ways to interface sustainable development concerns with success for women in science. They conceived a "double helix" approach to the two questions, pointing out that encouraging women to enter science education and careers was connected to making science responsive to local communities. In the United States, this approach may help not only to bring more women of color into science fields but also to respond to the hands-on learning mode that encourages girls and young women in general to feel at home with science and math.

References

Abir-Am, P. G., & Outram, D. (Eds.). (1987). *Uneasy careers and intimate lives: Women in science, 1789–1979.* New Brunswick, NJ: Rutgers University Press.

Amato, I. (1992). Profile of a field: Chemistry. *Science, 255,* 1372–1373.

Babco, E. L. (1990). *Salaries of scientists, engineers and technicians.* Washington, DC: Commission on Professionals in Science and Technology.

Bailyn, L. (1994, May). *Response to "Facing inequity: Women scientists in industry."* Paper presented at the Cross University Research in Engineering and Science (CURIES) Conference sponsored by the Alfred P. Sloan Foundation, Wellesley College, Wellesley, MA.

Baxandall, R., Gordon, L., & Reverby, S. (1976). *America's working women.* New York: Vintage Books.

Becker, G. (1957). *The economics of discrimination.* Chicago: University of Chicago Press.

Beechey, V. (1987). *Unequal work.* London: Verso.

Bem, S. L. (1993). *The lenses of gender: Transforming the debate on sexual inequality.* New Haven, CT: Yale University Press.

Beneria, L., & Stimpson, C. R. (Eds.). (1987). Women, households, and the economy. New Brunswick, NJ: Rutgers University Press.

Carre, F. (1992). Temporary employment in the eighties. In duRivage (Ed.), *New policies for the part-time and contingent workforce.* Armonk, NY: M. E. Sharp.

Catalyst. (1992). *Women in engineering: An untapped resource.* New York: Author.

Cohen, M., Woodward, C. A., & Ferrier, B. M. (1988). Factors influencing career development: Do men and women differ? *Journal of the American Women's Medical Association, 44,* 185–186.

Farnes, P. (1990). Women in medical science. In G. Kas-Simon & P. Farnes (Eds.), *Women of science: Righting the record.* Bloomington: Indiana University Press.

Grant, L. (1988). The gender climate in medical school: Perspectives of women and men students. *Journal of the American Women's Medical Association, 43,* 109–110, 115.

Grant, L., Simpson, L. A., & Rong, X. L. (1990). Gender, parenthood, and the work hours of physicians. *Journal of Marriage and the Family, 52,* 39–49.

Hacker, S. L. (1981). The culture of engineering: Women, workplace, and machine. *Women's Studies International Quarterly, 4*(3), 341–353.

Hartmann, H. (1974). *Capitalism and women's work in the home, 1900–1930.* New Haven, CT: Yale University Press.

Institute for Women's Policy Research. (1993, May 20). *State pay equity programs raise women's wages.* [News release]. Washington, DC: Author.

Kanter, R. M. (1977). *Men and women of the corporation.* New York: Basic Books.

Kessler-Harris, A. (1982). *Out to work.* New York: Oxford University Press.

Kessler-Harris, A. (1990). *A woman's wage: Historical meanings and social consequences.* Lexington: University of Kentucky Press.

Kuhn, S. (1980, May). *Computer programming and women's roles: A look at a changing occupation.* Cambridge, MA: Massachusetts Institute of Technology, Department of Urban Studies and Planning.

Lorber, J. (1993). Why women physicians will never be true equals in the American medical profession. In E. Riska & K. Wegar (Eds.), *Gender, work and medicine: Women and the medical division of labour.* London: Sage.

Matthaei, J. A. (1982). *An economic history of women in America: Women's work, the sexual division of labor, and the development of capitalism.* New York: Schocken.

Merton, R. K. (1957). Priorities in scientific discovery: A chapter in the sociology of science. *American Sociological Review, 22,* 635–659.

Merton, R. K. (1973). The normative structure of science. In *The sociology of science: Theoretical and empirical investigations.* Chicago: University of Chicago Press.

Miller, J. A. (1989, November). Daughters of Isis. *The Chemist.*

Moffat, A. S. (1993). Chemists at work. *Science, 261,* 1791.

National Bureau of Economic Research. (1964). *Human capital.* New York: Author.

National Research Council. Committee on Women in Science and Engineering, Office of Scientific and Engineering Personnel (1992).

Science and engineering programs: On target for women? Washington, DC: National Academy Press.

National Research Council. Committee on Women in Science and Engineering, Office of Scientific and Engineering Personnel. (1994). *Women scientists and engineers employed in industry: Why so few?* Washington, DC: National Academy Press.

National Science Board (NSB). (1991). *Science and engineering indicators* (NSB 91–1). Washington, DC: U.S. Government Printing Office.

National Science Foundation. (1986). *Women and minorities in science and engineering.* Arlington, VA: Author.

National Science Foundation. (1990). *Women and minorities in science and engineering* (NSF 90–301). Arlington, VA: Author.

National Science Foundation. (1992). *Women and minorities in science: An update* (NSF 92–303). Arlington, VA: Author.

O'Driscoll, M., & Anderson, J. (1994, June). *Women in science: Attitudes of university students towards a career in science: A pilot study* (Prism Report No. 4).

Perry, R., & Greber, L. (1990). Women and computers: an introduction. *Signs, 16*(1).

Preston, A. E. (1993, June). *Occupational departure of employees in the natural sciences and engineering.* Report to the Alfred P. Sloan Foundation, University of Colorado, Boulder.

Rayman, P. M. (1994, August). *Opening the doors: Pathways for women in the sciences, part II.* Report to the Alfred P. Sloan Foundation, University of Colorado, Boulder.

Rayman, P. M., & Brett, B. (1993). *Pathways for women in the sciences: The Wellesley Report (Part I).* Wellesley, MA: Wellesley Center for Research on Women.

Rayman, P. M., & Burbage, H. (1990). *Professional families: Falling behind while getting ahead.* Washington, DC: American Association for the Advancement of Science.

Reskin, B., & Padavic, I. (1994). *Women and men at work.* Thousand Oaks, CA: Pine Forge Press.

Roscher, N. M. (1990). *Women chemists 1990.* Washington, DC: American Chemical Society.

Rossi, A. (1965). Women in science: Why so few? *Science,* 148, 1196–1201.

Shannon, C. (1992). Working in the chemical industry. *Nature, 357,* 705–706.

Schiebinger, L. (1989). *The mind has no sex? Women in the origins of modern science.* Cambridge, MA: Harvard University Press.

Schor, J. B. (1992). *The overworked American.* New York: Basic Books.

Shaffer, P. (1980). *Amadeus*. New York: Harper and Row.

Shao, M. (1994, April 3). New U.S. workers: Flexible, disposable. *The Boston Globe*.

Spertus, E. (1991). *Why are there so few female computer scientists?* (An MIT Artificial Intelligence Laboratory Technical Report). Cambridge, MA: Massachusetts Institute of Technology.

Strober, M. H., & Arnold, C. L. (1987). Integrated circuits/segregated labor: Women in computer related occupations and high-tech industries. In Committee on Women's Employment and Related Issues, National Research Council (Ed.), *Computer chips and paper clips: Technology and women's employment*. Washington, DC: National Academy Press.

Tang, J. (1993). Whites, Asians, and blacks in science and engineering: A reconsideration of their economic prospects. *Research in Stratification and Mobility, 12,* 249–291.

Turkle, S. (1984). *The second self*. New York: Simon & Schuster.

U.S. Department of Labor. (1986). *Workforce 2000*. Washington, DC: U.S. Government Printing Office.

U.S. General Services Administration. (1990). *Code of federal regulations*. Washington, DC: U.S. Government Printing Office.

Vetter, B. M. (1989). *Professional women and minorities*. Washington, DC: Commission on Professionals in Science and Technology.

Vetter, B. M. (1994). *Professional women and minorities: A total human resource data compendium* (11th ed.). Washington, DC: Commission on Professionals in Science and Technology.

Willett, J., & Singer, J. (1988). *Doing data analysis with proportional hazards models: Model building, interpretation, and diagnosis*. Paper presented at the annual conference of the American Educational Research Association.

Zuckerman, H., Cole, J. R., & Bruer, J. T. (1991). *The outer circle: Women in the scientific community*. New York: W. W. Norton.

Chapter Ten

Ensuring Educational and Career Equity for Women: A Research and Policy Agenda

Carol S. Hollenshead, Stacy A. Wenzel,
Margaret N. Dykens, Cinda-Sue Davis,
Angela B. Ginorio, Barbara B. Lazarus, Paula M. Rayman

As we prepare for the twenty-first century, it is clear that the goals of our nation can be met only by drawing on the broadest possible pool of scientific and technical skills. We need the best minds available to help us safeguard the environment, reduce disease, and create new applications for industry. We need all the talented women and men we can recruit to the sciences to remain competitive in the global arena. We must act now to ensure that all our citizens—women and men alike—can enter, succeed, and progress in science, mathematics, and engineering.

Over the past years, our view of the factors discouraging girls and women from technical work has grown more complex. We are more aware of the institutional barriers; the interaction of race/ethnicity, class, and gender; variation within scientific fields; and differences among women. We need to know still more.

Some have questioned whether the United States should keep training scientists when demand continues to decrease. Regardless of what size the supply should be, however, we must strive for an equitable proportion of women at every level of scientific work. Far too many women are in entry-level positions; far too few women are in the top ranks. Our ultimate goal is to ensure that the best people who wish to serve as scientists, mathematicians, or engineers have full access to that opportunity.

The CURIES/Sloan Conference

The Cross University Research in Engineering and Science (CURIES) group on women and gender in science, mathematics, and engineering, together with the support of the Alfred P. Sloan Foundation, sponsored a conference in May 1994 to assess current knowledge and set an agenda for future research, practice, and policy. The goal was to build on work by the National Academy of Sciences, the American Association for the Advancement of Science, the National Science Foundation, the Association for Women in Science, and others. Bringing together a group of the country's most knowledgeable experts, the conference singled out research and policy changes needed to ensure equitable opportunities for all women in technical fields. After three days of intense discussion, conference participants developed a list of key recommendations with broad implications for both research and policy:

- Focus on action and accountability.
- Reframe problems and solutions to recognize the issue of diversity of people in science, mathematics, and engineering.
- Revise our view of the standard linear pipeline of science and engineering education and allow numerous possible entry points.
- Give top priority to sustainable improvements that become integral to institutional operations. This is especially important given the limited resources of time, energy, and funding available.

In addition, participants also developed specific recommendations for the separate agendas of researchers, funding agencies, employers, and others.

Research Agenda

We recommend that future research focus on five areas of need: collection and dissemination of disaggregated data, examination of nonacademic careers, evaluation of intervention programs, development of an institutional perspective, and examination of true entry points or gateways into science careers.

Collection and Dissemination of Disaggregated Data

Various agencies fund the collection of statistics on science and engineering students from K–12 through graduate education, as well as from professionals in academia, government, and industry. Meaningful analysis of this data requires that respondents' gender, race/ethnicity, and socioeconomic status be considered together. However, despite some attempts at disaggregation, many studies on women in science and engineering fail to collect or analyze data on their subjects' race/ethnicity and socioeconomic status. Even the federal government's primary indicator of educational achievement, the National Assessment of Educational Progress (NAEP) survey of K–12 students, publishes very little data disaggregated by gender within racial/ethnic categories. This must be remedied. In addition, those who do provide this data need—and rarely get—adequate funding. Conference attendees particularly recognized the critically valuable services of the Commission on Professionals in Science and Technology—a group that accomplishes tremendous work with meager resources.

Qualitative analysis can tease out the complex impact of race/ethnicity and class on women. For populations so small that statistical analysis is meaningless, qualitative analysis is the best tool available. Qualitative study has also proven effective in uncovering gender incquities in teacher-student interactions within the classroom. When combined with quantitative data, qualitative inquiry can be especially effective.

Little data exists on the impact of disabilities and sexual orientation for women going into science and engineering. Studies examining the experiences of these groups are especially needed.

Women are highly diverse, and theories developed without this realization are incomplete at best and misleading at worst. Programs based on incorrect or overgeneralized data can be wasteful.

Funding agencies should

- Support studies that collect, analyze, and disseminate findings with regard to the interactive effects of gender, race/ethnicity, and socioeconomic status.

- Support better qualitative and quantitative research seeking to understand the effects of race/ethnicity and socioeconomic status on the experiences of women.
- Support studies of the impact of disability and sexual orientation on the career success and satisfaction of women scientists and engineers. These studies must be designed to reflect an awareness of these groups' particular concerns.

Researchers should

- Examine the interactive effects of race/ethnicity, socioeconomic status, and gender for engineering and science students and workers.
- Examine the benefits to society that come from a wide diversity of people in science and engineering.

Examination of Nonacademic Careers

Research to date focuses primarily on academic scientists and engineers. We need to widen the perspective to industry, government, and other settings, to understand workplace issues for women in these fields. We need to investigate career issues for women in small businesses as well as for women in major corporations.

We need to examine longitudinal cohorts of women trained not only in linear paths from B.S. degrees through Ph.D. studies but also in vocational technical programs and two-year associate's degree programs. We must study the paths of technicians, physicians, and other workers who practice science or engineering but are not always recognized or rewarded as scientists or engineers.

Researchers should examine

- How diverse groups of women take both traditional and nontraditional paths with regard to education and career mobility in science and engineering. Longitudinal cohort studies are needed to answer this question.
- How policies aimed at providing support to caregivers (parental leave, child care, flex time) are utilized and affect women in technical and scientific work.
- How increased use of temporary workers, including postdoctoral scholars, affects women in scientific fields.

- How women in scientific fields work and relate to other workers at all levels in industry, from technicians to top management.
- How sexual harassment and other abusive behaviors disproportionately affect women in the workplace.

Evaluation of Intervention Programs

Institutional and multi-institutional projects for women in engineering and science have been funded by government and private agencies and by educational institutions themselves. Yet most of these projects have not been properly evaluated to learn if and why students and institutions benefit. If the investment of dollars into these intervention projects is to be productive, evaluation must be required, funded, conducted, and shared.

Appropriate evaluation requires various research methods including both quantitative and qualitative analysis, funded longitudinal follow-up, and control groups. Funding agencies must recognize that good evaluation takes both money and time. It also requires an expertise that not all administrators of intervention programs possess. Funders may need to provide assistance and advice in designing evaluation or require outside evaluators to examine programs. In addition, agencies should directly fund external evaluation studies of intervention projects.

Evaluation results need wide distribution so institutions can learn from each other. Currently, scholarly publications do not connect with the readership that would most benefit from this information. We need new means of sharing what is learned.

Care needs to be taken to avoid tempting grant recipients and applicants to evaluate their efforts in a way that overemphasizes success or denies failure. We need to know both what works and what does not work in programs designed to assist women and girls in science and engineering.

Government and private foundations should

- Fund intervention programs—and both require and fund appropriate evaluations to determine how these projects meet or do not meet their intended goals.
- Fund public dissemination of evaluation findings so others may learn what worked, what did not work, and why.

- Reexamine the ways in which findings are published and pilot new means of distribution using approaches such as electronic media and clearinghouses.

Researchers should examine the long-term relationships between interventions and practices and the retention and success of women in the sciences, mathematics, and engineering.

Institutional Perspectives

We must initiate more research on the institution—university, college, school, or employer—as a primary source of gender inequity and shaper of girls' and women's experiences. In the past, too much emphasis has been placed on telling women how to change to fit into a preexisting institutional culture, rather than finding ways to change institutions to make them more hospitable to women.

It can be very instructive to examine successful components of institutions and policies, to figure out how and why they work. We currently strive to create sustainable institutional change and to move successful intervention programs into the core of our institutions. The critical question of how change is best facilitated needs more work.

Researchers should examine

- How institutions might be structured if they were truly places where diverse groups experience equitable rewards and opportunities.
- How we can transform current institutions into those that provide an equitable environment for everyone interested in science and engineering.
- How institutional change occurs: What pressure points offer the most potential for initial change efforts? How have scientific institutions changed in the past? What have these changes meant for gender and race/ethnicity?

True Entry Points and Gateways

Researchers have conceptualized a pipeline for women in science and engineering: beginning with an abundant flow of girls and young women interested in the sciences, but losing participants at every educational and professional stage. At the highest levels of scientific endeavor, few if any women are left.

Although the concept of the pipeline is useful, it is also important to view science and engineering education as a more open, nonlinear system, with multiple entry points. Educational or career progress in such a system can proceed at different paces to different outcomes. We need to look beyond the experiences of women in the lockstep high-school-calculus-through-Ph.D. track.

We must learn how women who abandon college science majors regard science and what options are (or might be) open to industrial workers, community college students, and women returning to school. We need to examine the true entry points to success in science and engineering. For example, while the formal first job in an academic career is assistant professor, the true entry point may be graduate or postdoctorate fellow.

Researchers should examine

- The true entry points for gaining access to and success at different levels and in different disciplines in science and engineering education and careers.
- The ways women find or miss the entry points in science and engineering. How can we create entry points that are more accessible to diverse groups of women?
- The nontraditional paths open to community college students or older women returning to education.

Policy and Practice Agenda

The time for action, for institutional and systemic change, is now. We already have enough data to support several specific actions. We suggest changes in the awarding of grants and financial aid, in policies of educators and employers, and in efforts to promote broad public understanding of women's role in the sciences, mathematics, and engineering.

Accountability for Sex Equity Linked to Grants

Grants supporting basic, applied, and curricular research are the lifeblood of the science and engineering community in higher education. With approximately $11.4 billion of federal research support going to U.S. universities and colleges (National Science Board, 1993), policies directing grant awards and administration serve as the underpinning of the research infrastructure. These policies should be used to promote institutional change to facilitate the success of women in scientific fields.

The National Science Foundation (NSF) has acknowledged the importance of improving the distribution and effectiveness of the country's supply of scientists. As discussed in Chapter One, NSF criterion four calls for fund administrators to consider the effect of proposed research projects on the infrastructure of science and engineering, including its manpower base (National Science Foundation, 1990). The NSF's consistent use of this criterion when funding research projects, and the development of a similar criterion by private funding agencies, would help meet our goal of achieving a more diverse pool of scientific talent.

We suggest that grant applicants be required to provide data on their record in sex equity, including information about the participation of women of color. Funders should establish appropriate criteria for measuring progress, in keeping with the goals of their grant program. For example, each project supported by grants should keep records of recruitment, retention, and graduation rates of women. In addition, funders could use mechanisms such as cooperative agreements to provide ongoing assurance of progress and effort over the life of a project. Such agreements involve yearly reevaluation to ensure that recipients are continuing to meet the criteria set for the award. This kind of policy change would need to be made on an agency-by-agency basis.

Agencies also need to regularly review their own practices to see whether grants awarded to women are approximately proportionate to the number and value requested by women.

Federal, state, and private funding agencies should

- Develop criteria for measuring progress toward sex equity in keeping with the goals of their grant programs.
- Require applicants for funding (individual researchers and institutions) to supply longitudinal data on their record in regard to sex equity.
- Evaluate applicants' progress in achieving sex equity.
- Require that applicants show significant involvement in equity

    outreach interventions if they do not currently meet appropriate sex equity standards.

- Use alternative grant mechanisms such as cooperative agreements to ensure the accountability of grantees regarding sex equity standards and interventions.
- Review their own granting practices for gender equity.

Financial Aid Options

Financial aid for women qualified and interested in science and engineering education is critical. However, it is not enough to allocate money; financial resources must be targeted in ways that optimize women's chances for success. Women need an assortment of aid programs offering the flexibility to combine science and engineering studies with a variety of responsibilities.

The current practice of limiting most fellowship and scholarship programs to full-time students must be changed to allow part-time fellowships, to better accommodate women in science and engineering. To care for children or other dependents or to earn enough to support themselves and perhaps a family, some women need to pursue their studies on a part-time basis. Many women as well as men can not devote their full attention to their education—their lives include other responsibilities. We recognize that this recommendation challenges the view that successful science requires full-time dedication to scholarship. We also acknowledge that the length of time needed to earn a doctorate is already substantial. We do not think that a student's whole program is best done part-time, but part-time involvement should be available when necessary.

We recommend portable aid for graduate students in science and engineering. Independent national grants would give students greater bargaining power and the freedom to pursue their own research interests without complete reliance on receiving support from faculty projects. One important caveat: Institutions whose students participate in these programs should be required to provide resources and opportunities to students to ensure that they are not isolated from faculty or colleagues.

We recommend that financial support for girls and women in engineering and science be available early in education. We suggest a program similar to ROTC, which would provide financial support to undergraduates in return for the obligation to serve a number of years after graduation in capacities that meet national needs, such as the repair and improvement of the urban infrastructure. We also recommend programs to ensure select women sophomores or juniors financial support for graduate studies.

Studies of student success and persistence show that those with campus jobs are more likely to persist in science than those working off campus. Involving women science and engineering students in jobs such as assisting faculty in the laboratory or tutoring other students in mathematics, science, and engineering provides the benefits of financial aid, direct involvement with faculty, and valuable hands-on experience.

Women outside the traditional pipeline may have different types of financial needs. Women in community colleges or other regional institutions need better financial aid if they are to transfer to universities or colleges and successfully pursue the bachelor's degree in science, mathematics, or engineering.

Federal, state, and private agencies should

- Allow some scholarships and fellowship funds to go to promising women scientists, mathematicians, and engineers who pursue education on a part-time basis.
- Provide graduate women in science, mathematics, and engineering with more direct portable financial aid.
- Pilot an ROTC-like program that could allow women to commit to public service in science and engineering in return for guaranteed financial support through college.
- Pilot programs that guarantee matching graduate school funds to women juniors who successfully complete a summer research internship.
- Target financial assistance to programs that allow women students to earn salaries while becoming involved in the scientific community during college.
- Target funds to women in junior and community colleges.

Equitable Workplaces

Legislation protects the right of women to work in an environment free of harassment and discrimination, and with the same reward potential (salary, benefits, promotion opportunities) as men. Nevertheless, the glass ceiling is well documented in both industry and academia. Women do not appear in faculty ranks in proportion to the number of women Ph.D.'s. By the same token, women represent a very small percentage of the top management in industry. Neither higher education nor industry is free of harassment and discrimination against women employees. Furthermore, women of color may experience discrimination based on both gender and race.

We urge government agencies to enforce laws requiring equitable rewards for and opportunities to do work. All employers must be held accountable for compliance with our laws. Colleges/universities and industry should strive for female science, mathematics, and engineering employees in numbers resembling the percentage of women in the given field. Once hired, women should be retained, tenured, and/or promoted proportionately to men.

Recognizing personal and family responsibilities and needs is an essential part of providing an equitable work environment for women in science, mathematics, and engineering. Most women and men have partners and dependents who are important in their lives. While balancing career and family responsibilities is an issue for workers in all fields, it is particularly important for women in science and engineering. On average, women devote far more time to domestic duties than do men. Women face additional challenges, particularly in research-oriented institutions, because there is the expectation that they must spend a great deal of time in the laboratory, leaving them less time to spend with dependents. In addition, for most women faculty the tenure period occurs during prime childbearing years.

Policies need to ensure that new parents or persons with other dependent-care responsibilities, such as elder care, have equitable opportunities to remain and succeed in academia and industry. Departments, institutions, and companies can implement options such as generous family leave policies, paid time off, or extended tenure probationary periods to assist their employees. In addition, the employment status and situation of a spouse or partner may have a significant impact on some employees. Flexible work schedules must be available to allow employees time to care for dependents or other family members without jeopardizing their careers.

Policies need to be broadly formulated, keeping in mind that people have diverse needs in balancing their personal and professional lives.

Accountability is the key to the success of these initiatives. The top leadership of colleges, universities, and industry needs to give high priority to equity policies and hold managers and administrators accountable.

State and federal government should

- Hold institutions of higher education accountable for their records in hiring, promoting, and retaining women.
- Enforce laws that protect the right of women to work in environments free of harassment and discrimination, and with equal opportunity for advancement and reward.

Employers should

- Develop policies to assist women and men engineering and science researchers and other employees to deal effectively with work and home responsibilities.
- Make implementation of equity policies for women one of the aspects on which supervisors and, within academia, deans, directors, and chairs are evaluated and rewarded.
- Eliminate sexual harassment and work toward improving the climate for women.

Education of the Public

The education of the general public is essential to creating systemic improvement for girls and women in science, mathematics, and engineering and to clarifying the importance of science in the future of our nation. Voters and their elected legislators provide funding for public education and federal support for research. Parents influence the attitudes of their children toward education and career choices. Media sources shape public opinion. We recommend working with all these groups to promote a view of science, mathematics, and engineering that is as attractive to girls and women as to boys and men.

Funding agencies, professional organizations, institutions of higher education, and industry should

- Develop and fund a national campaign to educate the general public on the importance of science and engineering.
- Support efforts to educate teachers, parents, students, and the general public about the need to facilitate girls' and women's enjoyment and success in science, mathematics, and engineering.

Science and technology have become increasingly important in our everyday lives. Our dependence on scientific and technical skills, knowledge, and information will increase enormously over the next decades. To eliminate the remaining inequities for women in the sciences and engineering and to reap the full benefits of an educated and well-trained cadre of scientists, both men and women must make the challenges we suggest their priority. Our nation, as well as all its citizens, deserves nothing less.

References

National Science Board. (1993). *Science and engineering indicators—1993.* (NSB 93–1; pp. 134–135). Washington, DC: U.S. Government Printing Office.

National Science Foundation. (1990). *Grants for research and education in science and engineering: An application guide.* (NSF 90–77; pp. 8–9). Washington, DC: Author.

Name Index

Subject Index